D0638619

THE SCARECROW AUTHOR BIBLIOGRAPHIES

1. John Steinbeck (Tetsumaro Hayashi). 1973.
   See also no. 64.
2. Joseph Conrad (Theodore G. Ehrsam). 1969.
3. Arthur Miller (Tetsumaro Hayashi). 2nd ed., 1976.
4. Katherine Anne Porter (Waldrip & Bauer). 1969.
5. Philip Freneau (Philip M. Marsh). 1970.
6. Robert Greene (Tetsumaro Hayashi). 1971.
7. Benjamin Disraeli (R.W. Stewart). 1972.
8. John Berryman (Richard W. Kelly). 1972.
9. William Dean Howells (Vito J. Brenni). 1973.
10. Jean Anouilh (Kathleen W. Kelly). 1973.
11. E.M. Forster (Alfred Borrello). 1973.
12. The Marquis de Sade (E. Pierre Chanover). 1973.
13. Alain Robbe-Grillet (Dale W. Frazier). 1973.
14. Northrop Frye (Robert D. Denham). 1974.
15. Federico Garcia Lorca (Laurenti & Siracusa). 1974.
16. Ben Jonson (Brock & Welsh). 1974.
17. Four French Dramatists: Eugène Brieux, François de Curel, Emile Fabre, Paul Hervieu (Edmund F. Santa Vicca). 1974.
18. Ralph Waldo Ellison (Jacqueline Covo). 1974.
19. Philip Roth (Bernard F. Rodgers, Jr.). 2nd ed., 1984.
20. Norman Mailer (Laura Adams). 1974.
21. Sir John Betjeman (Margaret Stapleton). 1974.
22. Elie Wiesel (Molly Abramowitz). 1974.
23. Paul Laurence Dunbar (Eugene W. Metcalf, Jr.). 1975.
24. Henry James (Beatrice Ricks). 1975.
25. Robert Frost (Lentricchia & Lentricchia). 1976.
26. Sherwood Anderson (Douglas G. Rogers). 1976.
27. Iris Murdoch and Muriel Spark (Tominaga & Schneidermeyer). 1976.
28. John Ruskin (Kirk H. Beetz). 1976.
29. Georges Simenon (Trudee Young). 1976.
30. George Gordon, Lord Byron (Oscar José Santucho). 1976.
31. John Barth (Richard Vine). 1977.
32. John Hawkes (Carol A. Hryciw). 1977.
33. William Everson (Bartlett & Campo). 1977.
34. May Sarton (Lenora Blouin). 1978.
35. Wilkie Collins (Kirk H. Beetz). 1978.
36. Sylvia Plath (Lane & Stevens). 1978.
37. E.B. White (A.J. Anderson). 1978.

38. Henry Miller (Lawrence J. Shifreen). 1979.
39. Ralph Waldo Emerson (Jeanetta Boswell). 1979.
40. James Dickey (Jim Elledge). 1979.
41. Henry Fielding (H. George Hahn). 1979.
42. Paul Goodman (Tom Nicely). 1979.
43. Christopher Marlowe (Kenneth Friedenreich). 1979.
44. Leo Tolstoy (Egan & Egan). 1979.
45. T.S. Eliot (Beatrice Ricks). 1980.
46. Allen Ginsberg (Michelle P. Kraus). 1980.
47. Anthony Burgess (Jeutonne P. Brewer). 1980.
48. Tennessee Williams (Drewey Wayne Gunn). 1980.
49. William Faulkner (Beatrice Ricks). 1981.
50. Lillian Hellman (Mary Marguerite Riordan). 1980.
51. Walt Whitman (Jeanetta Boswell). 1980.
52. Jack Kerouac (Robert J. Milewski). 1981.
53. Herman Melville (Jeanetta Boswell). 1981.
54. Horatio Alger, Jr. (Scharnhorst & Bales). 1981.
55. Graham Greene (A.F. Cassis). 1981.
56. Henry David Thoreau (Boswell & Crouch). 1981.
57. Nathaniel Hawthorne (Jeanetta Boswell). 1982.
58. Jean Genet (R.C. Webb). 1982.
59. August Derleth (Alison Morley Wilson). 1983.
60. John Milton (Michael A. Mikolajczak). 1983.
61. Algernon Charles Swinburne (Kirk H. Beetz). 1982.
62. George Washington Cable (William H. Roberson). 1982.
63. Christine de Pisan (Edith Yenal). 1982.
64. John Steinbeck (Tetsumaro Hayashi). 1983.
    See also no. 1
65. John G. Neihardt (John Thomas Richards). 1983.
66. Yvor Winters (Grosvenor Powell). 1983.
67. Sean O'Casey (E.H. Mikhail). 1985.
68. Tennyson (Kirk H. Beetz). 1984.
69. Floyd Dell (Judith Nierman). 1984.
70. R.C. Hutchinson (Robert Green). 1985.
71. Charlotte Perkins Gilman (Gary Scharnhorst). 1985.
72. Maxwell Anderson (Alfred S. Shivers). 1985.
73. Theodore Dreiser (Jeanetta Boswell). 1986.
74. Ezra Pound (Beatrice Ricks). 1986.
75. Robert Bly (William H. Roberson). 1986.
76. Edward Albee (Richard Tyce). 1986.

EZRA POUND:
a bibliography of secondary works

compiled by
Beatrice Ricks

The Scarecrow Author Bibliographies,
No. 74

The Scarecrow Press, Inc.
Metuchen, N.J., & London
1986

PS
3531
.082
2459
1986

Library of Congress Cataloging-in-Publication Data

Ricks, Beatrice.
Ezra Pound, a bibliography of secondary works.

(The Scarecrow author bibliogaphies ; no. 74)
Bibliography: p.
Includes indexes.
1. Pound, Ezra, 1885-1972--Bibliography.
I. Title. II. Series.
Z8709.3.R53 1986 [PS3531.O82] 016.811'52 85-26140
ISBN 0-8108-1862-0

Copyright © 1986 by Beatrice Ricks

Manufactured in the United States of America

208849
OCLC: 12749759

Dedicated to the Staff of the

Ward Edwards Library

of

Central Missouri State University

PREFACE

Ezra Pound was chosen as the subject of this bibliography because he was very controversial during and after the Second World War. War arouses emotions, both political and personal, which are sometimes long lasting, and which often influence opinion as to the quality of a work, or character of a poet.

Despite the pain inflicted by the war, Ezra Pound's poetic influence awakened our love of poetry. History provides a record of the past, but poetry helps us to feel the emotions of those involved, and thus perhaps helps us to cope more efficiently with our own world and our own times.

B. R.

CONTENTS

Preface v

Abbreviations and Publications ix

I BIOGRAPHY 1
The Bollingen Award 10
The Case of Ezra Pound and His Confinement at St. Elizabeth's 17

II POETRY AND PROSE WORKS: ANALYSIS, CRITICISM, INTERPRETATION 29

III SUPPLEMENTAL WORKS 116

IV GENERAL CRITICISM 120

V INTERVIEWS 232

VI LETTERS 233

VII BIBLIOGRAPHY 242

Index of Critics 249

Index of Topics 272

ABBREVIATIONS AND PUBLICATIONS

ABnG	Amsterdamer Beitrage zur neueren Germanistik
Accent	Accent
ACF	Annali di Ca'Foscari
Agenda	Agenda
AI	American Imago: A Psychoanalytic Journal for Culture, Science and the Arts
AION-SG	Annali Istituto Universitario Orientale, Napoli Sezione Germanica
AJES	The Aligarh Journal of English Studies
Akzente	Akzente
AL	American Literature: A Journal of Literary History, Criticism and Bibliography
AmerDialog	American Dialogue
AmLS	American Literary Scholarship: An Annual
AmMerc	American Mercury
AmP	American Poetry
AmQ	American Quarterly
AmS	American Studies
AmsT	Amerikastudien/American Studies
Analyst	Analyst
AN&Q	American Notes & Queries (New Haven, Conn.)
AnRS	Annual Reports of Studies (Kyoto, Japan)
Antaeus	Antaeus
AntigR	Antigonish Review
Approdo	L'Approdo Letterario (Rome)
APR	American Poetry Review
AQ	American Quarterly
AR	The Antioch Review
ArAA	Arbeiten aus Anglistik und Amerikanistik
Archiv	Archiv für das Studium der neueren Sprachen und Literaturen
Arion	Arion (University of Texas)
ArionNS	Boston University
ArQ	Arizona Quarterly

ArtInt	Art International
AsSt	Asian Student
Atenea	Atenea
AtlM	Atlantic Monthly
ATQ	American Transcendental Quarterly
AUB-LG	Analele Universitatii, Limbi Germanice [formerly AUB]
Audit	Audit
AUMLA	Journal of the Australasian Universities' Language and Literature Association
Aut-Aut	Aut-Aut
AWR	The Anglo-Welsh Review (Pembroke Dock, Wales)
BA	Books Abroad
B&B	Books and Bookmen
Bachelor	The Bachelor (Wabash College, Crawfordsville, Ind.)
BColl	Book Collector
BJA	British Journal of Aesthetics (London)
BLM	Bonniers Litterära Magasin (Stockholm)
BNM	Book News Monthly
BNYPL	Bulletin of the New York Public Library
Booklist	Booklist
Bookman	Bookman
BookW	Bookweek
Borghese	Borghese
Boundary	Boundary I
BRH	Bulletin of Research in the Humanities
BRMMLA	Bulletin of the Rocky Mountain Modern Lang. Assn.
Brotéria	Brotéria
BSA	Bibliographical Society of America
BSAP	(See PBSA)
BSNotes	Browning Society Notes
BSUF	Ball State University Forum
BUJ	Boston University Journal
BuR	Bucknell Review
BUSE	Boston University Studies in English
CahiersdlH	Cahiers de l'Herne
CalcR	Calcutta Review
CamJ	Cambridge Journal
CaM	The Carleton Miscellany
CamQ	Cambridge Quarterly
CamR	Cambridge Review
CanForum	Canadian Forum
CanL	Canadian Literature
CanMusicJ	Canadian Music Journal
CaSE	Carnegie Studies in English
CathW	Catholic World

Cave	Cave
CdA	Camp de l'Arpa: Revista de Literatura
CdS	Cahiers du Sud
CE	College English
CEA	CEA Critic
CentR	The Centennial Review (Michigan State U.)
CHA	Cuadernos Hispanoamericanos (Madrid)
ChC	Chinese Culture
Chelsea	Chelsea
ChR	ChicagoR
ChrC	Christian Century
CimR	Cimarron Review (Oklahoma State U.)
Civ/n	Civ/n (Montreal)
CJ	Classical Journal
CJIS	Canadian Journal of Irish Studies (Vancouver)
CL	Comparative Literature
CLAJ	College Language Assn. Journal (Morgan State U., Baltimore)
CLit	Contemporary Literature (U. of Wisconsin, Madison)
CLS	Comparative Literature Studies
CollL	College Literature (Westchester State Coll.)
Coloquio	Coloquio
ColQ	Colorado Quarterly
Commentary	Commentary
CompLit	Comparative Literature
ConL	Contemporary Literature (Supersedes WSCL)
ConnR	Connecticut Review
ConP	Contemporary Poetry: A Journal of Poetry Criticism
ContempI	Contemporary Issues
ContP	Contemporary Poetry: A Journal of Poetry Criticism
CP	Classical Philology
ConP	Concerning Poetry (West. Wash. State Coll.)
Conv	Convivium (Barcelona)
ConvLit	Convorbiri literare (Jassy, Romania)
CRAS	The Centennial Review of Arts and Sciences (Michigan State U.)
Cresset	Cresset
CRevAS	Canadian Review of American Studies
Criterion	Criterion
Critic	Critic
Criticism	Criticism (Wayne State U.)
CritP	Critique: Revue Generale des Publication Francaises et Etrangeres (Paris)

CritQ	Critical Quarterly
Cronica	Cronica
Cronos	Cronos
CSMM	Christian Science Monitor Magazine
CurBio	Current Biography
Cw	Commonweal
DagensN	Dagens Nyheter
Delo	Delo (Belgrade)
DenQR	Denver Quarterly Review
Diagonale	Diagonale
Dial	Dialoghi
DilR	Diliman Review
Direction	Direction
DoshL	Doshisha Literature (Kyoto)
DQ	Denver Quarterly
DQR	Dutch Quarterly Review of Anglo-American Letters
DR	Dalhousie Review
Drama	Drama, The Quarterly Theatre Review
DramC	Drama Critique
DRund	Deutsch Rundschau
DSARDS	Dante Studies with the Annual Report of the Dante Society
DubM	Dublin Magazine
DubR	Dublin Review
DurhamUJ	Durham University Journal
DWB	Dietsche Warande en Belfort
E&S	Essays and Studies by Members of the English Association
Edda	Edda
Egoist	Egoist
EH	Eastern Horizons (Hong Kong)
EIC	Essays in Criticism
EIE	English Institute Essays
EigoS	Eigo Seinen [The Rising Generation] (Tokyo)
EJ	English Journal
ELH	English Literary History
ELN	English Language Notes (Univ. of Colorado, Boulder, Colorado)
ELWIU	Essays in Literature (Western Ill. Univ.)
EM	English Miscellany
EmoryUQ	Emory University Quarterly
Encounter	Encounter (London)
English	English
EngQ	English Quarterly
EngRec	English Record
EngRev	English Review
Epoch	Epoch (Cornell U.)
ES	English Studies

ESA	English Studies in Africa: A Journal of the Humanities (Johannesburg, South Africa)
ESPSL	O Estado de São Paulo, Suplemento Literário
Esquire	Esquire
Estaciones	Estaciones
Estafeta Literaria	Estafeta Literaria
Europa-Kurier	Europa-Kurier
Europe	Europe: Revue Litteraire Mensuelle
European	European
Evening Bulletin	Evening Bulletin
EvR	Evergreen Review
EWR	East-West Review (Doshisha U., Kyoto, Japan)
Expl	Explicator
Fantasy	Fantasy: A Literary Quarterly
FarP	Far Point
FDP	Four Decades of Poetry, 1890-1930
FH	Frankfurter Hefte
FlaRev	Florida Review
FLe	La Fiera Letteraria
FN	Filologičeskie Nauki
Forum	Forum (São Paulo)
ForumH	Forum (Houston)
Freeman	Freeman
Furioso	Furioso
FurmanMag	Furman Magazine
FurmS	Furman Studies (Furman U., Greenville, S.C.)
Gakujutsu Kenkyu Nempo	Gakujutsu Kenkyu Nempo
Galleria	Galleria (Italy)
GaR	Georgia Review
Genre	Genre (U. of Illinois at Chicago Circle)
Germanisch-Romanische	Germanisch-Romanische Monatsschrift, NS
GQ	German Quarterly
GR	Germanic Review
Greyfriar	Greyfriar: Siena Studies in Literature (Siena College, NY)
GRM	Germanisch-Romanische Monatsschrift
HA	Harvard Advocate
HAB	Humanities Association Bulletin/La Revue de l'Association des Humanites [Formerly: Humanities Association Bulletin (Canada)]
H&H	Hound and Horn
HAR	Hamilton Alumni Review

HarpB	Harper's Bazar
HarperW	Harper's Weekly
HINL	History of Ideas Newsletter
HJAS	Harvard Journal of Asiatic Studies
HLB	Harvard Library Bulletin
Hollins Critic	Hollins Critic
Horizon	Horizon
HSELL	Hiroshima Studies in English Language and Literature (Hiroshima, Japan)
HSL	University of Hartford Studies in Literature: A Journal of Interdisciplinary Criticism
HudR	The Hudson Review
Humanities	Humanities
Humanist	Humanist
HumR	Humane Review
Idea	Idea (Itlay)
IE	Interdisciplinary Essays
IJAS	Indian Journal of American Studies
Il Borghese	Il Borghese
Il Caffe	Il Caffe
Il Mare	Il Mare
Il Merle Giallo	Il Merle Giallo
Il Ponte	Il Ponte; Rivista mensile di politica e letteratura
Il Secolo d'Italia	Il Secolo d'Italia (Rome)
Il Tempo	Il Tempo
Imagi	Imagi
IM	Il Mondo
Indep	Independent
IndianLit	Indian Literature (New Delhi)
Intro	Intro
IowaR	Iowa Review (U. of Iowa, Iowa City)
IQt	Italian Quarterly
Ish	Ishmael
Isis	Isis
Irish Writing	Irish Writing
Italian Qt	Italian Quarterly
Izraz	Izraz: Časopis za Književnu i Umjetničku Kritiku (Sarajevo, Yugoslavia)
JA	Jahrbuch für Amerikastudien
JAAC	Journal of Aesthetics and Art Criticism
JAE	Journal of Aesthetic Education
JAmS	Journal of American Studies
JBeSt	John Berryman Studies
JEGP	Journal of English and Germanic Philology

JHS	Journal of Historical Studies
JJQ	James Joyce Quarterly
JML	Journal of Modern Literature
JoP	Journal of Politics
JPC	Journal of Popular Culture
JQ	Journalism Quarterly
Jubilee	Jubilee
KAL	Kyushu American Literature (Fukuoka, Japan)
KBAA	Kieler Beiträge zur Anglistik und Amerikanistik
KN	Kwartalnik Neofilologiczny (Warsaw)
KompH	Komparatistische Hefte (Formerly: Mainzer Komparatistische Hefte)
KR	Kenyon Review
KuL	Kunst und Literatur
KyR	Kentucky Review
L&I	Literature and Ideology (Montreal)
Landfall	Landfall
LC	Library Chronicle
LCUT	Library Chronicle of the University of Texas
LE&W	Literature East and West
Left Review	Left Review
Let	Letteratura
LetM	Letterature Moderne (Milan)
Lettere Italiane	Lettere Italiane
L'Europeo	L'Europeo
LGJ	Lost Generation Journal
LHR	Lock Haven Review (Lock Haven State College, Pa.)
LHY	Literary Half-Yearly
LibJ	Library Journal
Life	Life
Listener	Listener
L'Italia	L'Italia
LitD	Literary Digest
LitHY	Literary Half-Yearly (Mysore)
LitRev	Little Review
LitRNYEP	Literary Review, New York Evening Post
LJGG	Literaturwissenschaftliches Jahrbuch im Auftrage der Görres-Gesellschaft
LMS	Letopis Matice Srpske (Novi Sad)
LonM	London Magazine
LonMer	The London Mercury
LonSpec	London Spectator
Look	Look
Luc	Luceafărul (Bucharest)

LugR	Lugano Review
LWU	Literatur in Wissenschaft und Unterricht
Mainstream	Mainstream
MalahR	Malahat Review: An International Quarterly of Life and Letters (Victoria, British Columbia)
MalR	Malahat Review
M&M	Masses & Mainstream
MarkhamR	Markham Review
Martin	Martinella
MASJ	Midcontinent American Studies Journal (U. of Kansas, Lawrence)
MassR	Massachusetts Review
MdF	Mercure de France
Meanjin	Meanjin (U. of Melbourne)
MELUS	MELUS
Merkur	Merkur (Stuttgart)
Metrop	Metropolitan
MFS	Modern Fiction Studies
MGSL	Minas Gerais, Suplemento Literário
Midst	Midstream
MidwQ	Midwest Quarterly (Pittsburg, Kansas)
MinnR	Minnesota Review
MJSS	Montclair Journal of Social and Behavioral Sciences (Montclair State College, NJ)
MLN	Modern Language Notes
MLQ	Modern Language Quarterly
MLS	Modern Language Studies
MMN	Marianne Moore Newsletter
ModA	Modern Age (Chicago)
ModAmerG	Modern American Guide
ModR	Modern Review (Calcutta)
MoOc	Modern Occasions
Mosaic	Mosaic: A Journal for the Interdisciplinary Study of Literature
MP	Modern Philology
MPS	Modern Poetry Studies
MQ	Midwest Quarterly (Pittsburg, Kansas)
MQR	Michigan Quarterly Review
MR	Massachusetts Review
MSE	Massachusetts Studies in English
MSpr	Moderna Språk (Stockholm, Sweden)
NA	Nuova Antologia (Roma)
N&Q	Notes and Queries
NAR	North American Review
Nation	Nation
NatlR	National Review

Nazione	Nazione (Firenze)
NC	Nuova Corrente
NConL	Notes on Contemporary Literature
NDEJ	Notre Dame English Journal
NDH	Neue Deutsche Hefte
NDQ	North Dakota Quarterly
NE	Nueva Estafeta
NEQ	New England Quarterly
New Democracy	New Democracy
NEW	New English Weekly
NewF	New Freeman
NewSt	New Statesman
Nimbus	Nimbus
Ninepence	Ninepence
NL	Nouvelles Littéraires
NLB	Newberry Library Bulletin
NLH	New Literary History: A Journal of Theory and Interpretation (Charlottesville, VA)
NMAL	Notes on Modern American Literature
NMQ	New Mexico Quarterly
NOR	New Orleans Review
Novite	Novite
NR	New Republic
NR de DM	Nouvelle Revue des Deux Mondes
NS	Die Neueren Sprachen
NS&N	New Statesman and Nation
NSt	New Statesman
NWR	Northwest Review
NY	New Yorker
NYRB	New York Review of Books
NYT	New York Times
NYTBR	New York Times Book Review
NZZ	Neue Zürcher Zeitung (Zürich)
Obs	Observer
Occ	Occident (Berkeley, Calif.)
Oggi	Oggi (Milan)
OhR	The Ohio Review
OL	Orbis Litterarum: International Review of Literary Studies
OLR	Oxford Literary Review
OperaN	Opera News
OSA	Ohio State Argo
OT	Oakland Tribune
Outlook	Outlook
Paideuma	Paideuma: A Journal Devoted to Ezra Pound Scholarship
PaG	Pennsylvania Gazette
PaR	Pennsylvania Review
P&R	Philosophy and Rhetoric

Paragone	Paragone: Rivista Mensile di Arte Figurativa e Letteratura
ParisR	Paris Review
PBA	Proceedings of the British Academy
PBSA	Papers of the Bibliographical Society of America
Person	Personalist
Perspective	Perspective: A Magazine of Modern Literature
Plamen	Plamen (Praha)
Playboy	Playboy
PLL	Papers on Language and Literature (So. Ill. U.)
PM	PM Newspaper, Inc.
PMASAL	Papers of the Michigan Academy of Science, Arts, and Letters
PMLA	Publications of the Modern Language Association of America
PNR	PN Review
PoetA	Poetry Australia (New South Wales)
Poetica	Poetica (Tokyo)
Poet Lore	Poet Lore
Poetry	Poetry
PoetryN	Poetry Nation (Manchester, England)
PoundN	Pound Newsletter
PQ	Philological Quarterly
PR	Partisan Review
Prose	Prose
Prospects	Prospects: Annual of American Cultural Studies
Prospetti	Prospetti
PrR	Princeton Review
PrSch	Prairie Schooner
PsyToday	Psychology Today
PubW	Publisher's Weekly
PULC	Princeton University Library Chronicle
Purpose	Purpose
PUSA	Perspectives USA
QLS	Quarterly Journal of Speech
QL	La Quinzaine Littéraire (Paris)
QQ	Queen's Quarterly
QRL	Quarterly Review of Literature
Quadrant	Quadrant: An Australian Bi-Monthly
RAA	Revue Anglo-Américaine
RA&A	Recherches Anglaises et Américaines
RadioT	Radio Times
RALS	Resources for American Literary Studies
RBA	Revista de Bellas Artes
RdE	Rivista di Estetica (U. di Padova)
REL	Review of English Literature

Rendezvous	Rendezvous: Journal of Arts and Letters (Idaho State U)
Reporter	Reporter
RES	Review of English Studies
Review	Review: A Magazine of Poetry and Criticism
RevR	Review of Reviews
RGB	Revue Générale Belge (Brussels)
RL	Revista de Literatura
RLC	Revue de Littérature Comparée
RLM	Revue des Lettres Modernes
RLMC	Rivista di Letterature Moderne e Comparate (Florence, Italy)
RLV	Revue des langues vivantes (Bruxelles)
RN	Revue nouvelle
RNL	Review of National Literatures
RO	Revista de Occidente
RomLit	România literară (Bucharest)
RomN	Romance Notes (U. of North Carolina)
RPol	Review of Politics
RR	Romantic Review
RS	Research Studies (Pullman, WA)
RutgersRev	Rutgers Review
SA	Studi Americani (Roma)
Sal	Salmagundi
SAQ	South Atlantic Quarterly
SatRL	Saturday Review of Literature
SAVL	Studien zur Allgemeinen und Vergleichenden Literaturwissenschaft
SBHC	Studies in Browning and His Circle: A Journal of Criticism, History, and Bibliography
Sch&Soc	School and Society
SCR	South Carolina Review (Clemson U)
Scrutiny	Scrutiny
SCSML	Smith College Studies in Modern Languages
Secolul	Secolul
SEL	Studies in English Literature (Tokyo)
SELit	Studies in English Literature (English Literary Society of Japan, U. of Tokyo)
SELL	Studies in English Literature and Language (Kyushu U., Fukuoka, Japan)
Shan	Shantih: Journal of International Writing and Art
Shen	Shenandoah
SHR	Southern Humanities Review
SIR	Studies in Romanticism
SN	Studia Neophilologica: A Journal of

	Germanic and Romance Languages and Literature
SoR	Southern Review (Louisiana State U)
SoRA	Southern Review: Literary and Interdisciplinary Essays (Adelaide, Australia)
Sou	Sou'wester
Southerly	Southerly
SP	Studies in Philology
SPe	Lo Spettatore Italiano
Spect	Spectator (London)
Spectrum	Spectrum
Spirit	Spirit: A Magazine of Poetry
SR	Sewanee Review
Sreaua	Sreaua
SSMLN	Society for the Study of Midwestern Literature Newsletter (Michigan St. U., East Lansing)
Stagione	Stagione
Stand	Standpunte
StAR	StAR (St. Andrews Review, St. Andrews Presbyterian College)
StHum	Studies in the Humanities (Indiana U. of Pennsylvania)
Stony Brook	Stony Brook
Streven	Streven (Amsterdam)
Sumac	Sumac
SUS	Studi Urbinati di Storia, Filosofia e Letteratura
SWR	Southwest Review
SXX	Secolul XX (Bucharest)
TamR	Tamarack Review
T&T	Time and Tide
TC	Twentieth Century (Melbourne, Australia)
TCL	Twentieth Century Literature: A Scholarly and Critical Journal. (Hofstra U., Hempstead, NY)
Tel Quel	Tel Quel (Paris)
Tempo	Tempo (Rome)
TexQT	Texas Quarterly
Thought	Thought
ThQ	This Quarter (Paris)
Threshold	Threshold
Time	Time Magazine
TkR	Tamkang Review
TLS	Times Literary Supplement (London)
Today	Today
Topic	Topic: A Journal of the Liberal Arts
Townsend	Townsend

Townsman	Townsman
Trace	Trace
Transition	Transition
TriQ	Tri-Quarterly (Evanston, Ill.)
TSE	Tulane Studies in English
TSEN	T. S. Eliot Newsletter
TSER	T. S. Eliot Review
TSLL	Texas Studies in Language and Literature
TUSAS	Twayne United States Author Series
Tyro	Tyro
UDQ	University of Denver Quarterly
UES	UNISA English Studies: A Journal of the Department of English
UKCR	University of Kansas City Review
UMPAW	University of Minneapolis Pamphlets on American Writers
Universidad	Universidad de Mexico
Unser Tsait	Unser Tsait
UPortR	University of Portland Review
UR	University Review (Kansas City, MO)
UTQ	University of Toronto Quarterly
UWR	University of Windsor Review
Vanity Fair	Vanity Fair
Veltro	Veltro (Rome)
Verri	Il Verri
VLit	Voprosy Literature
Voices	Voices
Vort	Vort
VQR	Virginia Quarterly Review
VR	Viata Romaneasca (Bucharest)
VWQ	Virginia Woolf Quarterly (Calif. State U., San Diego)
WAL	Western American Literature
WASAL	Wisconsin Academy of Sciences, Arts, and Letters
WCR	West Coast Review
WCWN	William Carlos Williams Newsletter
WHR	Western Humanities Review
World	World Magazine
WR	Western Review (U. of Kansas, Lawrence)
WSCL	Wisconsin Studies in Contemporary Literature
WuW	Welt und Wort
WWR	Walt Whitman Review
WZ	Wort in der Zeit (Vienna)
XRev	X, A Quarterly Review

YCGL	Yearbook of Comparative and General Literature
YeA	Yeats Annual
YER	Yeats-Eliot Review
YES	Yearbook of English Studies
YFS	Yale French Studies
YLG	Yale Library Gazette
YLM	Yale Literary Magazine
YPR	Yale Poetry Review
YR	Yale Review
YSE	Yale Studies in English
YULG	Yale University Library Gazette
Zivot	Zivot: Casopis za Knjizevnost i Kulturu

I. BIOGRAPHY

1 Ackroyd, Peter. Ezra Pound and His World. New York: Charles Scribner, 1980.

2 Auden, W. H., et al. Ezra Pound at Seventy. Norfolk, Conn.: New Directions, 1956.

3 Baker, Carlos. "Pound in Venice," VQR, 50, #4 (Autumn, 1974), 597-605.

4 Banta, R. E. "Ezra Pound Among the Hoosiers," Wabash Bulletin, 49 (December, 1953), 11-13.

5 Berryman, John. "The Poetry of Ezra Pound," Partisan Review, 16, #4 (April, 1949), 377-394.

6 _____. "A Tribute," Agenda, Special Issue in Honor of Ezra Pound's Eightieth Birthday, IV, ii (October-November, 1965), 27-28.

7 Bibesco, H. "Lunch with Uncle Ez," AtlM, 240, #2 (August, 1977), 55-58.

8 Bottome, Phyllis. "Ezra Pound," From the Life. London: Faber & Faber, Ltd., 1944, pp. 70-82.

9 _____. "Ezra Pound--Happy Exile," This Week (December 1, 1935), 10-11.

10 Bowers, Faubion, and Carroll F. Terrell. "Memoir within Memoirs," Paideuma, 2, #1 (Spring, 1973), 49-66.

11 Boyd, Ernest L. "Ezra Pound at Wabash College," JML, 4 (September, 1974), 43-54.

12 Bradbury, Malcolm. "Pound of Flesh," NSt, 7 (August, 1970), 156-157.

13 Braidwood, John, et al. "Ezra Pound: A Commemorative Symposium," Paideuma, 3 (Winter, 1974), 151-168.

14 Brown, John L. "A Troubadour at Hamilton," Hamilton Literary Mag, 62 (November, 1932), 53-63.

15 Cann, Louise Beghard. "With the Pounds in Paris," Pound Newsletter, 8 (October, 1955), 24-27.

16 Capellan, Angel. "Ezra Pound (1885-1972), Estudio biografico," RO, 12, #132 (March, 1974), 309-342.

17 Capote, Truman, and Richard Avedon. "Observations on Ezra Pound," Esquire, 52 (September, 1959), 74-76.

18 Carruth, Hayden. "On a Picture of Ezra Pound," Poetry, 110, #2 (May, 1967), 103-105.

19 Clark, William Bedford, "'Ez sez': Pound's 'Pithy Promulgations,'" AntiochRev, 37 (Fall, 1979), 420-427.

20 Connolly, Cyril. "The Break-Through in Modern Verse," LonM, n.s., 1 (June, 1961), 27-40.

21 Cory, Daniel. "Ezra Pound: A Memoir," Encounter, 30, #5 (May, 1968), 30-39; repr., in Ezra Pound: A Critical Anthology. J. P. Sullivan, ed. Baltimore, MD., 1970, pp. 374-376.

22 Cournos, John. Autobiography. New York: G. P. Putnam's Sons, 1935, passim.

23 Cowley, Edmund. "Fox in Flight," Furioso, 6 (Spring, 1951), 7-10.

24 Dahlberg, Edward, and Herbert Read. "On T. S. Eliot and Ezra Pound," Truth Is More Sacred: A Critical Exchange on Modern Literature. New York: Horizon Pr., 1961, pp. 169-222.

25 Darrach, Brad. "Poetry and Poison," Review of Ezra Pound: The Last Rower by C. David Heymann. Time, 107 (March 8, 1976), pp. 74, 75, 77.

26 Davenport, Guy. "Ezra Pound, 1885-1972," Arion, n. s., 1 (1973), 188-196.

27 De Rachewiltz, Mary. Discretions: A Memoir by Ezra Pound's Daughter. London: Faber & Faber, 1971; Boston: Little Brown, 1971.

28 _____. "Ezra Pound at Eighty," Esquire, 65 (April, 1966), 114-116, 178-180.

29 Deutsch, Babette. "The Teacher," YLM, 126 (December, 1958), v, 10; repr., in A Casebook on Ezra Pound. Wm. Van O'Connor and Edward Stone, eds. New York: Crowell, 1959, pp. 151-152.

30 Devlin, Vianney M. "In Memoriam--Ezra Pound," Greyfriar, 13 (1972), 42-44.

31 Diesendorf, Margaret. "A Lume Spento: Ezra Pound (1885-1972)," Poetry Australia, 46 (1972), 4-5.

32 Doob, Eveline Bates. "Some Notes on Ezra Pound," Paideuma, 8 (1979), 69-78.

33 Doob, Leonard W., ed. "Ezra Pound Speaking," Radio Speeches of World War II. Westport, Conn.: Greenwood Pr., 1978.

34 Doody, M. A. "Elegy for Ezra Pound," AWR, 22 (Spring, 1973), 194-196.

35 Doolittle, Hilda [H. D.] An End to Torment: A Memoir of Ezra Pound by H. D. Norman Holmes Pearson and Michael King, eds. Foreword by Michael King. New York: New Directions Pub. Co., 1979.

36 Duncan, Ronald. "Pull Down Thy Vanity: A Visit to Ezra Pound," Sunday Times (February 11, 1962), p. 33, cols. 2-5.

37 Eastman, Barbara. "The 90th Birthday Symposium," Paideuma, 4, #2 & 3, (Fall and Winter, 1975), 519-523.

38 Edwards, John Hamilton. "A Critical Biography of Ezra Pound: 1885-1922," Diss. University of California, Berkeley, 1952.

39 Enright, D. J. "Dialect and Analect: A Life of Ezra Pound," Man Is an Onion: Reviews and Essays. The Library Press, U. S.; Distr. by Open Court Pub. Co., LaSalle, Ill., 1973, pp. 123-127.

40 Evans, Luther H. "A Letter from the Librarian of Congress," and "A Reply," SatRL, 32 (July 2, 1949), 20-23.

41 Fiedler, Leslie. "Traitor or Laureate: The Two Trials of the Poet," New Approaches to Ezra Pound. Eva Hesse, ed. Berkeley and Los Angeles: University of California, 1969, pp. 365-377.

42 Foote, Edward. "A Note on Ezra Pound," Prose, 7 (Fall, 1973), 71-78.

43 Ford, Ford Madox. It Was the Nightingale. New York: Farrar, Straus & Giroux; Octagon Books, 1975, pp. 203-205, passim.

44 Gallup, Donald Clifford. T. S. Eliot and Ezra Pound: Collaborators in Letters. New Haven, Conn.: Henry W. Wenning, 1970.

45 Gatter, Carl, and Noel Stock. "Ezra Pound's Pennsylvania," Poetry Australia, 46 (Spring, 1973), 5-36.

46 Geddes, Virgil. "A Visit to Ezra Pound," Paideuma, 7 (1924), 281-286.

47 Ginsberg, Allen. "Allen Verbatim," Paideuma, 3, #2 (Fall, 1974), 253-273.

48 _____. "The Death of Ezra Pound," Allen Verbatim: Lectures on Poetry, Politics, Consciousness. Gordon Ball, ed. New York: McGraw-Hill, 1974, pp. 179-187, passim.

49 Goacher, Denis. "Pictures of Ezra Pound," Nimbus, 3, #4 (1956), 24-32.

50 Goodwin, K. L. The Influence of Ezra Pound. London: Oxford U. P.; New York: Oxford, 1966.

51 Gordon, David. "Meeting E. P., and Then ...," Paideuma, 3, #3 (Winter, 1974), 343-360.

52 Grover, Philip, ed. Ezra Pound: The London Years, 1908-1920. New York: AMS Press, 1978.

53 Guthrie, Ramon. "Ezra Pound in Paris and Elsewhere," Nation, 185, #16 (November 16, 1957), 345.

H. D. [See Doolittle, Hilda]

54 Hall, Donald. "Fragments of Ezra Pound," and "The Paris Review Interviews with T. S. Eliot and Ezra Pound," Remembering Poets: Reminiscences and Reflections: Dylan Thomas, Robert Frost, T. S. Eliot, Ezra Pound. New York: Harper & Row, 1978, pp. 111-194, 201-244.

55 _____. "Pound's Death," Goatfoot Milktongue Twinbird: Interviews, Essays, and Notes on Poetry, 1970-1976. Ann Arbor: University of Michigan Pr., 1978, pp. 55-56.

56 Herzinger, Kim. "The Night Pound Ate the Tulips: An Evening at Ernest Rhys's," JML, 8, #1 (1980), 153-155.

57 Heymann, C. David. Ezra Pound, the Last Rower: A Political Profile. New York: Viking Pr., 1976.

58 Homberger, Eric. "A Glimpse of Pound in 1912 by Arundel del Re," Paideuma, 3, #1 (Spring, 1974), 85-88.

59 Hutchins, Patricia. "Ezra Pound as Journalist," TC, 167 (January, 1960), 39-48.

60 _____. Ezra Pound's Kensington: An Exploration, 1885-1913. London: Faber & Faber; Chicago: Regnery, 1965.

61 _____. "Yeats and Pound in England," TexQ, 4 (Autumn, 1961), 203-216.

62 _____. "Young Pound in London, Friends and Acquaintances," ConnR, 7 (1974), 86-93.

63 Iwasaki, Ryozo. "Pound Yuku," EigoS, 118 (1972), 624-625.

64 Kappel, Andrew J. "What Ezra Pound Says We Owe to Edward VIII, Duke of Windsor," JML, 9, #2 (May, 1982), 313-315.

65 Kazin, Alfred. Contemporaries. Boston: Little, Brown, 1962.

66 _____. "The Youngest Man Who Ever Was," Reporter, 21 (August 20, 1959), 43-46.

67 Kenner, Hugh. "D[orothy], P[ound] Remembered," Paideuma, 2, #3 (Winter, 1973), 485-493.

68 _____. "Ezra Pound and Money," Cf., #6, pp. 50-55.

69 _____. "Incurious Biography," NR, 163 (October 17, 1970), 30-32.

70 _____. "In Memoriam: Ezra Pound," SatRL, 55 (December 12, 1972), 30.

71 Knox, Bryant. "Allen Upward and Ezra Pound," Paideuma, 3 (Spring, 1974), 71-83; cf., A. D. Moody, "Pound's Allen Upward," Paideuma, 4, #1 (Spring, 1975), 55-70.

72 Lawrence, D. H. The Collected Letters of D. H. Lawrence. New York: Viking Pr., 1962, passim.

73 _____. Lawrence in Love: Letters to Louie Burrows. James T. Boulton, ed. University of Nottingham Pr., 1968, pp. 147-148, 165-166, passim.

74 Lewis, Wyndham. "Ezra: The Portrait of a Personality," QRL, 5, #2 (November 2, 1949), 136-144.

75 Livi, Grazia. "The Poet Speaks," Paideuma, 8 (1979), 243-247; Natalie Harris, trans., "Vi Parla Ezra Pound," Epoca (March 24, 1963).

76 Lottman, Herbert R. "The Silences of Ezra Pound," TexQ, 10, #4 (Winter, 1967), 105-128.

77 Lowell, Robert. "A Tribute," Cf., #6, p. 22.

78 McAlmon, Robert. Being Geniuses Together, 1920-1930. Rev.

with Supp. Chapters by Kay Boyle. Garden City, N.Y.: Doubleday, 1968, pp. 31-33, 99-101, 178-179, passim.

79 _____. McAlmon and the Lost Generation. Robert E. Knoll, ed. Lincoln: U. of Nebraska Pr., 1962. [Reprint of articles from books by Robert McAlmon.]

80 McCormick, John. "George Santayana and Ezra Pound," AL, 54, #3 (October, 1982), 413-433.

81 McCracken, Van. "Ezra Pound: The London Years," LGJ, 6, #3 (Winter, 1981), 12-14.

82 MacNaughton, William. "Pound, a Brief Memoir: 'Chi Lavora, Ora,'" Paideuma, 3, #3 (Winter, 1974), 319-324.

83 Maia, Joao. "Na Morte de Ezra Pound," Broteria, 95 (1972), 555-558.

84 Meacham, Harry. "I Remember Ezra," StAR, 1, #1 (Fall-Winter, 1970), 21-24.

85 Monroe, Harriet. "Ezra Pound," Poetry, 26 (May, 1925), 90-91.

86 _____. A Poet's Life: Seventy Years in a Changing World. New York: Macmillan, 1938, passim.

87 Montale, Eugenio. "Uncle Ez," IQ, 16, #64 (1973), 23-29; trans. of "Uncle Ez," Corriere della sera, Milan, 1953.

88 Montgomery, Marion. "Ezra Pound's Search for Family," GaR, 22 (Winter, 1968), 429-436.

89 _____. "Homage to Ezra Pound," UDQ, 3 (Winter, 1969), 1-17.

90 Moore, Marianne. "A Note," Cf., #6, p. 22.

91 Mullins, Eustace. "Ezra and America," Sou'w, 3-5 (1970), Special EP No.

92 _____. This Difficult Individual, Ezra Pound. New York: Fleet Pub. Corp., 1961.

93 Norman, Charles. Ezra Pound. New York: Macmillan, 1960; rev. ed., New York: Minerva Pr., 1960; London: 1969.

94 _____. The Magic-Maker: E. E. Cummings. New York: Macmillan, 1958, passim.

95 Olson, Charles. "Encounter with Ezra Pound," Antaeus, 17 (January, 1975), 72-92.

96 Oppen, George. "Pound in the U.S.A., 1969," Sagetrieb, 1, #1 (Spring, 1982), 119.

97 Palandri, Angela Jung. "Homage to a Confucian Poet," Paideuma, 3, #3 (Winter, 1974), 301-311; TkR, 5, #1 (1974), 129-142.

98 Patmore, Brigit. "Ezra Pound in England," TQ, 7, #3 (Autumn, 1964), 69-81.

99 _____. My Friends When Young: The Memoirs of Brigit Patmore. Ed. with Introduction by Derek Patmore. London: Heinemann, 1968.

100 Pearce, Donald. "A Wreath for Ezra Pound: 1885-1972," Shenandoah, 24, #3 (Spring, 1973), 3-14.

101 Pearlman, Daniel D. "Ezra Pound: America's Wandering Jew," Paideuma, 9 (1980), 461-480.

102 Peel, Robert. "The Poet as Artist and Citizen," CSMM (December 9, 1950), 7.

103 Pellizzi, Camillo. "Ezra Pound, uomo difficile," Il Tempo, (Rome: March, 1953), 3; translation: "Ezra Pound: A Difficult Man," Civ/n (Montreal), #4, pp. 20-22.

104 Pinck, Dan. "A Visit with Ezra Pound," Reporter, 10, 3 (February 2, 1954), 40-43.

105 Rader, James E., ed. "A Pound of Flesh," Wabash College Review, 6 (Spring, 1959), 5-10.

106 _____. "Ship in the Night," The Bachelor, 50 (May 9, 1958), 7-10.

107 Rattray, David. "Weekend with Ezra Pound," Nation, 185, #16 (November 16, 1957), 343-349; Reply by D. R. Wang, 185 [inside cover], (December 28, 1957); repr., in A Casebook on Ezra Pound, Cf., #29, pp. 104-117.

108 Reck, Michael. "A Conversation between Ezra Pound and Allen Ginsberg," EvergreenRev, 12 (June, 1968), 27-29, 84-86.

109 _____. Ezra Pound: A Close-up. London: 1967; New York: McGraw-Hill, 1967.

110 Redman, Tim. "The Repatriation of Pound, 1939-1942: A View from the Archives," Paideuma, 8 (1979), 447-457.

111 Regnery, Henry. "Eliot, Pound, and Lewis: A Creative Friendship," ModA, 16, #2 (Spring, 1972), 146-160.

112 Roche, Denis. "Pour Ezra Pound," Tel Quel (Paris), No. 2 (Autumn, 1962), 17-24.

113 Rogers, William D. "Ezra Pound and the Law," NR, 140 (June 1, 1959), 20-21; Reply: Weyl, Nathaniel. "Pound and US Treason Law," NR, 140, #25 (June 22, 1959), 3, 22-23.

114 Russell, Peter. Ezra Pound: A Collection of Essays to be Presented to Ezra Pound on His 65th Birthday. London: Peter Neville, 1950; and under title An Examination of Ezra Pound: A Collection of Essays. New York: New Directions, 1950.

115 _____. "Ezra Pound: The Last Years," MHRev, 29 (July, 1974), 11-44.

116 _____. "The Youth of Ezra Pound," SoR, II, #2 (Spring, 1966), 443-452.

117 Savery, Pancho. "Lie Quiet, Ezra Pound," Epoch (Cornell U.), 22 (1973), 364-365.

118 Schaffner, Perdita. "Merano, 1962," Paideuma, 4, #2-3 (Fall-Winter, 1975), 513-518.

119 Schultz, Robert. "A Detailed Chronology of Ezra Pound's London Years, 1908-1920; Part One: 1908-1914; Part Two: 1915-1920," Paideuma, 11, #3 (Winter, 1982), 456-472; 12, #2-3 (Fall-Winter, 1983), 357-373.

120 Sheldon, Michael. "Allen Upward: Some Biographical Notes," Agenda, 16, iii-iv (1978-79), 108-121.

121 Simpson, Louis A. Three on the Tower: The Lives and Works of Ezra Pound, T. S. Eliot, and William Carlos Williams. New York: Wm. Morrow, 1975.

122 Slocum, John J. "Remembering Ezra Pound," YULG, 57, #1-2 (October, 1982), 52-65.

123 Stern, Richard. "A Memory or Two of Mr. Pound," Paideuma, 1, #2 (Winter, 1972), 215-219.

124 Stock, Noel. "Danger: Biographers at Work," XRev, 2 (August, 1961), 144-149.

125 _____, ed. Ezra Pound: Perspectives--Essays in Honor of His Eightieth Birthday. Chicago: Henry Regnery, 1965.

126 _____. Ezra Pound's Pennsylvania. Toledo, Ohio: Friends of the Univ. of Toledo Libraries, 1976.

127 _____. The Life of Ezra Pound. New York; London: Routledge & Kegan Paul, 1970; New York: Pantheon Books [First American Edition], 1970; expanded edition, North Point Pr., 1982.

128 _____. "A Scholar's View--A Poet's Life and Content," Agenda, I, #11 (June, 1960), 1-2.

129 Sullivan, John Patrick, "An Afternoon with Ezra," Paideuma, 7 (Spring-Fall, 1978), 283-286.

130 Tanselle, G. Thomas. "Ezra Pound and a Story of Floyd Dell's," N&Q, 8 (September, 1961), 350-352.

131 _____. "The Lawrence Gomme Imprint," PBSA, 61 (Third Qt., 1967), 225-240.

132 Taylor, James, ed. "Ezra Pound Birthday Issue, October 30, 1970," Sou'wester (So. Ill. U.), #35 (October 30, 1970), 3-5.

133 Terrell, Carroll. "Ezra Pound," Paideuma, 3, #3 (Winter, 1974), 363-379.

134 _____. "Memoir within Memoirs," Paideuma, 2, #1 (Spring, 1973), 49-51.

135 Thayer, Mary Dixon. "Ezra Pound's Father Tells How Son Went to London with a Shilling and Found Fame," Philadelphia Evening Bulletin (February 20, 1928), p. 12.

136 Thomas, Edward. Letters from Edward Thomas to Gordon Bottomley. Edited with Introduction by George Thomas. London: Oxford U. Pr., 1968, pp. 185, 187, 197.

137 Thompson, Francis J. "Ezra in Dublin," UTQ, 21 (October, 1951), 64-67.

138 Thompson, Harold W. Body, Boots, and Britches: Folk Tales, Ballads and Speeches from Country New York. New York: Dover Pubs., c1939, 1962, pp. 11, 12, 85.

139 Torrey, E. Fuller. "The Protection of Ezra Pound," Psychlogy Today, 15, #1 (November, 1981), 57-66.

140 Uberti, Riccardo M. degli. "Ezra Pound and Ubaldo degli Uberti: History of a Friendship," IQ, 64 (1973), 95-107.

141 Wallace, Emily Mitchell. "Afterword: 'Grampaw'--Thaddeus Coleman Pound," WCWN, 2, i (Spring, 1976), 5-6. [Facts about Pound's grandfather.]

142 _____. "Penn's Poet Friends," Pennsylvania Gazette, 71 (February, 1973), 35.

143 _____. "Pound and Williams at the University of Pennsylvania," Pennsylvania Rev. (Spring, 1967), i, 41-53.

144 Whigham, Peter. "Ezra Pound and Catullus," Cf., #125, pp. 62-77.

145 _____. "Four from Martial for Ezra Pound's Eightieth Birthday," Cf., #6, p. 29.

146 _____. "Pound in the Classroom," Cf., #6, pp. 62-68.

147 Whittemore, Reed. "Ezra Pound, 1884-1972," NR, 167, #18, Issue, 3018 (November 11, 1972), 28.

148 Wieners, John. "Ezra Pound at the Spoleto Festival, 1965," Cf., #6, pp. 68-69.

149 Wigginton, Waller B. "A Homer Pound Letter," Rendezvous, 4, #2 (Winter, 1969), 27-29.

150 _____. "The Pounds at Hailey," Cf., #149, pp. 31-68.

151 Wilhelm, James J. "Ezra Pound's New York, 1887-1908: A Recreation," Paideuma, 12, #1 (Spring, 1983), 55-87.

152 _____. "The Wadsworths, the Westons, and the Farewell of 1911," Paideuma, 12, #2-3 (Fall-Wntr, 1983), 305-347.

153 Williams, William Carlos. "A Letter from William Carlos Williams to Norman Holmes Pearson Concerning Ezra Pound's Father and Grandfather," WCWN, 2, 1 (Spring, 1976), 4-5.

154 _____. "Some Notes toward an Autobiography," Poetry, 74 (May, 1949), 94-111.

155 _____. "Something for a Biography," General Magazine and History Chronicle, 50 (Summer, 1948), 211-213.

156 Yoder, Jonathan. "Pound as Odysseus, the Prisoner Psychotic," Rendezvous, 8, 1 (Summer, 1973), 1-11.

THE BOLLINGEN AWARD

157 Adams, Leonie, Secretary to the Fellows in American Letters.

"Statement of Procedure of the Jury for the Bollingen Award," Cf., #195, pp. 21-23.

158 Agnoletti, Enriques E. "Il Caso Ezra Pound," Il Ponto (Italy), (October, 1949), 1327.

159 Ames, Alfred C. "The Case of Ezra Pound," SatRL, 29, #11 (March 16, 1946), 34.

160 Auden, W. H. "The Question of the Pound Award," PR, 16, #5 (May, 1949), 512-513; repr., #371, 54-56.

161 Barrett, William. "A Prize for Ezra Pound," PR, 16, #4 (April, 1949), 344-345; 16, #5 (May-July, 1949), 512-522.

162 Benet, William Rose. "Ezra Pound," NR, 121, #16 (October 17, 1949), 4.

163 Berryman, John. "A Tribute," Agenda, Cf., #6, 27-28.

164 Blish, James. "The Pound Scandal," SR, 67, #4 (October-December, 1959), 703-706.

165 Brooks, Cleanth. "Letter to the Editor," SatRL, 32, #44 (October 29, 1949), 24.

166 Burt, Struthers. "Pro Bollingen Bosh," SatRL, 32, #35 (August 27, 1949), 21-23.

167 Canby, Henry Seidel. "Ezra Pound," SatRL, 28, #50 (December 15, 1945), 10.

168 Carruth, Hayden. "The Anti-Poet All Told," Poetry, 74, #5 (August, 1949), 274-285.

169 _____. "The Bollingen Award: What Is It?" Poetry, 74 (June, 1949), 154-156.

170 _____. "A Few Notes on the Recent Essays of Mr. Hillyer," Poetry, 74, #5 (August, 1949), 283-285.

171 Childs, Harwood Lawrence, and John B. Whitton, eds. Propaganda by Short Wave. Princeton: 1951, pp. 153-180.

172 Corrigan, Robert A. "Ezra Pound and the Bollingen Prize Controversy," MASJ, 8, #2 (Fall, 1967), 43-57.

173 _____. "Ezra Pound and the Bollingen Prize Controversy," The Forties: Fiction, Poetry, Drama. Deland, Fla.: Everett/Edwards, 1969, pp. 287-295.

174 _____. "'What's My Line': Bennett Cerf, Ezra Pound and the 'American Poet,'" AQ, 24 (March, 1972), 101-113.

175 Cousins, Norman, and Harrison Smith. "The Destruction of Art for Art's Sake," SatRL, 33, #14 (April 8, 1950), 22-23.

176 _____, and _____. "Ezra Pound and the Bollingen Award," SatRL, 32 (June 11, 1949), 20-21.

177 _____, and _____. "More on Pound," SatRL, 32, #31 (July 30, 1949), 22.

178 Cowley, Malcolm. "The Battle Over Ezra Pound," NR, 121 (October 3, 1949), 17-20.

179 Cummings, Annette. "The Case of Ezra Pound," SatRL, 29, #11 (March 16, 1946), 34-35.

180 Davidson, Gustav. "Cancellation of Prizes Protested," NYT (August 29, 1949), p. 16, col. 7.

181 _____. "Poet Protests Award to Pound," NYT (March 3, 1949), p. 24, col. 6.

182 Davis, Earle. "Ezra Pound, Traitor and Poet," Kansas Magazine [annual], 1951; repr., in A Casebook on Ezra Pound, Cf., #29, pp. 78-86.

183 Davis, Robert Gorham. John Dos Passos. Minneapolis: U. of Minn. Pr., 1962, passim.

184 _____. "The New Criticism and the Democratic Tradition," AmerScholar, 19 (Winter, 1949-50), 9-19.

185 _____. "The Pound Award," PR, 16, #5 (April, 1949), 513-515.

186 Deutsch, Babette. "Odi et Amo," PR, 16 (June, 1949), 668-670.

187 Diggins, John P. "The Arcadian Political Vision: Ezra Pound and John Horne Burns," Mussolini and Fascism: The View from America. Princeton U. Pr., 1972, pp. 240-269ff.

188 Dougherty, James P. "The Aesthetic and the Intellectual Analyses of Literature," JAAC, 22 (1964), 315-324.

189 Elliott, Robert C. "Moral Evil and Literary Value: The Case of Ezra Pound," Ohio State Argo (Spring, 1951), 27-36.

190 "Ezra Pound and the Bollingen Award," SatRL, 32 (June 11,

1949), 20; (June 25, 1949), 26; (July 2, 1949), 24-26; September 27, 1949), 22.

191 "Ezra Pound Awarded Bollingen Prize for Poetry," PubW, 155 (March 5, 1949), 1162-1163.

192 "Ezra Pound Crowned," LitD, 96 (January 14, 1928), 24-25.

193 Fitzgerald, Robert. "Further Comment on the Pound Award," Cf., #185, pp. 765-766.

194 Franzen, Erich. "T. S. Eliot und die Masken Ezra Pounds," Die Wandlung, 4 (August, 1949), 593-604.

195 "Further Remarks on the Pound Award," Cf., #160, pp. 666-670.

196 Gordon, David. "Zuk and Ez at St. Liz," Paideuma, 7, #3 (Winter, 1978), 581-584.

197 H. S. and N. C. "A Reply to Mr. Evans," SatRL, 32, #27 (July 2, 1949), 22-23.

198 Harnwell, Anna Jane. "The Case of Ezra Pound," Cf., #159, #11 (March 16, 1946), 32-33.

199 Hillyer, Robert. "The Case of Ezra Pound," Cf., #159, #11, p. 34.

200 _____. "Poetry's New Priesthood," SatRL, 32, #25 (June 18, 1949), 7-9, 38.

201 _____. "Treason's Strange Fruit: The Case of Ezra Pound and the Bollingen Award," SatRL, 32 (June 11, 1949), 9-11, 28.

202 Hopkins, Harry L. "The Case of Ezra Pound," Cf., #159 (March 16, 1946), 34.

203 Hoult, Thomas Ford. "More About the Pound Award," Cf., #160, #5 (1949), 767-768.

204 Howe, Irving. "The Question of the Pound Award," PR, Cf., #160, #5 (May, 1949), 516-517.

205 Huett, Richard. "Non-Sequitur," Cf., #160, #5 (1949), 671-672.

206 Hynes, Sam. "The Case of Ezra Pound," Cw, 63 (1955), 251-254.

207 James, Roberta. "The Case of Ezra Pound," SatRL, 29, #11 (March 16, 1946), 35.

208 Kapp, Jack. "The Case of Ezra Pound," Cf., #207, pp. 33-34.

209 Koch, Adrienne, and W. M. Lowry. "Evaluating the Pound Award," NYT (February 24, 1949), p. 22, col. 7.

210 Library of Congress. "Annex IV to the Statement: The Announcement of the Award: Library of Congress Press Release No. 542, February 20, 1949; repr., in The Case Against the Saturday Review, Cf., #215, pp. 29-38.

211 Loftus, Beverly J. G. "Ezra Pound and the Bollingen Prize: The Controversy in Periodicals," JQ, 39 (Summer, 1962), 347-354.

212 Louchheim, Aline B. "The State and Art," NYT (September 4, 1959), p. 8, cols. 1-3. Cf., also #352.

213 MacDonald, Dwight. "Homage to Twelve Judges," Politics (Winter, 1949); repr., in Memoirs of a Revolutionist. New York: Farrar, Straus & Cudahy, 1957; Meridian Bks., Inc., 1958; repr., Cf., #29, pp. 46-48.

214 McGuire, William. "The Bollingen Foundation: Ezra Pound and the Prize in Poetry," QJLC, 40, #1 (Winter, 1983), 16-25.

215 Meredith, William. "Letter of Protest," The Case Against The Saturday Review of Literature. Poetry [Modern Poetry Assn.]. Chicago: 1949, pp. 63-64. [Cf., #210]

216 Miller, Noland. "The Case of Ezra Pound," Cf., #159, p. 34.

217 Musselman, M. M. "The Case of Ezra Pound," Cf., #159, p. 35.

218 Norman, Charles. The Case of Ezra Pound. New York: The Bodley Pr., 1948; Funk & Wagnalls, 1968.

219 O'Connor, William Van. [Letter], Cf., #215, pp. 64-67.

220 O'Grady, Desmond. "Ezra Pound: A Personal Memoir," Agenda, 17, #3-4; 18, #1 (Autumn-Wntr-Spring., 1979-80), 285-299.

221 Olson, Paul A. "The Bollingen Controversy Ten Years After: Criticism and Content," Prairie Schooner, 33 (Fall, 1959), 225-229.

222 Orwell, George. "The Question of the Pound Award," PR, 16 (May, 1949), 517-518; repr., in A Casebook on Ezra Pound, Cf., #29, pp. 60-61.

223 Reit, Seymour V. "The Case of Ezra Pound," SatRL, 29, #11 (March 16, 1946), 34.

224 Ringer, Gordon. "More about the Pound Award," PR, 16, #7 (1949), 766-767.

225 Rosten, Norman. "The Case Against Ezra Pound," Cf., #159, p. 32.

226 Ruggeri, Cosimo. "Inveco del capestro il premio 'Bollingen,'" Momenta-Sera (February 2, 1949).

227 Shapiro, Karl. "Letter to the Editor," The Baltimore Sun, (February 25, 1949), 16.

228 _____. "More about the Pound Award," PR, 16, #7 (1949), 764.

229 _____. "The Question of the Pound Award," PR, 16, #5 (April, 1949), 518-519.

230 Sheerin, J. B. "The Pound Affair," Catholic World, 169 (August, 1949), 322-323.

231 Sillen, Samuel. "A Prize for Ezra Pound," M&M, 2 (April, 1949), 3-6. Cf., also, #1178.

232 Smith, Harrison. "End of Controversy," Sat RL, 32 (September 3, 1949), 23.

233 _____. "Lock, Stock, and Barrel," SatRL, 33 (March 4, 1950), 24.

234 _____, and Norman Cousins. "A Reply to Mr. Evans," SatRL, 32, #27 (July 2, 1949), 22-23.

235 Squires, Radcliffe. "Ambassador of Culture," Allen Tate: A Literary Biography. New York: Pegasus (A Division of Bobbs-Merrill Co.), 1971, pp. 184-189.

236 Struthers, Burt. "Pro Bollingen Bosh," SatRL, 32, #35 (August 27, 1949), 21-23.

237 Tate, Allen. "Annex I to the Statement: A Personal Statement on Fascism by Allen Tate," The Case Against the Saturday Review, Cf., #215, pp. 19-21.

238 _____. "Ezra Pound," Collected Essays. Denver: Allan Swallow, 1959, pp. 364-371, 532-536, passim.

239 _____. "Ezra Pound," An Examination of Ezra Pound. Rev. and Enl. Peter Russell, ed., Cf., #114, pp. 66-72.

240 _____. "Ezra Pound and the Bollingen Prize," Essays of Four Decades. Chicago: Swallow Pr., 1959, 1968, pp. 509-513.

241 _____. "Ezra Pound," The Forlorn Demon. Chicago: H. Regnery, 1953, pp. 156-160.

242 _____. "Ezra Pound," Ezra Pound: Perspectives. Noel Stock, ed., Cf., #125, pp. 86-89.

243 _____. "Ezra Pound and the Bollingen Prize," The Man of Letters in the Modern World. London: 1936; Meridian Bks., 1957, pp. 264-267.

244 _____. "Further Remarks on the Pound Award," PartisanRev, 16 (June, 1949), 666-668.

245 _____. "Poetry and Politics," NR, 75 (August 2, 1933), 308-311.

246 _____. "The Question of the Pound Award," PartisanRev, 5 (April, 1949), 520.

247 Tichenor, George H. "This Man Is a Traitor," PM (August 15, 1943), 3-5.

248 Van Doren, Mark. Letter [to Harrison Smith, Publisher of SatRL], May 26, 1949, Cf., #215, p. 62.

249 Viereck, Peter. "My Kind of Poetry," SatRL, 32 (August 27, 1949), 7-8, 35-36.

250 _____. "Pure Poetry, Impure Politics, and Ezra Pound," Commentary, 12 (April, 1951), 340-346; "Pure Poetry, Impure Politics: The Implications of Ezra Pound and the Bollingen Controversy," Dream and Responsibility: Four Test Cases of the Tension Between Poetry and Society. Washington, D.C., 1953, pp. 1-22.

251 _____. "Symbols: Hiss and Pound," Cw, 55 (March 28, 1952), 607-608.

252 Weissman, David L. "Ezra Pound," NR, 121, #16 (October 17, 1949), 4.

253 Wenning, Henry W. T. S. Eliot and Ezra Pound. New Haven: C. A. Stonehill, Inc., 1970.

254 West, Ray. "Excerpts from a Journal," Western Review, 14 (Winter, 1950), 82, 151-159; repr., Item #29, pp. 67-73.

255 Weyl, Nathaniel. "The Bollingen Award," Cf., #29, pp. 17-18.

256 Winters, Yvor. "Letter to Editors of Saturday Review of Literature," in The Case Against the Saturday Review, Cf., #215, pp. 69-71.

257 Woodfin, Henry A., Jr. "More about the Pound Award," PR, 16, #7 (July, 1949), 764-765.

258 Young, Gordon. "The Case of Ezra Pound," SatRL, 29, #11 (March 16, 1946), 35.

259 Young, Thomas Daniel. "The Little Houses against the Great," SR, 88 (Spring, 1980), 320-330.

THE CASE OF EZRA POUND AND HIS CONFINEMENT AT ST. ELIZABETH'S

260 Aiken, Conrad. Reviewer's ABC: Collected Criticism of Conrad Aiken from 1916 to the Present. New York: Meridian, 1958.

261 Allen, Robert L. "The Cage," Esquire (February, 1958); repr., Cf., #29.

262 Alvarez, A. "Ezra Pound: Craft and Morals," Stewards of Excellence: Studies in Modern English and American Poets. New York: Gordian Pr., 1971, pp. 48-72; repr., in Ezra Pound: Perspectives: Essays in Honor of His Eightieth Birthday. Noel Stock, ed., Cf., #125.

263 _____. "The Wretched Poet Who Lived in the House of Bedlam," SatRL, 53 (July 18, 1970), 27-39.

264 Arnold, Thurman. Fair Fights and Foul: A Dissenting Lawyer's Life. New York: Harcourt, Brace & World, 1965, pp. 236-242.

265 "An Artist Confined," Life Magazine, 40 (February 6, 1956), 30; repr., Cf., #291, pp. 121-122.

266 Barry, Iris. "Ezra Pound in London," Ezra Pound: Dichtung und Prosa. Eva Hesse, ed. Frankfurt: Athenaum, 1967, pp. 389-397.

267 Bayes, Ronald H. "Who Sprung Ezra? Continued Speculation," UPortR, 20, i (1968), 47-48.

268 Benet, William Rose. "The Case of Ezra Pound," SatRL, 26, #10 (March 6, 1943), 20-21.

269 _____. "Phoenix Nest," SatRL, 32 (July 23, 1949), 28.

270 Bishop, Elizabeth. "Visits to St. Elizabeth's," NC, #5-6 (1956), 28-34.

271 Blish, James. "The Pound Scandal," Cf., #164.

272 Bonfante, Jordan. "An Aging Genius in Exile," Life, 56 (March 27, 1964), 43-44, 46, 48.

273 Booth, Marcella Spann. "Through the Smoke Hole: Ezra Pound's Last Year at St. Elizabeth's," Paideuma, 3, #3 (Winter, 1974), 329-334.

274 Bosha, Francis J. "Faulkner, Pound, and the P.P.P.," Paideuma, 8 (1979), 249-256. [P.P.P., People-to-People Program]

275 Bradbury, Malcolm. "A Visit to Ezra Pound," TC, 159 (June, 1956), 604-606.

276 Breit, Harvey. "Birthday," NYTBR, 61, #39 (September 23, 1956), 8.

277 Bridson, D. G. "Ezra Pound's 'Four Steps,'" SoR, 13 (Autumn, 1977), 862-871.

278 Brooks, Cleanth. Letter to Editor of Saturday Review of Literature, (October 4, 1949), in The Case Against The Saturday Review, Cf., #215, pp. 68-69.

279 "Brought Back to Face Treason Charges," NYT (November 19, 1945), p. 12, col. 3.

280 Brown, Peter. "Revalued Pound," NSt, 86 (December 14, 1973), 904.

281 Canby, H. S. "Ezra Pound," SatRL, 28, #50, Cf., #167, p. 10.

282 Carruth, Hayden. "The Anti-Poet All Told," Poetry, 74, #5 (August, 1949), 274-282; repr., in The Case Against The Saturday Review, Cf., #215, pp. 46-55.

283 The Case Against The Saturday Review of Literature. Chicago: Poetry, [Pub.], Cf., #215.

284 Cerf, Bennett. "The Case of Ezra Pound," SatRL, 29, #6 (February 9, 1946), 26-27.

285 _____. "The Case of Ezra Pound," SatRL, 29, #11 (March 16, 1946), 32-36, 49-53.

286 Chilanti, Felice. "Ezra Pound Among the Seditious in the 1940's," Paideuma, 6 (Fall, 1977), 235-250.

287 Cohane, J. J., Jr. "Poet without a Country: Reply," Commonweal, 41 (November 10, 1944), 101.

288 Connolly, Cyril. "Ezra Pound: 1, 2, 3," The Evening Colonnade. New York; London: Harcourt, Brace, Jovanovich, 1973, pp. 217-221, 222-225, 226-228.

289 Cornell, Julien. "Letter to Bennett Cerf," (May 10, 1946), The Trial of Ezra Pound. New York: John Day Co., 1966, p. 115.

290 _____. "Letter to the Editor," SatRL, 31 (October 2, 1948), p. 21.

291 _____. The Trial of Ezra Pound: A Documented Account of the Treason Case by the Defendant's Lawyer. New York: John Day Co.,; London: Faber, 1967.

292 Corrigan, Robert A. "Ezra Pound and the Italian Ministry for Popular Culture," Journal of Popular Culture, 15, #4 (Spring, 1972), 767-781.

293 _____. "Literature and Politics: The Case of Ezra Pound Reconsidered," American Character and Culture in a Changing World. John A. Hague, ed. Westport, CT, 1964, pp. 81-98; see also: Prospects, 2 (1976), 463-482.

294 Cowley, Malcolm. "A Literary Odyssey of the 1920's," Exile's Return. New York: Viking Pr., 1934, 1959, pp. 119-124, passim.

295 _____. "Fox in Flight," Furioso, 6 (Spring, 1951), 7-10.

296 Cruvant, Bernard A. [Letter] "From Pound's Psychiatrist," SatRL, 32, #40 (October 1, 1949), 22.

297 Cummings, E. E. "Re: Ezra Pound: I--Ezra Pound: II: New York," E. E. Cummings: A Miscellany Revised. Ed. with Introduction and Notes by George J. Firmage. Foreword by E. E. Cummings. New York: October House, Inc., 1965, pp. 312, 313-315.

298 Davenport, Guy. "Il Vecchio," StAR, 1, #1 (Fall-Winter, 1970), 19-20.

299 Davis, Clyde Brion. "The Case of Ezra Pound," SatRL, 29, #11 (March 16, 1946), 33.

300 Delehanty, Elizabeth. "Day with Ezra Pound," NY, 16 (April 13, 1940), 76-77.

301 Deutsch, Albert. "Ezra Pound, Turncoat Poet, Seeks Release from Federal Mental Hospital," PM (January 25, 1947), 1, 24.

302 _____. "Pound Gets 'Unsound Mind' Verdict," PM (February 14, 1946), p. 7.

303 Dickey, R. P. "Ezra Pound," Sou'wester (So. Ill. U.) (October 30, 1970), 129.

304 Drummond, John. "Accusato non condannato," Paese Sera, 6 (June 16, 1954), 3.

305 _____. "I Passatempi dell' ambasciatore," Il Borghese, 7, 3 (Milano: January 21, 1955), 111.

306 _____. "Il Caso di Ezra Pound," Fiera Lettaria, 16 (April 17, 1949).

307 _____. "Il Dissenziente," Il Borghese, 49 (December 9, 1955), 882-883.

308 _____. "Pound's Lire," TLS (July 14, 1972), 819.

309 _____. "La verita sul caso Pound," FLe, 1 (January 7, 1951), 1.

310 Dudek, Louis. "Visit to Ezra Pound," Contemporary Verse (Summer, 1950), 20-23.

311 _____. "Why Is Ezra Pound Being Held in St. Elizabeth's Hospital, Washington, D.C.?" Civ/n, #4 (1953), 19.

312 [Editors of Hudson Review]. "Comment," HudR, 2, #3 (Autumn, 1949), 325-326; repr., in The Case Against The Saturday Review, Cf., #215, pp. 43-45.

313 Enriques Agnoletti, E. "Il Caso Ezra Pound," Il Ponte (Italy), (October, 1949), p. 1327.

314 Evans, David W. "Ezra Pound as Prison Poet," UKCR, 23 (Spring, 1957), 215-220.

315 Feldman, David. "Ezra Pound: A Poet in a Cage," Paideuma, 10, #2 (Fall, 1981), 361-365.

316 Feuchtwanger, Lion. "'Should Ezra Pound Be Shot?'-Five Writers Indict Him as a Traitor," New Masses (December 25, 1945), 5-6.

317 Fleming, William. "A Lone Ant from a Broken Ant-hill," Meanjin, 4 (Melbourne), 1954.

318 _____. "The Melbourne Vortex," Paideuma, 3, #3 (Winter, 1974), 325-328; also in AntigR, 9 (Spring, 1972), 74-77.

319 _____. "Prometheus Unbound: The Case of Ezra Pound," TCAus, 16 (1962), 208-213.

320 Friar, Kimon. "Politics and Some Poets," NR, 127 (July 7, 1952), 17-18.

321 Frost, Robert. "Statement of Robert Frost," United States of America, vs. Ezra Pound, Defendant. Criminal No. 76028; repr., in A Casebook on Ezra Pound. Wm. Van O'Connor and Edward Stone, eds. Cf., #29, pp. 135-138.

322 Gannett, Lewis. [Letter] New York Herald Tribune, repr., in SatRL, Cf., #284, pp. 26-27.

323 Garrison, Omar. "Ezra Pound's Italian Friends Campaign for His Release," The Mirror [Los Angeles], (April 21, 1954).

324 Giovannini, Giovanni. "The Strange Case of Ezra Pound," New Times (Melbourne), 21 (August 26, 1955), 194-196.

325 Glicksberg, Charles I. "Ezra Pound and the Fascist Complex," SAQ, 45 (July, 1947), 349-358.

326 _____. "Ezra Pound and the Commitment to Fascism," The Literature of Commitment. Bucknell U. Pr., Lewisburg, PA, 1977, pp. 100-110.

327 Gold, Michael. "A Bourgeois Hamlet of Our Time," New Masses, 11, #2 (April 10, 1934), 28-30.

328 _____. [Open Letter to Ezra Pound], New Masses (September, 1931), repr., New Masses (December 25, 1945).

329 Gordon, Arthur. "Intruder in the South," Look (February 19, 1957), 27-31.

330 Graham, John F. "Letter to the Editor," Paideuma, 4, #1 (Spring, 1975), 200-203. [Comment on C. F. Terrell's article on Pound at St. Elizabeth's, Cf., #133.]

331 Haley, Martin. "Is Ezra Pound, Modern Don Quixote, Really Mad?" Advocate (Melbourne), (September 13, 1951), 9.

332 Heymann, C. David. "The Case of Ezra Pound," Shantih: Journal of International Writing & Art (Brooklyn, New York), 3, #4 (1977), 48-52.

333 Holder, Alan. "Prisoner Ezra Pound," VQR, 44 (Spring, 1968), 337-341.

334 Homberger, Eric. "Pound and the Ostriches," CambridgeRev, 89 (November 4, 1967), 70-72; repr., in Ezra Pound: A Critical Anthology. J. P. Sullivan, ed. Baltimore, Md., 1970, pp. 350-353.

335 Howe, Irving. "The Case of Ezra Pound," The Critical Point: On Literature and Culture. New York: Horizon Pr., 1973, pp. 109-120.

336 _____. "The Return of the Case of Ezra Pound," World, 1, #9 (October 24, 1972), 20-24.

337 Humphries, Rolphe. "Poets, Traitors and Patriots," NR, 109, #22 (November 29, 1943), 748.

338 Hutchens, John K. "Round Two," New York Times (March 31, 1946), Section 7, 36.

339 Kavka, Jerome. "Ezra Pound's Sanity: The Agony of Public Disclosure," Paideuma, 4, #2 and 3 (Fall-Winter, 1975), 527-529.

340 Kenner, Hugh. "Ezra Pound on Visitors Day," NYT (November 19, 1972), 6.

341 Kimpel, Ben D., and T. C. Duncan Eaves. "More on Pound's Prison Experience," AL, 53, #3 (November, 1981), 469-476.

342 Knoll, Robert E. "Ezra Pound at St. Elizabeth's," PrS, 47 (Spring, 1973), 1-13.

343 Kutler, Stanley I. "'This Notorious Patient'--The Asylum of Ezra Pound," The American Inquisition: Justice and Injustice in the Cold War. New York: Hill & Wang of Farrar, Straus & Giroux, 1982, pp. 59-88.

344 Laughlin, James. "Letter to T. S. Eliot," Humanities Research Center, University of Texas, (December 23, 1945); (February 15, 1946).

345 Lawson, John Howard. "Inner Conflict and Proletarian Art--A Reply to Michael Gold," New Masses (April 17, 1934), p. 29.

346 LaZebnik, Jack. "The Case of Ezra Pound," NR, 136 (April 1, 1957), 17-20.

347 "Letters: The Case for Pound," LonM, 3, #4 (New Series), (July, 1963), 68-74. Cf., Conquest, Robert, "Letters," #2098.

348 "Letters to the Editor," SatRL, 32 (June 25, 1949), 26-27; (July 9, 1949), 23-25; (July 16, 1949), 21-22; (July 23, 1949), 22-23; (July 30, 1949), 23-24; (August 27, 1949), 21-23; (September 3, 1949), 26; (September 24, 1949), 27; (October 1, 1949), 22.

349 Lewis, Anthony. "U.S. Asked to End Pound Indictment: Court Told Poet's Insanity Is Incurable; Wife Would Take Him Back to Italy," NYT (Tuesday, April 15, 1958); repr., in A Casebook for Ezra Pound, Cf., O'Connor and Stone, eds., #29, pp. 132-134.

350 "Liberare Pound," in "Copialettere," Il Tempo, March 12, 1954; (report of Boris de Rachewiltz's reply to attack on Pound in "Una Storia d'Italia ed alcuni canti mazisti," by F. Fortini).

351 Lottman, Herbert R. "The Silences of Ezra Pound," Cf., #76, pp. 105-110.

352 Louchheim, Aline B. "The State of Art," Cf., #212, p. 8, cols. 1-3.

353 McCabe, Victoria. "Pound," [poem], Sou'wester (October 30, 1970), pp. 133-134.

354 MacDonald, Dwight. "Homage to Twelve Judges," Cf., #213, pp. 46-48.

355 McGrory, Mary. "Ezra Pound Still Sees Mad World Out of Step," Washington Star, April 30, 1958; repr., in A Casebook on Ezra Pound, Cf., O'Connor and Stone, eds., #29, pp. 144-148.

356 McKenzie, Donald. "T(h)inker Pound and Other Italian Legends," The Left, 1 (Summer-Autumn, 1931), 48-52.

357 MacShane, Frank, et al. "Letters: The Case for Pound," LonM, 3 (July, 1963), pp. 68-74.

358 Marshall, Margaret. "The Saturday Review Unfair to Literature," Nation, 169 (December 17, 1949), 598-599.

359 Matthiessen, F. O. [Response to Isidor Schneider], New Masses (December 25, 1945), p. 6.

360 Mayfield, John S. The Black Badge of Treason: An Account of Ezra Pound. Washington, D.C., Park Book Shop, 1944.

361 Meacham, Harry M. The Caged Panther: Ezra Pound at Saint Elizabeth's. New York: Twayne Pubs., 1967.

362 _____. "I Remember Ezra," Cf., #84, pp. 21-24.

363 Meyers, Jeffrey. "Shrinking Pound," Spectator (April 28, 1984), 25-26.

364 Mizener, Arthur. The Saddest Story: A Biography of Ford Madox Ford. New York; Cleveland: The World Pub. Co., 1971, passim.

365 Mullins, Eustace Clarence. This Difficult Individual: Ezra Pound. Cf., #92.

366 Neame, Alan. "Speech and Penalty," European, 10 (February, 1958), 351-360.

367 _____. "Typing Under the Bed," and "Neame Is Nuts," Agenda, 17, #3-4, and 18, #1 (Aut-Wntr-Spr., 1979-80), 194-196, 196-197.

368 Norman, Charles. "The Case for or against Ezra Pound," PM Newspaper, 6 (November 25, 1945), 12-17.

369 _____. "Pound in St. Elizabeth's," and "The Trial," Ezra Pound. Cf., #93, pp. 418-435; 436-458.

370 O'Connor, William Van, and Edward Stone, eds. A Casebook on Ezra Pound. Cf., #29.

371 Odlin, Reno. "Pound at St. Elizabeth's," AntigR, 51 (Autumn, 1982), 39-48.

372 Olmstead, Edwin G. "Usher Burdick and Ezra Pound," NDQ, 28 (Summer, 1960), 66-68.

373 Olson, Charles. Charles Olson and Ezra Pound: An Encounter at St. Elizabeth's by Charles Olson. Catherine Seelye, ed. New York: Grossman Pubs., 1975.

374 _____. "This is Yeats Speaking," PR, 13 (Winter, 1946), 139-142. Cf., #373, pp. 27-31.

375 Patchen, Kenneth. "Ezra Pound's Guilt," Renascence, 2 (February, 1946), 3-4.

376 Pearson, R. M. "Poet in a Cage," LGJ, 1, i (May, 1973), 26-29.

377 Pegler, Westbrook. "As Pegler Sees It," New York Journal-American (April 15, 1955).

378 _____. "Cult Lowdown: Ezra Pound Mystery," Boston Evening American (April 15, 1955).

379 _____. "History of the Case of Ezra Pound," San Francisco Call-Bulletin (September 16, 1955), 32.

380 Pepper, Bill. "It Happened in Italy," Rome Daily American (June 17, 1954).

381 "Pound Awaits Treason Trial," NYT (November 25, 1945), p. 7, col. 3.

382 "Pound Foolish," Newsweek, 27, No. 8 (February 25, 1946), 29; repr., in A Casebook on Ezra Pound, Cf., #29, p. 23.

383 Raddatz, Fritz J. "Poetischer Materialist. Zum Tode [Poetic Materialist. On the Death of] Ezra Pound," Merkur, 26, #296 (December, 1972), 1224-1232.

384 Reck, Michael. "Letter to the Editor," Paideuma, 3, #3 (Winter, 1974), 419-420.

385 Reinhold, Robert. "Ezra Pound Is Focus of New Dispute," NYT (July 5, 1972), Sec. 1, p. 29.

386 Rosenfeld, Paul. "The Case of Ezra Pound," AmMercury, 58 (January, 1944), 98-102.

387 Rovere, Richard. "The Contraries of Ezra Pound," Opinions and Speculations. New York: Harcourt, Brace & World, 1962, pp. 204-222.

388 _____. "The Question of Ezra Pound," Esquire, 48 (September, 1957), 66-80.

389 Russell, Francis. "Poet in the Madhouse," Observer (London), (March 1, 1953), 10.

390 Scarfoglio, Carlo. "Il caso Ezra Pound," Paeso Sera, 6 (June 16, 1954), 3.

391 Schneider, Isidor. "Should Ezra Pound Be Shot?" New Masses, 57, #11 (December 11, 1945), 5.

392 _____. "Traitor or Holy Idiot," New Masses, 57, #11 (December 11, 1945), 13.

393 Scott, Tom. "The Poet as Scapegoat," Agenda, 7, #2 (Spring, 1969), 49-58.

394 "The Seeker," Time, 46 (December 10, 1945), 22.

395 Shapiro, Karl. Beyond Criticism. Lincoln: University of Nebraska, 1953, pp. 1-6.

396 Sherman, William David. "The Case of Ezra Pound: A Documentary Play," AWR, 19 (Autumn, 1970), 85-108.

397 Shirer, William L. "The American Radio Traitors," Harper's Mag, 187 (October, 1943), 397-404.

398 Sieber, H. A., and Rudd Fleming. "The Case of Ezra Pound: A Cause Célèbre Is Ended," Washington Post & Times Herald (July 6, 1958), E-7.

399 _____, ed. The Medical, Legal, Literary and Political Status of Ezra Weston [Loomis] Pound, Selected Facts and Comments. Washington: The Library of Congress Legislative Reference Service, March 31, 1958; revised April 14, 1958.

400 Smith, Harrison. "Strange Paradox," SatRL, 35 (February 9, 1952), 20.

401 Spingarn, Natalie Davis. "St. Elizabeths, pace-setter for Mental Hospitals," Harpers (January, 1956), 58-63.

402 Stock, Noel. Poet in Exile: Ezra Pound. Manchester, 1964; New York: Barnes & Noble, 1964.

403 _____. "Why Is Ezra Pound Imprisoned?" New Times, Melbourne (March 9, 1956).

404 Szasz, Thomas S. "Politics and Mental Health: Some Remarks Apropos of the Case of Mr. Ezra Pound," American Journal of Psychiatry, 115 (1958), 508-511.

405 _____. "Politics and Psychiatry: The Case of Mr. Ezra Pound," Law, Liberty, and Psychiatry: An Inquiry Into the Social Uses of Mental Health Practices. New York: Macmillan, 1963, p. 228; Collier Books, 1968, pp. 199-211.

406 Terrell, Carroll F. "St. Elizabeths," Cf., #133.

407 Torrey, E. Fuller. The Death of Psychiatry. Radnor, Pennsylvania: Chilton Book Co., 1974, p. 81.

408 _____. The Roots of Treason: Ezra Pound and the Secret of St. Elizabeth's. New York: McGraw-Hill Book Co., 1984. Rev. by Jeffrey Meyers, "Shrinking Pound," Spectator (April 28, 1984), 25-26.

409 "Treason," Time, 46, #24 (December 10, 1945), 22; repr., Cf., #370, pp. 19-20.

410 Untermeyer, Louis. Letter to Charles Norman, October 8, 1945, Van Pelt Library, University of Pennsylvania; published

in [Charles Norman], "Ezra Pound," PM (November 15, 1945), 17.

411 Varney, H. L. "Mental Health, Fact and Fiction," AmMercury, 84 (April, 1957), 11-12.

412 "Vatican Radio Appeal for Pound Circulated," Paris Herald Tribune, (June 8, 1954).

413 Viator. "El Poeta Loco," La Universidad del Zulia, 2, #61 (May 6, 1958), 4.

414 Walton, Edna Lou. "Should Ezra Pound Be Shot?--Five Writers Indict Him as Traitor," New Masses (December 25, 1945), 5-6.

415 Watts, Harold H. "Philosopher at Bay," Cronos, 2 (March, 1948), 1-16.

416 "Wertham Assails Ezra Pound [Insanity] Ruling," NYT, (November 27, 1949), p. 33, col. 1, (I).

417 Wertham, Frederic. "For Ezra Pound's Release," SatRL, 34 (April 7, 1951), 22.

418 _____. "The Road to Rapallo: A Psychiatric Study," American Journal of Psychotherapy," 3 (1949), 585-600; survey of press comments, replies, and rejoinders appears in American Journal of Psychotherapy, 4, #1, pp. 123-140, and 4, #2, pp. 320-322.

419 Weyl, Nathaniel. "Pound and US Treason Law," NR, 140, #25 (June 22, 1959), 3, 22-23.

420 _____. "The Strange Case of Ezra Pound," Treason: The Story of Disloyalty and Betrayal in American History. Washington, D.C.: Public Affairs Pr., 1950; Cf., #370, pp. 5-18.

421 "What the Pound Case Means," Nation, 186, #16 (April 19, 1958), 335; repr., Cf., #370, pp. 130-131.

422 "Why Is Ezra Pound Being Held in St. Elizabeth's Hospital, Washington, D.C.?" Civ/n, No. 4 (Montreal: 1953), 19.

423 Williams, William Carlos. "Ezra Pound at St. Elizabeth's," The Autobiography of William Carlos Williams. New York: Random House, 1948, pp. 335-344; repr., in The William Carlos Williams Reader. New York: New Directions, 1966, pp. 308-318.

424 _____. "Poets and Critics Size up Pound as an Artist and as a Man," PM (November 25, 1945).

425 Wood, Lewis. "Pound Awaits Treason Trial," NYT (November 25, 1945), Sec. 4, p. 7.

426 "Your Witness: Ezra Pound," Scholastic, 48 (April 29, 1946), 20.

II. POETRY AND PROSE WORKS

CANTOS

427 Abiru, Shin. "Ezura Paundo no Kanto," [The Cantos of Ezra Pound], Shiho (Poetical Methods), #2 (1934), pp. 47-53.

428 Adams, Stephen Jon. "Are the Cantos a Fugue?" UTQ, 45 (Fall, 1975), 67-74.

429 _____. "Ezra Pound and Music," DAI, 37, #1 (Toronto: 1974), 7746.

430 _____. "The Soundscape of the Cantos: Some Ideas of Music in the Poetry of Ezra Pound," HAB, 28 (Spring, 1977), 177-181.

431 Alexander, Michael. "On Rereading the Cantos," Agenda, 4, #2 (October-November, 1965), 4-10.

432 _____. The Poetic Achievement of Ezra Pound. Berkeley: California U. Pr., 1979.

433 Amdur, Alice Steiner. "The Cantos," The Poetry of Ezra Pound. Cambridge, Mass., 1936; reissued, Russell & Russell, 1966.

434 Axelrod, Steven Gould. Robert Lowell, Life and Art. Princeton, New Jersey: Princeton U. Pr., 1978, pp. 74-75, 122-123, passim.

435 Baar, Ron. "Ezra Pound: Poet as Historian," AL, 42, #4 (January, 1971), 531-543.

436 Bachinger, Katrina. "A Make/Made Dialectic as a Key to Pound's Cantos," The Servant of the Muse: A Garland for Peter Russell on His Sixtieth Birthday. James Hogg, ed. Salzburg: Inst. für Anglistik & Amerikanistik, U. of Salzburg, 1981, VIII, pp. 207-224.

437 Bacigalupo, Massimo. "'Absolute' Timelessness: The Case of the Middle Cantos," The Formed Trace: The Later Poetry of Ezra Pound. New York: Columbia U. Pr., 1980, pp. 52-100.

438 _____. "Ezra Pound's Canto 106: A Late Mythologem," IQ, 16, #64 (1973), 77-93.

439 _____. "The Poet at War: Ezra Pound's Suppressed Italian Cantos," SAQ, 83, #1 (Winter, 1984), 69-79.

440 _____. "Sofocle e la danza tragica: Le Franchinie di Pound," Paragone, 334 (1976), 60-70.

441 _____. "Un tardo mitologema: Il canto 106 di Ezra Pound," Verri, Ser. 6, #1 (1976), 36-65.

442 Balagot, Thelma C. "A Guide to Ezra Pound's Cantos (VI)," Analyst, 3 (December, 1953), 1-9, 10.

443 Banerjee, R. D. K. "Formality and Intimacy in the Cantos of Ezra Pound," IJAS, 2, #2 (December, 1972), 2-11.

444 Barker, George. "Mr. Pound's New Cantos," Criterion, 14 (July, 1935), 649-651.

445 Baumann, Walter. "But to Affirm the Gold Thread in the Pattern (116/797): An Examination of Canto 116," Paideuma, 12, 2/3 (Fall-Winter, 1983), 199-221.

446 _____. "Pound and Layamon's Brut," JEGP, 68 (April, 1969), 265-276.

447 _____. The Rose in the Steel Dust: An Examination of the Cantos of Ezra Pound. Francke Verlag, Bern, 1967; Coral Gables, Florida: U. of Miami Pr., 1970.

448 _____. "The Structure of Canto IV," Cf., #52, pp. 117-137.

449 Bell, Ian F. A. "'Speaking in Figures': The Mechanical Thomas Jefferson of Canto 31," Ezra Pound: Tactics for Reading. Ian F. A. Bell, ed. London: Vision Pr.; Totowa, NJ: Barnes & Noble, 1982, pp. 148-186.

450 Berezin, Charles. "Poetry and Politics in Ezra Pound," PR, 48, #2 (1981), 262-279.

451 Bergonzi, Bernard. "From Imagism to Fascism," TLS (September 24, 1976), 1195-1196.

452 Bernstein, Michael André. "Distinguendum est inter et inter: A Defense of Calliope," Paideuma, 12, 2/3 (Fall-Wntr., 1983), 269-274.

453 _____. Ezra Pound and the Modern Verse Epic. Diss., Oxford U., 1975.

454 _____. "Identification and Its Vicissitudes: The Narrative Structure of Ezra Pound's Cantos," YR, 69 (Summer, 1980), 540-556.

455 _____. "Myths and Logos in Ezra Pound: The Splitting of the Realms," Paideuma, 8 (1979), 543-548.

456 _____. The Tale of the Tribe: Ezra Pound and the Modern Verse Epic. Princeton: Princeton U. Pr., 1980.

457 Bishop, John Peale. "The Talk of Ezra Pound," Nation, 151 (December 21, 1940), 637-639.

458 Bishop, Philip E. "Avatars of the Avant-Garde: Pound, Brecht, and Modern Culture," DAI, 43, #8 (Wisconsin: 1982), 2657A.

459 Blackmur, R. P. "An Adjunct to the Muses' Diadem: A Note on Ezra Pound," Poetry, 68, #6 (September, 1946), 338-347.

460 Blamires, David. "The Ordered World: The Anathemata of David Jones," Agenda, 5 (Spring-Summer, 1967), 101-111.

461 Blish, James. "The Rituals of Ezra Pound," SR, 58 (Spring, 1950), 185-226.

462 Bodenheim, Maxwell. "Isolation of Carved Metal," Dial, 72 (January, 1922), 87-91.

463 Bogan, Louise. "The Cantos," NY, 16 (November 9, 1940), 76-78.

464 _____. "The Cantos," NY, 24 (October 30, 1948), 107-109.

465 _____. "Pound's Later Cantos," Selected Criticism: Prose, Poetry. Noonday: 1955, pp. 178-183.

466 Bornstein, Daniel. "The Poet as Historian: Researching the Malatesta Cantos," Paideuma, 10, #2 (Fall, 1981), 283-291.

467 Bornstein, George. "The Forest of His Mind: Mauberley and The Cantos," The Postromantic Consciousness of Ezra Pound. (English Literary Studies), Victoria: U. of Victoria, 1977, pp. 60-72.

468 _____. "Yeats's 'Those Dancing Days Are Gone' and Pound's 'Canto 23,'" YeA, #2 (1983), 93-95.

469 Bosha, Francis J. "Canto LXXXIV: Pound's 'Henriot,'" Paideuma, 4, #1 (Spring, 1975), 99-100.

470 _____. "Pound's References to Borah and Stalin in Canto 84," Paideuma, 11, #2 (Fall, 1982), 284-286.

471 Bottrall, Ronald. "XXX Cantos of Ezra Pound," Scrutiny, 2 (September, 1933), 112-122.

472 _____. "XXX Cantos," Determinations: Critical Essays. F. R. Leavis, ed. London: Chatto & Windus, 1934, pp. 179-198.

473 _____. "XXX Cantos of Ezra Pound: An Incursion into Poetics," Ezra Pound: A Critical Anthology. J. P. Sullivan, ed. Baltimore, Md., 1970, pp. 133-143.

474 Bradford, Curtis B. Yeats at Work. Carbondale & Edwardsville: Southern Ill. U. Pr., 1965, p. 174. [Canto LXXXIII].

475 Bridson, D. G. "A Draft of XXX Cantos," New English Weekly, 3 (October 5, 1933), 593-595.

476 _____. "Italian Painting in the Cantos," Agenda, 17, #3-4 (Aut-Wintr-Spring, 1979-80), 210-217.

477 Brooker, Peter. A Student's Guide to the Selected Poems of Ezra Pound. London: Faber & Faber, 1979.

478 Brooke-Rose, Christine. "Ezra Pound: Piers Plowman in the Modern Waste Land," REL, 2, #2 (April, 1961), 74-88.

479 _____. "'Lay me by Aurelie': An Examination of Pound's Use of Historical and Semi-Historical Sources," Cf., #125, pp. 242-279.

480 _____. A Structural Analysis of Pound's Usura Canto: Jakobson's Method Extended and Applied to Free Verse. The Hague: Mouton, 1976.

481 _____. A ZBC of Ezra Pound. Berkeley and Los Angeles: U. of California Pr., 1971.

482 Brooks, David Gordon. "A Critical-Textual Study of Cantos I-XVI of Ezra Pound," DAI, 43, #3 (U. of Toronto: 1982), 796A.

483 Bunting, Basil. "Mr. Ezra Pound," New English Weekly, 1 (May 26, 1932), 137-138.

484 _____. "On the Fly-leaf of Pound's Cantos," Agenda, 4 (October-November, 1965), 28.

485 Burchardi, Johannis. "Extract from Diarium," Paideuma, 4, #1 (Spring, 1975), 107-110.

486 Burns, Gerald. "Intellectual Slither in the Cantos," SWR, 59 (Winter, 1974), 76-84.

487 Bush, Ronald L. "The Genesis of Ezra Pound's Cantos," DAI, 36, #3 (Princeton: 1974), 1499A; repr., by Princeton U. Pr., 1976.

488 Butterick, George. "On Maximus IV, V, VI," WCR, 4, #4 (April, 1970), 3-6.

489 Campbell, K. T. S. "The Purification of Poetry--A Note on the Poetics of Ezra Pound's Cantos," BJA, 8 (1968), 124-137.

490 Cantrell, Carol Helmstetter. "Obscurity, Clarity, and Simplicity in the Cantos of Ezra Pound," MQ, 23, #4 (1982), 402-410.

491 _____. "Quotidian to Divine: Some Notes on Canto 81," Paideuma, 12, #1 (Spring, 1983), 11-20.

492 Carne-Ross, D. S. "The Cantos as Epic," Cf., #114, pp. 134-153.

493 _____. "Ezra Pound," TLS (April 13, 1973), 420-421.

494 _____. "The Music of a Lost Dynasty: Pound in the Classroom," BUJ, 21, #1 (Winter, 1972), 25-41; Instaurations: Essays in and out of Literature. Berkeley: U. of Calif. Pr., 1979, pp. 193-217.

495 Casillo, Robert. "Plastic Demons: The Scapegoating Process in Ezra Pound," Criticism, 24, #4 (Fall, 1984), 355-382.

496 Cayley, John. "'New Mountains': Some Light on the Chinese in Pound's Cantos," Agenda, 20, #3-4 (1982-83), 122-158.

497 Chace, William M. "The Canto as Cento: A Reading of Canto 33," Paideuma, 1 (Spring-Summer, 1972), 89-100.

498 Cheadle, Brian. "The Rhythm of a Canto: A Reading of Canto 81," ESA, 23 (1980), 103-116.

499 Childs, John Steven. "Larvatus Prodeo: Semiotic Aspects of the Ideogram in Pound's Cantos," Paideuma, 9 (Fall, 1980), 289-307.

500 _____. "Modernist Form: Pound's Style in a Draft of XXX Cantos," DAI, 44, #6 (Arkansas: 1983), 1787A.

501 Clark, Thomas. "The Formal Structure of Pound's Cantos," EWR, #1 (1964), 97-144.

502 Connolly, Cyril. "A Short Commentary," Agenda, 8 (Autumn-Winter, 1970), 44-46.

503 Cook, Albert S. "Die Einheit des Selbstbewusstseins in den Cantos," Ezra Pound: 22 Versuche über einen Dichter. Eva Hesse, ed. Frankfurt: Athenaum, 1967, pp. 254-262; Cf., #41, pp. 349-364.

504 _____. Prisms: Studies in Modern Literature. Bloomington: Indiana U. Pr., 1967, pp. 93-98, 176-187.

505 Cookson, William. "Donald Davie on Ezra Pound," Agenda, 14, #3 (1976), 87-88.

506 _____. "Ezra Pound and Myth: A Reader's Guide to Canto II," Agenda, 15, #2 (1977), 87-92.

507 _____. "A Few Notes on 'Drafts and Fragments,'" Agenda, 8, #3-4 (Autumn-Winter, 1970), 5-6; 47-49; UES, 15, #2 (1977), 46.

508 _____. "Paradise of Just Rulers," T&T, 41, #21 (May 21, 1960), 584-585.

509 _____. "Some Notes on Hugh MacDiarmid," Agenda, 5, #4 (Aut-Wint., 1967-68), 35-41.

510 _____. "Some Notes on Rock-Drill and Thrones," Agenda, 4, (October-November, 1965), 30-37.

511 Cooney, Douglas L. "Ezra Pound: A Study of His Prosody," Sou'wester, (Special Pound No.), (October 30, 1970), 100-117.

512 Cory, Daniel. "Second Thoughts on Ezra Pound," Encounter, 37, #4 (October, 1971), 86-92.

513 Cowan, James C. "The Classical Figure as Archetype in Pound's Cantos, I-XXX," TCL, 6, #1 (April, 1960), 25-32.

514 Cowley, Malcolm. "Pound Reweighed," A Many-Windowed House: Collected Essays on American Writers and American Writing. Henry Dan Piper, ed. Carbondale: S. Ill. U. Pr., 1970, pp. 178-190; [a shorter version in Reporter, 24, #5 (March 2, 1961), 35-40.]

515 Cox, Kenneth. "New Things Seen," Agenda, 8, #3-4 (Autumn-Winter, 1970), 38-39.

516 Culver, Michael. "The Art of Henry Strater: An Examination of the Illustrations for Pound's A Draft of XVI Cantos," Paideuma, 12, #2-3, (Fall-Wntr., 1983), 447-478.

517 Cunard, Nancy. "Ezra Pound: XXX Cantos," These Were the Hours: Memories of My Hours Press, Reanville and Paris. Ed., & Foreword by Hugh Ford. Carbondale & Edwardsville: So. Ill. U. Pr., 1969, pp. 123-132.

518 D'Agostino, Nemi. "The Cantos," Italian Images of Ezra Pound: Twelve Critical Essays. Angela Jung and Guido Palandri, eds. & tr. Taipei, Taiwan: Mei Ya, 1979, pp. 37-54.

519 _____. "The Cantos," Ezra Pound. Rome: Edizioni di Storia e Letteratura, 1960, pp. 151-171.

520 _____. "Sulle origini dei Cantos," NC, #5-6 (January-June, 1956), 92-104.

521 Davenport, Guy. Cities on Hills: A Study of I-XXX of Ezra Pound's Cantos. Ann Arbor, Michigan: UMI Research Pr., 1983.

522 _____. "A Collation of Two Texts of the Cantos," Pound Newsletter, #6 (April, 1955), 5-13.

523 _____. "Ezra Pound's Radiant Gists: A Reading of Cantos II and IV," WSCL, 3, #2 (Spring-Summer, 1962), 50-64.

524 _____. "The House that Jack Built," Salmagundi, 43 (1979), 140-155.

525 _____. "Persephone's Ezra," Arion, 7 (Summer, 1967), 164-199; repr., #41, pp. 143-173.

526 _____. "A Reading of I-XXX of the Cantos of Ezra Pound," Diss., Harvard U., 1961.

527 _____. "Thrones [A Portion of the Cantos], Audit, I, #1 (February 22, 1960), 15-16.

528 Davidsen, Carol. "The Cantos and Culture," ConnR, 8, #2 (April, 1975), 55-62.

529 Davie, Donald. "Adrian Stokes and Pound's Cantos," TC, 160 (November, 1956), 419-436.

530 _____. "The Cantos: Towards a Pedestrian Reading," Paideuma, 1, #1 (Spring-Summer, 1972), 55-62.

531 _____. "Cypress Versus Rock-Slide: An Appreciation of Canto 110," Agenda, 8, #3-4 (Autumn-Winter, 1970), 19-26.

532 _____. Ezra Pound: Poet as Sculptor. London: 1965; New York: Oxford U. Pr., 1964.

533 _____. "'Form' and 'Concept' in Pound's Cantos," Irish Writing, 36 (Autumn, 1956), 160-173.

534 _____. "Ideas in The Cantos," and "Rhythms in The Cantos," Ezra Pound. Frank Kermode, ed. New York: Viking Pr., 1976, pp. 62-76, 77-98.

535 _____. "On Thrones: Cantos 96-109," Paris Review, 28 (Summer-Fall, 1962), 49; repr., in Critics on Ezra Pound. E. San Juan, Jr., ed. Coral Gables, Florida: U. of Miami Pr., 1972, pp. 95-96.

536 _____. "The Poet as Sculptor," Cf., #41, pp. 198-214.

537 _____. "Sicily in the Cantos," Paideuma, 6, #1 (Spring, 1977), 101-107.

538 _____. "The Significance of The Cantos," CamR, 94, #2214 (June 8, 1973), 165-166.

539 Davis, Earle. "The Man in The Cantos," Vision Fugitive: Ezra Pound and Economics. Lawrence: U. of Kansas Pr., 1968, pp. 1-16.

540 Davis, Helen Kathryn. "Fugue, Fresco, and Ideogram: Structures in Pound's Cantos," DAI, 43, #7 (Utah: 1982), 2347A.

541 Davis, Kay. "Fugue and Canto LXIII," Paideuma, 11, #1 (Spring-Summer, 1982), 15-38.

542 _____. "An Index to Canto References in Paideuma," Paideuma, 8 (1979), 317-324.

543 _____. "Ring Composition, Subject Rhyme, and Canto VII," Paideuma, 11, #3 (Winter, 1982), 429-439.

544 Deane, Hugh. "Ezra Pound's Chinese Translucencies," EH, 20, #4 (April, 1981), 39-41.

545 De Bedts, Ruth. "The Ideogrammatic Method in The Cantos of Ezra Pound," FlaR, 2 (Spring, 1958), 30-39.

546 Decavalles, Anthony M. "A Guide to Ezra Pound's Cantos (X)," Analyst, 11 (July, 1956), 1-18.

547 Dekker, George. The Cantos of Ezra Pound: A Critical Study. London: Routledge, 1963; New York: Barnes & Noble, 1963.

548 _____. "Poetic Motive and Strategy in The Cantos," Cf., Critics on Ezra Pound. E. San Juan, ed., #535, pp. 84-88.

549 _____. Sailing After Knowledge: The Cantos of Ezra Pound. London: Routledge; New York: Barnes & Noble, 1963.

550 Demetz, Peter. "Marginalien: Ezra Pound's Pisaner Gesange," Merkur, 12 (January, 1958), 97-100.

551 Demott, Robert. "Ezra Pound and Charles Bowlker: Note on Canto LI," Paideuma, 1, #2 (Winter, 1972), 187-198.

552 de Nagy, N. Christoph. Ezra Pound's Poetics and Literary Tradition: The Critical Decade. Bern: Francke Verlag, 1966.

553 _____. The Poetry of Ezra Pound: The Pre-Imagist Stage. Bern: Francke Verlag, 1960.

554 _____. "Pound and Browning," Cf., #503, pp. 231-251.

555 D'Epiro, Peter Francis. "Canto 74: New Light on Lucifer," Paideuma, 10, #2 (Fall, 1981), 297-301.

556 _____. "A Touch of Rhetoric: Ezra Pound's Malatesta Cantos," DAI, 42, #6 (Yale: 1981), 2673A.

557 _____. A Touch of Rhetoric: Ezra Pound's Malatesta Cantos. Ann Arbor, Mich.: UMI Research Pr., 1983.

558 de Rachewiltz, Boris. "Pagan and Magic Elements in Ezra Pound's Works," Cf., #41, pp. 174-197.

559 de Rachewiltz, Mary. "Traduzione Integrale," Arion, 6, #2 (Summer, 1967), 208-215.

560 _____. "Nota introduttiva al Canto 51 di Ezra Pound," L'Approdo Letterario (Rome), 38 (1967), 51-54.

561 Deutsch, Babette. "Chinese to Cleanthes," NY Herald Tribune (December 15, 1940), 17.

562 _____. "Ezra Pound's Sparks of Knowledge," NY Herald Tribune, (March 26, 1933), 4.

563 _____. "Odi et Amo," Cf., #186, pp. 668-670.

564 _____. "Poetry versus Politics," NY Herald Tribune (August 22, 1948), 7.

565 _____. "Pound Rises Again," NY Herald Tribune (March 13, 1938), 13. (Review: Fifth Decade of Cantos).

566 _____. "Speech and Song," Poetry in Our Time: A

Critical Survey of Poetry in the English-Speaking World, 1900-1960. 2nd ed., Rev. & Enl. Doubleday, 1963, pp. 133-145.

567 _____. "With Seven League Boots," [Eleven New Cantos] NY Herald Tribune (November 25, 1934), 18.

568 Dickey, R. P. "Introduction to the Esthetic and Philosophy of the Cantos," Sou'wester (Ezra Pound Birthday Issue), (October 30, 1970), 21-35.

569 Dilligan, Robert J., James W. Parins, and Todd K. Bender. A Concordance to Ezra Pound's Cantos. New York: Garland Pub. Co., 1981.

570 Dillon, George. "A Note on the Obvious," Poetry, 68 (September, 1946), 322-325.

571 Dodsworth, Martin. "The Marshall Plan," NSt, 84 (July 28, 1972), 129.

572 Donoghue, Denis. "Ezra Pound's School Book," LugR, 1, #3-4 (1965), 133-146; The Ordinary Universe: Soundings in Modern Literature. New York: Macmillan, 1968, pp. 291-308.

573 Doria, Charles. "Pound, Olson, and the Classical Tradition," Boundary, 2, #2 (Fall-Winter, 1973), 127-143.

574 Driscoll, John. "Canto LX and Ezra Pound's Use of Histoire générale de la Chine," SN, 50 (1978), 215-232.

575 _____. The China Cantos of Ezra Pound. Uppsala: Almqvist & Wiksell, 1983. (AUUSAU 46). [Cantos 52-61: Sources in Chinese literature].

576 Drummond, John. "La verità sul caso Pound," FLe, #1, 1 (January 7, 1951), 1.

577 Duclos, Jacques. "Cantos," RLV, 31, #1 (1955), 70-72.

578 Dudek, Louis. "Exotic Reference in the Cantos of Ezra Pound," AntigR, 11 (1972), 55-66; IJAS, 2, #2 (1972), 30-39.

579 Duffey, Bernard I. "The Experimental Lyric in Modern Poetry: Eliot, Pound, Williams," JML, 3 (July, 1974), 1085-1103.

580 Durant, Alan. Ezra Pound, Identity in Crisis: A Fundamental Reassessment of the Poet and His Work. New Jersey: Barnes & Noble, 1981; Sussex: The Harvester Pr., 1981.

581 Eastman, Barbara C. Ezra Pound's Cantos: The Story of the

Text, 1948-1975. Introduction by Hugh Kenner. Orono: Maine National Poetry Foundation, U. of Maine, 1979.

582 _____. "The Gap in The Cantos: 72 and 73," Paideuma, 8 (1979), 415-427; Agenda, 17, #3-4, and 18, #1 (Aut-Wntr-Spr., 1979-1980), pp. 142-156.

583 _____. "Unlocking The Cantos with Mauberley's Key," DQR, 9, #2 (1979), 82-100.

584 Eaves, T. C. Duncan, and Ben D. Kimpel. "The Birth of a Nation: A Note on Pound's Canto XIX," PQ, 62, #3 (Summer, 1983), 417-418.

585 Eder, Doris L. "Review: The Cantos of Ezra Pound: The Lyric Mode by Eugene Nasser," Paideuma, 5, #1 (1976), 195-197.

586 Edwards, John Hamilton. The Cantos of Ezra Pound. New York: New Directions, 1948.

587 _____. "Poet or Pooh-Bah?" KR, 14, #4 (Autumn, 1953), 684-689.

588 _____, and William V. Vasse. Annotated Index to the Cantos of Ezra Pound: Cantos I-LXXXIV. Berkeley: U. of Calif. Pr., 1957.

589 Eisenhauer, Robert G. "'Jeweler's Company': Topaz, Half-Light, and Bounding-Lines in The Cantos," Paideuma, 9 (1979), 249-270.

590 Eliot, T. S. After Strange Gods: A Primer of Modern Heresy. New York: Harcourt, Brace & Co., 1934, pp. 44-47.

591 _____. "The Method of Mr. Pound," Athenaeum, 4,669 (October 24, 1919), 1065-1066.

592 _____. "A Note on Ezra Pound," Today, 4, #19, (September, 1918), 3-9.

593 Elizondo, Salvador. "Il miglior fabbro: La poesia de Ezra Pound anterior a los Cantos," Estaciones, 5 (August, 1960), 3-15.

594 Elliott, Angela Pantaleone. "Light as Image in Ezra Pound's Cantos," DAI, 39 (Drew U: 1978), 2234A-35A.

595 _____. "Lucifer's Fall in Pound's Canto LXXIV," Paideuma, 8 (1979), 59-60.

596 Elliott, George P. "Poet of Many Voices," The Carleton Miscellany, 2 (Summer, 1961), 79-103; repr., in Ezra Pound: A Collection of Critical Essays. Walter Sutton, ed. Englewood Cliffs, N.J.: Prentice-Hall, 1963, pp. 152-162.

597 Ellmann, Maud. "Floating the Pound: The Circulation of the Subject in Pound's The Cantos," OLR, 3, #3 (1979), 16-27.

598 Ellman, Richard. "Ez and Old Billyum," KR, 28, #4 (September, 1966), 470-495.

599 Emerson, Dorothy. "Poetry Corner: Ezra Pound," Scholastic, 24 (May 12, 1934), 10.

600 Emery, Clark. Ideas into Action: A Study of Pound's Cantos. Coral Gables, Fl: U. of Miami Pr., 1958.

601 Espey, John J. "Addenda," Analyst (Northwestern U.), III (December, 1953), 10-11.

602 _____. "Note by John Espey," Paideuma, 4, #1 (1975), 181-185, 187.

603 _____. "Sidelights from the Italian and German Cantos," Paideuma, 8 (1979), 297-299.

604 Fang, Achilles. "Aspects of the Cantos: Notes on China and the Cantos," Pound Newsletter, 9 (January, 1956), 3-5.

605 _____, et al. "A Guide to Ezra Pound's Cantos I-VIII: Addenda," Analyst (Northwestern), VI (January, 1955). (Entire Issue).

606 Feldman, A. Bronson. "The Critical Canons of Ezra Pound," Poet Lore, 57 (Summer, 1953), 226-246.

607 Fender, Stephen. "Ezra Pound and the Words off the Page: Historical Allusions in Some American Long Poems," YES, 8 (1978), 95-108.

608 Fink, Jon-Stephen. "Ezekial Ton and Isaih Ounce (E. P. Perspective)," St. Andrew's Rev, 3, #4 (1976), 31-35.

609 Fitts, Dudley. "Music Fit for the Odea," H&H, 4 (January-March, 1931), 278-289.

610 _____. "Pound and the Cantos," SatRL, 8 (December 26, 1931), 416.

611 Fitzgerald, Edward J. "Eleven New Cantos," American Poetry Journal (March, 1935), 23.

612 Fitzgerald, Robert. "Gloom and Gold in Ezra Pound," Encounter, 7 (July, 1956), 16-22.

613 _____. "Mr. Pound's Good Governors," Accent, 1 (Winter, 1941), 121-122.

614 _____. "A Note on Ezra Pound, 1928-1956," KR, 18, #4 (Autumn, 1956), 505-518.

615 _____. "Notes on Ezra Pound, 1928-1956," NC, Nos. 5-6 (January-June, 1956), 35-57.

616 _____. "What Thou Lovest Well Remains," NR, 119 (August 16, 1948), 21-23.

617 Fleming, William. "Ezra Pound's 'Thrones': Its Place in the Cantos," TC (Australia), (Autumn, 1961), 252-259.

618 Fletcher, John Gould. "The Neglected Assessment," Criterion, 8 (April, 1929), 513-524.

619 Flint, R. W. "Pound and Modern Poetry," HudR, 8, #1 (Spring, 1955), 134-135.

620 Flory, Wendy Stallard. "Alexander Del Mar: Some Additional Sources," Paideuma, 4, #2-3 (Fall-Winter, 1975), 325-327.

621 _____. Ezra Pound and The Cantos: A Record of a Struggle. New Haven; London: Yale U. Pr., 1980.

622 _____. "Pound's Blake and Blake's Dante: 'The Circle of the Lustful' and Canto 20," Paideuma, 6 (Fall, 1977), 155-165.

623 Foster, John L. "Pound's Revision of Cantos I-III," MP, 63 (August 1, 1948), Sec. 7, p. 14.

624 Frankenberg, Lloyd. "Ezra Pound and His Magnum Opus," NYT (August 1, 1948), Sec. 7, p. 14.

625 Freudenheim, Richard Jesse. "Ezra Pound: Canto 85," DAI, 39, #2 (Calif., Berkeley: 1977), 871A.

626 Friar, Kimon, and John Malcolm Brinnin. "The Cantos," Modern Poetry, American and British. New York: Appleton-Century-Crofts, 1951, pp. 525-531.

627 Frohock, W. M. "Ezra Pound: Images of Revolt," Strangers to This Ground: Cultural Diversity in Contemporary American Writing. Dallas: Southern Methodist U. Pr., 1961, pp. 111-131.

628 _____. "The Revolt of Ezra Pound," SWR, 44 (Summer, 1959), 190-199.

629 Fuller, Dorothy V. "Ezra Pound and the Cantos," ArQ, 8, #4 (Winter, 1952), 361-362.

630 Furia, Philip. "Pound and Blake on Hell," Paideuma, 10, #3 (Winter, 1981), 599-601.

631 _____. Pound's Cantos Declassified. University Park, Pa.: Pa. State U. Pr., 1984.

632 Fussell, Edwin. "Dante and Pound's Cantos," JML, I, 1 (1970), 75-87.

633 _____. "The Waste Land and The Cantos," Lucifer in Harness: American Meter, Metaphor, and Diction. Princeton: Princeton U. Pr., 1973, pp. 80-88.

634 Galigani, Giuseppe. "Montis Pascuorum," YLM, 126, #5 (December, 1958), 18-23.

635 Gall, Sally M. "Pound and the Modern Melic Tradition: Towards a Demystification of 'Absolute Rhythm,'" Paideuma, 8 (1979), 35-47.

636 Géfin, Laszlo. "Ideagram: The History of a Poetic Method," DAI, 40 (McGill U.: 1979), 3299A.

637 Gibbs, Alonzo. "The Sports Department," Voices, 173 (September-December, 1960), 38-41.

638 Giovannini, Giovanni. Ezra Pound and Dante. Nijmegen, Utrecht, Netherlands: Dekker and Van de Vegt, 1961.

639 Glenn, Edgar M. "Addenda," Analyst (Northwestern U.), No. 2 (July, 1953), 8-9.

640 _____. "Association and the Cantos of Ezra Pound," DAI, 15 (Stanford: 1955), 1853-54. [Cf., Pound Newsletter, 8 (October, 1955), 28.]

641 _____. "A Guide to Canto I of Ezra Pound (Revised and Enlarged)," Analyst, 8, #4 (June, 1955). [Entire Issue.]

642 _____. "A Guide to Ezra Pound's Cantos (I-IV)," Analyst, 1 (March, 1953), 1-7.

643 _____. "Pound and Ovid," Paideuma, 10, #3 (Winter, 1981), 625-634.

644 Goacher, Denis. "Ezra Pound's Cantos," Listener, 68 (September 6, 1962), 357-358.

645 _____. Reading the Cantos. New York: Random House, 1966.

646 Goodspeed, George. "Corrections and a Clarification," The Month at Goodspeed's, 33 (January-February, 1962), 98-99.

647 Goodwin, K. L. "Ezra Pound: The Formal Structure of the Later Cantos," Australasian Universities Language and Literature Association: Proceedings and Papers of the Thirteenth Congress Held at Monash University, August 12-18, 1970. J. R. Ellis, ed. Melbourne: AULLA and Monash U., 1971, pp. 154-156.

648 _____. "The Structure of Pound's Later Cantos," SoRA, 4, #4 (1971), 300-307.

649 Gordon, David M. "'Confucius, Philosophe': An Introduction to the Chinese Cantos 52-61," Paideuma, 5, #3 (Winter, 1976), 387-403.

650 _____. "Corpus Juris and Canto XCIV," Paideuma, 11, #2 (Fall, 1982), 313-324.

651 _____. "Edward Coke: The Azalea Is Grown," Paideuma, 4, #2 & 3 (Fall-Winter, 1975), 223-229.

652 _____. "A Place for Buddhism in Canto 99," Paideuma, 5, #2 (Fall, 1976), 275-278.

653 _____. "Pound's Use of the Sacred Edict in Canto 98," Paideuma, 4, #1 (Spring, 1975), 121-168.

654 _____. "The Sacred Edict: Thought Built on Sagetrieb," Paideuma, 3, #2 (Fall, 1975), 169-190.

655 _____. "The Sources of Canto LIII," Paideuma, 5, #1 (Spring-Summer, 1976), 123-152.

656 Graham, Robin. "Will and Sensibility in the Cantos," ESA, 21 (1978), 87-97.

657 Gregory, Horace. "The Search for a Frontier," NR, 75 (July 26, 1933), 292-294.

658 Grigsby, Gordan Kay. "The Modern Long Poem: Studies in Thematic Form," DA, 21 (Wisconsin: 1960), 622-623.

659 _____. "Newspeak in Pound's Cantos," SAQ, 62, #1 (Winter, 1962), 51-56.

660 Grigson, Goeffrey. "Aspects of Modern Poetry," NS&N, 8 (December 15, 1934), 899.

661 _____. "The Methodism of Ezra Pound," New Verse, #5 (October, 1933), 17-22.

662 Gross, Harvey. "The Cantos of Ezra Pound," The Contrived Corridor: History and Fatality in Modern Literature. Ann Arbor: Michigan U. Pr., 1971, pp. 100-123.

663 _____. "Pound's Cantos and the Idea of History," BuR, 9, #1 (March, 1960), 14-31.

664 Gugelberger, Georg M. "By No Means an Orderly Dantescan Rising," IQ, 64 (1973), 31-48.

665 Guiliani, Alfredo. "Le ragioni metriche de Ezra Pound," NC, 5-6 (January-June, 1956), 105-110.

666 Haberstroh, Patricia Boyle. "The Two Worlds of the Cantos," DAI, 38, #9 (Bryn Mawr: 1977), 5461A.

667 Halawatsch, Wolfhard. "Ezra Pound's Weg sum Licht: Eine Interpretation von Canto XV," NS, 18 (November, 1969), 551-557.

668 Hall, Donald. "The Art of Poetry V," ParisR, 7, #28 (Summer-Fall, 1962), 22-51.

669 _____. "The Cantos in England," NS&N, 59 (March 12, 1960), 368.

670 Hall, Ian Roger. "Murdering the Time: A Study of Temporal Order in Selected Works of Henry Thoreau, Nathaniel Hawthorne, T. S. Eliot, and Ezra Pound," DAI, 36, #9 (Kent State: 1975), 6099A.

671 Halperen, Max. "How to Read a Canto," The Twenties: Fiction, Poetry, Drama. Warren French, ed. Deland, Florida: Everett/Edwards, Inc., 1975, pp. 335-350.

672 _____. "Old Men and New Tools: The Chinese Cantos of Pound," Trace, 52 (Spring, 1964), 1-8.

673 _____. "The Structural Reading of The Cantos of Ezra Pound," DA, 20 (Florida St., 1960), #4659.

674 Hankins, John E. "Notes and Queries," Paideuma, 2, #1 (Spring, 1973), 141-145.

675 _____. "Notes and Queries," Paideuma, 3, #1 (Spring, 1974), 135-137.

676 Harmon, William. Time in Ezra Pound's Work. Chapel Hill: U. of North Carolina Pr., 1977.

677 _____. "Visions of Perfection: Some Recurrent Figures in the Poems of Eliot and Pound," Yeat-EliotRev, 5, #1 (1978), 18-20.

678 Harper, Michael F. "Truth and Calliope: Ezra Pound's Malatesta," PMLA, 96, #1 (January, 1981), 86-103.

679 Harrison, John. The Reactionaries: Yeats, Pound, Eliot, Lawrence: A Study of the Anti-Democratic Intelligentsia. New York: Schocken, 1967.

680 Hartley, Anthony. "The Cantos of Ezra Pound," Spectator (July 23, 1954), 124-126.

681 Helmling, Steven. "Del Mar Material in Canto 97: Further Annotations," Paideuma, 5, #1 (Spring, 1976), 53-57.

682 _____. "Pound, Del Mar, and Canto 97," UES, 15, #2 (1977), 26-34.

683 Hénault, Marie, ed. Studies in the Cantos. Columbus, Ohio: Charles E. Merrill Pub. Co., 1971.

684 Heppenstall, Rayner. "Poetry," New English Weekly, 7 (April 18, 1935), 10.

685 Herdeck, Donald Elmer. "The Golden Bitch: A Study of Ezra Pound's 'Anti-Semitism' and 'Fascism' as Affecting Structure, Theme, and Imagery in The Cantos," DAI, 29, #10 (Penn. U: 1968), 3613A.

686 Hesse, Eva. "Answers to Queries on Canto 38; and Letters to the Editor," Paideuma, 5, #2 (Fall, 1976), 345-352.

687 _____. "Answers to Queries and Letters to the Editor," Paideuma, 5, #3 (Winter, 1976), 493-500.

688 _____. "Baedeker zu einer Kontinent: Ein Versuch über die Cantos von Ezra Pound," Akzente, 11 (1964), 79-95.

689 _____. "Books Behind The Cantos, Part One: Cantos I-XXX," Paideuma, 1 (Winter, 1972), 137-151.

690 _____, ed. "Canto XIII übertragen von Eva Hesse," Merkur, #87 (September, 1963), 833-836.

691 _____. "Franco Sacchetti in Canto 22/106:110," Paideuma, 5, #3 (Winter, 1976), 413-414.

692 _____. "Frobenius as Rainmaker," Paideuma, 1, #1 (Spring-Summer, 1972), 85-88.

693 _____. "'Kadzu, Arachidi, Acero' in Canto XCVII/683: A Matter of Coherence," Paideuma, 8 (1979), 53-54.

694 _____. "Klages in Canto LXXV/450: A Positive Identification," Paideuma, 10, #2 (Fall, 1981), 295-296.

695 _____. "Margarethe von Taufers," Paideuma, 2, #3 (Winter, 1973), 497-502.

696 _____. "Notes and Queries," Paideuma, 3, #3 (Winter, 1974), 413-416.

697 _____. "A Redefinition of the Problem of mo in Canto LXXIV/430 in the Light of Its Source," Paideuma, 8 (1979), 407-408.

698 _____. "Smaragdos, Chrysolihos ... Reflexionen zu Canto VII," Jahresring (Stuttgart), 62/63, pp. 90-109.

699 Heyen, William. "John Berryman: A Memoir and an Interview," OhR, 15, #2 (Winter, 1974), 46-65.

700 Highet, Gilbert. "Beer-Bottle on the Pediment," Horizon, 3, #13 (January, 1961), 116-118.

701 Hildesheimer, Wolfgang. "Die Wirklichkeit der Reaktionäre: Uber [The Reality of the Reactionary: About] T. S. Eliot und Ezra Pound," Merkur, 28 (July, 1974), 630-647.

702 Hlawatsch, Wolfhard. "Ezra Pounds Weg zum Light: Eine Interpretation von Canto XV," NS, 18 (1969), 551-557.

703 Hoffa, William W. "Ezra Pound and George Antheil: Vorticist Music and the Cantos," AL, 44 (March, 1972), 52-73.

704 Hoffman, Daniel. "Poetry: After Modernism," Harvard Guide to Contemporary American Writing. Daniel Hoffman, ed. Cambridge, Mass.; London: Belknap Pr., 1979, pp. 439-453.

705 Holaday, Woon-Ping Chin. "Ezra Pound's Use of Moyriac de Mailla's Histoire generale de la Chine: A Source Study of the Chinese History Cantos," DAI, 38 (Toledo: 1977), 2789A.

706 Holder, Alan. "The Lesson of the Master: Ezra Pound and Henry James," AL, 35, #1 (March, 1963), 71-79.

707 _____. "Three Voyagers in Search of Europe: A Study of Henry James, Ezra Pound, and T. S. Eliot," DA, 26, #3 (Columbia: 1965), 1646-47.

708 _____. Three Voyagers in Search of Europe: A Study of Henry James, Ezra Pound, and T. S. Eliot. Philadelphia: U. of Pa. Pr., 1966.

709 Hopes, David Brendan. "Turbulent Form: The Vortex in The Cantos of Ezra Pound," DAI, 41, #6 (Syracuse: 1980), 2612A.

710 Horrocks, R. J. "Mosaic: A Study of Juxtaposition in literature, as an Approach to Pound's Cantos and Similar Modern Poems," Diss. U. of Auckland, New Zealand, 1976.

711 Houston, John Porter. "The Cantos," French Symbolism and the Modernist Movement: A Study of Poetic Structures. London; Baton Rouge: La. St. U. Pr., 1980, pp. 166-172.

712 Hugen, Dorothy Jean. "Ezra Pound's Use in Canto XXIV of Luchino Dal Campo's Viaggio a Gerusalemme," DAI, 40, #4 (Los Angeles: 1979), 2091A.

713 _____. "... Small Birds of Cypress," Paideuma, 3, #2 (Fall, 1974), 229-238.

714 Hughes, Robert. "Amarili," Paideuma, 2, #1 (Spring, 1973), 39.

715 Hynes, Samuel. "Pound and the Prose Tradition," YR, 51 (June, 1962), 532-546.

716 Ismail, Jamila. "News of the Universe: Muan Bpo and The Cantos," Agenda, 9, #2-3 (Spring-Summer, 1971), 70-87.

717 Iwasaki, Ryozo. "The Cantos e no approach," EigoS, 119 (1973), 2-4.

718 Jackson, Thomas. "The Adventures of Messire Wrong-Head," ELH, 32 (June, 1965), 238-255.

719 Jarrell, Randall. "Five Poets," YR, 46 (September, 1956), 103-106.

720 _____. "Poets: Old, New and Aging," NR, 103 (December 9, 1940), 798-800.

721 Jenner, E. A. B. "Some Notes on the Poetry and Technique of the Later Cantos of Ezra Pound," Cave, 3 (February, 1973), 67-69.

722 John, Roland. "A Note on the Meaning of the Cantos," Agenda, 17, #3-4; 18, #1 (Aut-Wntr-Spr., 1979-80), 257-263.

723 Joyce, James. "From James Joyce," The Cantos of Ezra Pound:

Some Testimonials. New York: Farrar & Rinehart, Inc., 1933, pp. 12-13.

724 Juhasz, Suzanne. "Metaphor in The Cantos of Ezra Pound," Metaphor and the Poetry of Williams, Pound, and Stevens. Lewisburg: Bucknell U. Pr., 1974. pp. 75-131, passim.

725 Kappel, Andrew J. "Napoleon and Talleyrand in The Cantos," Paideuma, 11, #1 (Spring-Summer, 1982), 55-78.

726 Kearns, George. "Guide to Ezra Pound's Selected Cantos," DAI, 42, #1 (Boston U: 1976), 210A.

727 _____. Guide to Ezra Pound's Selected Cantos. New Brunswick, NJ: Rutgers U. Pr., 1980.

728 Keith, Nobuko T. "Ezra Pound's Relationship with Fenollosa and the Japanese Noh Plays," MarkhamR, 3 (1972), 21-27.

729 Kenner, Hugh. "Art in a Closed Field," VQR, 38 (Autumn, 1962), 597-613.

730 _____. "Blood for the Ghosts," TexQt, 10, #4 (Winter, 1967), 67-79.

731 _____. "The Broken Mirrors and the Mirror of Memory," Cf., #771, pp. 3-32.

732 _____. "The Cantos-1," and "Cantos-2," The Pound Era. Berkeley, LA. & London: U. of Calif. Pr., 1971, pp. 349-381, 414-436.

733 _____. "Drafts and Fragments and the Structure of the Cantos," Agenda, 8, #3-4 (Autumn-Wntr., 1970), 7-19.

734 _____. "Gold in the Gloom," Poetry, 81, #2 (November, 1952), 127-132.

735 _____. "More on the Seven Lakes Canto," Paideuma, 2, #1 (Spring, 1973), 43-46.

736 _____. "Motz El Son," StBr, 3/4 (Fall, 1969), 371-377.

737 _____. "Plea for Metrics," Poetry, 86, #1 (April, 1955), 41-45.

738 _____. The Poetry of Ezra Pound. London: Faber & Faber; New York: New Directions, 1951, pp. 185-304.

739 _____. "Pound's Cantos, I," Expl, 11 (December, 1952), Item 20.

740 _____. "Pound on Going and on Ending," Spectrum, 15 (May, 1973), 55-59.

741 _____. "Prophets of Renaissance," HudR, 3 (Fall, 1950), 474-478.

742 _____. "The Rose in the Steel Dust," HudR, 3 (Spring, 1950), 66-124.

743 _____. "Schema for XXX Cantos," Paideuma, 2 (Fall, 1973), 201.

744 Kenny, Herbert A. "Pound's Cantos: The Failure of an Epic," Critic, 19 (June-July, 1961), 9-10, 72.

745 Kimpel, Ben, and T. C. Duncan Eaves. "American History in Rock-Drill and Thrones," Paideuma, 9 (1980), 417-439.

746 _____ and _____. "Ezra Pound's Use of Sources and Illustrated by His Use of Nineteenth-Century French History," MP, 80 (1982-83), 35-52.

747 _____ and _____. "A Note to Ezra Pound's Canto 85," ELN, 17 (June, 1980), 292-293.

748 _____ and _____. "Pound's Canto LXXX," Expl, 41, #3 (Spring, 1983), 43-44.

749 _____ and _____. "Pound's 'Ideogrammatic Method,' as Illustrated in Canto 99," AL, 51 (May, 1979), 205-237.

750 _____ and _____. "Pound's Research for the Malatesta Cantos," Paideuma, 11, #3 (Winter, 1982), 406-419.

751 _____ and _____. "Pound's Use of Sienese Manuscripts for Cantos 42 and 43," Paideuma, 8 (1979), 513-518.

752 _____ and _____. "Some Curious 'Facts' in Ezra Pound's Cantos," ELH, 50, #3 (Fall, 1983), 627-635.

753 _____ and _____. "The Source of Canto L," Paideuma, 8 (1979), 81-93.

754 _____ and _____. "The Sources of Cantos 42 and 43," Paideuma, 6 (Winter, 1977), 333-358.

755 _____ and _____. "The Sources of the Leopoldine Cantos," Paideuma, 7 (Spring and Fall, 1978), 249-277.

756 _____ and _____. "Two Notes on Ezra Pound's Cantos," MP, 78 (February, 1981), 285-288.

757 King, George T. "Janequin's 'Song of the Birds' in Pound's Canto 75," UES, 15, #2 (1977), 31-34.

758 Knight, Robert. "Thomas Jefferson in Canto 31," Paideuma, 5, #1 (Spring-Summer, 1976), 79-94.

759 Kodama, Sinehide. "The Eight Scenes of Sho-Sho," Paideuma, 6 (Fall, 1977), 131-145.

760 Kohli, Raj K. "'Epic of the West': Some Observations on American History and the Cantos," IJAS, 2, #2 (December, 1972), 40-54.

761 Koppenfels, Werner von. "Ezra Pound: Der Modernist als Elegike," Archiv, 212, #2 (1975), 280-302.

762 Korg, Jacob. "Jacob Epstein's Rock Drill and the Cantos," Paideuma, 4 (Fall-Winter, 1975), 301-313.

763 Kostelanetz, Richard. "Ezra Pound: The Cantos," Cw, 96 (July 28, 1972), 410-411, 413.

764 _____. "Impounding Pound's Milestone," The Old Poetries and the New. Ann Arbor: U. of Michigan Pr., 1981, pp. 48-51.

765 Kwan-Terry, John. "Pound and the Limits of Prosody: Some Notes on the Cantos," SELit (Eng. No.), (1979), 95-113.

766 Landini, Richard G. "Confucianism and The Cantos of Ezra Pound," Topic, 6 (Fall, 1966), 30-42.

767 _____. "A Guide to the Economic Thought in Ezra Pound's Cantos," DA, 24, #2 (Fla.: 1959), 747.

768 _____. "Vorticism and The Cantos of Ezra Pound," WHR, 14 (Spring, 1960), 173-181.

769 Lauber, John. "Pound's Cantos: A Fascist Epic," JAmS, 12 (April, 1978), 3-21. Reply: D. Murray, JAmS, 13 (April, 1979), 109-113.

770 Law, Richard. "The Seventh Canto Initial," Paideuma, 8 (1979), 411.

771 Leary, Lewis, ed. Motive and Method in The Cantos of Ezra Pound. New York: Columbia U. Pr., 1954; 1961.

772 _____. "Pound-Wise, Penny Foolish," Paideuma, 1, #2 (Winter, 1972), 153-159.

773 Leavis, Frank R. "Ezra Pound," Ezra Pound: A Collection of Critical Essays. Walter Sutton, ed. Englewood Cliffs, NJ: Prentice-Hall, Inc., 1963, pp. 26-40.

774 _____. "Ezra Pound," New Bearings in English Poetry: A Study of the Contemporary Situation. Ann Arbor: U. of Michigan Pr., 1960, pp. 133-157.

775 Leibowitz, Herbert. "The Muse and the News," HudR, 22 (Autumn, 1969), 501-502.

776 Lennig, Arthur George. "An Analysis of the Cantos of Ezra Pound," DA, 22 (Wisconsin: 1961), 1179-80.

777 Levi, Peter. "Pound and the Classics," Agenda, 4, 2 (October-November, 1965), 42-45.

778 Lewis, Wyndham. "Ezra Pound, Etc.," Time and Western Man. Boston: Beacon Pr., 1957, pp. 38-48.

779 Libera, Sharon Mayer. "Casting His Gods Back into the Nous: Two Neoplationists and the Cantos of Ezra Pound," Paideuma, 2, #3 (Winter, 1973), 355-377.

780 _____. Ezra Pound's Paradise: A Study of Neoplatonism in the Cantos. Diss. Harvard U., 1972.

781 Logue, Christopher, and Alan Neame, assisted by Jared Shlaes. "Commentary: The Sixth Canto of Ezra Pound," Merlin, I, #2 (Autumn, 1952), 104-109.

782 MacDiarmid, Hugh. "The Esemplastic Power," Agenda, 8, #3-4 (Autumn-Winter, 1970), 27-30.

783 McDowell, Colin. "'The Toys ... at Auxerre': Canto 77," Paideuma, 12, #1 (Spring, 1983), 21-30.

784 McNaughton, William. "Ezra Pound's Meters and Rhythms," PMLA, 78, #1 (March, 1963), 136-146.

785 _____. "The 1976 'Summer at Brunnenburg': Reading the Cantos," Paideuma, 5, #3 (Winter, 1976), 457-460.

786 _____. "A Note on the Main Form in The Cantos," Paideuma, 6, #2 (Fall, 1977), 147-152.

787 MacNeice, Louis. Modern Poetry: A Personal Essay. Oxford: Clarendon Pr., 1968, pp. 162ff.

788 Madge, Charles. "Pound's Odyssey," NS&N, 40 (September 30, 1959), 328-329.

789 Malkoff, Karl. Escape from the Self: A Study in Contemporary American Poetry and Poetics. New York: Columbia Pr., 1977, pp. 48-64, passim.

790 Mandanis, Alice Subley. "Pound and Longinus: The Didactic Element in The Cantos," DAI, 32 (Catholic U. of America: 1970), 2095A.

791 Manganaris-Decavailes, Anthony. "A Guide to Ezra Pound's Cantos (X)," Analyst, 11 (July, 1956), 1-18.

792 Mangum, Geoff. "A Note on Canto LXXIX: Cimbica, Sacred Puma of the Baja Peninsula," Paideuma, 9 (1980), 323-326.

793 Martin, B. K. "Ezra Pound and T. E. Lawrence: 74/444:472," Paideuma, 6 (Fall, 1977), 167-173. [Canto 74]

794 Materer, Timothy. "H. D., serenitas, and Canto LXIII," Paideuma, 12, #2-3 (Fall-Winter, 1983), 275-280.

795 _____. "Henry Gaudier's 'Three Ninas,'" Paideuma, 4 (Fall-Winter, 1975), 323-324. [Canto 107]

796 _____. "A Reading of 'From Canto CXV,'" Paideuma, 2, #2 (Fall, 1973), 205-207.

797 Mayo, Robert. "A Guide to Ezra Pound's Cantos (VIII)," Analyst, 5, (October, 1954). [Entire issue].

798 _____. "A Guide to Ezra Pound's Cantos (XI)," Analyst, 13 (July, 1957), 1-4.

799 _____, and Sybil Wuletich. "A Guide to Ezra Pound's Cantos (IX)," Analyst, 7 (April, 1955), [Entire issue].

800 Merchant, Moelwyn. "The Coke Cantos," Agenda, 17, #3-4 & 18, #1 (Aut-Wntr-Spr., 1979-80), 76-85.

801 Michaels, Walter B. "Lincoln Steffens and Pound," Paideuma, 2, #2 (Fall, 1973), 209-210.

802 Miller, James Edwin. "An Epic Is a Poem Containing History: Ezra Pound's 'Cantos,'" The American Quest for a Supreme Fiction. Chicago: U. of Chicago Pr., 1979, pp. 68-98.

803 Miller, Vincent. "Pound's Battle with Time," YR, 66, #2 (December, 1976), 193-208.

804 Millett, Fred B. "Ezra Pound and The Cantos," AL, 25, #4 (January, 1954), 517-519.

805 Miner, Earl. "Ezra Pound," The Japanese Tradition in British and American Literature. Princeton: Princeton U. Pr., 1958.

806 Miyake, Akiko. "Between Confucius and Eleusis: Ezra Pound's Assimilation of Chinese Culture and Writing the Cantos I-LXXI," DAI, 31 (Duke: 1971), 5416A-17A.

807 _____. "The Greek-Egyptian Mysteries in Pound's 'The Little Review Calendar' and in Cantos 1-7," Paideuma, 7 (Spring-Fall, 1978), 73-111.

808 Monroe, Harriet. "Ezra Pound," Poets and Their Art. Freeport, NY: Bks. for Libraries Pr., 1967, pp. 12-20.

809 Moody, A. D. "Cantos I-III: Craft and Vision," Agenda, 17, #3-4, and 18, #1 (Aut-Wntr-Spr., 1979-80), 103-117.

810 _____. "The Democracy of the Cantos," TLS, #4038 (August 15, 1980), 917.

811 Moore, Marianne. "A Draft of XXX Cantos," Poetry, 39 (October, 1931), 37-50.

812 _____. "A Draft of Cantos," Criterion, 13 (April, 1934), 482-485.

813 _____. "Ezra Pound: The Cantos," A Marianne Moore Reader. New York: Viking Pr., 1961, pp. 149-166.

814 _____. "Ezra Pound: The Cantos," Predilections. New York: Viking Pr., 1955, pp. 62-75.

815 _____. "A Note," Agenda, 4 (October-November, 1965), 22.

816 _____. "A Tribute," Cf., #125, p. 21.

817 Moramarco, Fred. "Concluding an Epic: The Drafts and Fragments of the Cantos," AL, 49 (November, 1977), 309-326.

818 _____. "Italian Imagery in The Cantos," Contributi dell' Istituto di filologia moderna. Sergio Rossi, ed. Milano: Vita e Pensiero, Univ. Cattolica. [1974?]

819 _____. "The Malatesta Cantos," Mosaic, 12, #1 (1978), 107-118.

820 _____. "Schiavoni: 'That Chap on the Wood Barge,'" Paideuma, 4, #1 (Spring, 1975), 101-104.

821 Morrow, Bradford. "De Lollis' Sordello and Sordello: Canto 36," Paideuma, 4, #1 (Spring, 1975), 93-98.

822 _____. "A Source for 'Palace in smoky light': Pound and Dryden's Virgil," Paideuma, 3, #2 (Fall, 1974), 245-246.

823 Morse, Jonathan. "What's His Name," Paideuma, 10, #3 (Winter, 1981), 595-597.

824 Muir, Edwin. "Experimental Poetry," LonM, 31 (April, 1935), 594-595.

825 _____. "Recent Poetry," Purpose, 12 (July-December, 1940), 149-150.

826 _____. "Review: Fifth Decade of Cantos," Criterion, 17 (October, 1937), 148-149.

827 Mullins, Eustace Clarence. Cf., #92, pp. 176-179, passim.

828 Murphy, Richard. "Books and Writers," Spectator, 185 (November 17, 1950), 516.

829 Myers, Peter. "The Metre of Canto 47," Paideuma, 11, #1 (Spring-Summer, 1982), 91-92.

830 Namjoshi, Suniti Manohar. "Ezra Pound and Reality: A Study of the Metaphysics of the Cantos," DAI, 34, #2 (McGill (Canada): 1972), 785A.

831 Nanny, Max. Ezra Pound: Poetics for an Electric Age. Bern: Francke, 1973.

832 _____. "Ezra Pound's Cantos: The Tale of the Tribe," NZZ, (November, 1972), 51-52.

833 _____. "Oral Dimensions in Ezra Pound," Paideuma, 6 (Spring, 1977), 13-26.

834 Nassar, Eugene Paul. The Cantos of Ezra Pound: The Lyric Mode. Baltimore and London: Johns Hopkins U. Pr., 1975.

835 _____. "'This Stone Giveth Sleep': 'Io son la lune,'" Paideuma, 1, #2 (Winter, 1972), 207-211.

836 Neidhardt, Frances E. "From Apelles to Pound's 'Usury' Canto: Botticelli's 'La Calumnia' Goes Modern," Paideuma, 12, #2-3 (Fall-Winter, 1983), 427-445.

837 Nicholls, P. Ezra Pound: Politics, Economics, and Writing: A Study of the Cantos. England: Macmillan Pr., 1984.

838 Nicolescu, Vasile. "Ezra Pound: tragism si iluminare," Cantos, si alte poeme. Bucharest: Univers, 1975, pp. 5-10.

839 Niikura, Toshikazu. "Berryman's Significance," JBeSt, 1, #2 (April, 1975), 14-18.

840 Nolde, John J. "The Sources for Canto 54: Part One," Paideuma, 5, #3 (Winter, 1976), 419-453; "Part Two," Paideuma, 6, #1 (Spring, 1977), 45-98.

841 _____. "The Sources for Canto 55," Paideuma, 7 (Spring-Fall, 1978), 189-247.

842 _____. "The Sources for the Chinese Dynastic Canto 56," Paideuma, 8 (1979), 263-292, 485-511.

843 Norman, Charles. "Pound's Cantos and His Economic," Cf., #93, pp. 335-354.

844 Oakes, Lois Ann. "An Explication of 'Canto 75' by Ezra Pound," WSCL, 5 (Summer, 1964), 105-109.

845 O'Connor, William Van. Ezra Pound. Minneapolis: U. of Minnesota Pr., 1963; also: #26 Pamphlets of American Writers.

846 Odlin, Reno. "Dinklage," Paideuma, 11, #2 (Fall, 1982), 283.

847 Olson, Charles. "First Canto," Paideuma, 3, #3 (Winter, 1974), 295-300.

848 Olson, Paul A. "Pound and the Poetry of Perception," Thought, 35, #138 (Autumn, 1960), 331-348; repr., #535, pp. 72-73.

849 Olsson, Theodore C. A. "Usura: Economics and Ethics in the Cantos of Ezra Pound," DAI, 35, #6 (Calif., Santa Barbara: 1974), 3758A.

850 Overland, Orm. "Ezra Pound and Wilfrid Scawen Blunt: A Footnote to Canto 81," N&Q, 14 (July, 1967), 250-252.

851 Owen, Earl Ben. "Social Credit and The Cantos," Pound Newsletter, 2 (April, 1954), 6-10.

852 Paige, D. D. "Aspects of the Cantos: Three New Cantos," Pound Newsletter, 6 (April, 1955), 2-4.

853 Paz, Octavio. The Bow and the Lyre. Trans. Ruth L. C. Simms. New York: McGraw-Hill, 1973, pp. 66-68.

854 _____. Children of the Mire: Modern Poetry from Romanticism to the Avant-Garde. Tr. by Rachel Phillips. Cambridge, Mass.: Harvard U. Pr., 1974, pp. 123-130, 132-138, passim.

855 Peachy, Frederic. "Aspects of the Cantos: The Greek Element in the Cantos," Pound Newsletter, 8 (October, 1955), 8-10.

856 Peacock, Alan J. "Pound, Horace and Canto IV," ELN, 17 (June, 1980), 288-292.

857 Pearce, Roy Harvey. "'The Cantos,'" The Continuity of American Poetry. Princeton, N.J.: Princeton U. Pr., 1961, pp. 83-101, 286-289.

858 _____. "Toward an American Epic," HudR, 12, #3 (Autumn, 1959), 362-377.

859 Pearlman, Daniel. "Alexander Del Mar in The Cantos: A Printout of the Sources," Paideuma, 1, #2 (Winter, 1972), 161-180.

860 _____. The Barb of Time: On the Unity of Pound's Cantos. New York: Oxford U. Pr., 1969.

861 _____. "The Blue-Eyed Eel: Dame Fortune in Pound's Later Cantos," Agenda, 9, #4-10 (Fall-Wntr, 1971-72), 60-77.

862 _____. "Canto 52: The Vivante Passage," Paideuma, 10, #2 (1981), 311-314.

863 _____. "Canto 74: 'Lucifer' Elucidated," Paideuma, 9 (1980), 313-317.

864 _____. Review: [Cf., #834], MLQ, 37, #3 (1976), 298-300.

865 _____. "The Inner Metronome: A Genetic Study of Time in Pound," Agenda, 8, #3-4 (Autumn-Wntr., 1970), 51-58.

866 _____. "Time and Major Form in the Cantos of Ezra Pound," DAI, 31, #9 (Columbia U: 1968), 4789A.

867 Peck, John. "'Get a Dictionary': The Festus Behind Pound's Festus," Paideuma, 2, #2 (Fall, 1973), 211-213.

868 _____. "Landscape as Ceremony in the Later Cantos: From The Roads of France to Rock's World," Agenda, 9, #2-3 (Spr.-Summer, 1971), 26-69.

869 _____. "Pound's Lexical Mythography," Paideuma, 1, #1 (Spring-Summer, 1972), 3-36.

870 Perlès, Alfred. "From an Ancient Diary," Nimbus, 3, #1 (Summer, 1955), 6-11.

871 Peterson, Leland D. "Ezra Pound: The Use and Abuse of History," AQ, 17 (Spring, 1965), 33-47.

872 Pevear, Richard. "Notes on the Cantos of Ezra Pound," HudR, 25, #1 (Spring, 1972), 51-70.

873 Powell, James A. "The Light of Vers Libre," Paideuma, 8, #1 (Spring, 1979), 3-34.

874 Pritchard, William. "Two-tone Epic," TLS (July 23, 1976), 926-927.

875 Quinn, Bernetta, O. S. F. "'All That Sandro Knew': The Boticellian Vision in The Cantos," Greyfriar, 20 (Fall, 1979), 29-55.

876 _____. "The Cantos: From Erebus to Pisa," and "The Cantos: The Perilous Ascent," Ezra Pound: An Introduction to the Poetry. London; New York: Columbia U. Pr., 1972, pp. 101-128, 129-167.

877 _____. "Light from the East: The Cantos and Chinese Art," Greyfriar, 18 (1977), 49-63.

878 _____. "The Metamorphoses of Ezra Pound," WR, 15 (Spring, 1951), 169-181; repr., EIE (1953), pp. 60-100; Cf., #771.

879 _____. "A Note on Richard of St. Victor and the Moon Goddess," Paideuma, 5, #1 (Spring-Summer, 1976), 59-61.

880 Raaberg, Gloria Gwen. "Toward a Theory of Literary Collage: Literary Experimentalism and Its Relation to Modern Art in the Works of Pound, Stein, and Williams," DAI, 39, #5 (U. of Calif., Irvine: 1978), 2932A.

881 Rabaté, Jean-Michel. "Pound anathème," Degrés, (Spring-Summer, 1981), 26-27.

882 _____. "'Sounds Pound': History and Ideology in the China Cantos," Myth and Ideology in American Culture. Regis Durand, ed. (Cahiers Amer. 1.) Villeneuve d'Ascq: U. de Lille, III, pp. 21-41.

883 Raboni, Giovanni. "Appunti per una lettura dei Cantos," Let, Nos. 39-41 (maggio-agosto, 1959), 52-61.

884 Racey, Edgar Francis, Jr. "Pound's Cantos: The Structure of a Modern Epic," DA, 24, #6 (Claremont: 1963), 2484.

885 Read, Forrest, Jr. "A Man of No Fortunes," EIE, (1953), pp. 101-123; repr., #771, pp. 101-123.

886 _____. "The Mathematical Symbolism of Ezra Pound's Revolutionary Mind," Paideuma, 7 (Spring-Fall, 1978), 7-72.

887 _____. "Pound, Coke, or Gordon? Venus, Aeneas, or Tmesis? That's What's Wrong with Paideuma," Paideuma, 5, #1 (Spring, 1976), 199-208.

888 _____. "'76: The Cantos of Ezra Pound," StAR, 1, #1 (Fall-Winter, 1970), 11-16.

889 _____. '76: One World and the Cantos of Ezra Pound. Chapel Hill: U. of North Carolina Pr., 1981.

890 Read, Herbert E. "Ezra Pound," Cf., #125, pp. 7-20.

891 _____. "Ezra Pound," The Tenth Muse: Essays in Criticism. London: Routledge & Kegan Paul, c1957; Freeport, NY: Books for Libraries Pr., 1969, pp. 260-275.

892 _____. "Ideas in Action: Ezra Pound," True Voice of Feeling: Studies in English Romantic Poetry. New York: Pantheon Pr., 1953, pp. 116-138.

893 _____. "The Limits of Permissiveness," MalR, 9 (January, 1969), 37-50.

894 Reboni, Giovanni. "Appunti per una lettura dei Cantos," Let, 7 (1959), xxxix-xl, 52-61.

895 Reche, Denis. "Pour Ezra Pound," Tel Quel, #11 (Fall, 1962), 17-24.

896 Reck, Michael. "Reading the Cantos: Pound's Fugal Music," Cw, 83 (October 22, 1965), 93-95.

897 Reed, Victor B. "Toward The Cantos of Ezra Pound," DA, 28 (Columbia: 1965), 1445A-46A.

898 Regier, W. G. "Ezra Pound, Adam Smith, Karl Marx," MinnR, n.s., 12 (1979), 72-76.

899 Revell, Peter. "'Toward the Great Healing': The Cantos of Ezra Pound," Quest in Modern American Poetry. London: Vision Pr.; NJ: Barnes & Noble, 1981, pp. 98-136.

900 Rice, Philip Blair. "The Education of Ezra Pound," Nation, 139 (November 21, 1934), 599-600.

901 Riddel, Joseph N. "Pound and the Decentered Image," GaR, 29, #3 (Fall, 1975), 565-591.

902 Roberts, Michael. "A Draft of XXX Cantos," Adelphi, 7 (December, 1933), 226-228.

903 _____. "Mr. Pound's Cantos," Spectator, 151 (October 13, 1933), 492.

904 Rosenthal, M[acha] L[ouis]. "Canto XVI," Poetry and the Common Life. New York: Oxford U. Pr., 1974, p. 87.

905 _____. "The Cantos," A Primer of Ezra Pound. New York: Macmillan, 1960, pp. 42-51; repr., in Ezra Pound: A Collection of Critical Essays. Walter Sutton, ed. Englewood Cliffs, NJ: Prentice-Hall, Inc., 1963, pp. 57-63; and in Ezra Pound: A Collection of Criticism. Grace Schulman, ed. NY: McGraw-Hill, 1974, pp. 125-131.

906 _____. "Dimensions of Pound: The Structuring of The Cantos," and "Voyage of Sensibility: Pound's Canto 47," Sailing Into the Unknown: Yeats, Pound, and Eliot. New York: Oxford U. Pr., 1978, pp. 69-115, pp. 12-25.

907 _____. "The New Poets," American and British Poetry Since World War II. New York: Oxford U. Pr., 1967, passim.

908 _____. "The Pleasures of Pound," Nation, 190 (1960), 368-371.

909 _____. "Poetic Means and Meanings," Nation, 182 (May 5, 1956), 385.

910 _____. "Pound at His Best: Canto 47 as a Model of Poetic Thought," Paideuma, 6 (Winter, 1977), 309-321.

911 _____. "Some Notes on The Cantos," The Modern Poets: A Critical Introduction. New York: Oxford U. Pr., 1960, pp. 66-74.

912 _____. "The Structuring of Pound's Cantos," Paideuma, 6, #1 (Spring, 1977), 3-11.

913 Rosenthal, Marilyn. "The Impact of Confucius on Ezra Pound's Canto XIII: An Explication de Texte," ChC, 18 (1977), 41-48.

914 Roskolenko, Harry. "The Cant in Pound's Cantos," Congress Weekly (April 11, 1949), 5-7.

915 Rubin, Louis D., Jr. "The Search for Lost Innocence," Hollins Critic, I, #5 (December, 1964), 1-16.

916 Russell, Francis. "The Cantos of Ezra Pound," ContemplI, 10 (May-June, 1960), 117-142.

917 Sanders, Frederick K. "The 'French Theme' of Canto 70: An Examination of Ezra Pound's Use of Historical Sources," Paideuma, 2, #3 (Winter, 1973), 379-390.

918 Sawyer, Richard James. "The Great Periplus: A Study of the Structure of Ezra Pound's Cantos," DAI, 45, #2 (Toronto: 1983), 517A.

919 Schafer, Murray. "Ezra Pound and Music," Canadian Music Journal, 5, #4 (Summer, 1961), 15-43.

920 Schimmel, Harold. "Historical Grit Gestation," Sagetrieb, 1, (1982), 220-254.

921 Schmidt, Gerd. "A Note on Canto CX," Paideuma, 8 (1979), 55-56.

922 Schneidau, Herbert N. Ezra Pound: The Image and the Real. Baton Rouge: Louisiana St. U. Pr., 1969, pp. 126-127, 136-145.

923 Schneideman, Robert. "A Guide to Ezra Pound's Cantos (VII)," Analyst, No. 4 (June, 1954), 1-14.

924 Schwartz, Delmore. "Ezra Pound and History," NR, 142, #6 (February 8, 1960), 17-19; Cf., #926, pp. 113-119.

925 _____. "Ezra Pound's Very Useful Labors," Poetry, 51, #6 (March, 1938), 324-339; Cf., #926, pp. 102-112.

926 _____. Selected Essays of Delmore Schwartz. Donald A. Dike and David H. Zucker, eds., with an appreciation by Dwight MacDonald. Chicago: U. of Chicago Pr., 1970.

927 _____. "Notes on the Verification of the Cantos," Notes on Ezra Pound's Cantos: Structure and Metric. Norfolk, Conn.: New Directions, 1940, pp. 90-91.

928 Scott, Tom. "Two Plus Two Would Equal Four but for the Shadow," Agenda, 8, #3-4 (Autumn-Winter, 1970), 35-37.

929 Seferis, George. "A Note Appended to His Translation of Three Cantos," Cf., #239, pp. 77-83.

930 Shaheen, Mohammed Y. "A Note on the Spelling 'Habdimalich' for 'Abd-al-Malik' in The Cantos," Paideuma, 11, #2 (Fall, 1982), 287-288.

931 _____. "The Story of Abd-el-Melik's Money in Canto XCVI and XCVII," Paideuma, 11, #3 (Winter, 1982), 420-428.

932 Shaw, Peter. "Ezra Pound on American History," PR, 44 (1977), 112-124.

933 Shere, Charles. "Eastbay Artists Score Record Triumph," Oakland Tribune (September 17, 1972), 7-9; Paideuma, 2 (Spr., 1973), 7-9.

934 Sieburth, Richard. "Canto 119: Francois Bernouard," Paideuma, 4, #2-3 (Fall-Winter, 1975), 329-332.

935 _____. "Ideas into Action: Pound and Voltaire," Paideuma, 6, #3 (Winter, 1977), 365-390.

936 Singh, G. "The 'Cantos' of Ezra Pound," TLS, No. 3,497 (March 6, 1969), p. 241; No. 3498 (March 13, 1969), p. 271; No. 3,500 (March 27, 1969), p. 327; No. 3,501 (April 3, 1969), p. 368; No. 3,502 (April 10, 1969), p. 390.

937 _____. "Dante and Pound," CritQ, 17, #4 (Winter, 1975), 311-328.

938 _____. "Ezra Pound Symposium," Paideuma, 3, (Fall, 1974), 151-168.

939 _____. "Four Views of Ezra Pound," BA, 46 (Winter, 1972), 61-63.

940 _____. "Meeting Ezra Pound," BA, 46 (Summer, 1972), 403-409.

941 _____. "Pound and Cavalcanti," Essays in Honour of John Humphreys Whitfield Presented to Him on His Retirement from the Serena Chair of Italian at the University of Birmingham. Davis, H. C., D. G. Rees, J. M. Hatwell, and G. W. Slowey, eds. London: St. George's, 1975, 268-284.

942 Sitwell, Edith. "Ezra Pound," Aspects of Modern Poetry. London: Duckworth, 1934; repr., Freeport, NY: Bks. for Libraries Pr., 1970, pp. 178-214.

943 _____. "Ezra Pound," English and American Book of English and American Poetry. Edith Sitwell, ed. Boston: Little, Brown & Co., 1958, pp. 993-1003.

944 _____. "Preface to Ezra Pound," YLM, 126, #5 (December, 1958), 42-44.

945 Slatin, Myles. "A History of Pound's Cantos, I-XVI, 1915-1925," AL, 35, #2 (May, 1963), 183-195.

946 Smith, P. H., and A. E. Durant. "Pound's Metonymy: Revisiting Canto 47," Paideuma, 8 (1979), 327-333.

947 Snodgrass, W. D. "Four Gentlemen; Two Ladies," HudR, 13, #1 (Spring, 1960), 120-125.

948 Spann, Marcella. "Beauty in Fragments," Agenda, 8, #3-4 (Autumn-Winter, 1970), 40-43; repr., under title "Ezra Pound: Drafts and Fragments of Cantos CX-CXVII," Sou'wester (So. Ill. U.), Special Ezra Pound, Birthday Issue (October 30, 1970), 55-58.

949 Spender, Stephen. "The Fifth Decad of Cantos," Left Review, 3 (July, 1937), 361.

950 Splitter, Randolph. "Pound's Dream of the Gods: A Baker's Half-Dozen of the Cantos," Sou'wester, Special Ezra Pound, Birthday Issue, (October 30, 1970), 81-99.

951 Stauffer, Donald A. "Poetry as Symbolic Thinking," SatRL, 30 (March 22, 1947), 9-10.

952 Steven, James C. "Modernist Form: Pound's Style in a Draft of XXX Cantos," DAI, 44, #6 (U. of Arkansas: 1983), 1787A.

953 Stock, Noel. "Balancing the Books," PoetA, 30 (October, 1969), 42-52.

954 _____. Reading the Cantos: A Study of Meaning in Ezra Pound. London: Routledge & Kegan Paul; NY: Random House, 1966.

955 Stoicheff, Richard Peter. "Ezra Pound's 'Drafts & Fragments': A Study in Composition," DAI, 44, #9 (U. of Toronto: 1983), 2768A.

956 _____. "CX/778 Revisited," Paideuma, 12, #1 (Spring, 1983), 47-50.

957 Stone, Douglas. "Pound's 'Mr. Corles': Canto XXXV," Paideuma, 2, #3 (Winter, 1973), 411-414.

958 Surette, Philip Leon. "The City in the Cantos of Ezra Pound: A Study of a Modern Epic," DAI, 32 (Toronto: 1969), 458A-459A.

959 _____. "The City of Dioce, U.S.A.: Pound and America," BuR, 20, #2 (Fall, 1972), 14-34.

960 _____. "Ezra Pound's John Adams: An American Odyssey," Prospects: Annual of American Cultural Studies, 2 (1976), 483-495.

961 _____. "'Having His Own Mind to Stand by Him,'" HudR, 27 (Winter, 1974-75), 491-510.

962 _____. "Helen of Tyre," Paideuma, 2, #3 (Winter, 1973), 419-421.

963 _____. "The Historical Pattern in Ezra Pound's Cantos," HAB, 22, #3 (1971), 11-21.

964 _____. "A Light from Eleusis," Paideuma, 3, #2 (Fall, 1974), 191-216.

965 _____. A Light from Eleusis: A Study of Ezra Pound's Cantos. Oxford: Clarendon Pr.; NY: New York U. Pr., 1979.

966 Sutton, Walter E. "Criticism as a Social Act," Modern American Criticism. Englewood Cliffs, NJ: Prentice-Hall, 1963, pp. 281-283.

967 _____. "Ezra Pound: The Cantos," American Free Verse: The Modern Revolution in Poetry. New York: New Directions, 1973, pp. 65-80.

968 Swabey, Henry. "Towards an A.B.C. of History," Cf., #239, pp. 186-202.

969 Tate, Allen. "Ezra Pound," Collected Essays, Cf., #238, pp. 350-357.

970 _____. "Ezra Pound," Essays of Four Decades. Chicago: Swallow Pr., 1968, pp. 364-371.

971 _____. "Ezra Pound, 1931," On the Limits of Poetry: Selected Essays: 1928-1948. New York: Swallow Pr., and Wm. Morrow Co., pp. 350-357.

972 _____. "Ezra Pound," Reactionary Essays on Poetry and Ideas. New York: Charles Scribner's Sons, 1936.

973 _____. "Ezra Pound," Literary Opinion in America: Essays Illustrating the Status, Methods, and Problems of Criticism in the United States in the Twentieth Century. M. D. Zabel, ed., 3rd ed. revised, Harper, 1951, pp. 237-242.

974 _____. "Ezra Pound's Golden Ass," Nation, 132 (June 10, 1931), 632-634; An Examination of Ezra Pound. New York: New Directions, 1950, pp. 66-72.

975 _____. "Il vero cuore dei Cantos," FLe, 8, #43 (October 25, 1953), 3-4.

976 _____. "On Ezra Pound's Cantos," Essays of Four Decades, Cf., #970, pp. 364-371.

977 _____. "Poetry and Politics," NR, 75 (August 2, 1933), 308-311.

978 Tay, William Shu-san. "The Sun on the Silk: Ezra Pound and Confucianism," DAI, 38 (U. of Calif., San Diego: 1977), 5450A.

979 Terrell, Carroll F. "Cabranez, the Mystery Man," Paideuma, 11, #3 (Winter, 1982), 451-453.

980 _____. "Canto XXXIV: The Technique of Montage," Paideuma, 6 (Fall, 1977), 186-232.

981 _____. "The Chinese Dynastic Cantos Generale de la Chine, 100-121," Paideuma, 5 (Spring-Summer, 1976), 95-99.

982 _____. A Companion to the Cantos of Ezra Pound. Published in cooperation with the National Poetry Foundation of California Pr., Berkeley: U. of Calif. Pr., 1980; Vol. 2, 1984.

983 _____. "A Commentary on Grosseteste with an English Version of De Luce," Paideuma, 2, #3 (Winter, 1973), 449-470.

984 _____. "A Couple of Glosses," Paideuma, 12, #1 (Spring, 1983), 51-52.

985 _____. "The Eparch's Book," Paideuma, 2, #2 (Fall, 1973), 223-311.

986 _____. "History, de Mailla, and the Dynastic Cantos," Paideuma, 5, #1 (Spring-Summer, 1976), 95-99.

987 _____. "John Adams Speaking: Some Reflections on Technique," Paideuma, 4, #2&3 (Fall-Winter, 1975), 533-538.

988 _____. "Magna Carta, Talbots, The Lady Anne, and Pound's Associative Technique in Canto 80," Paideuma, 5, #1 (Spring, 1976), 69-76.

989 _____. "The Na-Khi Documents, I: The Landscape of Paradise," Paideuma, 3, #1 (Spring, 1974), 91-122.

990 _____. "The Periplus of Hanno: Edited with a Commentary," Paideuma, 1, #2 (Winter, 1972), 223-232.

991 _____. "The Sacred Edict of K'ang-hsi," Paideuma, 2, #1 (Spring, 1973), 69-112.

992 _____, and David M. Gordon. "The Sources of Canto 53," Paideuma, 5, #1 (Spring, 1976), 95-152.

993 Thaniel, George. "George Seferis' Thrush and the Poetry of Ezra Pound," CLS, 11, #4 (December, 1974), 326-336.

994 Theroux, Paul. "Christopher Okigbo," Transition, 5, #22 (1965), 18-20.

995 Thompson, J. S. "The Political Theme of Pound's Cantos," L&I, 8 (1971), 43-56.

996 Trevisan, Lucio. "Il Canto 74 e el metodo poundiano," SA, 17 (1971), 167-193.

997 Tritschler, D. M. "A Guide to Ezra Pound's Cantos (V)," Analyst, 2 (July, 1953), 1-7.

998 Tseng, Yueh-nung. "On Ezra Pound's Canto XIII," Chinese Cult (Taiwan), 2 (1959), 1-3.

999 Ullyatt, A. G. "Judging the Cantos: Paradox as Unity," UES, 15, #2 (1977), 52-61.

1000 Untermeyer, Louis, "Poet in Extremis," SatRL, 17 (January 29, 1938), 10.

1001 _____. "Yeats and Others," YR, 30 (Winter, 1941), 380-382.

1002 Vasse, William W. "Aspects of the Cantos: II: American History and the Cantos," PoundN, 5 (January, 1955), 13-19.

1003 _____. "A Note on the Text of the China Cantos," PoundN, 6 (April, 1955), 15-19.

1004 _____. "Traveler in a Landscape: The Structure of History in Ezra Pound's Cantos," DAI, 31 (Calif., Berkeley: 1969), 772A.

1005 _____, and William W. Edwards. The Annotated Index to the Cantos of Ezra Pound. Berkeley and Los Angeles, Calif., 1957.

1006 Vettori, Vittorio. "Premessa" [for "Dai Cantos di Ezra Pound"], Dial, 6 (1958), 3-9.

1007 _____. "Pound in Italia," Il fiore dei Cantos: 18 Interpretazioni con un saggio introduttivo de Vittorio Vettori. Pisa: Giardini Editore, 1962.

1008 Véza, Laurette. "Les Cantos de Pound: Un Voyage au bout de la nuit," Le Voyage dans la littérature anglo-saxonne. Actes du Congres de Nice (1971): Soc. des Anglicistes de l'Enseignement Supérieur. Paris: Didier, 1972.

1009 Vidan, Ivo. "Znanje Pounda i glas 'Pjevanja,'" [Pound's knowledge and the voice of the Cantos.] Kritika (Zagreb), (12), (1970), 417-423.

1010 Von Hendy, Andrew John. "The Form and Principal Themes of Pound's Cantos," DA, 24 (Cornell: 1962), 306.

1011 Wagstaff, A. Christopher. "Make It New: A Study of the American Aspects of Ezra Pound's Cantos," DAI, 34 (Calif., Davis: 1973), 6668A.

1012 Wain, John. "The Reputation of Ezra Pound," LonM, II, #10 (October, 1955), 55-64.

1013 _____. "The Shadow of an Epic," Spectator, #6872 (March 11, 1960), 360.

1014 Walkiewicz, E. P. "A Reading of Pound's Canto CXX," NMAL, 4 (1980), Item 28.

1015 Walton, Eda Lou. "Eleven New Cantos by Ezra Pound," NYTBR, 5 (November 18, 1934), 4.

1016 _____. "Obscurity in Modern Poetry," NYTBR, 5 (April 2, 1933), 2.

1017 Wand, David Hsin-Fu. "To the Summit of the Tai Shan: Ezra Pound's Use of Chinese Mythology," Paideuma, 3, #1 (Spring, 1974), 3-12.

1018 Wanning, Andrews. "Current Letters: III: Ezra Pound, Poetry in an Ivory Tower," The Harkness Hoot, 3 (April, 1933), 33-39.

1019 Warren, Eugene. "The Temple Is Not for Sale,"--Canto 97, Sou'wester (So. Ill. U.), (October 30, 1970), 125-126.

1020 Watts, Harold H. "The Devices of Pound's Cantos," QRL, V, #2 (1949), 147-173.

1021 _____. Ezra Pound and the Cantos. Chicago: Henry Regnery, 1952; London: Routledge & Kegan Paul, 1951.

1022 _____. "Pound's Cantos: Means to an End," YPR, #6 (1947), 9-20.

1023 Wees, William C. "Ezra Pound as a Vorticist," WSCL, 6 (Winter-Spring, 1965), 56-72.

1024 Westcott, Glenway. "A Draft of Cantos," Dial, 79 (December, 1925), 501-503.

1025 Weston, K. Noel. "Cantos LII-LXXI," The Townsman, 3, #11 (July, 1940), 27-29.

1026 Whigham, Peter. "Il Suo Paradiso Terrestre," Agenda, 8 (Spring, 1970), 31-34.

1027 Wilhelm, James J. "The Dragon and the Duel: A Defense of Pound's Canto 88," TCL, 20 (April, 1974), 114-125.

1028 _____. "Guido Cavalcanti as a Mask for Ezra Pound," PMLA, 89, #2 (March, 1974), 332-340.

1029 _____. "In Praise of Anselm: An Approach to Canto 105," Paideuma, 2, #3 (Winter, 1973), 399-407.

1030 _____. The Later Cantos of Ezra Pound. New York: Walker, 1977.

1031 _____. "Notes and Queries," Paideuma, 2, #2 (Fall, 1973), 333-339.

1032 _____. "Pound's Middle Cantos as an Analogue to Dante's Purgatorio: Purgatories Fictive and Real," IQ, 16, #64 (1973), 49-66.

1033 _____. "Two Heavens of Light: Paradise to Dante and to Pound," Paideuma, 2, #2 (Fall, 1973), 175-191.

1034 Williams, John K., Jr. "The Hell-Cantos as Source of Satiric Imagery," IE, 4 (1975), 1-7.

1035 Williams, William Carlos. "Excerpts from a Critical Sketch: A Draft of XXX Cantos of Ezra Pound," Symposium, 2 (April, 1931), 257-263; repr., in Ezra Pound: A Collection of Critical Essays. Walter Sutton, ed. Englewood Cliffs, N.J.: Prentice-Hall, 1963, pp. 11-16; also repr., in Ezra Pound: A Critical Anthology. J. P. Sullivan, ed. Baltimore: Penguin Bks., 1970, pp. 116-122.

1036 _____. "The Later Pound," MassR, 14, #1 (Winter, 1973), 124.

1037 _____. "Pound's Eleven New Cantos," New Democracy, 3 #10-11 (January 15-February 1, 1935), 191-192.

1038 _____. "A Study of Ezra Pound's Present Position," MassR, 14, #1 (Winter, 1973), 118-123.

1039 Wilson, T. C. "Rhythm and Phrase," SatRL, 9 (July 1, 1933), 677.

1040 Winters, Yvor. "Ezra Pound's Techniques," Cf., #535, pp. 31-33.

1041 _____. "Primitivism and Decadence," The Anatomy of Nonsense. Norfolk, Conn.: New Directions, 1943; repr., in In Defense of Reason: Primitivism and Decadence. New York: Wm. Morrow & Co., 1947, pp. 95, 101-102.

1042 _____. "Problems of the Modern Critic of Literature," The Function of Criticism: Problems and Exercises. Denver: Allen Swallow, 1967, pp. 12, 46-47.

1043 Witemeyer, Hugh. "The Flame-style King," Paideuma, 4, #2-3 (Fall-Winter, 1975), 333-335.

1044 _____. "Pound and the Cantos: 'Ply over Ply,'" Occident, 7, #1 (1973), 229-235; Paideuma, 8 (1979?), 229-235.

1045 _____. Review, Paideuma, 5, #1 (1976), 191-193, [Cf., #724]

1046 _____. "Ruskin and the Signed Capital in Canto 45," Paideuma, 4, #1 (Spring, 1975), 85-88.

1047 Wolfe, Humbert. "Yes or No," EngRev, 57 (December, 1933), 664-666.

1048 Yueh-nung, Tseng. "On Ezra Pound's Canto XIII," Chinese Culture, II (Taiwan), (March, 1959), 1-3.

1049 Zapatka, Francis E. "Crommelyn and del Valle: A Note on Canto 105," Paideuma, 2, #3 (Winter, 1973), 423.

1050 Zolla, Elémire. "I 'Cantos' di Ezra Pound," SPe, 8 (November, 1955), 465-467.

1051 Zukovsky, Louis. "American Poetry, 1920-1930," Symposium, 2, #1 (January, 1930), 71-73, 74.

1052 _____. "Cantos d'Ezra Pound," Echanges, 3 (June, 1930), 145-172.

1053 _____. "The Cantos of Ezra Pound," Criterion, 10 (April, 1931), 424-440.

1054 _____. "Ezra Pound," Prepositions: The Collected Critical Essays of Louis Zukovsky. Expanded Ed. Berkeley & Los Angeles: 1981, pp. 67-83.

1055 _____. "Ezra Pound: His Cantos," Observer (Memphis, Tenn.), 2 (January-February, 1934), 3-4, 8.

1056 _____. "Ezra Pound's XXX Cantos," Front, 4 (Amsterdam), (June, 1931), 364-369.

1057 _____. "Cantos di Ezra Pound," L'Indice, (Genoa: 10, April 25, May 10, 1931).

The Adams Cantos

1058 Davis, Kay. "Eleusis and the Structure of the Adams Cantos," ConP, 5, #1 (1982), 45-55.

1059 Gordon, David M. "Coke in the Adams and Pisan Cantos," Paideuma, 4, #2&3 (Fall-Winter, 1975), 223-299.

1060 McDonald, James R. "The 'Adams Cantos': Fact or Fiction," AntigR, 21 (1975), 97-107.

1061 _____. "'Norm of Spirit': The Adams Cantos of Ezra Pound," DAI, 34, #10 (Toledo: 1973), 6650A.

1062 Sanders, Frederick Kirkland. John Adams Speaking: Pound's Sources for the Adams Cantos. Orono: U. of Maine Pr., 1975.

1063 _____. "A Source Book for the 'Adams Cantos' of Ezra Pound," DAI, 32 (Georgia: 1971), 5805A-06A.

1064 Terrell, C. F. "John Adams Speaking: Some Reflections on Technique," Paideuma, 4, #2&3 (Fall-Winter, 1975), 533-538.

The Pisan Cantos

1065 Amaral, José Vázquez. Introduction. Los Cantares de Pisa. Mexico: Universidad Nacional de Mexico, 1956, p. 14.

1066 _____. "Words from Ezra Pound," RutgersRev, 3 (Winter, 1968), 40.

1067 Astaldi, Maria Luisa. "I Canti Pisani," Il Giornale d'Italia. Rome: January 21, 1954.

1068 Bacigalupo, Massimo. "The Pisan Poem and Its Genesis," Cf., #437, pp. 1-4.

1069 Barton, David. "Difficult Methods: The Pisan Cantos," NConL, 8, iv (1978), 8-9.

1070 Benet, William Rose. "Phoenix Nest," Cf., #269.

1071 Berryman, John. Cf., #5.

1072 Bertacchini, Renato. "I Canti Pisani," Gazzetta dell-Emilia, Modena: (January 2, 1954).

1073 Bogan, Louise. Cf., #464.

1074 Bowra, C. M. "More Cantos from Ezra Pound," NS&N, 38 (September 3, 1949), 250.

1075 Cantrell, Carol Helmstetter. Cf., #490.

1076 Caparelli, Giuseppe. "I Canti Pisani di Ezra Pound," La Giustizia. Rome: December, 1953.

1077 Chace, William M. "The Pisan Cantos: 'Paradise,'" The Political Identities of Ezra Pound and T. S. Eliot. Stanford, Calif.: Stanford U. Pr., 1973, pp. 86-105.

1078 Contino, Vittorugo. Ezra Pound in Italy: From the Pisan Cantos. Venice: G. Ivancich, 1970.

1079 Corrigan, Robert A. Cf., #172.

1080 Corsare, Antonio. "I Pisan Cantos," Il Giornale di Sicilia. Cantania: (April 12, 1954).

1081 Cousins, Norman, and Harrison Smith. Cf., #177.

1082 Cowley, Malcolm. Cf., #178.

1083 Crino, Anna Maria. "Observations on the Italian Translation of the Cantos by Alfredo Rizzardi," Idea, 5 (December 27, 1953), 4.

1084 Davie, Donald. "The Pisan Cantos," Ezra Pound: A Collection of Criticism. Grace Schulman, ed. New York: McGraw-Hill, 1974, pp. 114-124.

1085 _____. "The Pisan Cantos," TLS (January 11, 1957), 23.

1086 Decavalles, Anthony M. "Elysium in Fragments," IJAS, 2, #2 (December, 1972), 17-29.

1087 Dennis, Helen M. "The Elusinian Mysteries as an Organising Principle in The Pisan Cantos," Paideuma, 10, #2 (Fall, 1981), 273-282.

1088 Deutsch, Babette. Cf., #562, p. 4.

1089 _____. Cf., #563, pp. 668-670.

1090 _____. Cf., #564, p. 7.

1091 Diggory, Terrence. "A Live Tradition: Ezra Pound," Yeats and American Poetry: The Tradition of the Self. Princeton: Princeton U. Pr., 1983, pp. 31-58.

1092 DuPlessis, Rachel Blau. "The Endless Poem: Paterson of William Carlos Williams and The Pisan Cantos of Ezra Pound," DAI, 31 (Columbia: 1970), 5396A.

1093 Eberhart, Richard. "An Approach to the Cantos," See #535, pp. 34-35.

1094 _____. Of Poetry and Poets. Urbana: U. of Illinois Pr., 1979, pp. 126-140.

1095 _____. "Pound's New Cantos," QRL, 5, #2 (1949), 174-191.

1096 Emery, Clark. [Pisan Cantos]. Ideas Into Action. Coral Gables, Fla.: U. of Miami Pr., 1958, pp. 79ff.

1097 Fang, Achilles. "Materials for the Study of Pound's Cantos," Diss., Harvard U., 1958. [Pisan Cantos]

1098 Ferril, Thomas Harnsby. "The New Poetry," San Francisco Chronicle, (November 7, 1948), 11.

1099 Fitzgerald, Robert. "Addendum on Pound," NR, 119, #8 (August 23, 1948), 26.

1100 _____. "What Thou Lovest Well Remains," NR, 119 (August 16, 1948), 21-23.

1101 Fleming, William. Cf., #318, pp. 325-328.

1102 Flory, Wendy Stallard. "The 'Tre Donne' of the Pisan Cantos," Paideuma, 5, #1 (Spring, 1975-76), 45-52.

1103 Frankenberg, Lloyd. Cf., #624, Sec. 7, p. 14.

1104 Gerhardt, Rainer M. "Die Pisaner Gesange," Hossischer Rundfunk, (March, 1952). [A radio program]

1105 Giovacchini, Graziella. "I Canti Pisani de Ezra Pound," Posta Letteraria (Lodi: April 3, 1954).

1106 Golffing, Francis. Pisan Cantos: Review. Furioso, 4 (Winter, 1949), 64.

1107 Gordon, David M. "Edward Coke: The Azalia Is Grown," Cf., #651.

1108 Greenspan, Cory Robert. "Charles Olson and Ezra Pound: Modes of Language and Thought in Modern Poetry," DAI, 34 (Buffalo: 1973), 5172A.

1109 Gregory, Horace. "Ezra Pound in Progress," NR, 94 (March 23, 1938), 200-201.

1110 _____. "The Search for a Frontier," Cf., #657.

1111 _____, and Marya Zaturenska. A History of American Poetry, 1900-1940. New York: Harcourt, Brace & Co., 1946.

1112 Guidacci, Margherita. "Canti Pisani," Il Ponte, 10, #4 (Florence: 1954).

1113 Guidi, Augusto. "I Pisan Cantos e la corrispondenza di Pound," Occasioni americane. Rome: 1958, pp. 92-99.

1114 _____. "Pound nei 'Pisan Cantos' e nella corrispondenza," Letteratura, I (December, 1953), 153-159.

1115 Guidotti, Mario Colombi. "Canti Pisani," Gazzetta de Parma, (December 29, 1953).

1116 Hamburger, Michael. Pisan Cantos. [Review], World Review, 8 (October, 1949), 78.

1117 Healy, J. V. "Pound and Tate," WR, 13, #2 (Winter, 1949), 115-118.

1118 Hesse, Eva, tr. Die Pisaner Gesange. With Concluding Essay. Zurich: Die Arche, 1956.

1119 _____. "New Light on Old Problems," Paideuma, 7 (Spring-Fall, 1978), 179-183.

1120 Humphries, Rolfe. "Jeffers and Pound," Nation, 167 (September 25, 1948), 349.

1121 Hutchins, Patricia. "Ezra Pound's Pisa," SoR, 2, #1, n.s. (Winter, 1966), 77-93.

1122 Kennedy, Leo. "Poet Who Was 'Mad as a Fascist,'" Chicago Sun, (August 9, 1948).

1123 Kenner, Hugh. "In the Caged Panther's Eyes," HudR, 1, #4 (Winter, 1949), 580-586.

1124 _____. Cf., #738, pp. 185ff.

1125 _____. "Pound's Cantos I," Expl, 11, #3 (December, 1952), Item 20.

1126 _____. "The Rose in the Steel Dust," Cf., #742, pp. 66-124.

1127 Kimpel, Ben D., and T. C. Duncan Eaves. "Pound's Canto LXXX," Explicator, 41, #3 (Spring, 1983), 43-44.

1128 _____ and _____. "Pound's Pisan Cantos," Expl, 40 (Fall, 1981), #43.

1129 King, Michael. "Ezra Pound at Pisa: An Interview with John L. Steel," TQ, 21, #4 (Winter, 1978), 48-61.

1130 Kurumisawa, Atsuo. "The 'Center of the World' as Implied in The Pisan Cantos," SELL, 31 (January, 1981), 19-37.

1131 Larkin, Greg. "From Noman to Everyman: Chinese Characters in the Pisan Cantos," TkR, 11, #3 (Spring, 1981), 307-315.

1132 Lenberg, Lore Marianne. The Coherence of the Pisan Cantos and Their Significance in the Context of Ezra Pound's "Poem of Some Length." Diss. Freiburg, 1958.

1133 _____. Rosen aus Feilstaub: Studien zu den Cantos von Ezra Pound. Wiesbaden: Limes, 1966.

1134 MacLeish, Archibald. Letter. The Case Against The Saturday Review of Literature. Cf., #215, pp. 59-62.

1135 _____. Poetry and Opinion: The Pisan Cantos of Ezra Pound: A Dialog on the Role of Poetry. Urbana: U. of Illinois Pr., 1950.

1136 Madge, Charles. "The Ellipse in the Pisan Cantos," An Examination of Ezra Pound: A Collection of Essays. Rev. & Enl. Peter Russell, ed. New York: Gordian Pr., 1973, pp. 119-133.

1137 Martz, Louis L. "Recent Poetry," YR, 38, #1 (Autumn, 1948), 144-151.

1138 Monk, Donald. "Intelligibility in The Pisan Cantos," JAmS, 9 (1975), 213-227.

1139 Montale, Eugenio. "Ezra Pound," Corriere della sera (Milan),

(November 19, 1953), p. 3; repr., in Nuova corrente, Nos. 5-6 (Genn.-giugno, 1956), pp. 21-27.

1140 _____. "Lo zio Ez," Studi e Opinioni su Ezra Pound. Alfredo Rizzardi, ed., NC, Nos. 5-6 (January-June, 1956), 21-27.

1141 _____. "Uncle Ez," NER, 4, #2 (Spring, 1982), 358-362.

1142 Moody, A. D. "The Pisan Cantos: Making Cosmos in the Wreckage of Europe," Paideuma, 11, #1 (Spring-Summer, 1982), 135-146.

1143 Moramarco, Fred. "Thirty Years with The Pisan Cantos: A Reading," MPS, 9 (Spring, 1978), 1-17.

1144 Mowrer, Deane. "Some Current Poetry," NMQ, 18 (Winter, 1948), 463-464.

1145 Nassar, Eugene Paul. "The Pisan Cantos," Cf., #834, pp. 71-98.

1146 Neame, Alan. "The Pisan Cantos: An Approach," The European, #4 (June, 1953), 37-46. (Annotations to Canto LXXIV, 11, 1-43.)

1147 _____. "The Pisan Cantos. II. Considerations in Criticism," European, #10 (December, 1953), 13-26.

1148 _____. "The Pisan Cantos: III," European (September, 1954), 17-29.

1149 _____. "The Pisan Cantos, IV: Construction Part I," European (January, 1955), 23-34.

1150 _____. "The Pisan Cantos, VI: Speech and Penalty," European, 10 (February, 1958), 351-360.

1151 Niikura, Shunichi. "Pound wo Motomete: Pisa Shihen no Sekai," EigoS, 121 (1975), 407-408. ["In Search of Pound: World of Cantos.]

1152 Niikura, Toshikazu. "The Pisan Cantos and Noh Drama," American Literature in the 1940's. Annual Report, 1975. Tokyo: Tokyo and Chapter, Amer. Lit. Soc. of Japan, 1976, pp. 132-140.

1153 Norman, Charles. The Case of Ezra Pound, Cf., #219.

1154 Nyren, Dorothy, ed. "Ezra Pound," A Library of Literary Criticism: Modern American Literature. New York: Ungar Pub. Co., 1960, pp. 380-385.

1155 O'Connor, William Van, and Edward Stone. A Casebook on Ezra Pound. Cf., #29.

1156 Olson, Paul A. Cf., #221.

1157 Patmore, Brigit. "Ezra Pound in England," Cf., #98.

1158 Pecorino, Jessica Prinz. "Resurgent Icons: Pound's First Pisan Canto and the Visual Arts," JML, 9, #2 (May, 1982), 159-174.

1159 Petrocchi, Giorgio. "I Canti Pisani," Il Giornale d'Italia, Rome: (December 2, 1953).

1160 Pritchard, William H. "Pisan Cantos," Lives of the Modern Poets. New York: Oxford U. Pr., 1980, pp. 144, passim.

1161 Raine, Kathleen. "There Is No Trifling," NR, 126 (March 24, 1952), 17, 22.

1162 Ratte, Eva. "Ezra Pound: I Canti Pisani," Umana (Trieste: January, 1954).

1163 Read, Forrest. "The Pattern of the Pisan Cantos," SR, 65 (Summer, 1957), 400-419. Cf., E. San Juan, Jr., ed., #535, pp. 49-52.

1164 Rebora, Piero. "Ezra Pound: Canti Pisani," Italia Che Scrive. Rome (January, 1954).

1165 Reck, Michael. "The Pisan Cantos," Cf., Michael Reck, #109, pp. 11-12, 64-65.

1166 Rizzardi, Alfredo. "La maschera e la poesia di Ezra Pound," Canti pisani di Ezra Pound. Bologna: Guanda, 1953, pp. vii-xlv. Cf., #518, Jung, Angela, and Guido Palandri, eds., pp. 55-76.

1167 _____. "The Mask of Experience: A Chapter upon Ezra Pound's Pisan Cantos," SUS, 35 (1960), 135-159.

1168 Rosenthal, Macha Louis. "The Pisan Cantos," A Primer of Ezra Pound. Cf., #905, p. 49.

1169 Roskolenko, Harry. "The Cant in Pound's Cantos," Cf., #914, pp. 5-7.

1170 Rossi, Alberto. "I Canti Pisani," La Stampa (Turin: March 31, 1954).

1171 Sanesi, Roberto. "I Canti Pisani," Aut-Aut, 18 (November, 1953).

1172 Sanguineti, Edoardo. "I 'Canti Pisani,'" Aut-Aut, #22 (luglio, 1954), 329-334.

1173 Scalero, Liliano. "I 'Canti Pisani' di Ezra Pound," La Giustizia, (Juno 1, 1954), 3.

1174 Schlauch, Margaret. "The Anti-Humanism of Ezra Pound," Science and Society, 13 (Summer, 1949), 258-269; repr., in Critics on Ezra Pound. E. San Juan, ed., Cf., #535, pp. 44-46.

1175 Schuldiner, Michael. "Pound's Progress: The Pisan Cantos," Paideuma, 4, #1 (Spring, 1975), 71-81.

1176 Shapiro, Karl. "Letter to the Editor," Cf., #227, p. 16.

1177 Sieburth, Richard. "He Do the Enemy in Different Voices," Poetry, 134 (August, 1979), 292-302.

1178 Sillen, Samuel. "A Prize for Ezra Pound," Cf., #231.

1179 Smith, Harrison. "Lock, Stock, and Barrel," Cf., #233.

1180 Spagnoletti, Giacinto. "Canti Pisani di Ezra Pound," Epoca, Milan (May 2, 1954).

1181 Squires, Radcliffe. "Ambassador of Culture," Cf., #235.

1182 Stevens, Peter. "Climbing the Poundian Alps," CRevAS, 12, #3 (Winter, 1981), 355-360.

1183 Stock, Noel. "The Pisan Cantos, 1948," Cf., #954, pp. 72-90.

1184 Surette, Philip Leon. "Also Sprach Ezra: Pound Exposed," Mosaic, 15 #2 (June, 1982), 57-62.

1185 _____. "'Having His Own Mind to Stand by Him.'" Cf., #961.

1186 Sutton, Walter. "Ezra Pound: The Pisan Cantos," American Free Verse. Cf., #967, pp. 77-86.

1187 _____. "The Pisan Cantos: The Form of Survival," Sense and Sensibility in Twentieth Century Writing: A Gathering in Memory of William Van O'Connor. Brom Weber, ed. Carbondale and Edwardsville: So. Ill. U. Pr., 1970, pp. 118-129.

1188 Tay, William. "Confucianism as Leitmotif: The Four Books in the Pisan Cantos," TkR, 9 (1978), 235-267.

1189 Viereck, Peter. "My Kind of Poetry," Cf., #249.

1190 _____. "Parnassus Divided," AtlM, 184 (October, 1949), 69-70.

1191 Watts, Harold H. "Points on the Circle," SR, 57, #2 (Spring, 1949), 303-306.

1192 Weissman, David L. ["The Pisan Cantos"], Cf., #252.

1193 Whittemore, Reed. "Pound on Pound," Poetry, 73 (November, 1948), 108-110.

1194 Williams, David Park. "The Background of The Pisan Cantos," Poetry, 73, #4 (January, 1949), 216-221.

1195 Williams, William Carlos. "The Fistual of the Law," Imagi, 4, #4 (Spring, 1949), 10-11.

1196 Woods, John. "Brief: In William Duffy's Hammock," NWR, 15, #1 (Summer, 1975), 15-20.

1197 Woodward, Anthony. Ezra Pound and The Pisan Cantos. Boston: Routledge & Kegan Paul, 1980.

1198 Woodward, Kathleen M. "Ezra Pound and the Pisan Cantos: The Teachings of Confucius, the Teachings of Ezra Pound," At Last, the Real Distinguished Thing: The Late Poems of Eliot, Pound, Stevens, and Williams. Ohio State U. Pr., 1980, pp. 69-98.

The Rock-Drill Cantos

1199 Alvarez, Alfred. "Rock-Drill Cantos," Observer (March 3, 1957), 3.

1200 Bacigalupo, Massimo. "Rock-Drill--'In the Sibyl's Cave'" The Formed Trace: The Later Poetry of Ezra Pound. New York: Columbia U. Pr., 1980, pp. 219ff.

1201 Baumann, Walter. "Secretary of Nature, J. Heydon," New Approaches to Ezra Pound: A Co-ordinated Investigation of Pound's Poetry and Ideas. Eva Hesse, ed. Berkeley; Los Angeles: U. of Calif., 1969, pp. 303-319.

1202 Cambon, Glauco. "Ezra Pound: Section: Rock-Drill 85-95 de los cantares," Il Verri (Autunno 1956), 98-102.

1203 Ciardi, John. "For Ezra Pound: Section: Rock-Drill," The

Yale Literary Magazine, 127, #5 (December, 1958), 17; The Poetry Circus. New York: Hawthorn Bks., 1967, p. 139.

1204 Cookson, William. "Some Notes on Rock-Drill and Thrones," Agenda (London), 4, (October-November, 1965), 30-37.

1205 Davie, Donald. "Bed-Rock," NS&N, 53 (March 9, 1957), 316-317.

1206 _____. "The Rock-Drill Cantos," Modern Poetry: Essays in Criticism. John Hollander, ed. London; New York: Oxford U. Pr., 1968, pp. 447-472.

1207 _____. "Res and Verba in Rock-Drill and After," Paideuma, 11, #3 (Winter, 1982), 382-394.

1208 Fitts, Dudley. "Prelude to Conclusion," SatRL, 39 (May 12, 1956), 18-19.

1209 Gordon, David. "Ezra Among the Old Bones," Paideuma, 4, #2-3 (Fall-Winter, 1975), 355-359.

1210 Grieve, Thomas. "Annotations to the Chinese in Section: Rock-Drill," Paideuma, 4, #2-3 (Fall-Winter, 1975), 362-508.

1211 Kenner, Hugh. "Homage to Musonius," Poetry, 90, #4 (July, 1957), 237-243. Reply: J. R. Hendrickson, Poetry, 91 (December, 1957), 209-211.

1212 _____. "Rock-Drill by Ezra Pound," HudR, 9 (1957), 457.

1213 _____. "Rock-Drill: A Review of Cantos 88-89," Pound Newsletter, 8 (October, 1955), 15-17.

1214 _____. "Rock Drill, Cantos 88-89," Studi e Opinioni su Ezra Pound. Alfredo Rizzardi, ed. Nuova Corrente, Nos. 5-6 (January-June, 1957), 197-204.

1215 _____. "Rock-Drill," The Pound Era. Berkeley and Los Angeles, Calif.: U. of Calif. Pr., 1971, pp. 528-532, passim.

1216 _____. "Under the larches of Paradise," Gnomon: Essays on Contemporary Literature. New York: McDowell-Obolensky, 1958, pp. 280-296.

1217 Kimpel, Ben, and T. C. Duncan Eaves. "American History in Rock-Drill and Thrones," Cf., #745, pp. 417-439.

1218 Korg, Jacob. "Jacob Epstein's Rock-Drill and the Cantos," Paideuma, 4, #2&3 (Fall-Winter, 1975), 310-313.

1219 _____. "The Music of Lost Dynasties: Browning, Pound and History," ELH, 39 (1972), 420-440.

1220 Lewis, Wyndham. "The Rock-Drill," Ezra Pound: Perspectives. Noel Stock, ed. Cf., #125, pp. 198-203.

1221 Lucas, John. "Our Foreign Agents: Rock Drill Dinner-Date," Carleton Miscellany, I, #3 (Summer, 1960), 91-94.

1222 Neault, D. James. "Apollonius of Tyana: The Odyssean Hero of Rock-Drill as a Doer of Holiness," Paideuma, 4, #1 (Spring, 1975), 3-36.

1223 _____. "Richard of St. Victor and Rock-Drill," Paideuma, 3, #2 (Fall, 1974), 219-227.

1224 _____. "Spring Ice and Tiger's Tail: A Study of Major Sources in Ezra Pound's Rock-Drill," DAI, 35 (Ohio: 1974), 7916A.

1225 Rosen, Aaron. "The Enormous Dream--Its Rhetoric," Pound Newsletter, 10 (April, 1956), 6-9.

1226 Rosenthal, M. L. "Poetic Means and Meanings," Nation, 182, #18 (May 5, 1956), 384-386.

1227 Stock, Noel. "Rock-Drill," Meanjin, 15 (March, 1956), 112-114.

1228 _____. "Rock-Drill, 1955," Reading the Cantos: A Study of Meaning in Ezra Pound. London: Routledge & Kegan Paul, 1967, pp. 91-103.

1229 Tay, William. "History as Poetry: The Chinese Past in Ezra Pound's Rock-Drill Cantos," TkR, 10 (1979), 97-125.

Seven Lakes Canto

1230 Kenner, Hugh. "More on the 'Seven Lakes Canto,'" Paideuma, 2 (Spring, 1973), 43-46.

1231 Palandri, Angela J. "The 'Seven Lakes Canto' Revisited," Paideuma, 3, #1 (Spring, 1974), 51-54.

CATHAY

1232 Ford, Ford Madox. "On Ezra Pound's Cathay," Agenda, 20, #3-4 (Autumn-Winter, 1982-83), 65-66.

1233 Lee, Pen-Ti, and Donald Murray. "The Quality of Cathay: Ezra Pound's Early Translations of Chinese Poems," LE&W, 10 (September, 1961), 264-277.

1234 Orage, A[lfred] R[ichard]. "Mr. Pound's 'Cathay,'" The Art of Reading. New York: Farrar & Rinehart, 1930, pp. 143-146.

1235 Sanehide, Kodama. "Cathay and Fenollosa's Notebooks," Paideuma, 11, #2 (Fall, 1982), 207-240.

1236 Toki, Tsuneji. "Technique of Ezra Pound--on Cathay," Metropolitan, 7 (March, 1962), 17-22.

1237 Wells, Tanya. "Ezra Pound's Cathay and the American Idea of China," DAI, 44, #11 (Arizona State: 1983), 3381A.

1238 Yip, Wai-Lim. "Ezra Pound's 'Cathay,'" DA, 29 (Princeton: 1967), 280A.

1239 _____. Ezra Pound's Cathay. Princeton: University of Princeton Pr., 1969.

CLASSIC ANTHOLOGY

1240 Blissett, William. Classic Anthology. Review: Canadian Forum, 34 (October, 1954), 166-167.

1241 "Classic Anthology," Review: NY, 30, #38 (November 6, 1954), 195-196.

1242 Cookson, William. "A Note on The Classic Anthology," Agenda, 17 #3-4, (Autumn-Winter-Spring, 1979-80), 218-219.

1243 Fitts, Dudley. "From Some Three Millennia," NYT (September 12, 1954), 42.

1244 Ford, Ford Madox. "'From China to Peru,'" Outlook, 35 (June 19, 1915), 800-801.

1245 Fussell, Paul. "The Book of Odes Made New," Pound Newsletter, 5 (January, 1955), 10-13.

1246 Garcia Terres, Jaime. Classic Anthology. Universidad de Mexico, 9, #5-6 (January-February, 1955), 31-32.

1247 Jung, Angela. "Classic Anthology," Review: Comparative Literature, 7, #1 (Winter, 1955), 91-93.

1248 _____. "Pound's Translation of 'Book of Poetry' Is a Recreation," Asian Student, 3, #2 (San Francisco: September 21, 1954), 4.

1249 Liu, Wu-Chi. Classic Anthology. LE&W, 2 (Summer, 1955), 36-37.

1250 Muir, Edwin. "Odes from the East," Observer (March 6, 1955).

1251 Smith, G. D. Gilling. [Under initials H. B.] Review: Classic Anthology, European (June, 1955).

EXULTATIONS

1252 Bennett, John. "Ezra Pound's Exultations: A Study in Structure," AmerS (Taiwan), 7, #3 (September, 1977), 27-39.

1253 Brenner, Milton. "A Panel of Poets," Bookman, 35 (April, 1912), 156-161.

1254 "Current Poetry," LitD, 50, #9 (February 26, 1910), 402-404.

1255 Flint, F. S. "Publications Received," EngRev, 4 (December, 1909), 160-161.

1256 _____. "Verse," New Age, 6 (January 6, 1910), 233-234.

GAUDIER-BRZESKA

1257 Ede, H. S. A Life of Gaudier-Brzeska. London: William Heinemann, 1930.

1258 "Gaudier-Brzeska." Review: American Review of Reviews, 54 (August, 1916), 238.

1259 "Gaudier-Brzeska," Review: Dial, 61 (August 15, 1916), 112

1260 "Gaudier-Brzeska," Review: Nation, 103 (August 31, 1916), 207.

1261 "Gaudier-Brzeska," Review: NYTBR (August 13, 1916), 314.

1262 "Gaudier-Brzeska," Review: TLS (August 27, 1916), 199.

1263 "Gaudier-Brzeska," Review: Pittsburg, 21 (November, 1916), 485.

1264 Materer, Timothy. "Ezra Pound and Gaudier-Brzeska: Sophie's Diary," JML, 6 (April, 1977), 315-321.

1265 _____. "Gaudier's 'Three Ninas,'" Cf., #795, pp. 323-324.

1266 Matthias, John E. "Statement," Sou'wester (October 30, 1970), 135-136.

1267 Perloff, Marjorie. "The Portrait of the Artist as Collage-Text: Pound's Gaudier-Brzeska and the 'Italic' Texts of John Cage," APR, 11, #3 (May-June, 1982), 19-29.

GUIDE TO CULTURE (American, 1938)
GUIDE TO CULTURE (England, 1938)

1268 Bogan, Louise. "Make It New," Nation, 148 (April 29, 1939), 504-505.

1269 _____. "Make It New," Cf., #465, pp. 138-141.

1270 "Briefly Noted: Fiction," NY, 28, #33 (October 4, 1952), 137.

1271 Deutsch, Babette. "A Baedeker in Code," NY Herald Tribune (Book Rev.), (February 26, 1939), 18.

1272 Fitts, Dudley. "Right Thinking," SatRL, 20 (Mary 13, 1939), 16.

1273 Friedrich, Otto. "Ezra Pound: The Guide to Kulchur," New World Writing, 17 (1960), 161-202.

1274 Healy, J. V. "The Pound Problem," Poetry, 57, #3 (December, 1940), 200-214.

1275 Jack, Peter Monroe. "Ezra Pound's Culture," NYT (February 26, 1939), 14.

1276 Kenner, Hugh. "Pound and the Provision of Measures," Poetry, 83, #1 (October, 1953), 29-35.

1277 Queneau, Raymond. "Guide to Kulchur," Nouvelle Revue Francaise (October, 1939).

1278 Williams, William Carlos. "Penny Wise, Pound Foolish," NR, 99 (June 28, 1939), 229-230.

GUIDO CAVALCANTI

1279 Anderson, David. "Cavalcanti: Canzone to Fortune," Paideuma, 12, #1 (Spring, 1983), 41-46.

1280 _____. "The Techniques of Critical Translation: Ezra Pound's Guide Cavalcanti, 1912," Paideuma, 8 (Fall, 1979), 215-226.

1281 Gilson, Etienne. "Books of the Quarter," Criterion, 12 (October, 1932), 106-112.

1282 Henderson, Archie. "Ezra Pound: Composer," Paideuma, 12, #2-3 (Fall-Winter, 1983), 499-509.

1283 Mangan, Sherry. "Poetry for Scholars, Scholarship for Poets," Poetry, 41 (March, 1933), 336-339.

1284 Mayor, A. Hyatt. "Cavalcanti and Pound," H&H, 5 (April-June, 1932), 468-471.

1285 Oderman, Kevin. "'Cavalcanti': That the Body Is Not Evil," Paideuma, 11, #2 (Fall, 1982), 257-279.

HOMAGE TO SEXTUS PROPERTIUS

1286 Blackmur, R. P. "Masks of Ezra Pound," H&H, 7 (January-March, 1934), 184-191; repr., in The Double Agent. Gloucester, Mass., 1962; also in Language as Gesture. New York: Harcourt, Brace, 1952.

1287 Bush, Ronald. "Gathering the Limbs of Orpheus: The Subject of Pound's Homage to Sextus Propertius," Ezra Pound and William Carlos Williams: The University of Pennsylvania

Conference Papers. Daniel Hoffman, ed. Philadelphia: U. of Pennsylvania Pr., 1983, pp. 61-78.

1288 Chauvet, Paul. Review: Homage to Sextus Propertius and Make It New," RAA (June, 1934), 445-446.

1289 Drew-Bear, Thomas. "Ezra Pound's 'Homage to Sextus Propertius,'" AL, 37, #2 (May, 1965), 204-210.

1290 Espey, John. "Towards Propertius," Paideuma, 1, #1 (Spring-Summer, 1972), 63-74.

1291 _____. "Vers Propertius," Les Cahiers de l'Herne. D. de Roux, ed. Paris: 1965, Vol. 2, pp. 502-507.

1292 Fletcher, John Gould. "Some Contemporary Poets," Chapbook: A Monthly Miscellany. No. 11 (May, 1920), 23-25.

1293 Forbes, Clarence A. "Ezra Pound and Sextus Propertius," CJ, 42, #3 (December, 1946), 177-179.

1294 Friar, Kimon. "On Translation," CLS, 8, #3 (September, 1971), 197-213.

1295 Hale, William G. "Pegasus Impounded," Poetry, 14, #1 (April, 1919), 52-55.

1296 Heppenstall, Rayner. "Homage to Sextus Propertius," Adelphi, 9 (January, 1935), 253-254.

1297 Hesse, Eva. "Pound oder der Verlängerie Konflikt [Pound: or, the Protracted Battle]," Diagonale, 5 (1967), 26-29.

1298 Highet, Gilbert. "Beer-bottle on the Pediment," Cf., #700.

1299 Holder, Alan. "Anne Bradstreet Resurrected," CP, 2, #1 (Spring, 1969), 11-18.

1300 Iwasaki, Ryozo. "Ezura Paundo no 'Puroperuchiusu' Santan," [Pound's Homage to Propertius], Shiho (Poetical Methods), 2, #2 (February 1, 1935), 74-76.

1301 Joseph, Terry Brint. "Ezra Pound's Approaches to the Long Poem in 'Near Propertius' and 'Hugh Selwyn Mauberly,'" DAI, 42, #9 (U. of Calif., Irvine: 1981), 4000A.

1302 Kenner, Hugh. The Poetry of Ezra Pound, Cf., #738, pp. 146-163.

1303 _____. "Scatter," StAR, 1, #1 (Fall-Winter, 1970), 51-55.

1304 Laughlin, James. "Ezra Pound's Propertius," SR, 46 (October-December, 1938), 480-491. Cf., #1545, pp. 320-329.

1305 Levi, Peter. "Pound and the Classics," Cf., #777, pp. 42-45.

1306 Lewis, Wyndham. "Mr. Ezra Pound," Observer (October 18, 1920), 5. See also #778, pp. 169ff.

1307 MacDiarmid, Hugh. "The Esemplastic Power," Cf., #782, pp. 27-30.

1308 _____. "The Master Voyager of Our Age," Agenda, 10 (1972-73), 139-145.

1309 _____. "The Return of the Long Poem," Cf., #125, pp. 90-108.

1310 _____. "Tribute to Ezra Pound," CamR, 94 (June 8, 1973), 168-170.

1311 Messing, Gordon M. "Pound's Propertius: The Homage and the Damage," Poetry and Poetics from Ancient Greece to the Renaissance: Studies in Honor of James Hutton. G. M. Krikwood, ed. Cornell Studies in Classical Philology, 38. Ithaca: Cornell U. Pr., 1975, pp. 105-133.

1312 Miller, Vincent E. "The Serious Wit of Pound's Homage to Sextus Propertius," ConL, 16 (Autumn, 1975), 452-462.

1313 Nichols, Robert. "Poetry and Mr. Pound," Observer (January 11, 1920), 6.

1314 Orage, A[lfred], R[ichard]. "Mr. Ezra Pound as Metricist," The New Age. New Age Press, 1918; repr., in Readers and Writers (1917-1921). London: Allen & Unwin, 1922, pp. 57-60.

1315 _____. "Readers and Writers," New Age, 16, #3 (November 19, 1914), 69.

1316 Porteus, Hugh Gordon. "Propertius Transmuted," New English Weekly, 6 (March 7, 1935), 432-433.

1317 Richardson, Lawrence. "Ezra Pound's Homage to Propertius," YPR, 6 (1947), 21-29.

1318 Rosenthal, M. L. The Modern Poets: A Critical Introduction. New York: Oxford U. Pr., 1960, pp. 55-56.

1319 Ruthven, K. K. "Propertius, Wordsworth, Yeats, Pound and Hale," N&Q, 15, #2 (February, 1968), 47-48.

1320 Sinclair, May. "The Reputation of Ezra Pound," NAR, 211 (May, 1920), 658-668.

1321 Speirs, John. "Mr. Pound's Propertius," Scrutiny, 3 (September, 1934), 409-418.

1322 Spender, Stephen. "Homage to Sextus Propertius," Review. Spectator, 153 (December 14, 1934), 938.

1323 Sullivan, John Patrick. Ezra Pound and Sextus Propertius: A Study in Creative Translation. London: Faber & Faber; Austin, Texas: U. of Texas Pr., 1964.

1324 _____. "Ezra Pound's Classical Translations," TQ, 10, #4 (Winter, 1967), 57-62.

1325 _____. "The Poet as Translator: Ezra Pound and Sextus Propertius," KR, 23 (Summer, 1961), 462-481.

1326 _____. "Pound and Propertius: Some Techniques of Translation," Hereditas: Seven Essays on the Modern Experience of the Classical. Will, Frederic, ed. Austin, Texas: U. of Texas Pr., 1964, pp. 95-129.

1327 _____. "Pound's Homage to Propertius: The Structure of a Mask," EIC, 10 (July, 1960), 239-249; Agenda (London), 4, #2 (October-November, 1965), 57-61.

1328 Turner, Mark. "Propertius through the Looking Glass: A Fragmentary Glance at the Construction of Pound's Homage," Paideuma, 5, #2 (Fall, 1976), 241-265.

HOW TO READ

1329 Brulé, A. "Active Anthology," RA&A (October, 1934), 76-77.

1330 _____. "Revue of How to Read," RA&A (August, 1932), 559-560.

1331 Ford, Ford Madox. "Pound and 'How to Read,'" New Review, 11 (April, 1932), 39-45.

1332 Leavis, Frank Raymond. How to Teach Reading: A Primer for Ezra Pound. Cambridge, England: Heffer, (Minority Press Pamphlet), 1932.

1333 _____. How to Teach Reading: Education and the University. London: Chatto & Windus, 1943.

1334 _____. New Bearings on English Poetry, Cf., #774, pp. 133-157.

1335 McGreevy, Thomas. "Pound and How to Read," New Review, 2 (April, 1932), 45-48.

1336 Stafford, Clayton. "Reading and Writing," H&H, 7 (July-September, 1934), 731-736.

1337 Tate, Allen. "How Is Writing Taught," Poetry, 44 (April, 1934), 53-55.

1338 _____. "Laundry Bills," Poetry, 41 (November, 1932), 107-112.

HUGH SELWYN MAUBERLEY

1339 Bacigalupo, Massimo. "Lineaments of Space: From Hugh Selwyn Mauberley to the Early Cantos," Cf., #437, pp. 5-51.

1340 Bell, Ian F. A. "In the Real Tradition: Edgar Lee Masters and Hugh Selwyn Mauberley," Criticism, 23, #2 (Spring, 1981), 141-154.

1341 _____. "Instruments for Design: Mauberley's Sieve," ELN, 17 (June, 1980), 294-297.

1342 _____. "Mauberley's Barrier of Style," Ezra Pound: The London Years: 1908-1920. Philip Grover, ed., Cf., #52, pp. 89-115.

1343 _____. "The Phantasmagoria of Hugh Selwyn Mauberley," Paideuma, 5, #3 (Winter, 1976), 361-385.

1344 Berryman, Jo Brantley. "The Art of the Image: Allusions in Pound's 'Medallion,'" Paideuma, 6 (Winter, 1977), 295-308.

1345 _____. Circe's Craft: Ezra Pound's 'Hugh Selwyn Mauberley.' UMI Research Press, Ann Arbor, Michigan, 1983.

1346 _____. "Ezra Pound Versus Hugh Selwyn Mauberley: A Distinction," DAI, 34, #10 (So. Calif.: 1973), 6624A.

1347 _____. "Mauberley, Logopoeia, and the Language of Modernism,: SAQ, 83, #1 (Winter, 1984), 18-43.

1348 _____. "'Medallion': Pound's Poem," Paideuma, 2, #3 (Winter, 1973), 391-398.

1349 _____ and Donald Davie. "'Medallion': Some Questions," Paideuma, 8 (1979), 151-157.

1350 Bornstein, George. "The Forest of His Mind: Mauberley and The Cantos," Cf., #467, pp. 60-72.

1351 Brumm, Anne-Marie. "Mouths Biting Empty Air: Ezra Pound's 'Hugh Selwyn Mauberley' and Henry James's 'Lambert Strether,'" RLC, 54 (January-March, 1980), 47-70.

1352 Bueltmann, Faith. "Mauberley's 'Medallion,'" N&Q, 7, #4 (n.s.), (April, 1960), 148.

1353 Campos, Augusto de. "Nota Sobre 'Hugh Selwyn Mauberley,'" ESPSL, (October 30, 1965), 3.

1354 Connolly, Thomas E. "Further Notes on Mauberley," Accent, 16 (Winter, 1956), 59-67.

1355 D'Agostino, Nemi. "La Sequenza di Hugh Selwyn Mauberley," La Fiera Letteraria, 8, #43 (October 25, 1953), 3-4.

1356 Davie, Donald. Ezra Pound. Frank Kermode, ed. New York: Viking Pr., 1975.

1357 _____. "Ezra Pound's Hugh Selwyn Mauberley," The Modern Age. Boris Ford, ed. Pelican Guide to English Literature. New York: Penguin Books, 1961, VII, pp. 315-329.

1358 DeCampos, Augusto. "Nota sobre 'Hugh Selwyn Mauberley,'" ESPSL, (October, 1965), 3.

1359 Demirovic, Hamdija. "Tekst i kaos: Slika umjetnika u svijetu rasapa vrijednosti u poemi 'Hugh Selwyn Mauberley' Ezre Pounda," Izraz, 22 (1978), 1557-1602.

1360 Deutsch, Babette. This Modern Poetry. New York: W. W. Norton, Inc., 1935, pp. 115-118, passim.

1361 Donoghue, Denis. "James's The Awkward Age and Pound's Mauberley," N&Q, 17 (February, 1970), 49-50.

1362 Duffey, Bernard. "Ezra Pound's Mauberley," AL, 27 (January, 1956), 601-602.

1363 Duncan, Ronald. "A Supervision with Dr. Leavis on Mauberley," All Men Are Islands: An Autobiography. London: Rupert Hart-Davis, 1964, pp. 84-87.

1364 Egudu, R. N. "'The Idyll Sham: Ezra Pound and Nigerian Wole Soyinka on War,'" Paideuma, 5, #1 (Spring, 1976), 31-41.

1365 Emery, Clark M. "Pound as Mauberley," HINL, 4 (January, 1958), 6-8.

1366 Emslie, Macdonald. "Pound's 'Hugh Selwyn Mauberley,' I, iii, 13-16," Expl, 14, #4 (January, 1956), Item 26.

1367 Espey, John. Ezra Pound's Mauberley: A Study in Composition. London: Faber & Faber, 1955; Berkeley and Los Angeles: U. of Calif. Pr., 1955.

1368 Faas, Egbert. "Formen der Bewusstseinsdarstellung in der dramatischen Lyrik Pounds und Eliots," GRM, 18, #2, n.s. (April, 1968), 172-191.

1369 Feder, Lillian. Ancient Myth in Modern Poetry. Princeton, N.J.: Princeton U. Pr., 1971, pp. 99-105.

1370 Findley, Timothy. Famous Last Words. New York: Delacorte Pub. Co., 1982.

1371 Fraser, G. S. "Pound: Masks, Myth and Man," Cf., #114, pp. 172-185.

1372 French, A. L. "'Olympian Apathein': Pound's Hugh Selwyn Mauberley and Modern Poetry," EIC, 15, #4 (October, 1965), 428-445.

1373 _____. "Mauberley: A Rejoinder," EIC, 16 (July, 1966), 356-359. Cf., #1407.

1374 Friar, Kimon, and John Malcolm Brinnin. "Hugh Selwyn Mauberley," Cf., #626, pp. 525-531.

1375 Giovannini, G. "'Pound's Hugh Selwyn Mauberley,' I, iii, 22," Expl, 16 (March, 1958), Item 35.

1376 Gregory, Horace. "This Side of Poetry," Poetry, 44 (August, 1934), 291-294.

1377 Grover, Philip, ed. "Mauberley's Barrier of Style," Ezra Pound: The London Years, 1908-1920. Philip Grover, ed. Cf., #52, pp. 89-115, 155-164.

1378 Hoffman, Frederick J. "The Text: Ezra Pound's Hugh Selwyn Mauberley," The Twenties: American Writing in the Postwar Decade. New York: Viking, 1955, pp. 36-46.

1379 Holbrook, David. "The Lack of a Creative Theme: Ezra Pound's Stone Mouths Biting Empty Air and Eliot's Hollow Men," Lost Bearings in English Poetry. London: Vision Pr., 1977, pp. 64-91; New York: Barnes & Noble, 1977, pp. 58-100.

1380 Holder, Alan. "The Lesson of the Master: Ezra Pound and Henry James," Cf., #706, pp. 71-79.

1381 Homberger, Eric. "Towards 'Mauberley,'" AntigR, 13 (Spring, 1973), 35-44.

1382 Hombitzer, Eleonore. "Ezra Pound: 'Medallion,'" NS, 16, #10 (October, 1967), 499-503.

1383 Houston, John Porter. "Hugh Selwyn Mauberley," French Symbolism and the Modernist Movement, Cf., #711, pp. 46-48.

1384 Jenner, E. A. B. "'Medallion': Some Questions," Paideuma, 8 (1979), 153-157.

1385 Joseph, Terri Brint. "The Decentered Center of Ezra Pound's Hugh Selwyn Mauberley," REALB, 1 (1982), 121-151.

1386 _____. "Ezra Pound's Approaches to the Long Poem in 'Near Perigord,' Homage to Sextus Propertius, and Hugh Selwyn Mauberley," Cf., #1301, p. 4000A.

1387 Kenner, Hugh. "Broken Mirrors and the Mirror of Memory," Cf., #731, p. 26, and #771.

1388 _____. "Critic of the Month: III--Ghosts and Benedictions," Poetry, 113, #2 (November, 1968), 109-125.

1389 _____. "Mauberley," The Poetry of Ezra Pound, Cf., #738, pp. 164-182.

1390 _____. "Mauberley," Ezra Pound: A Collection of Critical Essays. Walter Sutton, ed. Englewood Cliffs, NJ, Prentice-Hall, Inc., 1951, pp. 41-56.

1391 Knox, George. "Glaucus in Hugh Selwyn Mauberley," ES, 45, #3 (June, 1964), 236-237.

1392 _____. "Pound's Hugh Selwyn Mauberley': A Vortex Name," Spirit, 36, #2 (1969), 23-28.

1393 Leavis, F. R. "Ezra Pound--Mauberley," New Bearings in English Poetry. Cf., #774, pp. 133-157.

1394 Libby, Gary R. "Image or Image: An Unnoticed Allusion in 'Hugh Selwyn Mauberley,'" Paideuma, 1, #2 (Winter, 1972), 205-206.

1395 Link, Franz H. "A Note on Samothrace in Pound's Hugh Selwyn Mauberley," Paideuma, 6 (Winter, 1977), 329.

1396 Long, Richard A. "Pound's Hugh Selwyn Mauberley," Expl, 10 (June, 1952), Item 56; repr., in The Explicator Cyclopedia, Vol. I, p. 231.

1397 McCuaig, Ronald. "Mauberley Again," The Bulletin, (Sydney), (May 4, 1955), p. 2.

1398 Madge, Charles. "The Ellysse in the Pisan Cantos," An Examination of Ezra Pound. Peter Russell, ed., Cf., #1136, pp. 121-123.

1399 Malkoff, Karl. "Allusion as Irony: Pound's Use of Dante in Hugh Selwyn Mauberley," MinnR, 7, #1 (1967), 81-88.

1400 _____. Escape from the Self: A Study in Contemporary American Poetry and Poetics. New York: Columbia U. Pr., 1977, pp. 31-32, 106-107, passim.

1401 Mazzeno, Laurence W. "A Note on Hugh Selwyn Mauberley," Paideuma, 4, #1 (Spring, 1975), 89-91.

1402 Mills, Lloyd L. "English Origin of 'Still-born' and 'Dumb-born' in Mauberley," AN&Q, 10, #5 (January, 1972), 67-68.

1403 Muir, Edwin. "Hugh Selwyn Mauberley," [Review], New Age, 21 (October, 1922), 288.

1404 Pratt, William C. "Ezra Pound and the Image," Ezra Pound: The London Years: 1908-1920, Cf., #52, pp. 15-30.

1405 Quartermain, Peter. "'Blocked. Make a Song out of That': Pound's 'E.P. Ode pour l'élection de son sépulchre,'" KRev, 1, i (1980), 32-48.

1406 Quinn, Sr. M. Bernetta. "A Poem Too Interesting for Burial," Pound Newsletter, 7 (July, 1955), 1-3. [Review: John J. Espey's Ezra Pound's Mauberley, #1367.]

1407 Reiss, Christopher. "In Defence of Mauberley," EIC, 16 (July, 1966), 351-355; Rejoinder by A. L. French, Cf., #1373, pp. 356-359.

1408 Rosenthal, M. L. "Ezra Pound: The Poet as Hero, ... Mauberley: Alienation of the Citizen-Artist," The Modern Poets: A Critical Introduction. New York: Oxford U. Pr., 1960, pp. 49-74.

1409 _____. "The Mauberley Sequence," A Primer for Ezra Pound, Cf., #905, pp. 29-41.

1410 San Juan, E[pifanio], Jr., ed. "Ezra Pound's Craftsmanship:

An Interpretation of Hugh Selwyn Mauberley," Critics on Ezra Pound, Cf., 535, pp. 106-124.

1411 Sanavio, Piero. "'Hugh Selwyn Mauberley,'" Nuova corrente, Nos. 5-6 (genn.-giugno, 1956), 165-183.

1412 Schmidt, A. V. C. "Crumpets in Coriolan, Muffins in Pickwick," N&Q, 23 (July, 1976), 298-299.

1413 Sergeant, Howard. Review: John J. Espey's Ezra Pound's Mauberley English, 10, #59 (Summer, 1955), 192-193. [John J. Espey: #1367].

1414 Sitwell, Edith. "Ezra Pound," An Examination of Ezra Pound. Peter Russell, ed. Cf., #114, pp. 44-50.

1415 Spanos, William V. "The Modulating Voice of Hugh Selwyn Mauberley," WSCL, 6 (Winter-Spring, 1965), 73-96.

1416 Sparrow, John. "Doubts about Pound and 'Mauberley,'" Sense and Poetry: Essays on the Place of Meaning in Contemporary Poetry. London: Constable, 1934, pp. 122-132.

1417 Sutton, Walter E. "Ezra Pound: Early Poems and Mauberley," American Free Verse: The Modern Revolution in Poetry. New York: New Directions, 1973, pp. 47-64.

1418 _____. "Mauberley, The Waste Land, and the Problem of Unified Form," WSCL, 9, #1 (Winter, 1968), 15-35.

1419 Tillyard, E. M. W. Poetry, Direct, and Oblique. London: Chatto and Windus, 1934, pp. 34-35.

1420 Wallace-Crabbe, Chris. "Auden's New Year Letter and the Fate of Long Poems," Melbourne Critical Rev, 5 (1962), 129-136.

1421 Widmer, Kingsley. "The Waste Land and the American Breakdown," The Twenties: Fiction, Poetry, Drama. Warren French, ed. Cf., #671, pp. 479-480.

1422 Witemeyer, Hugh. "Hugh Selwyn Mauberley as Bhlooming Ulysses," The Poetry of Ezra Pound: Forms and Renewal, 1908-1920. Berkeley and Los Angeles: U. of Calif. Pr., 1969, pp. 161-195.

IMPACT: ESSAYS ON IGNORANCE AND THE DECLINE OF AMERICAN CIVILIZATION

1423 Fitts, Dudley. "Impact," New York Times Book Review (July 3, 1960), Review.

1424 _____. The Caged Panther: Ezra Pound at St. Elizabeth's by Harry M. Meacham. Cf., #361, p. 88.

1425 Heymann, C. David. "Impact," Ezra Pound: The Last Rower, Cf., #57, pp. 268, 348.

1426 Kenner, Hugh. "Apples, Planets, Dollars," National Review, 10 (March 25, 1961), 183-185.

1427 Stock, Noel, Ed., with Introduction. Impact: Essays on Ignorance and the Decline of American Civilization. Chicago: H. Regnery Co., 1960.

1428 _____. "Impact," Poet in Exile: Ezra Pound. Cf., #402, pp. 12, 175.

IN A STATION OF THE METRO

1429 Beck, Warren. "Boundaries of Poetry," CE, 4 (March, 1943), 346-347.

1430 Bell, Ian F. A. "'In a Station of the Metro' and Carpenterian Transformations," N&Q, 29, #4 (August, 1982), 345-346.

1431 Bevilaqua, Ralph. "Pound's 'In a Station of the Metro': A Textual Note," ELN, 8 (June, 1971), 293-296.

1432 Brooks, Cleanth, and Robert Penn Warren. Understanding Poetry. New York: 1938, pp. 175-176; Revised Ed., New York: Holt, 1951, pp. 78-80.

1433 Bryer, Jackson R., ed. Fifteen Modern American Authors: A Survey of Research and Criticism. Durham, N.C.: Duke U. Pr., 1969, pp. 335ff.

1434 _____. Sixteen Modern American Authors: A Survey of Research and Criticism. Durham, N.C.: Duke U. Pr., 1974, pp. 457ff.

1435 Espey, John J. "Pound's 'In a Station of the Metro,'" Expl, 11 (June, 1953), #59.

1436 Friend, Joseph H. "Teaching the 'Grammar of Poetry,'" CE, 27 (February, 1966), 362-363.

1437 Haefner, Gerhard. "Zur Wandlung des Imagismus Ezra Pounds," Poetica, 4, #3 (1971), 325-332.

1438 Hanzo, Thomas A. "Pound's 'In a Station of the Metro,'" Expl, 11 (February, 1953), No. 26.

1439 Kann, Hans-Joachim. "Translation Problems in Pound's 'In a Station of the Metro,'" LWU, 6 (1973), 234-240.

1440 Lasser, Michael L., and Yoshiyuki Iwamoto. "Pound's 'In a Station of the Metro,'" Expl, 19 (February, 1961), No. 30.

1441 Link, Franz H. "A Note on the Apparition of These Faces ... in 'In a Station of the Metro,'" Paideuma, 10, #2 (Fall, 1981), 327.

1442 Nicolaisen, Peter. "Ezra Pounds 'In a Station of the Metro,'" LWU, 1, #3 (1968), 198-204.

1443 Rosenthal, Machia Louis, and A. J. M. Smith. Exploring Poetry. New York: Macmillan, 1955, pp. 157-158.

1444 Smith, Richard Eugene. "Ezra Pound and the Haiku," CE, 26, #7 (April, 1965), 522-527.

1445 Wilson, Donald D. "Penny-Wise Pound," Paideuma, 1, #2 (Winter, 1972), 203-204.

1446 Wimsat, W. K. ["In a Station of the Metro"], Day of the Leopards: Essays in Defense of Poems. New Haven and London: Yale U. Pr., 1976, p. 217.

INSTIGATIONS

1447 Blum, W. C. "Super Schoolmaster," Dial, 69 (October, 1920), 422-423.

1448 Brooks, Van Wyck. "Reviewer's Notebook," Freeman, 1 (June 16, 1920), 334-335; repr., in Van Wyck Brooks: The Early Years, A Selection from His Works, 1908-1921. Claire Sprague, ed. New York: Harper & Row, 1968.

1449 Colum, Padriac. "Studies in the Sophisticated," NR, 25 (December 8, 1920), 52-54.

1450 Dale, Peter. "Pound and De Gourmont," Agenda, 17, #3-4 (1979-80), 284.

1451 Kay, Bernard. "The Singing Sinologue," NS&N, 44 (June 4, 1955), 788.

1452 Sieburth, Richard. Instigations: Ezra Pound and Remy de Gourmont. Diss., Cambridge: Harvard UP., 1978.

JEFFERSON AND/OR MUSSOLINI

1453 A. M. "For Mussolini, God, Moscow and Major Douglas," New Verse, #16 (August-September, 1935), 18-20.

1454 Falbo, Ernest S. "Ezra Pound's 'Lombard Writer, Friend,'" Paideuma, 3, #2 (Fall, 1974), 247-249.

1455 Hawkins, A. Desmond. "Prejudices," NS&N, 10 (August 31, 1935), 284-285.

1456 Kenner, Hugh. "Jefferson and/or Mussolini," The Poetry of Ezra Pound. Cf., #738, pp. 320-323.

1457 Olson, Charles. "This Is Yeats Speaking," Cf., #374.

LITERARY ESSAYS

1458 Bloom, E. A. "Literary Essays," Review. SatRL, 37 (April 3, 1945), 30.

1459 Brown, Ashley. "The Translations and Literary Essays," Review. Shenandoah, 5, #3 (Summer, 1954), 61-65.

1460 Carter, Thomas H. "Ezra Pound the Critic," KR, 16, #3 (Summer, 1954), 490-496.

1461 Cole, Thomas. "Literary Essays," Review. Imagi, 6, #4 (1955).

1462 Davie, Donald. "Instigations to Procedures," NS&N, 47 (March 27, 1954), 410, 412.

1463 Deutsch, Babette. "Pound's Enduring Criticism," NY Herald Tribune Book Review (June 6, 1954), 14.

1464 Duclos, Jacques. "Personae, Literary Essays, Translations," Revue Des Langues Vivantes, 21, #1 (1955), 70-72.

1465 Eliot, T. S., ed. Introduction by T. S. Eliot. The Literary Essays of Ezra Pound. Norfolk, Conn.: New Directions, 1954.

1466 Freedman, Ralph. "The Serious Artist and the Verbal Icon," WR, 19, #3 (Spring, 1955), 221-229.

1467 Fuller, Roy. "Literary Essays." Review. London Magazine, 1 (May, 1954), 94, 96, 99, 100.

1468 "The Greatness of Critics," TLS (May 28, 1954), 345.

1469 "Literary Essays," Review. The Listener, 51 (April 29, 1954), 749.

1470 "Literary Essays of Ezra Pound," Review, NY, 30, #6 (March, 1954), 118-119.

1471 "Literary Essays." Review. St. Louis Post-Dispatch (March 15, 1954).

1472 McLuhan, Marshall. "The Criticism of Ezra Pound," Cw, 60, #20 (August 20, 1954), 492-493.

1473 "Pound as Critic," Nation, 178, #18 (May 1, 1954), 388-389.

1474 Robson, W. W. "Literary Essays." Review. Blackfriars, 35 (April, 1954), 184-185.

1475 Stanford, Derek. "Sun-Spots and Blind-Spots," Month, 197 (April, 1954), 239-241.

1476 Stock, Noel. "Literary Essays," Review. Meanjin, 2 (Melbourne, 1955), 273-277.

1477 Tomlinson, Charles. "Literary Essays." Review. Spectator, 192 (February 19, 1954), 212.

LUSTRA

1478 Bodenheim, Maxwell. "A Poet's Opinion," Little Review, 4 (June, 1917), 28.

1479 Buss, Kate. "Ezra Pound: Some Evidence of His Rare

Chinese Quality," Boston Evening Transcript (December 6, 1916), Sec. 3, p. 5.

1480 Cronin, G. W. "Classic Free Verse," New York Call (December 20, 1917), 18.

1481 "Current Poetry," LitD, 55 (December 29, 1917), 51-52.

1482 Deutsch, Babette. "Ezra Pound: Vorticist," Ready's Mirror (St. Louis), 26 (December 21, 1917), 860-861.

1483 Grover, Philip. "Manuscript Corrections in Lustra," Paideuma 9, (1980), 357-358.

1484 Hasegawa, Mitsuaki. "Sexual Mockery in Lustra," HSELL, 19, #2 (1973), 33-44.

1485 "Lustra," LitD, 55, #24 (December 15, 1917), 38.

1486 M. T. "Ezra Pound and Others," NR, 13, #168 (January 19, 1918), 352-353.

1487 Michelson, Max. "A Glass-Blower of Time," Poetry, 11 (March, 1918), 330-333.

1488 Orage, A. R. "Readers and Writers," New Age, 23 (July 25, 1918), 201.

1489 Reid, B. L. The Man from New York: John Quinn and His Friends. New York: Oxford U. Pr., 1968, p. 340.

1490 Rittenhouse, J. B. "Contemporary Poetry," Bookman, 46 (January, 1918), 577-578.

1491 Thomas, Ronald E. "Catullus, Flaminius, and Pound in 'Blandula, Tenella, Vagula,'" Paideuma, 5, (Winter, 1976), 407-412.

1492 Untermeyer, Louis. "China, Provence, and Points Adjacent," Dial, 63 (December 20, 1917), 633-635.

1493 Witemeyer, Hugh. "Aspects of Lustra," The Poetry of Ezra Pound: Forms and Renewal, 1908-1920. Berkeley: U. of Calif. Pr., 1969, pp. 122-160.

MAKE IT NEW

1494 C. R. A. "Make It New," Review. AL, 9, #3 (November, 1937), 393.

1495 Chauvet, Paul. "Make It New," Review, RAA (June, 1934), 445-446.

1496 Chesterton, G. K. "Make It New," Review, Listener, 12 (November 28, 1934), 921.

1497 Deutsch, Babette. "Indomitable Ezra Pound," NYHBR (June 2, 1935), 18.

1498 Dobree, Bonamy. "Make It New," Criterion, 14 (April, 1935), 523-526.

1499 DuBois, Arthur E. "Make It New," Review, SR, 44, #2 (April-June, 1936), 254-256.

1500 Gregory, Horace. "Pound as Essayist," YR, 24 (March, 1935), 608-610.

1501 John, K. "The Eternal Schoolboy," NS&N, 8 (November 3, 1934), 630-632.

1502 King, William. "Essays," EngRev, 59 (December, 1934), 745-746.

1503 McCole, Camille. "Make It New," CathW, 141 (May, 1935). 244.

1504 Powell, Dilys. "The Jackdaw of Paris," LonMer, 31 (November, 1934), 81-82.

1505 Roberts, Michael. "Off with the Motley," Spect, 153 (November 2, 1934), 684-686.

1506 S. C. C. "Make It New," Review, CSMM (April 3, 1935), 10.

1507 Walton, Eda Lou. "Mr. Pound as a Critic Is Not Bound by Any Group," NYT, 6 (June 30, 1935), 3.

1508 Wilson, T. C. "Pound as Critic," NR, 85 (November 27, 1935), 80-81.

1509 Young, G. M. "Make It New," Review, Observer (October 7, 1934), 7.

1510 _____. "Ezra Pound Again," Springfield Republican (October, 1934), 7e.

NEAR PERIGORD

1511 Connolly, Thomas E. "Ezra Pound's 'Near Perigord': The Background of a Poem," CL, 8 (Spring, 1956), 110-121.

1512 Joseph, Terry Brint. "'Near Perigord': A Perplexity of Voice," Paideuma, 11, #1 (Spring-Summer, 1982), 93-98.

1513 Kenner, Hugh. "The Broken Mirrors and the Mirror of Memory," Cf., #731, #771.

1514 Schmidt, Gerd. "Ezra Pound: 'Near Perigord,'" NS, 18 (October, 1969), 502-512.

THE NOH PLAYS

1515 Eliot, T. S. "The Noh and the Image," Egoist, 4 (August, 1917), 102-103.

1516 Keith, Nobuko T. "Ezra Pound and Japanese Noh Plays: An Examination of Sotoba Komachi and Nishikigi," LE&W, 15-16 (1971-72), 662-679.

1517 _____. "Ezra Pound's Relationship with Fenollosa and the Japanese Noh Plays," Cf., #728.

1518 Lewin, Bruno. "Literarische Begegnungen zwischen Amerika und Japan," JA, 14 (1969), 25-39.

1519 Miller, Felicia. "Pound, Fenollosa, and the Noh," Occident, 7, #1 (1973), 63-65.

1520 Packard, William. "An American Experiment in Noh," First Stage 4, #2 (Summer, 1965), 60-61.

1521 Saitoh, Kuniharu. "Some Critical Comments on 'Fenollosa-Pound' Translations of Noh Plays," Meiji Gakuin Review (1966), referred to in Sixteen Modern American Authors, Jackson R. Bryer, ed., Cf., #1434, p. 459.

1522 Sato, Toshihiko. "A Study of Noh, The Robe of Feathers," CLAJ, 16 (September, 1972), 72-80.

1523 Taylor, Richard. "Ezra Pound: Editor of Nō," Paideuma, 4, #2-3 (Fall-Winter, 1975), 345-353.

1524 Teele, Roy E. "A Balance Sheet on Pound's Translation of Noh Plays," BA, 39 (Spring, 1965), 168-170.

1525 _____. "Translations of Noh Plays," CL, 9, #4 (Fall, 1957), 345-368.

1526 Tsukui, Nobuko. "Ezra Pound and the Japanese Noh Plays," DAI, 28 (Nebraska: 1967), 2267A-68A; United Pr. of America, Inc., Washington, D.C., 1983.

A PACT

1527 D'Avanzo, Mario L. "Pound's 'A Pact,'" Expl, 24 (February, 1966), Item 51.

1528 Kahn, Sholom J. "Whitman's 'New Wood,'" WWR, 15, #4 (December, 1969), 201-214.

PAPYRUS

1529 Byrnos, Robert S. "Modern Poetry," The Courier Mail (Brisbane), (March 31, 1954). (An attack on Pound's "Papyrus" and a reply by Roger Covell.)

1530 Collinge, N. E. "Gongyla and Mr. Pound," N&Q, n.s., 5, #6 (June, 1958), 265-266.

1531 Daniels, Earl. "Papyrus," The Art of Reading Poetry. New York: Farrar & Rinehart, Inc., 1941; Bks. for Libraries Pr., 1969, p. 9.

1532 Dawson, Christopher M. "Pound's Papyrus," Expl, 9 (February, 1951), Item 30.

1533 Fang, Achilles. "A Note on Pound's Papyrus," MLN, 67, #3 (March, 1952), 188-190.

1534 _____. "Metaphysics and Money-Making," NMQ, 23, #1 (Spring, 1953), 91-94.

1535 Highet, Gilbert. "The Symbolist Poets ...," The Classical Tradition: Greek and Roman Influences on Western Literature. New York: Oxford U. Pr., 1957, p. 517, passim.

1536 Murray, Robert Duff, Jr. "A Note on Sappho and Ezra Pound," Classical Journal, 46 (March, 1951), 304-305.

PATRIA MIA

1537 Deutsch, Babette. "Ezra Pound's Early Credo," NY Herald Tribune Bk. Review (September 17, 1950), 19.

1538 Kenner, Hugh. "Prophets of Renaissance," HudR, 3 (Fall, 1950), 474-478.

1539 MacFall, Russell. "Patria Mia," Review. Chicago Sunday Tribune, (July 2, 1950), 5.

1540 Richie, Donald. "Belles-Lettres Notes," SatRL, 33 (October 14, 1950), 42.

1541 Runnquist, Åke. "Notiser från vöster," Dagens-Nyheter (Stockholm), (August 21, 1950).

1542 Wilson, Edmund. "Patria Mia," NY, 26 (August 5, 1950), 64-67.

PAVANNES AND DIVISIONS

1543 Aiken, Conrad. "A Pointless Pointillist," Dail, 65 (October 19, 1918), 306-307.

1544 Carnevali, Emanuel. "Irritation," Poetry, 15 (January, 1920), 211-221.

1545 Hale, W. G. "Pegasus Impounded," Poetry, 14 (April, 1919), 52-55; repr., in Ezra Pound: The Critical Heritage. Eric Homberger, ed. London; Boston: Routledge & Kegan Paul, 1972, pp. 155-157.

1546 "Mr. Pound as Critic," TLS (September 19, 1918), 437; repr., in American Writing Today: Its Independence and Vigor. Allan Angoff, ed. New York U. Pr., 1957, pp. 332-335.

1547 Untermeyer, Louis. "Ezra Pound, Proseur," NR, 16 (August 17, 1918), 83-84.

PERSONAE

1548 Aiken, Conrad. "Personae," Review. Indep, 118 (February 26, 1927), 246.

1549 _____. "Personae," Poetry, 44, #5 (August, 1934), 276-279.

1550 _____. "Vagabondia," NR, 51, #655 (June 22, 1927), 131-132.

1551 Benet, William Rose. "Personae," The Collected Poems of Ezra Pound, Review. YR, 17 (January, 1928), 366-374.

1552 Blackmur, R. P. "A Variety of Masks," SatRL, 3, #40 (April 30, 1927), 784.

1553 Braybrooke, Neville. "Personae," Review. English, 9, #51 (Autumn, 1952), 108-109.

1554 Bronner, Milton. "A Panel of Poets," Bookman, 35 (April, 1912), 156-158.

1555 Brooke, Rupert. "Personae," Review. CamR, 31 (December 2, 1909), 166-167.

1556 _____. The Letters of Rupert Brooke. Chosen and edited by Geoffrey Keynes. New York: Harcourt, Brace & World, 1968, pp. 332, 470.

1557 Courtney, W. L. "Personae," Review. Daily Telegraph (April 23, 1909), 6.

1558 "Current Poetry," LitD, 60 (February 26, 1910), 402-404.

1559 Deutsch, Babette. "Personae," Review. Bookman, 65 (April, 1927), 220.

1560 Eliot, T. S. Ezra Pound: His Metric and Poetry. New York: Alfred A. Knopf, 1917; repr., in To Criticize the Critic. New York: Farrar, Straus & Giroux, 1965, pp. 162-182.

1561 _____. "Isolated Superiority," Dial, 84 (January, 1928), 4-7.

1562 Flint, F. S. "Verse," The New Age, 5 (May 27, 1909), 101-102.

1563 Ford, Ford Madox. "Personae," NY Herald Tribune BR (January 9, 1927), 1, 6.

1564 Gorman, H. S. "Personae," Review. NYTBR (January 23, 1927), 2.

1565 Harris, Frank. "L'Homme Moyen Sensuel," The Little Review, 4 (October, 1914), 40.

1566 Hassall, Christopher. Rupert Brooke: A Biography. New York: Harcourt, Brace & World, 1964, p. 210.

1567 Hollander, John. "The Poem in the Eye," Shenandoah, 23 (Spring, 1972), 24.

1568 McFarland, Ronald E. "A Note on Monsieur Verog," Paideuma, 11, #3 (Winter, 1982), 446-448.

1569 Mathews, Elkin. Personae: Die Masken Ezra Pounds. Verlag der Arche, Zürich, 1959, pp. 12-15.

1570 Nanny, Max. "Context, Contiguity and Contact in Ezra Pound's Personae," ELH, 47 (Summer, 1980), 386-398.

1571 Petter, C. G. "Pound's Personae: From Manuscript to Print," Studies in Biblio. Vol. 35, pp. 111-132. Fredson Bowers, ed. Published for the Biblio Soc. of University of Virginia by University Pr. of Virginia, 1982, pp. 111-132.

1572 Ruthven, K. K. A Guide to Ezra Pound's Personae. Berkeley; Los Angeles: U. of Calif. Pr., 1969.

1573 Sitwell, Edith. "Ezra Pound," An Examination of Ezra Pound. Peter Russell, ed. Rev. and Enlarged. New York: Gordian Pr., 1973, pp. 39-40.

1574 Thomas, Edward. "Two Poets," English Review, 2 (June, 1909), 627-632.

1575 Van Doren, Mark. "First Glance," Nation, 124 (February 2, 1927), 120.

1576 Williams, W. C. "Personae," Review. LiteraryRev (February, 1927), 1.

1577 Wright, George T. "Modern Poetry and the Personae: The Device and Its Aesthetic Context, as Exhibited in the Work of Eliot, Yeats and Pound," Diss. U. of Calif., at Berkeley, 1956.

1578 _____. The Poet in the Poem: The Personae of Eliot, Yeats, and Pound. Berkeley. U. of Calif. Pr., 1960.

PHANOPOEIA

1579 Hombitzer, Eleonore. "Ezra Pound: 'Phanopoeia': Hinweise zu einer Interpretation," NS, 14, #7 (July, 1965), 568-578.

POEMS: 1918-1921

1580 Bishop, John Peale. "The Intelligence of Poets," Vanity Fair, 17 (January, 1922), 13-14.

1581 Bodenheim, Maxwell. "Isolation of Carved Metal," Cf., #462.

1582 Geddes, Virgil. "Ezra Pound Today," Poetry, 21 (November, 1922), 95-100.

1583 Howard, Brian. Brian Howard: Portrait of a Failure. Marie-Jacqueline Lancaster, ed. London: Anthony Blond, 1968, p. 56.

1584 LeGallienne, Richard. "Poems: 1918-1921," Review. NYT (February 5, 1922), 2.

1585 McClure, John. "New Poems of Ezra Pound," Double Dealer, 2 (May, 1922), 269-271.

1586 Monroe, Harriet. "Ezra Pound," Cf., #85.

1587 Wilson, Edmund. "Mr. Pound's Patchwork," NR, 30, #385 (April 19, 1922), 232-233; repr., in The Shores of Light: A Literary Chronicle of the Twenties and Thirties. New York: Farrar, Straus & Young, Inc., 1952, pp. 44-48.

POLITE ESSAYS

1588 Brown, E. K. "Mr. Pound's Conservatism," Canadian Forum, 20 (April, 1940), 24.

1589 Evans, B. I. "Polite Essays." Review. Manchester Guardian (March 25, 1937), 7.

1590 Healy, J. V. "The Pound Problem," Cf., #1274, p. 75.

1591 Mortimer, Raymond. "Polite Essays," Review. NS&N, 13 (May 15, 1937), 813-814.

1592 Mowrer, Deane. "Pound Wise," NR, 102 (February 12, 1940), 220.

1593 "Polite Essays," Review. CSMM (March 16, 1940), 10.

1594 "Polite Essays," Review. Nation, 150 (March 23, 1940), 401.

1595 "Polite Essays," Review. New Yorker, 15 (January 20, 1940), 64.

1596 "Polite Essays," Review. Time, 35 (January 1, 1940), 47.

1597 Roberts, Michael. "Mr. Pound's Criticism," Spectator, 158 (February 19, 1937), 324.

1598 Wright, Cuthbert. "Criticism," Cw, 31 (February 23, 1940), 390.

PORTRAIT D'UNE FEMME

1599 Barry, Elaine. "'Portrait d'une Femme,' Frost's Comments on Pound," Robert Frost on Writing. New Brunswick, New Jersey: Rutgers U. Pr., 1973, pp. 170-172.

1600 Giannone, Richard J. "Eliot's 'Portrait of a Lady' and Pound's 'Portrait d'une Femme,'" TCL, 5 (October, 1959), 131-134.

1601 Grieder, Josephine. "Robert Frost on Ezra Pound, 1913: Manuscript Corrections of 'Portrait d'une Femme,'" NEQ, 44 (June, 1971), 301-305.

1602 Hagelstango, Rudolf. "Ezra Pound und die fallstricke der Politik," Suddeutsche Zeitung (July 24/25, 1954).

PROFILE

1603 Arns, K. "How to Read," Deutsche Schulzeitung. Hannover: 1931, pp. 307-308.

1604 _____. "Profile," Englische Studien, 69 (1934), 281-282.

1605 Parkes, H. B. "Two Pounds of Poetry," New English Weekly, 2 (December 22, 1932), 227-228.

PROVENÇA

1606 Dell, Floyd. "Provença," Ezra Pound: The Critical Heritage. Eric Homberger, ed. Cf., #1545, pp. 70-72.

1607 _____. "Friday Literary Review," Chicago Evening Post, (January 6, 1911), p. 5.

1608 Mencken, H. L. "Provença," Review in Smart Set (April, 1911), Repr., in Ezra Pound: The Critical Heritage. Eric Homberger, ed., Cf., #1545, pp. 73-74.

1609 Nolte, William H., ed. H. L. Mencken's Smart Set Criticism. Cornell U. Pr., 1969, pp. 76-78.

1610 Stock, Noel. "Provença," The Life of Ezra Pound. Cf., #127, pp. 80, 90, 92-93.

1611 Tanselle, G. Thomas. "Two Early Letters of Ezra Pound," AL, 34, #1 (March, 1962), 114-119.

THE RETURN

1612 Deutsch, Babette. "The Return," Poetry in Our Time. New York: Henry Holt & Co., 1952, pp. 124-125.

1613 "Experiment in Verse--'The Return,'" TLS (August 17, 1956), Special Number, #3.

1614 Friar, Kimon, and John Malcolm Brinnin, eds. "The Return," Modern Poetry. New York: Appleton-Century-Crofts, 1951, pp. 138, 531.

1615 Israel, Calvin. "Imitation and Meaning in Ezra Pound's 'The Return,'" LHR, 8 (1966), 31-36.

1616 Kenner, Hugh. "The Return," Cf., #738, p. 122.

1617 M. M. "Pound's 'Return,'" Expl, 12, #3 (December, 1953), Q. 1.

1618 Rosenthal, M. L. "The Return," The Modern Poets, Cf., #911, pp. 51-53.

1619 Taupin, René. L'Influence de Symbolisme Français sur la Poèsie Américaine, (de 1910 à 1920). Paris: 1929, pp. 114, 133-158.

RIPOSTES

1620 Alden, Raymond Macdonald. "The New Poetry," Nation, 96 (April 17, 1913), 386-387.

1621 Bell, Ian F. A. "Pound's 'Silet,'" Expl, 38, #4 (Summer, 1980), 14-16.

1622 Child, Harold. Ripostes. Review. TLS (December 12, 1912).

1623 Flint, F. S. "The 'Ripostes' of Ezra Pound with 'The Complete Poetical Works' of T. E. Hulme," Poetry and Drama, I, #1 (March, 1913), 60-62.

1624 Ingber, Richard Geoffrey. "Ezra Pound and the Classical Tradition Backgrounds and Formative Influences," DAI, 44, #9 (U. of Toronto: Canada, 1983), 2759A.

1625 Kenner, Hugh. "Ripostes," The Pound Era, Cf., #732, passim.

1626 Monroe, Harriet. "In Defense of Poetry," Dial, 54 (May 16, 1913), 106-107, 409.

1627 _____. A Poet's Life, Cf., #86, passim.

1628 Rice, Wallace. "Pound and Poetry," Dial, 54 (May 1, 1913), 370-371.

1629 Witemeyer, Hugh. "Ripostes: Recapitulations and Innovations," Cf., #1422, pp. 140-121.

SEAFARER

1630 Adams, S. J. "A Case for Pound's Seafarer," Mosaic, 9, #2 (Winter, 1976), 127-146.

1631 Alexander, Michael. "Ezra Pound's 'Seafarer,'" Agenda, 13, iv-14; i (Winter, 1975; Spring, 1976), 110-126.

1632 Bessinger, J. B. "The Oral Text of Ezra Pound's 'The Seafarer,'" QJS, 47 (April, 1961), 173-177.

1633 Chaplin, Sherry. "Pound's Seafarer: An Assessment of Value," UES, 15, #2 (1977), 42-45.

1634 Herzbrun, Philip. "Mr. Pound and The Seafarer," TLS (August 20, 1954), 529. [Letter concerning "The Greatness of Criticism," TLS (May 28, 1954).]

1635 Hesse, Eva, ed., with Introduction. New Approaches to Ezra Pound, Cf., #41, pp. 35, 332-334, passim.

1636 Kenner, Hugh. The Poetry of Ezra Pound, Cf., #738, pp. 134, 140, 316.

1637 _____. The Pound Era, Cf., #732, pp. 349-354, passim.

1638 _____. "Song's Sooth Reckoned," Poetry, 111, #6 (March, 1968), 395-399.

1639 Lucas, F. L. Criticism and Poetry. (The Wharton Lecture, British Academy) Oxford U. Pr., 1933.

1640 _____. "Translation," TLS (September 10, 1954), 573. [Letter has mention of Pound's Seafarer]

1641 Robinson, Fred C. "'Might of the North': Pound's Anglo-Saxon Studies and The Seafarer," YR, 71, #2 (Winter, 1982), 199-224.

1642 Sarang, Vilas. "Pound's Seafarer," CP, 6, #2 (Fall, 1973), 5-11.

1643 Savoia, Dianella. "Traduzione e poesia nel Seafarer di Ezra Pound," Contributi dell'Instituto di filologia moderna. Sergio Rossi, ed. Milano: Vita e Pensiero. U. of Cattolica, 1974, pp. 210-238.

1644 Sisam, Kenneth. "Mr. Pound and the Seafarer," TLS (June 25, 1954), 409.

1645 Sutherland, James R. "Mr. Pound and 'The Seafarer,'" TLS, (July 9, 1954), 447. [Reply to Kenneth Sisam, TLS (June 25, 1954).]

SELECTED POEMS (1928; 1949)

1646 Bowra, C. M. "More Cantos from Ezra Pound," NS&N, 38 (September 3, 1949), 250.

1647 Burford, William. "On Louis Coxe's Review of Ezra Pound," Poetry, 92, #3 (June, 1958), 195-196.

1648 Cole, Thomas. "Ends and Means," Imagi, 5 (1949), 11.

1649 Coxe, Louis O. "Temperament and Subject," Poetry, 91, #6 (March, 1958), 389-393; repr., Discussion, 92 (June, 1958), 195-197.

1650 Duncan, Robert. "On Louis Coxe's Review of Ezra Pound," Poetry, 92, #3 (June, 1958), 196-197.

1651 Eliot, T. S. "Introduction," Selected Poems (by Ezra Pound). London: Faber & Gwyer, 1928, pp. vii-xxv.

1652 Espey, John. "Ezra Pound: 'Selected Poems,'" Fifteen Modern American Authors. Jackson R. Bryer, ed. Cf., #1433, p. 324.

1653 _____. "Ezra Pound: 'Selected Poems,'" Sixteen Modern American Authors. Jackson R. Bryer, ed., Cf., 1434, p. 446.

1654 Ferril, Thomas Harnsby. Review: Selected Poems. San Francisco Chronicle (January 8, 1950), 25.

1655 Fletcher, John Gould. Review: "Selected Poems," Cf., #618.

1656 Froula, Christine. A Guide to Ezra Pound's "Selected Poems." New York: New Directions, 1983.

1657 Lucas, F. L. "The Criticism of Poetry," (Warton Lecture on English Poetry). Proceedings of the British Academy. London: Oxford U. Pr., 1933, pp. 171-172.

1658 McDonald, Gerald. Review: Selected Poems. Library Journal, 74 (December 15, 1949), 1909.

1659 Meyer, G. P. "A Sampling of Pound and Modern Man," SatRL, 32 (December 24, 1949). 14.

1660 Roberts, Michael. "Ezra Pound's Unpopularity," NEW, 1 (May 5, 1932), 67-69.

1661 Roskolenko, Harry. "What Manner of Man Is This?" Voices, 141 (1950), 41-43.

1662 Russell, Peter. Review: Selected Poems. WorldRev, 7 (September, 1949), 76.

SELECTED PROSE, 1909-1965

1663 Cookson, William, ed. Introduction. Selected Prose, 1909-1965. New York: New Directions, 1973.

1664 Read, Forrest. Review: Ezra Pound: Selected Prose, 1909-1965. Paideuma, 3, #1 (Spring, 1974), 125-128.

SEPARATION ON THE RIVER KIANG

1665 Graham, D. B. "From Chinese to English: Ezra Pound's 'Separation on the River Kiang,'" LE&W, 13 (June, 1969), 182-195.

1666 Meyer, William J. "The Imagist and the Translator: Ezra Pound's 'Separation on the River Kiang,'" Sou'wester (So. Ill. U), (October 30, 1970), 72-80.

THE SPIRIT OF ROMANCE

1667 Coffman, Stanley K., Jr. Review: Spirit of Romance. BA, 27, #4 (Autumn, 1953), 385.

1668 Espey, "Ezra Pound: 'Spirit of Romance,'" Fifteen Modern American Authors, Cf., #1433, p. 324; Cf., #1434, p. 446.

1669 Halsband, Robert. "Pound Revisited," SatRL, 36, #19 (May 9, 1953), 47-48.

1670 Kenner, Hugh. "Pound and the Provision of Measures," Poetry, 83, #1 (October, 1953), 29-35.

1671 Littlefield, Walter. Review: The Spirit of Romance, NYT (November 17, 1910), 714.

1672 "Pound Revisited," Review: The Spirit of Romance, SatRL, 36 (May 9, 1953), 47-48.

1673 "The Spirit of Romance," Review: NY, 29 (May 23, 1953), 138.

1674 Stern, Richard G. "Pound as Translator," Accent, 13, #4 (Autumn, 1953), 265-268.

1675 Thomas, Edward. Review: "The Spirit of Romance," Morning Post (August 1, 1910); repr., Ezra Pound: The Critical Heritage. Eric Homberger, ed. Cf., #1545, pp. 68-69.

LE TESTAMENT DE VILLON

1676 Antheil, George. "Salons de Paris," Bad Boy of Music. Garden City, New York: Doubleday, Dorn & Co., 1945, pp. 117-123.

1677 _____. "Why a Poet Quit the Muses," Paideuma, 2, #1 (Spring, 1973), 3-6.

1678 Hughes, Robert. "Ezra Pound's Opera: Le Testament de Villon," Paideuma, 2, #1 (Spring, 1973), 11-16.

1679 Lucas, John. "'Villon'--Made New and Well," CaM, 13 (1973), 78-84.

1680 Lyall, Larry. "Pound/Villon: Le Testament de François Villon," Paideuma, 2, #1 (1973), 17-22.

1681 Rodker, John. "Pound's 'Villon' on the Radio," Transatlantic-Rev, I, #4 (Winter, 1931), 389.

1682 Straus, H. "American Music via Europe," Nation, 119 (September 10, 1924), 268.

THE TRANSLATIONS

1683 Alvarez, A[lfred]. "Ezra Pound: The Qualities and Limitations of Translation-Poetry," EIC, 6 (1956), 171-189.

1684 Davie, Donald. "Translation Absolute," NS&N, 46 (September 5, 1953), 262.

1685 De Schloezer, Boris. "Stravinsky: His Technique," (Trans. by Ezra Pound), Dial, 86 (1929), 9-26, passim.

1686 Dudek, Louis. Review: The Translations, CIV/n, No. 4 (Montreal: 1953), 17-18.

1687 Edwards, John. "Pound's Translations," Poetry, 83, #4 (January, 1954), 233-238.

1688 Ferlinghetti, Lawrence. "Among the New Books," San Francisco Chronicle, (October 4, 1953), 26.

1689 Fiedler, Leslie. "Sufficient Unto the Day," PR, 22 (Winter, 1955), 118-122; repr., in Partisan Review Anthology. William Phillips and Philip Rahv, eds. New York: Holt, Rinehart & Winston, 1962, pp. 457-459.

1690 Fitts, Dudley. "The Tea-Shop Aura," NR, 130 (January 4, 1954), 18-19.

1691 Graham, Stephen. "Pound Sterling," Poetry Review, 44, #4 (October-December, 1953), 472-473.

1692 Guenther, Charles. "Eloquent Scholarship," St. Louis Post-Dispatch, (November 30, 1953), 2E.

1693 Haley, Martin. Review: Translations, TC (Australia), (Autumn, 1954).

1694 Keith, Nobuko Tsukui. "Aoi no Ue and Kinuta: An Examination of Ezra Pound's Translations," Paideuma, 8 (1979), 199-214.

1695 Kenner, Hugh. "Introduction." The Translations of Ezra Pound. London: Faber; New York: New Directions, 1953.

1696 McNaughton, William. "Pound's Translations and Chinese Melopoeia," TQ, 10, #4 (Winter, 1967), 52-56.

1697 Muir, Edwin. "New Poems for Old," Observer (August 2, 1953).

1698 Murphy, Richard. "The Art of a Translator," Spectator, 190 (September 18, 1953), 303-304.

1699 Sontag, Susan. "Translation as Art," New Leader (June 28, 1954), 26-27.

1700 Stern, Richard G. "Pound as Translator," Cf., #1674.

1701 Stevenson, Anne. Review: "The Translations." Michigan Daily, (March 4, 1954).

1702 "Translations." Review: New Yorker, 30 (May 1, 1954), 112.

1703 Ward, Charlotte, ed. "Translations," IowaR, 12, #1 (Winter, 1981), 37-49.

1704 Whicher, George F. Review: "Translations," AL, 26, #1 (March, 1954), 119-121.

1705 _____. "Translations and Poetry," NY Herald Tribune Book Review (October 25, 1953). 25.

THE UNWOBBLING PIVOT and THE GREAT DIGEST

1706 Breit, Harvey. "Repeat Performances Approved," NYT Bk. Rev., (February 3, 1952), 29.

1707 Chan, Wing-tsit. "The Unwobbling Pivot and The Great Digest," Philosophy, East & West, 3, #4 (January, 1954), 371-373.

1708 Fang, Achilles. "Metaphysics and Money-Making," Cf., #1534.

1709 Ferlinghetti, Lawrence. "Poetry Shelf," San Francisco Chronicle (February 3, 1952), 27.

1710 Raine, Kathleen. "There Is No Trifling," Cf., #1161.

1711 Tay, William. "Between Kung and Eleusis: Li Chi, The Eleusinian Rites, Erigena and Ezra Pound," Paideuma, 4, #1 (Spring, 1975), 37-54.

1712 _____. "Cheng Ming: The New Paideuma of Ezra Pound," Asian Cult, 7 (1979), 29-46.

1713 "The Unwobbling Pivot." NY, 28 (May 31, 1952), 98.

1714 "The Unwobbling Pivot," San Francisco Chinese World (January 21, 1954), (English Section), p. 2.

WOMEN OF TRACHIS

1715 Bowra, C. M. "The Women of Trachis: A Symposium," Pound Newsletter, 2 (January, 1955), 3-8.

1716 Dick, Bernard F. "Sophocles Com-Pounded," Classical World, 54 (1961), 236-237.

1717 Donoghue, Denis. "Ezra Pound and Women of Trachis," The Third Voice: Modern British and American Verse Drama. Princeton, N.J.: Princeton U. Pr., 1959, pp. 213-222.

1718 Earp, F. R. "The Women of Trachis: A Symposium," Pound Newsletter, 5 (January, 1955), 3-8.

1719 Eliot, T. S. "The Women of Trachis," Cf., #1718.

1720 Espey, John. "Ezra Pound--'Women of Trachis,'" Cf., #1433, pp. 340-341.

1721 _____. "Ezra Pound: Women of Trachis," Cf., #1434, pp. 462-463.

1722 Goacher, Denis. "The Critics and the Master," European, 15 (May, 1954), 24-37.

1723 _____. "Notes from Abroad: London," Shenandoah, 6, #1 (Winter, 1954), 84-87.

1724 Ingber, Richard. "Ezra Pound's Women of Trachis: A Song for the Muses' Garden," AmS, 23 (1978), 131-146.

1725 Kenner, Hugh. "Some Elders," Poetry, 83, #6 (March, 1954), 357-366.

1726 _____. "Homage to Musonius," Cf., #1211.

1727 Lattimore, Richmond. "The Women of Trachis: A Symposium," Cf., #1718.

1728 Levi, Peter. "Ezra Pound's Translation of Sophokles' Women of Trachis," Agenda, 7, #1 (1969), 17-22.

1729 _____. "Pound and the Classics," Cf., #777.

1730 Mason, H. A. "The Women of Trachis," Arion, 2 (1963), 59-81, 105-121; revised version, Cambridge Qt, 4 (1969), 244-272.

1731 "Melpomene in the West," TLS (August 27, 1954), 537-538.

1732 Pasquier, Marie-Claire, tr. "Les Femmes de Trachis," CRB, 103 (1982), 67-150.

1733 Peachy, Frederic. "The Women of Trachis: A Symposium," Pound Newsletter, 5 (January, 1955), 3-8.

1734 "Pound Takes on Sophocles: Women of Trachis Staged," The Times, (November 23, 1962), p. 16, col. 7.

1735 Slavitt, David. "Eliot, Pound Played in Three Quarter Round," Yale Daily News (March 24, 1955), 8. (Review of the Yale performance of the Women of Trachis, March 23-25, 1955.)

1736 Sutherland, Donald. "Ezra Pound or Sophocles," ColQ, 8, #2 (Autumn, 1959), 182-191.

1737 Trewin, J. C. "Women of Trachis," Review of Performance. Listener, 51 (April 29, 1954), 755.

III. SUPPLEMENTAL WORKS

ABC OF ECONOMICS

1738 Coulter, John W. "Reviews," Adelphi (May 6, 1933), 142-144.

1739 Gregory, Horace. "The ABC of Ezra Pound," Poetry, 46 (August, 1935), 279-285.

1740 Hazlitt, Henry. "Studies in Money and Power," New York Times (April 7, 1940), 22.

1741 Healy, J. V. "The Pound Problem," Cf., #1274.

ABC OF READING

1742 Arvin, Newton. "Primer for Pedants," NR, 82 (February 20, 1935), 54.

1743 B[regy], K[atherine]. Review of ABC of Reading, Catholic World, 140 (December, 1934), 371.

1744 Bridson, D. G. "ABC OF READING," Criterion, 14 (October, 1934), 123-125.

1745 Brown, Ivor. "Ezra Pound Speaks," Springfield Republican, 22 (July, 1934), 7e.

1746 Burke, Kenneth. "Gastronomy of Letters," Nation, 139 (October, 1934), 458-459.

1747 Deutsch, Babette. "With Seven League Boots," New York Herald Tribune (November 25, 1934), 18.

1748 Gregory, Horace. "The ABC of Ezra Pound," Cf., #1739.

1749 _____. "Pound as Essayist," Yale Review, 24 (March, 1935), 608-610.

1750 Haley, Martin. "Ezra Pound as Literary Teacher Writes Sensibly," Advocate (Melbourne), (August 26, 1954), 9.

1751 Halsband, Robert. "Belles-Lettres Notes," SatRL, 34 (July 14, 1951), 48.

1752 John, K. "Mr. Pound's Exhibits," NSt&N, 7 (June 23, 1934), 952.

1753 Mairet, Philip. Review: ABC of Reading. New English Weekly (June 14, 1934).

1754 Palmer, Leslie H. "Matthew Arnold and Ezra Pound's ABC of Reading," Paideuma, 2, #2 (Fall, 1973), 193-198.

1755 Peel, Robert. Review: ABC of Reading, CSMM (October 31, 1934), 12.

1756 Peschman, Herman. "ABC of Reading," Poetry Review, 42, #5 (September-October, 1951), pp. 273-275.

1757 Rainer, Dachine. "ABC of Reading," Retort, 5 (1951), 48.

1758 Ransom, John Crowe. "ABC of Reading," SatRL, 11 (January 19, 1935), 434-435.

1759 Sjostrand, Osten. "Konsten all lasa," Morgon-Tindningen (Stockholm) (August 1, 1951).

THE ALCHEMIST

1760 Materer, Timothy. "Ezra Pound and the Alchemy of the Word," JML, 11, #1 (March, 1984), 109-124.

1761 Rosenthal, M[achia], L[ouis]. "The Alchemist--Ezra Pound: The Poet as Hero," The Modern Poets: A Critical Introduction. Cf., #911, p. 53.

A LUME SPENTO

1762 Accrocca, E. F. "'A Lume Spento' di Ezra Pound, nel cinquantenario del primo libro," FLe, 13 (November 16, 1958), 1-2.

1763 Diesendorf, Margaret. Cf., #31.

1764 Falck, Colin. "A Lume Spento," Encounter, 27 (August, 1966), 82.

1765 Levi, Peter, S. J. "Ezra Pound Assessed," Jubilee, 13, #10 (February, 1966), 56-57.

1766 Schmidt, Gerd. "Pound's 'In Epitaphium Eius,'" Expl, 40, #3 (Spring, 1982), 44-45.

ANTHEIL AND THE TREATISE ON HARMONY

1767 Engel, Carl. "Views and Reviews," Musical Quarterly, 12, #4 (October, 1926), 631-641.

1768 Frank, Mortimer H. "Ezra Pound's Musical Excursions," UWR, 15, i-ii (1979-80), 5-12.

1769 Haggin, Bernard H. "Antheil and the Treatise on Harmony, with Supplementary Notes," Music in the Nation. New York: Wm. Sloane Associates, Inc., 1949, pp. 325-327.

1770 Robinson, E. "Antheil," NY Evening Post (November 5, 1927), 12.

1771 Rorem, Ned. "Introduction," Antheil and the Treatise on Harmony by Ezra Pound. New York: Da Capo Pr., 1968, pp. 1-16.

1772 Schafer, Murray. "Ezra Pound and Music," Cf., #919.

THE APPROACH TO PARIS

1773 Hutchins, Patricia. "Ezra Pound's Approach to Paris," SoR, 6, #2 (New Series), (April, 1970), 340-355.

THE BALLAD OF THE GOODLY FERE

1774 Abad, Gemino H. "Ballad of the Goodly Fere," A Formal

Approach to Lyric Poetry. Quezon City, Philippines: U. of Philippines Pr., 1978, pp. 168-169, 172-173, passim.

1775 Buxbaum, Katherine. "Ezra Pound's 'Ballad of the Goodly Fere,'" Poet's Lore, 40 (Spring, 1929), 142-143.

1776 Hughes, Glenn. "Ezra Pound: 'Ballad of the Goodly Fere,'" Imagism and the Imagists: A Study in Modern Poetry. New York: Humanities Pr., 1960, pp. 230-231.

1777 Link, Franz H. "Two Notes on the Early Poetry," Paideuma, 7 (Fall, 1978), 185-186.

1778 Mencken, H. L. "Ezra Pound," H. L. Mencken's Smart Set Criticism. Sel., and ed., by William H. Nolte. Ithaca, New York: Cornell U. Pr., 1968, pp. 77-78.

1779 Riding, Laura, and Robert Graves. "Ballad of the Goodly Fere," A Survey of Modernist Poetry. New York: Doubleday, Doran & Co., 1928, pp. 140-142.

1780 Schneidau, Herbert N. "Style and Sacrament in Modernist Writing," GeorgiaRev, 31, #2 (Summer, 1977), 427-452.

1781 Tanselle, G. Thomas. ["Ballad of the Goodly Fere"], "Two Early Letters of Ezra Pound," AL, 34, #1 (March, 1962), 114-119.

BLANDULA, TENELLA, VAGULA

1782 McDougal, Stuart. "The Presence of Pater in 'Blandula, Tenella, Vagula," Paideuma, 4, 2&3 (Fall-Winter, 1975), 317-321.

1783 Thomas, Ronald. "Catullus, Flaminius, and Pound in 'Blandula, Tenella, Vagula," Cf., #1491.

IV. GENERAL CRITICISM

1784 Aaron, Daniel. Writers on the Left: Episodes in American Literary Communism. New York: Harcourt, Brace & World, 1961, 114-116, 201-202, passim.

1785 Abbs, Peter, ed. The Black Rainbow: Essays on the Present Breakdown of a Culture. London: Heineman, 1975, passim.

1786 Abse, Dannie. "Ezra Pound," [Poem about Ezra Pound], Commentary, 26 (November, 1958), 410.

1787 _____. "Ezra Pound and My Father," TC, 176 (1st Qt., 1968), 42-44.

1788 Accrocca, Elio Filippo. "Pound e l'ideogramma," Stagione, 2, #7 (Rome: 1955), 4.

1789 Ackroyd, Peter. Ezra Pound and His World. Cf., #1.

1790 Adams, Robert M. "A Hawk and a Handsaw for Ezra Pound," Accent, 8 (Summer, 1948), 205-214.

1791 _____. "The Pound in Your Pocket," Review: Ezra Pound by Donald Davie. TLS (February 6, 1976), 128-129.

1792 Adams, Stephen J. "Ezra Pound and Music," DAI, Cf., #429.

1793 _____. "Ezra Pound and Provencal Melopoeia," FDP, 2 (1978), 27-48.

1794 _____. "More on Pound," CRevAS, 13, #2 (Fall, 1982), 245-251.

1795 _____. "Musical Neofism: Pound's Theory of Harmony in Context," Mosaic, 13, #2 (Winter, 1980), 49-69.

1796 _____. "Pound, Olga Rudge, and the 'Risveglio Vivaldiano,'" Paideuma, 4, #1 (Spring, 1975), 111-118.

1797 _____. "Pound's Quantities and 'Absolute Rhythm,'" ELWIU, 4 (1977), 95-109.

1798 _____. "T. S. Eliot's So-Called Sestina: A Note on 'The Dry Salvages,' II," ELN, 15, #3 (March, 1978), 203-208.

1799 Agresti, Olivia Rosetti. "The Ambassador," Pound Newsletter, #8 (October, 1955), 19-20.

1800 _____. "Ezra Pound: A Tribute," Civ/n (Canada), 6 (1954), 25-27.

1801 _____. "Ricordo di Ezra Pound," Il Secolo d'Italia (December 1, 1953), 3.

1802 Aiken, Conrad. "Ezra Pound: 1914," Ezra Pound: Perspectives. Cf., #125, pp. 2-6.

1803 _____. "The Place of Imagism," NR, 3, #29 (May 22, 1915), 75-76.

1804 _____. "A Pointless Pointillist: Ezra Pound," Cf., #1543, pp. 136-142.

1805 _____. "Ezra Pound," Reviewer's ABC, Cf., #260, pp. 323-327.

1806 _____. Selected Letters of Conrad Aiken. Joseph Killorin, ed. New Haven and London: Yale U. Pr., 1978, pp. 21-23, passim.

1807 Aldington, Richard. "The Art of Poetry," Dial, 69 (August, 1920), 168-180.

1808 _____. "Blast," Egoist, 1 (July 15, 1914), 272-273.

1809 _____. "A Book for Literary Philosophers," Poetry, 16 (July, 1920), 213-216.

1810 _____. "Des Imagistes," SatRL, 21 (March 16, 1940), 3-4.

1811 _____. "Des Imagistes," The Saturday Review Gallery. New York: Simon & Schuster, 1959, pp. 269-275.

1812 _____. Ezra Pound and T. S. Eliot: A Lecture. Hurst, Berkshire: The Peacocks Pr., 1954.

1813 _____. Ezra Pound: Perspectives. Noel Stock, ed., Cf., #125, pp. 122-124.

1814 _____. "Farewell to Europe," AtlM, 166 (October, 1940), 518-530.

1815 _____. Life for Life's Sake. New York: Viking Pr., Inc., 1941, pp. 134-135.

1816 _____. "Modern Poetry and the Imagists," Egoist, I, ii (June 1, 1914), 201-203.

1817 _____. "Penultimate Poetry: Xenophilometropolitania," Egoist, I, 2 (January 15, 1914), 36.

1818 _____. Literary Studies and Reviews. London; New York: Allen & Unwin, and Dial Press, 1924; repr., Books for Libraries Pr., 1968.

1819 _____. "The Poetry of Ezra Pound," Egoist, 2 (May 1, 1915), 71-72.

1820 Aleksic, Branko. "X-Ray Pound i poetika imazizma," Izraz, 42 (1977), 1202-1231.

1821 Alexander, Michael. The Poetic Achievement of Ezra Pound. Cf., #432.

1822 _____. "Two Reviews," Agenda, 17, #3-4, and 18, #1 (Autumn-Winter-Spring, 1979-80), 122-129.

1823 Alpert, Barry S. "Ezra Pound, John Price, and The Exile," Paideuma, 2, #3 (Winter, 1973), 427-448.

1824 _____. "Permanence and Violence: Ezra Pound, The English Review, and BLAST," Occident, 8 (Spring, 1974), 80-96.

1825 _____. "The Unexamined Art: Ezra Pound and the Aesthetic Mode of the Little Magazine," DAI, 32 (Stanford: 1971), 5771A.

1826 Alsterlund, B. "Ezra Pound," Wilson Library Bulletin, 20 (January, 1946), 326.

1827 _____. "Newsmen and Their Wares," Wilson Library Bulletin, 18 (September, 1943), 6.

1828 Altieri, Charles. "Objective Image and Act of Mind in Modern Poetry," PMLA, 91 (1976), 101-114.

1829 Alvarez, A[lfred]. "Ezra Pound: Craft and Morals," The Shaping Spirit: Studies in Modern English and American Poets. London: Chatto & Windus, 1958; American Edition, entitled Stewards of Excellence. New York: Scribner, 1971.

1830 _____. "Ezra Pound: The Qualities and Limitations of Translation-Poetry," Cf., #1683.

1831 _____. "Two Faces of Pound," Observer (March 6, 1960).

1832 Amaral, José Vazquez. "Ezra Pound: Poeta del mundo nuevo," Universidad de Mexico, 8, #11 (July, 1954), 9-11.

1833 _____. "Notes from Abroad," Shenandoah, 6, #2 (Spring, 1955), 88-89.

1834 _____. "Words from Ezra Pound," Cf., #1066.

1835 Amdur, Alice Steiner. The Poetry of Ezra Pound. Cambridge, Mass., 1936; New York: Russell & Russell, 1966.

1836 Anant, Victor. "'Pop' Fiction," London Spectator, 14 (February, 1958), 197-198.

1837 Anceschi, Luciano. "Ezra Insegna Ancora," Stagione, 2, #7 (Rome: 1955), 3.

1838 _____. "Ezra Pound y el humanismo Americano," Cuadernos Hispanoamericanos, 32 and 35 (Madrid: August-November, 1953).

1839 _____. "Palinsesti del Protoumanesimo americano," Litteratura Arte Contemporanea (August, 1950), 34-44; (December, 1950), 30-38.

1840 _____. "Palinsesti del protoumanesimo poetico Americano," Poetica americana e altri studi contemporanei de poetica. Pisa: Nistri-Lischi, 1953, pp. 13-50, 131-133.

1841 Anderson, David. "Breaking the Silence: The Interview of Vanni Ronsisvalle and Pier Paolo Pasolini with Ezra Pound in 1968," Paideuma, 10, #2 (Fall, 1981), 331-345.

1842 _____. "Rapallo, 1941," Paideuma, 8 (1979), 431-442.

1843 Anderson, Margaret. My Thirty Years' War. New York: Covici, Friede, 1930, pp. 158-172, 174-175.

1844 Angoff, Allan, ed. "The Poems of Ezra Pound," American Writing Today: Its Independence and Vigor. New York: New York U. Pr., 1957, pp. 365-368.

1845 Angoff, Charles. "The Mystique of The Smart Set," Literary Review, 11, #1 (Autumn, 1967), 49-60.

1846 Antheil, George. "Salons de Paris," Bad Boy of Music. New York: Doubleday, Doran & Co., Inc., 1945, pp. 117-123.

1847 _____. "Why a Poet Quit the Muses," Paideuma, 2 (Spring, 1973), 3-6.

1848 Antonini, A. "A Lume Spento," Book News Monthly, 27 (May, 1909), 719.

1849 Apter, Ronnie Susan. "Creative Translation: The Influence of Ezra Pound on the Translation of Poetry," DAI, 40, #12, Part 1 (Fordham: 1980), 6285A.

1850 Arce, Armando Uribe. "Pound," Santiago: Centro de Investigaciones de Literatura Comparada de la Universidad de Chile. [1963]. Rev. by Bernard F. Engel, AL, 37, #1 (March, 1965), 89-90.

1851 Arendt, Hannah. Men in Dark Times. New York: Harcourt, Brace & World, 1968, pp. 211-212.

1852 Armanini, Ante. "Ezra Pound," Delo, 22, #10 (1976), 91-109.

1853 Ashleigh, Charles. "Des Imagistes," Little Review, 1 (July, 1914), 15-17.

1854 Avedon, Richard, and Truman Capote. "Observations on Ezra Pound," Cf., #17, pp. 74, 76.

1855 Awiszus, Sabine. "Kurg in Venedig: Die Erscheinung Ezra Pounds," Vergleichen und Verändern. Festschrift für Helmut Motekat. Albrecht Goetze and Pflaum Gunther, eds. München: Hueber, 1970, pp. 385-393.

1856 _____. "The Poet Professorially Examined," Agenda, 17, #2 (1979), 64-67.

1857 _____. "Statements on Pound's Prose," Agenda, 17, #3-4; 18, #1 (Autumn-Winter-Spring, 1979-80), 266-272.

1858 Axelrod, Steven Gould. Robert Lowell: Life and Art. Cf., #434.

1859 Ayscough, Florence, and Amy Lowell. Correspondence of a Friendship. Harley F. MacNair, ed. Chicago: U. of Chicago Pr., 1945, pp. 253-256.

1860 Baar, Ron. "Ezra Pound: Poet as Historian," Cf., #435.

1861 Bab, Julius. [Essay on Pound]. Amerikas Dichter der Gegenwart. Berlin: Christian Verlag, 1951, pp. 128-134.

1862 Bacigalupo, Massimo. The Formed Trace: The Later Poetry of Ezra Pound. Cf., #437.

1863 _____. "The Later Pound, [Ezra Pound's Poetry, 1945-1960]," DAI, 36, #5 (Columbia U.: 1975), 2817-2818A.

1864 Baconsky, A. E. "Ezra Pound," Panorama Poeziei universale contemporane. [The scene of the world contemporary poetry.] Burcuresti: Albatros, 1972, pp. 629-632.

1865 Bailey, Bruce. "T. S. Eliot's The Waste Land in Parody, Travesty, and Satire," Yeats-Eliot Review, 5, #1 (1978), 3.

1866 Baisch, Dorothy R. "Ezra Pound," London Literary Circles, 1910-1920, with Special Reference to Ford Madox Ford, Ezra Pound, D. H. Lawrence, and Virginia Woolf. Diss. Cornell U., 1950.

1867 Baker, Carlos. "Pound in Venice, 1965," Cf., #3.

1868 Baldner, Ralph W. "Ezra Pound: Image of Theophile Gautier," ArQ, 14, #3 (Autumn, 1958), 246-256.

1869 Banerjee, Ron D. K. "Dante Through the Looking Glass: Rossetti, Pound, and Eliot," CL, 24, #2 (Spring, 1972), 136-149.

1870 Barbour, Douglas. "Ezra Pound's Legacy: 'What Thou Lovest Well Remains,'" QQ, 80 (Autumn, 1973), 450-454.

1871 Barbour, Linda Lee. "Lyric Definition: Poetry as Definitive Play," DAI, 43, #9 (U. of Calif., Irvine: 1982), 2987A.

1872 Barfoot, Gabriels. "Dante in T. S. Eliot's Criticism," EM, 23 (1972), 231-246.

1873 _____. "The Theme of Usury in Dante and Pound," RLMC, 30 (1977), 254-283.

1874 Barilli, Renato. Poetica e Retorica. Milano: Mursia, 1969.

1875 Barnard, Harry. "The Lost Liberals," Cw, 56, #8 (May 30, 1952), 198-199. (Cf., Peter Viereck, "Symbols: Hiss and Pound," Cf., #251.)

1876 Barnard, Mary. "A Communication on Greek Metric, Ezra Pound, and Sappho," Agenda, 16, #3-4 (1978-79), 62-68.

1877 Barricalli, Gian Piero. "A Poet of a Poet: Comments on Pound's Translation of Leopardi's 'Sopra il Ritratto di una Bella Donna,'" IQ, 16:64 (July, 1973), 68-75.

1878 Barry, Elaine. "Frost's Comments on Pound," Cf., #1599, pp. 170-172.

1879 Barry, Iris. "The Ezra Pound Period," Bookman, 74, #2 (October, 1931), 159-171.

1880 Batavia, Ludovico von. "USA--Botschaft, Schwedische Akademie: zu Ezra Pound und dem nobel-Preis [American Ambassador, Swedish Academy: of Ezra Pound and the Nobel Prize], Diagnole, 8 (1969), 28-31.

1881 Bates, Eveline. "Ezra Pound and the Critics," ChR, 24, #4 (Spring, 1973), 108-115.

1882 Bates, Margaret. "Ezra Pound: Maker of Connections," Paideuma, 6 (1977), 114-115.

1883 Baumann, Walter, "Carleton, Paquin and Salzburg," Paideuma, 11, #3 (Winter, 1982), 442-445.

1884 _____. "Ezra Pound and Magic: Old World Tricks in a New World Poem," Paideuma, 10, #2 (Fall, 1981), 209-224.

1885 _____. "Gerhart--with the Standebuch of Sachs in Yr/ Luggage," Paideuma, 10, #3 (Winter, 1981), 589-594.

1886 _____. "Pound and Layamon's Brut," JEGP, 68, #2 (April, 1969), 265-276.

1887 _____. "Secretary of Nature, J. Heydon," New Approaches to Ezra Pound. Eva Hesse, ed., Cf., #41, pp. 303-318.

1888 Beach, Joseph Warren. "Ezra Pound," Obsessive Images: Symbolism in Poetry of the 1930's and 1940's. Minneapolis, Minn.: Lund Pr., Inc., 1960, passim.

1889 _____. "Pound, the Imagists, Sandburg," Concept of Nature in Nineteenth-Century English Poetry. New York: Pageant Book Co., 1956, pp. 547-559.

1890 Beach, Sylvia. "Mr. and Mrs. Pound," Shakespeare and Company. London; New York: Harcourt, Brace & Co., 1959, pp. 26-27, passim.

1891 _____. "Une lettre sur Ezra Pound," Mercure, 306 (June, 1949), 379-380.

1892 Beaujour, Michel. "Pound in France," Punto de Contacto/ Point of Contact. (New York), 1, #2 (1976), 61-68.

1893 Bednář, Kamil. "Malé úvahy nad dílem Ezry Pounda," Plamen, 10, #8 (1968), 66-70. [Considering Pound's work.]

1894 Beer, J. B. "Ezra Pound," TLS, #3, 710 (April 13, 1973), 421.

1895 Bell, Ian F. A. Critic as Scientist: The Modernist Poetics of Ezra Pound. London; New York: Methuen, 1981.

1896 _____. "Divine Patterns: Louis Agassiz and American Men of Letters," JAmS, 10, #3 (December, 1976), 372-373.

1897 _____. "Pound, Emerson and 'Subject Rhyme,'" Paideuma, 8 (1979), 237-239.

1898 _____. "Pound's Vortex: Shapes Ancient and Modern," Paideuma, 10, #2 (Fall, 1981), 243-271.

1899 _____. "'Red Bloods': Pound's 'The Condolence' and William James," N&Q, 30 [228], #4 (August, 1983), 333-334.

1900 Benet, William Rose. "Poetry by the Pound," Dial, 54 (June 1, 1913), 450.

1901 _____. "Poets in Collected Editions," Cf., #1551.

1902 Bennett, Mitchell Bruce. "In Altera Persona: The Dramatic Monologue in the Poetry of Pound, Eliot and Frost," Diss. Harvard: 1967.

1903 Benton, Richard P. "A Gloss on Pound's 'Four Poems of Departure,'" LE&W, 10 (September, 1966), 292-301.

1904 Berezin, Charles. "The Quest for Disconnection in the Poetry of George Oppen," Research Studies, 48, (1980), 167-182.

1905 Berger, T. L. "Orwell as Essayist: Pound as Correspondent," Intro, I (1951), 98-100.

1906 Bergman, Herbert. "Ezra Pound and Walt Whitman," AL, 27 (March, 1955), 56-61.

1907 Bergonzi, Bernard. "From Imagism to Fascism," Cf., #451.

1908 Bernard, Mary. "A communication on Greek Metric, Ezra Pound, and Sappho," Agenda, 16 (1978), 62-68.

1909 Berri, Pietro. "Una tradizione che non si spengne," Il Mare (Rapallo, 7) (November 7, 1945), 2-3.

1910 Berryman, John. "The Poetry of Ezra Pound," Critics on Ezra Pound. E. San Juan, Jr., ed. Cf., #535, pp. 38-43.

1911 _____. "The Poetry of Ezra Pound," The Freedom of the Poet. New York: Farrar, Straus and Giroux, 1976, pp. 253-269.

1912 Bertacchini, Renato. "Saggi letterari," Lettere Italiane (genn.-marzo, 1958), pp. 106-112.

1913 _____. "Saggismo di Ezra Pound," Idea, 15 (1959), 622-628.

1914 Berti, Luigi. "Ezra Pound," Storia della letteratura americana. Milano: 1964, Vol. IV, pp. 102-127.

1915 _____. "Poesia e memetismo con Ezra Pound," Boccaporto secondo, Florence: Parenti, 1940, pp. 117-164; also in Letteratura, 4 (1940), 140-145; 5 (1941), 123-134.

1916 Bertolucci, Attilio. "Riterno di Pound," Illustrazione italiana, (sett. 1958), pp. 33-39.

1917 Betocchi, Carlo. "Ragioni mie per Pound," Stagione, 2, #7 (Rome), (1955), p. 5.

1918 Bewley, Marius. The Complex Fate. New York: Gordian Pr., 1952; 1967, pp. 166-167.

1919 _____. "Eliot, Pound, and History," Masks and Mirrors: Essays in Criticism. New York: London: Chatto & Windus, 1970, pp. 302-323.

1920 Beyer, W. H. "Contemporary Literature in Review," Sch&Soc, 74, (July 7, 1951), 8-10.

1921 Bhatnagar, I. "Rabindranath Tagore and Ezra Pound," AsSt, 12 (October 5, 1974).

1922 Bianchi, Ruggero. "Aspetti dell'estetica del primo Pound," RdE, 8 (1963), 88-108.

1923 _____. "Fenollosa, Hulme e gli Imagisti," EM, 12 (1961), 123-145.

1924 Bigongiari, Piero. "Appunti," Paragone, 72 (December, 1955), 126.

1925 _____. "Per Ezra Pound," Stagione, 2, #7 (Rome: 1955), 5-6.

1926 Bilenchi, Romano. "Rapallo, 1941," Paideuma, 8 (1979), 431-432.

1927 _____. Amici: Vittorini, Rosae, e altre incontre. Torino: Einaudi, 1976, p. 18.

1928 Bishop, John Peale. "Homage to Hemingway," NR, 89, #1145 (November 11, 1936), 39-42.

1929 _____. "Intelligence of Poets," and "Talk of Ezra Pound," Collected Essays of John Peale Bishop. Ed. with Introduction by Edmund Wilson. New York: Scribners, 1948, pp. 263-269, 327-330. See also #457.

1930 Blackburn, Paul. "Das Kennerbuch," NMQ, 23, #2 (Summer, 1953), 215-219.

1931 Blackburn, Thomas. "Ezra Pound," The Price of an Eye. London: Longmans, Green, 1961; New York: Wm. Morrow & Co., 1961, pp. 66-68.

1932 Blackmur, R. P. "An Adjunct to the Muses' Diadem: A Note on Ezra Pound," American Critical Essays: Twentieth Century. Harold L. Beaver, ed. Oxford, 1959, pp. 202-210. Cf., #459.

1933 _____. "A Critic's Job of Work," Form and Value in Modern Poetry. New York: Anchor Books, 1957, pp. 113-120.

1934 _____. "Lord Tennyson's Scissors: 1912-1950," KR, 14, #1 (Winter, 1952), 1-20.

1935 Bly, Robert. "On English and American Poetry," MFS, 5, #2 (Summer, 1959), 45-47.

1936 Bock, Layeh Aronson. "The Birth of Modernism: Des Imagistes and the Psychology of William James," DAI, 41, #2 (Stanford: 1980), 666A.

1937 Bode, Carl, ed. The New Mencken Letters. New York: Dial Pr., 1977, passim.

1938 Boensch, Maria R. "Colloqui con Ezra Pound," Borghese, (31 luglio, 1958), 181-183.

1939 Boer, Charles. Charles Olson in Connecticut. Chicago: Swallow Pr., 1975, pp. 84-87.

1940 Bogan, Louise. Achievement in American Poetry--1900-1950. Chicago: Henry Regnery Co., 1951, passim.

1941 _____. "Modernism in American Literature," Selected Criticism: Prose, Poetry. New York: Noonday, 1955, pp. 178-180.

1942 _____. "Poetry," America Now: An Inquiry into Civilization in the United States by Thirty-six Americans. Harold Edmund Stearns, ed. New York: Scribners, 1938, pp. 48-61.

1943 _____. A Poet's Alphabet: Reflections on the Literary Art and Vocation. Robert Phelps and Ruth Limmer, eds. New York: McGraw-Hill, 1970, passim.

1944 _____. "Verse," NY, 32, #28 (September 1, 1956), 32-92.

1945 Bonner, Paul Hyde. "Goodby to Good Manners," Esquire, 12 (December, 1939), 271-272.

1946 Booth, Frederick Joseph. "Ovid and Pound: Myth and Metamorphosis," DAI, 44, #12, Pt. 1 (New Jersey, New Brunswick: 1983), 3676A-77A.

1947 Booth, Marcella, and Carroll F. Terrell. "An Interlude: Creating and Sweeping Up," Paideuma, 4, #1 (Spring, 1975), 189-195.

1948 Bornstein, George. "The Last Romanticism of W. B. Yeats," Transformations of Romanticism in Yeats, Eliot, and Stevens. Chicago: U. of Chicago Pr., 1976, pp. 79-80, passim.

1949 _____. "Pound and Eliot," AmLS (1977), pp. 119-134.

1950 _____. "'What Porridge Had John Keats?' Pound's 'L'Art' and Browning's 'Popularity,'" Paideuma, 10, #2 (Fall, 1981), 303-306.

1951 _____, and Stuart Y. McDougal. "Pound and Eliot," AmLS (1978), pp. 111-126.

1952 _____, and _____. "Pound and Eliot," AmLS (1979), pp. 115-132.

1953 _____, and Hugh H. Witemeyer. "From 'Villain' to Visionary: Pound and Yeats on Villon," CL, 19, #4 (Fall, 1967), 308-320.

1954 Boselli, Mario. "Alcune osservazioni sui saggi critici di Ezra Pound," NC, Nos. 5-6 (January-June, 1956), 70-80.

1955 _____. "Some Observations on the Critical Essays of Ezra Pound," Italian Images of Ezra Pound: Twelve Critical Essays. Angela Jung and Guido Palandri, eds., and trs., Cf., #518, pp. 77-86.

1956 Bosschère, Jean de. "Ezra Pound," Egoist, 4 (January-February, April, 1917), 7-8, 27-29, 44.

1957 Bottrall, Ronald. "Ezra Pound," Adelphi, 28 (2nd Qt., 1952), 16-24.

1958 Boussard, Leon. "Ezra Pound ou le poète déraciné," Nouvelle Revue des Deux Mondes (December, 1972), 735-737.

1959 Boveri, Margaret. "Klassizist und Revolutionar--Ezra Pound," Der Verrat im 20. Jahrhundert, 1 (1956), 125-130.

1960 Bowen, Stella. Drawn from Life. London: Collins Pubs., 1941, pp. 142-143.

1961 Bowers, Frederick. "Arthur Hugh Clough: The Modern Mind," SELit, 6 (1967), 709-716.

1962 Bowra, Cecil Maurice. Poetry and Politics, 1900-1960. Cambridge: Cambridge U. Pr., 1966, p. 32.

1963 Boyers, Robert. R. P. Blackmur: Poet-Critic: Toward a View of Poetic Objects. A Literary Frontier Edition. Columbia; London: U. of Missouri Pr., 1980, pp. 82-84.

1964 Bradbrook, Muriel C. "The Roles of Pound and Quinn," T. S. Eliot: The Making of "The Wasteland," Published for The British Council by Longman Group, Ltd., 1972, pp. 26-36.

1965 Bradbury, Malcolm. "The Scenario for Modernism," NSt, 78, #2010 (September 19, 1969), 378-379.

1966 _____. The Social Context of Modern English Literature. Oxford: Basil Blackwell; New York: Schocken Bks., 1971, passim.

1967 Bradley, Edward Sculley, Richard Croom Beatty, and Ed. Hudson Long, eds. The American Tradition in Literature. Vol. 2. New York: W. W. Norton Co., 1956, pp. 881-889.

1968 Braithwaite, Willian Stanley. "Imagism: Another View," NR, 3 (June 12, 1915), 154-155.

1969 Brandabur, Edward. "Ezra Pound and Wassily Kandinsky: A Language in Form and Color," JAE, 7, #2 (1973), 91-107.

1970 Breslin, James E. "Whitman and the Early Development of William Carlos Williams," PMLA, 82 (December, 1967), 613-621.

1971 Breunig, Le Roy. "F. S. Flint, Imagism's 'Maitre d'Ecole,'" CL, 4 (Spring, 1952), 118-136.

1972 Bridgman. Richard. "Ernest Hemingway," Ernest Hemingway: Five Decades of Criticism. Linda Welshimer Wagner, ed. East Lansing: Michigan State U. Pr., 1974, pp. 162, 165-166.

1973 Bridson, D. G. "Ezra Pound," TLS, #3892 (October 15, 1976), 1306.

1974 _____. "Ezra Pound: Translater of Sophocles," Radio Times (April 25, 1954), 4.

1975 _____. "The Genius of Ezra Pound," Radio Times (August 13, 1954), 8.

1976 Brinnin, John Malcolm. The Third Rose: Gertrude Stein and Her World. Gloucester, Mass.: Peter Smith, 1968, passim.

1977 Brooker, Peter. "The Lesson of Ezra Pound: An Essay on Poetry, Literary Ideology and Politics," Ezra Pound: Tactics for Reading. Ian F. A. Bell, ed. Cf., #449, pp. 9-49.

1978 _____. A Student's Guide to the Selected Poems of Ezra Pound. Cf., #477.

1979 Brooke-Rose, Christine. "'Legt mich zu Aurelie, den Sonnenaufgang zu Stonehenge,'" Ezra Pound: 22 Versuche über einen Dichter. Eva Hesse, ed. and trans. Frankfurt: Athenaum, 1967, pp. 304-331.

1980 Brooks, Van Wyck. An Autobiography. New York: E. P. Dutton & Co., Inc., 1965, passim.

1981 _____. The Confident Years, 1885-1915. New York: E. P. Dutton & Co., 1952, pp. 513-538, passim.

1982 _____. The Opinions of Oliver Allston. New York: E. P. Dutton & Co., Inc., 1941, p. 240.

1983 _____. "Religion of Art," SatRL, 34 (December 1, 1951), 13-14, 48-52.

1984 Brown, C. "The Color Symphony before and after Gautier," CL, 5 (Fall, 1953), 289-309.

1985 Brown, John. "Larbaud et al jeune poésie amércaine," Valery Larbaud et la littérature de son temps. Actes du colloque de Vichy, 17-19, juin 1977, pp. 39-39. (Assn. Internat. des Amis de Valery Larbaud) Paris: Klincksieck, 1978.

1986 Brown, John L. "Ezra Pound, Comparatist," YCGL, 20 (1971), 37-47. Cf., Actes du VIe Congres de l'Association Internationale de Litterature Comparee/Proceedings of the 6th Congress of the International Comparative Literature Association. Michel Cadot, et al., eds. Stuttgart: Bieber, 1975, pp. 727-729.

1987 _____. "Ezra Pound and the Social Responsibility of the Artist," World Lit. Today, 51 (Spring, 1977), 233-234.

1988 Brown, Merle. "Criticism as the Animus of Poetry," Stand, 8 (1967), 45-52.

1989 Browne, Robert. "Convention in Productive Theories: Ezra Pound and T. S. Eliot," Theories of Convention in Contemporary American Criticism. Diss. Catholic U. of America, Washington, D.C., 1956, pp. 44-69.

1990 Broyard, A. [Pound and Eliot], New York Times Bk. Rev., 87 (May 30, 1982), 27.

1991 Bruce, Elizabeth Esther. Pound and Vorticism. Diss., U. of Alberta, Canada, 1968.

1992 Bruns, Gerald L. Modern Poetry and the Idea of Language. New Haven: Yale U. Pr., 1974, p. 195.

1993 Bryer, Jackson R., ed. Fifteen Modern American Authors. Cf., #1433, pp. 323-344.

1994 _____. "Joyce, 'Ulysses' and the 'Little Review,'" SAQ, 66 (Spring, 1967), 148-164.

1995 _____, ed. Sixteen Modern American Authors. Cf., #1434, pp. 445-472, passim.

1996 Bryher, [Annie Winifred Ellerman]. The Heart to Artemis: A Writer's Memoirs. London: Collins, 1963, pp. 194, 195-197, 210.

1997 Bullaro, John Joseph. "The Dantean Image of Ezra Pound, T. S. Eliot and Hart Crane," DA, 22 (Wisconsin: 1962), 4012.

1998 Bullough, Geoffrey. "The Individual and the Racial Image in Modern Poetry," Mirror of Minds: Changing Psychological Beliefs in English Poetry. London; Toronto: U. of Toronto Pr., 1962, pp. 212-213, 216.

1999 Burgess, Anthony. "The Milton Revolution," Spectator, #7244 (April 28, 1967), 487-488.

2000 Burne, Glenn S. Remy de Gourmont: His Ideas and Influence in England and America. Carbondale: So. Ill. U. Pr., 1963, passim.

2001 Bush, Douglas. "American Poets," Mythology and the Romantic Tradition in English Poetry. New York: Pageant Bk. Co., 1957, pp. 481-525.

2002 _____. Pagan Myth and Christian Tradition in English Poetry. American Philosophical Soc., Independence Square, Philadelphia, 1968, pp. 89-92, passim.

2003 Bush, Ronald. "Pound and Spengler: Another Look," Paideuma, 5, #1 (Spring, 1976), 63-65.

2004 Butor, Michel. "La Tentative Poétique d'Ezra Pound," Critique (Paris), 14 (March, 1956), 206-219; repr., in Butor's Répertoire: Etudes et Conferences 1948-1959 (1960).

2005 Butturff, Douglas R. "Ezra Pound and the Medieval Tradition," Paideuma, 4, #2&3 (Fall-Winter, 1975), 539-545.

2006 Bynner, Witter. Journey with Genius: Recollections and Reflections Concerning the D. H. Lawrences. New York: John D. Co., 1951, pp. 144-145, 194-195.

2007 Byrd, Don. "The Poetry of Production," Sagetrieb, 2, #2 (Summer-Fall, 1983), 7-43.

2008 Cady, Frank C. "The Unitary Phenomenon: The Phenomenology of Martin Heidegger and the Poetry of Ezra Pound, William Carlos Williams, and Charles Olson," DAI, 33 (Stanford: 1973), 6903A.

2009 Caesar, Terry Paul. "'Violating the Shrine': Parody Inside and Outside Literature," DAI, 40 (Washington: 1979), 3311A.

2010 Călinescu, Matei. "Conceptual Modern de poezie--modernism şi tradiţie: Ezra Pound şi 'imagismul,'" SXX, 13, #5 (1970), 8-28.

2011 _____. "După simbolism: modernism şi tradite in poetica lui Ezra Pound şi u liŭ T. S. Eliot," Conceptul Modern de Poezie. De la romantism la avangardă. Bucureşti: Editura Eminescu, 1972, pp. 141-177.

2012 Callaghan, Morley. That Summer in Paris: Memories of Tangled Friendships with Hemingway, Fitzgerald, and Some Others. New York: Coward-McCann, Inc., 1963, passim.

2013 Caloro, Bonaventura. "Chi ha paura di Ezra Pound?" FLe, 48, #25 (1972), 8-11.

2014 Cambon, Glauco. "Dante's Presence in American Literature," Dante's Craft: Studies in Language and Style. Minneapolis: U. of Minn. Pr., 1969, pp. 127-136, passim.

2015 _____. "Ezra Pound as Translator of Italian Poetry," SA, 19-20 (1976), 201-236.

2016 _____. The Inclusive Flame: Studies in Modern American Poetry. Bloomington, Indiana: U. of Indiana Pr., 1963, passim.

2017 _____. "La poesia di Pound come experienza spaziale," NC, Nos. 5-6 (genn.-giugno, 1956), 81-91; repr., in La Lotta con Proteo. Milan: 1963, pp. 245-255.

2018 _____. "Poesie di Pound scelte dal poeta, tradotte da Rizzardi, introdotte da Eliot," FLe, 15 (November 6, 1960), 5.

2019 _____. "Pound's Poetry as Spatial Experience," in Italian Images of Ezra Pound. Angela Jung and Guido Palandri, eds. & trs., Cf., #518, pp. 112-122.

2020 _____. "Sulla strada di Joyce," FLe (February 7, 1954).

2021 _____. "La Testimonianza epistolare di Pound," Aut-Aut, 33 (May, 1955), 221-230.

2022 _____. "The Waste Land as Work in Progress," Mosaic, 6, #1 (Fall, 1972), 191-200.

2023 _____. "William Carlos Williams and Ezra Pound: Two Examples of Open Poetry," CE, 22, #6 (March, 1961), 387-389.

2024 Campbell, Sue Ellen. "The Enemy Attacks: Wyndham Lewis Versus Ezra Pound," JML, 10, #2 (June, 1983), 247-256.

2025 Campos, Augusto de. "Ezra Pound aos oitenta anos," ESPSL, 30 (1965), 2.

2026 _____, and Haroldo de Campos. "Ezra Pound: a beleza e dificil," Diario de São Paulo (August 16, 1953), 8; (August 23, 1953), 8-10.

2027 Campos, Haroldo de. "Ezra Pound: La vida, texto," Plural, 50 (1975), 23-27.

2028 Capellán Gonzalo, Angel. "La obra poética de Ezra Pound," CHA (1974), 32-87.

2029 _____. "Sobre Ezra Pound," CdA, 10 (1974), 36-38.

2030 Caproni, Giorgio. "Due 'pesci d'oro': Ezra Pound e Luciano Erba," FLe, 14 (November 8, 1959), 1-2.

2031 _____. "Omaggio a Pound e a Guillén," FLe, 14 (January 11, 1959), 3.

2032 _____. "Ricordo di Pound," Stagione, 2, #7 (Rome: 1955), 6.

2033 Cargill, Oscar. "American Decadence--[Ezra Pound]," Intellectual America: Ideas on the March. New York: Macmillan, 1941, pp. 229-238, passim.

2034 Carleton, Samuel. "Trachiniae 1046-1063: Sophocles, Cicero, and Ezra Pound," Proceedings: Pacific Northwest Conference on Foreign Languages. Walter C. Kraft, ed. Twenty-third Annual Meeting, April 28-29, 1972. Corvallis: Oregon State U., 1972, pp. 19-23.

2035 Carmichael, Frank Charles, Jr. "Ezra Pound, Romanticism, and Explanation," DAI, 36 (South Carolina: 1975), 7418A-19A.

2036 Carne-Ross, D. S. "New Metres for Old: A Note on Pound's Metric," Arion, 6 (Summer, 1967), 216-232.

2037 Carruth, Hayden. "Ezra Pound and the Great Style," SatRL, 49 (April 9, 1966), 21-22, 56; excerpt: "Vision and Style," in Critics of Ezra Pound. E. San Juan, Jr., ed. Cf., 535, pp. 100-101.

2038 _____. "Here Today: A Poetry Chronicle," HudR, 24 (1971), 320-336.

2039 _____. "La poesia di Ezra Pound," Prospetti, #16 (1956), 137-166; "The Poetry of Ezra Pound," PUSA, #16 (Summer, 1956), 129-159.

2040 Carruthers, Ian, tr. "A Translation of Fifteen Pages of Ito Michio's Autobiography, Uksukushiku naru Kyoshito," CJIS, 2, #1 (1976), 32-43.

2041 Cary, Joseph. "Evangelism, Epic and Ethical," Pound Newsletter, 10 (April, 1956), 11-12.

2042 Casamayor, Enrique. "Ezra Pound, un poeta encadenado a la política de los EE.UU," CHA, 49 (January, 1954), 104-107.

2043 Casillo, Robert. "Anti-Semitism, Castration, and Usury in Ezra Pound," Criticism, 25, #3 (Summer, 1983), 239-265.

2044 Casillo, Robert Faulkner. "The Parallel Design in John Ruskin and Ezra Pound," DAI, 38 (Johns Hopkins: 1978), 6712A.

2045 Casper, Leonard. "Apprenticed in Provence," Poetry, 81 (December, 1952), 203-211.

2046 Cassell, Richard A. Ford Madox Ford: A Study of His Novels. Baltimore: Johns Hopkins Pr.; London: Oxford U. Pr., 1961, passim.

2047 _____. "A Visit with Ezra Pound," Paideuma, 8 (1979), 64-67.

2048 Castellani, Leonardo. "Ezra Pound Recitante," Il Mondo (Rome), (January 3, 1956), 12.

2049 Cenci, Lino. "Pound e la politica," FLe, 13, #3 (May 4, 1958), 3.

2050 Cerf, Bennett. "Ezra Pound and the American Poet," AmQ, 34 (March, 1972), 101-113.

2051 Chace, William M. "Ezra Pound and the Marxist Temptation," AQ, 22 (Fall, 1970), 714-725.

2052 _____. "'Make It Not So New,' The Waste Land Manuscript," SoR, 9, #1 (January, 1973), 476-480.

2053 _____. "Modern Poetry," ConL, 17 (1976), 570-590.

2054 _____. "The Political Affinities of T. S. Eliot and Ezra Pound," DA, 29, #12 (Berkeley, Calif.: 1968), 4479A-80A.

2055 _____. "Talking Back to Ezra Pound," SoR, 8 (1972), 225-233.

2056 Chakravarty, Amiya. "A Note on Pound," IJAS, 2, #2 (December, 1972), 12-14.

2057 Chapman, Robert T. Wyndham Lewis: Fictions and Satires. New York: Barnes & Noble, 1973, passim.

2058 Charlesworth, Barbara. "Pound und die Tradition des ungeteilten Lichtes," Ezra Pound: 22 Versuche über einen Dichter. Eva Hesse, ed. Cf., #1979, pp. 217-226.

2059 _____. The Tensile Light: A Study of Ezra Pound's Religion. MA Diss: Coral Gables Fla., U. of Miami, 1957.

2060 Charters, Jimmie. "The White Winers," Esquire, 2 (August, 1934), 42-43, 126.

2061 Chase, Richard. "Pound of Flesh," PR, 18, #5 (September-October, 1951), 586-590.

2062 Cherchi, Luciano. "Un appello per Ezra Pound," Conv, 24 (July-August, 1955), 503-504.

2063 Chiara, Piero. "Ezra Pound," L'Italia (Milan: March 11, 1954).

2064 Chiareno, Aldo. "Saggismo di Ezra Pound," Idea, 15 (1959), 622-631.

2065 Chiari, Joseph. T. S. Eliot: Poet and Dramatist. New York: Harper & Row, 1973, pp. 56-59, passim.

2066 Chilanti, Felice. Ezra Pound fra i sediziosi degli anni quaranta. Milan: All'insegna del pesce d'oro, 1972. Cf., #286.

2067 Chisolm, Lawrence W. Fenollosa: The Far East and American Culture. New Haven, Conn.: Yale U. Pr., 1963.

2068 Christensen, Paul. Charles Olson: Call Him Ishmael. George F. Butterick, ed. Austin, Texas: U. of Texas Pr., 1975, pp. 14-15, 75-79, passim.

2069 _____. "The New American Romances," TCL, 26 (Fall, 1980), 269-277.

2070 Chung, Ling. "Ezra Pound's Interpretation of 'cheng ming' and His Literary Theories," Kushner, Eva, and Roman Struc, eds. Actes du VIIe congrès de l'Association Intérnationale de Litterature Comparée/Proceedings of the 7th Congress of the International Comparative Literature Association, II: La Littérature comparée aujourd'hui: Théorie et pratique/ Comparative Literature Today: Theory and Practice. (Lib. of CRCL 3.) Stuttgart: Bieber, 1979, pp. 689-692.

2071 Chute, Desmond. "Poets in Paradise," Listener, 55 (January 5, 1956), 14-15.

2072 _____. "Poet's Paradise," Pound Newsletter, 8 (October, 1955), 12-14.

2073 Cianci, Giovanni. "Futurism and the English Avant-Garde: The Early Pound between Imagism and Vorticism," ArAA, 6, #1 (1981), 3-39. [Sum., 3; tr. and revision of "Futurismo e Avanguadia Inglese: il Primo Pound tra Imagismo e Vorticismo," Quarderno 9, (1979), 9-66.]

2074 Ciardi, John. "For Ezra Pound," [poem], Sou'wester (October 30, 1970), 137-138.

2075 Cimatti, Pietro. "La patria di Pound," FLe, 13 (December 7, 1958), 5.

2076 Claes, Paul. "Ezra Pound: Apologia voor 'a poet's poet,'" Streven, 26 (1973), 355-361.

2077 Clare, John. "Form in Vers Libre," English, 27 (1978), 450-470.

2078 Clark, David R. "Stretching and Yawning with Yeats and Pound," MalR, 29 (1974), 104-117.

2079 Clarkson, William Ellis. "A Rage for Order: The Development of Ezra Pound's Poetics and Politics, 1910-1945," DAI, 35, #8 (Virginia: 1974), 5391A.

2080 _____. "Ezra Pound LTD," SR, 85, #4 (Fall, 1977), 667-670.

2081 Clearfield, Andrew. "Pound, Paris, and Dada," Paideuma, 7 (Spring-Fall, 1978), 113-140.

2082 Clemons, Walter. "A Tough, Wrongheaded Genius," Newsweek, 85, #20 (November 13, 1972), 63.

2083 Coblentz, Stanton A. "Freedom Through Dictatorship," The Poetry Circus. New York: Hawthorn Bks, Inc., 1967, pp. 13-14, 45-46, 177-178, passim.

2084 Coffman, Stanley K., Jr. "Imagism: The Contribution of T. E. Hulme and Ezra Pound to English Poetry, 1908-1917," DA, 57 (Ohio State, 1948), 39-45.

2085 _____. "Imagism and Symbolism," and "Ezra Pound and Imagist Theory," Imagism: A Chapter for the History of Modern Poetry. Norman, Oklahoma: U. of Okla. pr., 1951, pp. 74-103, 120-162, passim.

2086 Cohen, J. M. "Virgin Soil," Poetry of This Age, 1908-1958. Philadelphia: Dufour Eds., 1962, pp. 210-216.

2087 Colaneri, John. "Reflection of a Man: Guido Cavalcanti," Paideuma, 1, #2 (Winter, 1972), 199-204.

2088 Cole, Thomas. "William Carlos Williams," SatRL, 32, #40 (October 1, 1949), 22.

2089 _____. "Williams and Pound Remembered," William Carlos Williams Rev, 7, #2 (Fall, 1981), 4-20.

2090 Coles, R. "Pound Speaking," NYTimes Bk. Rev, 84 (January 14, 1979), 9ff.

2091 Colinas, Antonio. "Ezra Pound: Una poética con rigor," NE, 4 (1979), 47-50.

2092 Colum, Mary M. From These Roots: The Ideas That Have Made Modern Literature. New York: Chas. Scribner's Sons, 1938, pp. 178, 338.

2093 _____. Life and the Dream. Garden City, New York: Doubleday & Co., 1947, pp. 306-308, passim.

2094 Conarroe, Joel. "'You Can't Steal Credit': The Economic Motif," William Carlos Williams' Paterson: Language and Landscape. Philadelphia: U. of Penn. Pr., 1970, pp. 117-118.

2095 Connolly, Cyril. "The Breakthrough in Modern Verse," Previous Convictions. New York: Harper & Row, 1963, pp. 235-251; Cf., #20.

2096 _____. "Ezra Pound: 1, 2, 3," The Evening Colonnade. New York: Harcourt, Brace & Jovanovich, 1975, pp. 217-221, 221-225, 226-228.

2097 _____. "Ezra Pound as Critic," Previous Convictions. Cf., #2095, pp. 255-257.

2098 Conquest, Robert. "Ezra Pound," London Magazine, 3, #1 (new series), (April, 1963), 33-49.

2099 Contini, Gianfranco. "From Dante to the Duce," TLS, #3916 (April 1, 1977), 395-396.

2100 Cook, Howard Willard. "Ezra Pound," Our Poets of Today. New York: Moffat, Yard & Co., 1919, pp. 139-142.

2101 Cook, Reginald L. "Robert Frost in Context," Frost: Centennial Essays III. Jac Tharpe, ed. Jackson: Miss U. Pr., 1978, pp. 157-162.

2102 Cookson, William. "Notes on Pound's Confucian Odes," Agenda, 20, #3-4 (Autumn-Winter, 1982-83), 61-64.

2103 Cork, Richard, ed. Vorticism and Abstract Art in the First Machine Age. Berkeley and Los Angeles: U. of Calif., 1976, 2 vols., passim.

2104 Cornevali, Emanuel. "Irritation," Poetry, 15 (January, 1920), 211-221.

2105 Coronel-Urtecho, Jose. "Ezra Pound's Case," Universidad de México (Mexico City), (February, 1957).

2106 Corrigan, Matthew. "The Poet's Intuition of Prose Fiction: Pound and Eliot on the Novel," UWR, 2, #1 (Fall, 1965), 33-51.

2107 Corrigan, Robert A. "Ezra Pound Criticism, 1904-1917: Additions and Corrections," Paideuma, 2, #1 (Spring, 1973), 115-130.

2108 _____. "The First Quarter Century of Ezra Pound Criticism" RALS, 2 (Autumn, 1972), 157-207.

2109 _____. "A Yankee in King Edward's Court: The Critical Response to Ezra Pound's Early Verse," Paideuma, 1 (Winter, 1972), 229-260.

2110 _____. "'What Thou Lovest Well Remains,' Ezra Pound and America 1940-1958," DA, 28 (Pennsylvania: 1967), 4985A.

2111 Corsini, Renato. "Ezra Pound economista," Il Secolo d'Italia (Rome: May 4, 1955); repr., "Ezra Pound, Economist: Justice the Final Goal," New Times (Melbourne: December 15, 1955), 7.

2112 Cory, Daniel. Santayana: The Later Years: A Portrait with Letters. New York: Braziller, 1963, pp. 186-188.

2113 Cowley, Malcolm. "The Art of Fiction," ParisR, 24, #84 (Summer, 1982), 53-75.

2114 _____. "Books and People," NR, 109, #1511 (November 15, 1943), 689-690.

2115 _____. "Ezra Pound," After the Genteel Tradition: American Writers Since 1910. New York: W. W. Norton & Co., 1937, passim.

2116 _____. "Laforgue in America: A Testimony," SR, 71 (January-March, 1963), 62-74.

2117 _____. "What the Poets Are Saying: 1941," Think Back on Us. Henry Dan Piper, ed. Carbondale: So. Ill. U. Pr., 1967, II, pp. 372-377.

2118 Cox, Kenneth. "Allen Upward," Agenda, 16, #3-4 (1978-79), 87-107.

2119 Craig, Cairns. "The Continuity of the Associationist Aesthetic: From Archibald Alison to T. S. Eliot (and Beyond)," DR, 60 (1980), 20-37.

2120 _____. Yeats, Eliot, Pound, and the Politics of Poetry: Richest to Richest. (Critical Essays in Modern Literature Set.) Pittsburgh, Pa.: U. of Pittsburgh, 1982.

2121 Craig, David. The Real Foundations: Literature and Social Change. New York: Oxford U. Pr., 1974, pp. 182-184, passim.

2122 Crane, Hart. The Letters of Hart Crane, 1916-1932. Brom Weber, ed. Berkeley and Los Angeles: U. of Calif. Pr., 1965, passim.

2123 Creeley, Robert. "A Note," IJAS, 2, #2 (December, 1972), 15-16.

2124 _____. "A Note on Ezra Pound," A Quick Graph:

Collected Notes and Essays. San Francisco: Four Seasons Foundation, 1970, pp. 95-98.

2125 _____. "Robert Creeley in Conversation with Charles Tomlinson," Review, #10 (January, 1964), 24-35.

2126 _____. "Why Pound!?!" Agenda, 17, #3-4; 18, #1 (Aut-Winter-Spring, 1979-80), 198-199.

2127 Crick, Bernard. "Poets and Partisans," TLS, #3821 (May 30, 1975), 586.

2128 Cronin, Anthony. "A Question of Modernity," XR, 1 (1960), 283-292.

2129 Crosman, Robert. "Do Readers Make Meaning?" The Reader in the Text: Essays on Audience and Interpretation. Susan R. Suleiman and Inge Crosman, eds. Princeton U. Pr., 1980, pp. 151-154.

2130 Crowder, Richard. "Poetry: 1900 to the 1930's," Mon/AmLS, No. 9 (1971), 277-298.

2131 Cummings, E. E. "Re Ezra Pound," We Moderns. Gothic Book Mart, 1940, p. 69.

2132 Cunard, Nancy. "The Hours Press," Book Collector, 13, #4 (Winter, 1964), 488-496.

2133 Cunha, Carlos. "Camões num ensaio de Ezra Pound," Colóquio, 22 (1963), 65-66.

2134 Cunliffe, Marcus. "Poetry and Criticism Since World War I," The Literature of the United States. Baltimore: Penguin Bks., Inc., 1955, pp. 321-326, passim.

2135 Curtui, Aurel. "Brancusi as Seen by Ezra Pound," Romanian Bulletin (New York Romanian Library), (December, 1976), p. 6.

2136 D'Agostino, Nemi. Ezra Pound. Cf., #519, pp. 315-316.

2137 _____. "La 'fin de siècle' inglese e il giovane Ezra Pound," EM, 6 (1955), 135-162.

2138 _____. "La fin de siècle francese e la poesia di Pound e Eliot," Galleria (Italy), 4 (December, 1954), 327-339.

2139 _____. "La 'poetiche della crisi' in Inghilterra," Letteratura (Florence), Nos. 11-12 (sett-dic, 1954), 29-49.

2140 Dahlberg, Edward. The Confessions of Edward Dahlberg. New York: Geo. Braziller, 1971, passim.

2141 _____. Epitaphs of Our Times: The Letters of Edward Dahlberg. New York: Geo. Braziller, 1967, pp. 96-99, 275-278, passim.

2142 Daiches, David. "Literature and Belief," A Study of Literature: For Readers and Critics. New York: Norton, 1964, pp. 212-226.

2143 _____. "War Poetry, The Imagists, Post-War Satire, The Sitwells," Poetry and the Modern World: A Study of Poetry in England Between 1900 and 1939. Chicago: U. of Chicago Pr., 1940, pp. 61-89.

2144 Dale, Peter. "Some Translations from Jules Laforgue," Agenda, 17, #3-4, and 18, #1 (Autumn-Winter-Spring, 1979-80), 86-102.

2145 Damon, S. Foster. Amy Lowell: A Chronicle. With Extracts from Her Correspondence. Boston and New York: Houghton Mifflin Co., 1935, passim.

2146 Daniels, Earl. The Art of Reading Poetry. Cf., #1531, pp. 9, 161.

2147 Danojlić, Milovan. "Poezija Ezre Paunda," LMS, 415 (1975), 639-674.

2148 Dasenbrock, Reed Way. "Dante's Hell and Pound's Paradiso: 'Tutto spezzato,'" Paideuma, 9 (1980), pp. 501-504.

2149 _____. "Literary Vorticism: Painting and the Modernist Aesthetic of Wyndham Lewis and Ezra Pound," DAI, 42, #9 (Johns Hopkins: 1982), 4005A.

2150 Davenport, Guy. "Ezra Pound," ConL, 11 (1970), 579-585.

2151 _____. "Frobenius and Pounds Sextant," Ezra Pound: 22 Versuche über einen Dichter. Eva Hesse, ed. Cf., #1979, pp. 186-202.

2152 _____. "The Nuclear Venus: Dr. Williams' Attack upon Usura," Perspective, 6, #4 (Autumn-Winter, 1953), 183-190.

2153 _____. "The Perpendicular Honeycomb: Pound, De Gourmont, Frobenius," Meanjin, 14 (December, 1955), 492-501.

2154 _____. "The Pound Vortex," NatlR, 24 (May 12, 1972), 525-526.

2155 _____. "The Real Lucifer," Paideuma, 8 (1979), 335-336.

2156 _____. "Poet's Romance," NYTBR, 15 (July 12, 1979), 33-34.

2157 Davey, Frank. "Black Days on Black Mountain," Tamarack Rev, 35 (Spring, 1965), 62-71.

2158 Davidson, Peter. "Giulio Romano at the Spring Marriage," Paideuma, 11, #3 (1982), 503-510.

2159 _____. "Heracles & m'la calata," Paideuma, 8 (1979), 413-414.

2160 Davie, Donald. "The Adventures of a Cultural Orphan," Listener, 86 (December 23, 1971), 876-877.

2161 _____. Articulate Energy: An Inquiry into the Syntax of English Poetry. London: Routledge & Kegan Paul, 1955; St. Clair Shores, Michigan: Scholarly Pr., 1971, pp. 154-158, passim.

2162 _____. Ezra Pound. London: Fontana/Collins, 1975; New York: Viking and Penguin, 1976.

2163 _____. "Ezra Pound," Modern Masters: Ezra Pound. Frank Kermode, ed. New York: Viking Pr., 1976.

2164 _____. "Ezra Pound Abandons the English," Poetry Nation, (Manchester, England), No. 4, 1975; repr., in Trying to Explain. Ann Arbor: U. of Michigan Pr., 1979, pp. 114-128.

2165 _____. "Ezra Among the Edwardians," Paideuma, 5, #1 (Spring, 1976), 3-14.

2166 _____. "Ezra Pound and the English," Paideuma, 7 (Spring/Fall, 1978), 297-307; Cf., Trying to Explain, #2164, pp. 150-164.

2167 _____. "Ezra Pound: Der Dichter als Bildhäuer," Ezra Pound: 22 Versuche über einen Dichter. Eva Hesse, Ed. Cf., #1979, pp. 267-279.

2168 _____. "Poetry and the Other Modern Arts," MQR, 7, #3 (Summer, 1968), 193-198.

2169 _____. "A Poetry of Protest," New Statesman, (February 11, 1966), 198-199.

2170 _____. "Pound and Eliot: A Distinction," Eliot in Perspective: A Symposium. Graham Martin, ed. New York: Humanities, 1970, pp. 62-82.

2171 _____. "Pound and Eliot: Eine Unterscheidung," Zur Aktualität T. S. Eliot. Helmut Viebrock and Armin Paul Frank, eds. Frankfort: Suhrkamp, 1975, pp. 118-145.

2172 _____. "Pound and 'The Exile,'" Trying to Explain, Cf., #2164, pp. 128-133.

2173 _____. "Pound and Fascism," NYRB (April 1, 1976), 32-33.

2174 _____. "Davie's Review of The Pound Era," Paideuma, 2, (1972), pp. 263-269; Cf., #732.

2175 _____. "Res and Verba in Rock-Drill and After," Paideuma, 11, (1982), 382-394.

2176 _____. "Six Notes on Pound," Trying to Explain, Cf., #2164, pp. 95-164.

2177 _____. "Two Kinds of Magnanimity," NYRB, 1975; repr., in Trying to Explain, #2164, pp. 143-149.

2178 _____. "The Universe of Ezra Pound," Paideuma, 1 (1972), 263-269; CritQ, 15 (1973), 51-57.

2179 _____. "Yeats and Pound," DublinMag., 30, #4 (October-December, 1955), 17-21.

2180 Davis, Earle. "Ezra Pound: New Emphasis on Economics," Paideuma, 2 (Winter, 1973), 473-478; Cf., Notation by Dennis R. Klinck, Paideuma, 4, #2&3 (Fall-Winter, 1975), 552-553.

2181 Davis, Gary. "Pound's 'Cino' and the Poetics of Process," ContP, 2, #1 (Spring, 1975), 28-39.

2182 Davis, Kay. "Fugue and Canto LXIII," Paideuma, 11 (1982), 15-38.

2183 _____. "Ring Composition, Subject Rhyme, and Canto VI," Paideuma, 11 (1982), 429-439.

2184 Davis, Robert G. "Pound: The Poem and the Poet," New Leader (December 11, 1950), 17-18.

2185 Day, Douglas. "The Background of the New Criticism," Jour. of Aesthetics and Art Criticism, 24, #3 (Spring, 1966), 429-440.

2186 de Bosschère, Jean. "Ezra Pound," Egoist, 4 (1917), 28.

2187 De Campos, Augusto. "Ezra Pound aos oitenta anos," ESPSL (October 30, 1965), 2.

2188 de Chasca, Edmund S. John Gould Fletcher and Imagism. London; Columbia: U. of Missouri Pr., 1978, passim.

2189 Dell, Floyd. "To a Poet," Chicago Evening Post, Literary Review (April 4, 1913), 4.

2190 Delmer, F. Sefton. "Ezra Pound," Zeitschrift für französischen und englischen Unterricht, Vol. 29 (1930), 92-110.

2191 de Mailla, Père Joseph. "Histoire Générale de la Chine," Paideuma, 5 (Spring, 1976), 100-121.

2192 Dembo. L. S. The Confucian Odes of Ezra Pound: A Critical Appraisal. Berkeley and Los Angeles: U. of California Pr., 1963.

2193 _____. "Ezra Pound: Fac Deum," Conceptions of Reality in Modern American Poetry. Berkeley and Los Angeles: U. of California Pr., 1966, pp. 151-182.

2194 Demetz, Peter. "Ezra Pound's German Studies," GR, 31, #4 (December, 1956), 279-292.

2195 de Nagy, N. Christoph. "The Place of Laforgue in Ezra Pound's Literary Criticism," Jules Laforgue: Essays on a Poet's Life and Work. Carbondale: Southern Illinois U. Pr., 1969.

2196 Denlin, Vianney M. "In Memoriam Ezra Pound," Greyfriar, 13 (1972), 42-44.

2197 Dennis, H. M. "A New Approach to the Poetry of Ezra Pound through the Medieval Provencal Aspects," DAI, 43, #4 (1982), 4286C.

2198 de Rachewiltz, Boris. L'Elemento Magico in Ezra Pound. Milano: Scheiwiller, 1965.

2199 _____. "Magische und heidnische Symbole in der Dichtung Ezra Pounds," Ezra Pound: Versuche über einen Dichtung. Eva Hesse, ed. Cf., #1979, pp. 283-301.

2200 de Rachewiltz, Mary. "Fragments of an Atmosphere," Agenda, 17, #3-4; 18, #1 (Aut-Wntr-Spr., 1979-80), 157-170.

2201 _____. "Pound and Frobenius," KompH, 2 (1980), 92-101.

2202 _____. "Tempus Loquendi," TQ, 10, #4 (Winter, 1967), 36-39.

2203 _____, and D. S. Carne-Ross. "Pound in Texas," Arion, 6 (1967), 207-232.

2204 Di Canzio, William. "Pound and the Pateresque Renaissance," DAI, 39, #4 (Johns Hopkins: 1978), 2253A.

2205 Dilworth, Thomas. "Virgil Thomson on George Antheil and Ezra Pound, A Conversation," Paideuma, 12, #2-3 (Fall-Winter, 1983), 349-356.

2206 Dodworth, Edmund. "Ezra Pound in un giudizio di Gino Saviotti," Il Mare, 26 (January 7, 1933), 3.

2207 Donath, Andreas and Hans-Christian Kirsch. "Ezra Pound: ein Proträt in Briefen," Frankfurter Hefte, 9, #5 (May, 1954), 373-379.

2208 Donati, Franco. "Un lottatore stanco," FLe, 15 (March 13, 1960), 3.

2209 Donoghue, Denis. "Ezra Pound," PR, 44, #3 (1977), 452-458. [Review of Ezra Pound by Donald Davie. New York: Viking Pr., 1977.]

2210 _____. "Mediterranean Man," PR, 44, #3 (1977), 452-457.

2211 Doolittle, Hilda. Bid Me to Live. New York: Grove Pr., 1960, passim.

2212 Dos Passos, John, et al. "Aftermath: The Question of Ezra Pound," Esquire, 48 (December, 1957), 12-20.

2213 Drew, Elizabeth. Poetry: A Modern Guide to Its Understanding and Enjoyment. New York: Norton & Co., 1959, passim.

2214 _____, in collaboration with John L. Sweeney. Directions in Modern Poetry. New York: W. W. Norton & Co., 1940, passim.

2215 Drummond, Donald F. "On Ezra Pound," Sou'wester (October 30, 1970), 130.

2216 Drummond, Roberto. "Vicissitudes Vividas por um certo James Joyce," MGSL, 18 (January, 1975), 2-3.

2217 Duberman, Martin. Black Mountain: An Exploration in Community. New York: E. P. Dutton & Co., 1972, passim.

2218 Dudek, Louis. "Lunchtime Reflections on Frank Davey's Defence of the Black Mountain Fort," TamarackRev, 36 (Summer, 1965), 58-63.

2219 _____. "Poetry as a Way of Life," EngQ, 1, #1 (June, 1968), 7-19.

2220 Duffey, Bernard I. "Ezra Pound and the Attainment of Imagism," Toward a New American Literary History. L. J. Budd, E. H. Cady, and C. L. Anderson, eds. Durham, N.C.: Duke U. Pr., 1980, pp. 181-194.

2221 _____. "The Whole Poem and the Image: Pound, Williams, and Minor Imagists," and "Values in Time: Pound, Eliot, Hart Crane," Poetry in America: Expression and Its Values in the Times of Bryant, Whitman and Pound. Durham, N.C.; Duke U. Pr., 1978, pp. 196-200, 298-305.

2222 Duncan, Robert. "The Lasting Contribution of Ezra Pound," Agenda, Special Issue in Honor of Ezra Pound's Eightieth Birthday," 4, ii (October-November, 1965), 23-26.

2223 Duncan, Ronald. "Poet's Poet," An Examination of Ezra Pound: A Collection of Essays. Peter Russell, ed. Cf., #114, pp. 154-164.

2224 _____. "Il professore di Rapallo," FLe, 46 (November 16, 1950), 4.

2225 _____. "Religio," Agenda, 4, #2 (October-November, 1965), 56.

2226 Duran, Manuel. "Ezra Pound and the Spanish-Speaking World," YLM, 126, #5 (December, 1958), 11-16.

2227 Dyson, William. "The Fluctuation of Ezra Pound," B&B, 16, #12 (September, 1971), 22-27.

2228 Eastham, Scott Thomas. "Paradise and Ezra Pound: The Poet as Psychopomp," DAI, 41, #7 (U. of Calif., Santa Barbara: 1979), 3148A.

2229 _____. Paradise and Ezra Pound: The Poet as Shaman. Lanham, MD: U. Pr. of America, 1983.

2230 Eckman, Frederick. "Imagism: The Radiant Center," Itinerary 3: Criticism. Frank Baldanza, ed. Bowling Green, OH: Bowling Green U. Pr., 1977, pp. 109-119.

2231 Eder, Doris L. Three Writers in Exile: Pound, Eliot, and Joyce. Troy, New York: Whitson Pub. Co., 1984.

2232 Edwards, Thomas R. Imagination and Power: A Study of Poetry on Public Themes. London: Chatto & Windus, 1971, pp. 185, 202.

2233 Egudu, Romanus N. "Ezra Pound in African Poetry: Christopher Okigbo," CLS, 8, #2 (June, 1971), 143-154.

2234 Ehrenpreis, Irvin. "Love, Hate, and Ezra Pound," NYRB (May 27, 1976), 6-12.

2235 Eliot, T. S. "American Literature and the American Language," SR, 74, #1 (January-March, 1966), 1-20.

2236 _____. "Clemenza per Ezra Pound: una lettera di T. S. Eliot," Il Mare, (Rapallo: October 31, 1954), 1.

2237 _____. "Disjecta Membra," Egoist, 5 (April, 1918), 55.

2238 _____. "Ezra Pound," An Examination of Ezra Pound. Peter Russell, ed., Cf., #114, pp. 25-36.

2239 _____. "Ezra Pound," Poetry, 68 (September, 1946), 326-328; repr., in New English Weekly (October 31-November 7, 1946).

2240 _____. "Ezra Pound," Ezra Pound: A Collection of Critical Essays. Walter Sutton, ed., Englewood Cliffs, NJ: Prentice-Hall, Inc., 1963, pp. 17-25.

2241 _____. "Ezra Pound nel 1945," NC, 5-6 (1956), 9-20.

2242 _____. "Five Points on Dramatic Writing," Townsman, I, #3 (July, 1938), 10.

2243 _____. "The Letters of W. B. Yeats," The Egoist, 4 (July, 1917), 89-90.

2244 _____. "Mr. T. S. Eliot's Quandaries," New English Weekly, 4 (April 12, 1934), 622-623.

2245 _____. "Mr. Eliot's Virginian Lectures," New English Weekly, 4 (March 15, 1934), 528.

2246 _____. "Omaggio a Ezra Pound," FLe, 46 (November 16, 1950), 1.

2247 _____. "On a Recent Piece of Criticism," Purpose, 10, #2 (April-June, 1938), 90-94.

2248 _____. "Studies in Contemporary Criticism II," Egoist, 5 (November-December, 1918), 131-133.

2249 _____. "The Three Provincialities," Tyro, #2 (1922), 13.

2250 Elliott, Angela. "Pound's Lucifer: A Study in the Imagery of Flight and Light," Paideuma, 12, #2-3 (Fall-Winter, 1983), 237-266.

2251 Elliott, George P. "Poet of Many Voices," Carleton Miscellany, 2, #3 (Summer, 1961), 79-103; repr., in Ezra Pound: A Critical Anthology. J. P. Sullivan, ed. Baltimore, Md.: Penguin, 1970, pp. 251-277.

2252 Ellis, Stephen Paul. "Dante in Pound's Early Career," Paideuma, 8 (1979), 549-561.

2253 Ellmann, Richard. "Gazebos and Gashouses," Eminent Domain: Yeats Among Wilde, Joyce, Pound, Eliot, and Auden. New York: Oxford U. Pr., 1967, pp. 97-126.

2254 _____. Golden Codgers: Biographical Speculations. London; New York: Oxford U. Pr., 1973, passim.

2255 _____. The Identity of Yeats. New York: Oxford U. Pr., 1954, pp. 182-183, 320-321, passim.

2256 _____. James Joyce. New York: Oxford U. Pr., 1959, passim.

2257 _____. New Approaches to Ezra Pound. Eva Hesse, ed., Cf., #41, pp. 55-85.

2258 _____. "Two Faces of Edward," Literary Criticism: Idea and Act. Ed. with Introd. by W. K. Wimsatt. Berkeley & Los Angeles: London: U. of Calif. Pr., 1974, pp. 561-575, passim.

2259 _____. Yeats: The Man and the Masks. New York: Macmillan, 1948; New York: Norton, 1978, pp. 211-214, passim.

2260 Emery, Clark. "Räude und Marasmus: Der wirtschaftpolitische Angriff," Ezra Pound: 22 Versuche über einen Dichter. Eva Hesse, ed., Cf., #1979, pp. 354-375.

2261 Engel, Bernard F. "Ezra Pound, 1885-1972," SSMLN, 3, #1 (1973), 3-4.

2262 Engel, Carl. "Poet as Prophet," Discords Mingled: Essays on Music. New York: A. A. Knopf, 1931, pp. 172-183.

2263 Engel, Ilse. "Story of a Meeting with Ezra Pound," Paideuma, 8 (1979), 257-260; YULG, 55, #4 (April, 1981), 195-198.

2264 Engelking, Leszek. "Ezra Pound in Poland," Paideuma, 11 (1982), 105-131.

2265 Enright, D. J. Conspirators and Poets. Chester Springs, Pa.: Dufour, 1966; London: Chatto & Windus, 1966, passim.

2266 Eoyang, Eugene. "The Confucian Odes: Ezra Pound's Translations of the Shih Ching," Paideuma, 3, #1 (Spring, 1974), 33-47; Actes du VII congrès de l'Association Internationale de Littérature Comparée/Proceedings of the 7th Congress of the International Comparative Literature Association, II: La Littérature comparée aujourd'hui: Théorie et pratique/Comparative Literature Today: Theory and Practice. (Lib. of CRCL 3.) Eva Kushner and Roman Struc, eds. Stuttgart: Bieber, 1979, pp. 637-644.

2267 Epstein, Jacob. Let There Be Sculpture. New York: G. P. Putnam's Sons, 1940; an extended version: Epstein: An Autobiography, 2nd ed., Introduction by Richard Buckle. London: Vista Books, 1963, pp. 44-45, 57-58.

2268 Epstein, Joseph. "The Small-eyed Poet," NR, 160 (June 7, 1969), 23-28.

2269 Eriksson, Pamela. "Pound and Imagism," UES, 15, #2 (1977), 48-51.

2270 Espey, John J. "Das Vermächtlnis von Tó Kalón," Ezra Pound: 22 Versuche über einen Dichter. Eva Hesse, ed. Cf., #1979, pp. 90-100.

2271 _____. "Ezra Pound," Fifteen Modern American Authors. Jackson R. Bryer, ed., Cf., #1433, pp. 323-344.

2272 _____. "Ezra Pound," Sixteen Modern American Authors. Jackson R. Bryer, ed., Cf., #1434, pp. 445-471.

2273 _____. "The Inheritance of To Kalon," New Approaches to Ezra Pound. Eva Hesse, ed., Cf., #41, pp. 319-330.

2274 _____. "A Note on 'Nils Lykke,'" Paideuma, 6 (Spring, 1977), 39-40.

2275 _____. "Pound as Subject," Approaches to Twentieth-Century Literature, 2 (1964), 111-124; Approaches to the Study of Twentieth Century Literature. East Lansing: Michigan State U. Pr., 1964.

2276 _____, and William Tay. "Notes and Queries," Paideuma, 4, 2-3 (Winter, 1975), 547, 549.

2277 Espmark, Kjell. "Ezra Pounds 'kejsarsnitt,' Hans roll vid redigeringen av 'The Waste Land,'" [Pound's 'Caesarean operation,'], [His role in editing 'The Waste Land,'], Tidskrift for litteratur litteraturvetenskap, 2 (1973), 225-239.

2278 Essary, Loris. "On Language and Visual Language," Visual

Literature Criticism: A New Collection. Carbondale: So. Ill. U. Pr., 1979, pp. 93-102.

2279 Evans, Oliver W. "Ezra Pound: Poet without a Country," Cw, 41 (October 20, 1944), 10-16.

2280 Everett, B. "Eliot's 'Marianne': The Waste Land and Its Poetry of Europe," RES, 31, #121 (February, 1980), 41-53.

2281 Faas, Egbert. "Formen der Bewusstseinsdarstellung in der dramatischen Lyrik Pounds und Eliots," Cf., #1368.

2282 Fabiani, Enzo. "Il signore dei monti pallidi," Gente, 6 dic, (1958), pp. 24-26.

2283 Fabri, Renata. "Un giudizio di Pound su una traduzione umanistica di Omero," Annali di Ca'Foscari, 12 (1973), 21-44.

2284 Fairchild, Hoxie N. Religious Trends in English Poetry, 1880-1920. Vol. 5, New York: Columbia U. Pr., 1962, pp. 446-456, 551-558; 1920-1965, Vol. 6, 1968, pp. 489-497, passim.

2285 Fallacara, Luigi. "Il poeta in Prigione," Stagione, 2, #7 (Rome: 1955), 6.

2286 Falqui, Enrico. "Marinetti, Pound e l'ultimissimo," FLe, 19 (1964), 1-2.

2287 Fang, Achilles. "Fenollosa and Pound," HJAS, 20 (June, 1957), 213-238.

2288 _____. "Introduction," The Confucian Odes. The Classic Anthology Defined by Confucius. (Trans. by Ezra Pound). New York: New Directions, 1959.

2289 _____. "Some Reflections on the Difficulty of Translation," Studies in Chinese Thought. Arthur F. Wright, ed. Chicago: U. of Chicago Pr., 1953, pp. 263-285, passim.

2290 Farmer, David R. Ezra Pound: An Exhibition Held in March, 1967. The Academic Center and Undergraduate Library, U. of Texas, Austin, 1967.

2291 Fauchereau, Serge. "Ezra Pound," QL, 152 (November 16, 1972), 11-12.

2292 _____. "Où Pound et Eliot recontrent Goumilev, Mandelstam et Akhmatova," Europe, 601 (1979), 57-73.

2293 _____. "La Prose d'Ezra Pound," Critique (Paris), 30 (February, 1974), 189-190.

2294 Faulkner, Peter. "Yeats, Ireland and Ezra Pound," Threshold, #18 (1963), 58-68.

2295 Feder, Lillian. "Ezra Pound: The Messianic Vision," Ancient Myth in Modern Poetry. Cf., #1369, pp. 293-307.

2296 _____. "Ezra Pound: Rebirth and Reversion," Ancient Myth in Modern Poetry. Cf., #1369, pp. 200-219.

2297 _____. "The Voice from Hades in the Poetry of Ezra Pound," MQR, 10 (Summer, 1971), 167-186.

2298 Fender, Stephen. "Works in Progress in the United Kingdom," Paideuma, 7 (Spring-Fall, 1978), 289-294.

2299 Fenton, Charles. The Apprenticeship of Ernest Hemingway. New York: Farrar, Straus & Young, 1954, p. 227.

2300 Ferkiss, Victor L. "Ezra Pound and American Fascism," Journal of Politics, 17 (May, 1955), 173-197.

2301 Ferlinghetti, Lawrence. "Pound at Spoleto," SatRL, 48, #36 (September 4, 1965), 20.

2302 Ferran, Jaime. "Ezra Pound," Estafeta Literaria, No. 507 (January 1, 1973), 10-11.

2303 Fiedler, Leslie A. The Collected Essays of Leslie Fiedler. New York: Stein & Day, 1971, Vol. II, passim.

2304 _____. An End to Innocence: Essays on Culture and Politics. Boston: Beacon Pr., 1948, 1955, passim.

2305 _____. "Lyrik ist eine sterbende Kunst: Uber den Dichter in der amerikanischen Gesellschaft," DRund, 90, #1 (January, 1964), 34-41.

2306 _____. Waiting for the End: The Crisis in American Culture. New York: Stein & Day, 1964, pp. 184-191, passim.

2307 Fields, Kenneth Wayne. "The Rhetoric of Artifice: Ezra Pound, T. S. Eliot, Wallace Stevens, Walter Conrad Arensberg, Donald Evans, Mina Loy, and Yvor Winters," DA, 28 (Stanford: 1967), 4627A.

2308 Fields, Rick. "'No Oblivion in the Orange Poppy': Ernest Fenollosa and Turn of the Century Orientalism," Zero, 4 (1980), 8-24.

2309 Figgis, Darrell. "Mr. Ezra Pound," New Age, 7 (August 18, 1910), 373-375.

2310 Filler, Louis. "Book Notes," AntiochR, 9 (December, 1949), 553-555.

2311 Finkelstein, Norman Mark. "The Utopian Invariant: Interiority and Exteriority in the Twentieth-Century Poetic Consciousness," DAI, 41, #7 (Emory, 1980), 3104A-05A.

2312 Finkelstein, Sidney. "Ezra Pound's Apologists," Mainstream, 14, #1 (January, 1961), 19-34.

2313 Firchow, P. E. "Ezra Pound's Imagism and the Tradition," CLS, 18, #4 (September, 1981), 379-385.

2314 Fischer, Walther L. "Ezra Pounds chinesische Denkstrukturen," Ezra Pound: 22 Versuche über einen Dichter. Eva Hesse, ed., #1979, pp. 167-181.

2315 Fisher, Esther Safer. "The Pound-Abercrombie Feud," FDP, 1 (1976), 66-69.

2316 Fitts, Dudley. "O dulce convivium!" Poetry, 79 (December, 1951), 150-157.

2317 _____. "The Too-Good Friend," NR, 125 (December 10, 1951), 30.

2318 Fitzgerald, Robert. "Mirroring the Commedia: An Appreciation of Laurence Binyon's Version," Paideuma, 10, #3 (Winter, 1981), 489-508.

2319 Fleming, William. "Ezra Pound and the French Language," Ezra Pound: Perspectives, Essays in Honor of His Eightieth Birthday. Noel Stock, ed., #125, pp. 129-150.

2320 _____. "How to Write Poetry, I," Meanjin, 14, #3 (Melbourne: Spring, 1955), 379-389; II, 14, #4 (Summer, 1955), 550-564.

2321 _____. "Programme for a Manifesto: Why not imagism?" Direction, 1, #2 (Melbourne: December, 1952), 34-37.

2322 Fletcher, John Gould. "'Hard' and 'Soft,'" Poetry, 12 (May, 1918), 111-112.

2323 _____. Life Is My Song: The Autobiography of John Fletcher. New York: Toronto: Farrar & Rinehart, Inc., (1937), pp. 284, passim.

2324 _____. "The Orient and Contemporary Poetry," The Asian Legacy and American Life. Arthur Christy, ed. New York: John Day, 1942, pp. 152-161, passim.

2325 Flint, F. S. "The History of Imagism," Egoist, 2, #5 (May 1, 1915), 70-71.

2326 _____. "Imagisme," Poetry, 1, #6 (March, 1913), 198-200.

2327 _____. "Letter to Robert Frost," Selected Letters of Robert Frost. New York: Holt, Rinehart & Winston, (1964), 86-87.

2328 _____. "Verse," New Age, 6 (December 9, 1909), 137-138.

2329 Flint, R. W. "Pound and the Lyric," HudR, 4, #2 (Summer, 1951), 293-304.

2330 _____. "Pound, Poetry, and Politics," Commentary, 12, #1 (July, 1951), 85-86.

2331 Flory, Wendy Stallard. "The Pound Problem," Ezra Pound and William Carlos Williams: The University of Pennsylvania Conference Papers. Daniel Hoffman, ed. Philadelphia: U. of Pennsylvania Pr., 1983, pp. 107-127.

2332 _____. "Pound's Prose Works as a Guide to His Thought," DAI, 31 (Austin, Texas: 1971), 6054A.

2333 _____ and Jo Berryman. "Report on the MLS Special Session, 1977," Paideuma, 7 (Spring-Fall, 1978), 317-324.

2334 Ford, Ford Madox. "Enter Ezra Pound ...," Your Mirror to My Times: The Selected Autobiographies and Impressions of Ford Madox Ford. Ed. with Introduction by Michael Killigrew. New York; Chicago: Holt, Rinehart & Winston, 1971, pp. 175-177.

2335 _____. New York Essays. New York: William Edwin Rudge, Inc., 1927, pp. 35-37, passim.

2336 _____. "The Poet's Eye [I-II]," New Freewoman, I, #6 (September 1, 1913), 107-110.

2337 _____. "Reviews," Return to Yesterday. New York: Liveright, 1932, pp. 373-375, passim.

2338 _____. Thus to Revisit. London: Chapman & Hall, 1921, passim.

2339 Forde, S. Victoria M. "Basil Bunting's Debt to Ezra Pound and the Classics," CML, 1 (1980), 25-37.

2340 Forgue, Guy J. Letters of H. L. Mencken: Selected and Annotated by Guy J. Forgue. New York: Alfred A. Knopf, 1961, passim.

2341 Forrest-Thomson, Veronica. "The Disconnected Image-Complex: Pound and Eliot," Poetic Artifice: A Theory of Twentieth-Century Poetry. New York: St. Martin's Press, 1978, pp. 65-80.

2342 Forsell, Lars. "Ezra Pound," Bonniers Litterära Magasin (Stockholm), 18 (October, 1949), 608-618.

2343 _____. "Rader från Rapallo," Dagens Nyheter (Stockholm), (June 2, 1953).

2344 _____. "Sider av Pound," Dagens Nyheter (Stockholm), (August 9, 1954). 2.

2345 Fraire, Isabel. "Pound and Cardenal," Review, 18 (1976), 36-42.

2346 Franciosa, Massimo. "Ezra Pound, leader di tutti," FLe, 46, #6 (November 16, 1950), 4.

2347 Franck, J. "Ezra Pound ou la recherche désespérée d'un monde des bénédictions," RGB (December, 1972), 25-34.

2348 Frankel, Haskell. "The San Francisco Beat," SatRL, 48, #36 (September 4, 1965), 20-21.

2349 Frankenberg, Lloyd. "Ezra Pound," Pleasure Dome: On Reading Modern Poetry. Boston: Houghton Mifflin Co., 1949, pp. 273-285.

2350 Fraser, George S. Ezra Pound. Edinburgh and London: Oliver & Boyd, 1960; New York: Barnes & Noble, 1960.

2351 _____. "The Last English Imagist: On Sir Herbert Read," Encounter, 28, #1 (January, 1967), 86-90.

2352 _____. The Modern Writer and His World. London: D. Verschoyle, Ltd.; New York: Criterion Books & Derek Verschoyle, 1953, passim.

2353 _____. "Poetic Politics," TSER, 2, #1 (1975), 4-7.

2354 _____. "Pound," Vision and Rhetoric: Studies in Modern Poetry. New York: Barnes & Noble, 1959, 1960, pp. 84ff.

2355 French, Warren G., ed. The Forties: Fiction, Poetry, Drama. Deland, Florida: Everett/Edwards, 1969, passim.

2356 _____. The Thirties: Fiction, Poetry, Drama. Deland, Florida: E. Edwards, 1967, pp. 123-131, passim.

2357 French, William. "For 'Gentle Graceful Dorothy,' a Tardy Obit," Paideuma, 12, #1 (Spring, 1983), 89-112.

2358 _____. "'Saint Hilda,' Mr. Pound, and Rilke's Parisian Panther at Pisa," Paideuma, 11 (1982), 79-87.

2359 _____, and Timothy Materer. "Far Flung Vortices and Ezra's 'Hindoo' Yogi," Paideuma, 11 (1982), 39-53.

2360 Friedman, Melvin J. "The Creative Writer as Polyglot." Wisconsin Academy of Sciences, Arts & Letters, 49 (1960), 229-236.

2361 Frost, Robert. "To Ezra Pound," Selected Letters of Robert Frost. Lawrance Thompson, ed. New York: Holt, Rinehart & Winston, 1964. pp. 85-86.

2362 _____. "Letter to John T. Bartlett," Cf., #2361, pp. 69-71.

2363 _____. "Letter to Thomas B. Mosher," The New Colophon, Part 8 (March, 1950), 316-317; Cf., #2361, pp. 96-97.

2364 _____. "Part of a letter dated December 14, 1932," Thomas Madigan's Autograph Album, Vol. 1 (December, 1933), 56.

2365 Froula, Christine. "Ezra Pound: Fragment, 1944," YR, 71, #2 (January, 1982), 161-174.

2366 Frye, Northrup. "Phalanx of Particulars," HudR, 4, #4 (Winter, 1952), 627-631; repr., in Northrop Frye on Culture and Literature: A Collection of Review Essays. Robert D. Denham, ed. Chicago; London: U. of Chicago Pr., 1978, pp. 197-203.

2367 Fuchs, Daniel. "Ernest Hemingway, Literary Critic," Ernest Hemingway: Five Decades of Criticism. Linda Welshimer Wagner, ed. Michigan State U. Pr., 1974, pp. 40, 44, 56n.

2368 Fukuda, Rikutaro. "Ezra Pound and the Orient: Some Oriental Figures behind Ezra Pound," TamkR, 2 (October, 1971), 61-69; EigoS, 119 (1973), 13-16; Proceedings from the International Comparative Literature Conference Held on July 18-24, 1971 at Tamkang College of Arts and Sciences, Taipei, Taiwan, Republic of China. Yen Yuan-Shu, ed. TkR, 2, #2-3, i (October, 1971-April, 1972), pp. 61-69.

2369 _____. "Japanese Elements in Western Literature," Yearbook of Comparative and General Literature, No. 11, Supplement (1962), 204-210.

2370 Fuller, Buckminster. "Pound, Synergy, and the Great Design," Agenda, 16, #iii-iv (1978-1979), 130-164.

2371 Fuller, Roy. Owls and Artificers: Oxford Lectures on Poetry. New York: The Library Pr., 1971, pp. 45, 46, 128.

2372 _____. "Philistines and Jacobins," TLS, #3495 (February 20, 1969), 183-184.

2373 _____. "Poetic Memories of the Thirties," MQR, 12, #3 (Summer, 1973), 217-231.

2374 Fussell, Edwin. "Ezra Pound: A Note on the International Theme," Pound Newsletter, 10 (April, 1956), 1-3.

2375 _____. "From Imagism to 'The Waste Land,'" VWQ, 1, #4 (1973), 58-68.

2376 Fussell, Paul. Abroad: British Literary Traveling Between the Wars. New York: Oxford U. Pr., 1980, passim.

2377 Gage, John T. In the Arresting Eye: The Rhetoric of Imagism. Baton Rouge: La. St. U. Pr., 1981, passim.

2378 _____. "Paradoxes of Objectivity and Argument in Imagist Theory," P&R, 12 (1979), 153-175.

2379 Gall, Sally M. "Domestic Monologues: The Problem of Voice in Contemporary American Poetry," MR, 23 (1982), 489-503.

2380 Gallup, Donald. "'Boobliography,' and Ezra Pound," TQ, 10, #4 (Winter, 1967), 80-92.

2381 _____. "The Search for Mrs. Wood's Program," Ezra Pound: Perspectives, Cf., #125, pp. 78-85.

2382 _____. "Some Notes on Ezra Pound and Censorship," YLM, 126 (December, 1958), 37-41.

2383 _____. "T. S. Eliot and Ezra Pound: Collaborators in Letters," AtlM, 225, #1 (January, 1970), 48-62; repr., Poetry (Australia), 32 (February, 1970), 58-80.

2384 Gardner, Helen. "The Waste Land: Paris, 1922," Eliot in His Times: Essays on the Occasion of the Fiftieth Anniversary of 'The Waste Land.' Princeton, N.J.: Princeton U. Pr., 1973, pp. 67-94.

2385 Garelick, Judith Spritzer. "Marianne Moore, Modern Poet: A Study of Miss Moore's Relationships with William Carlos Williams, E. E. Cummings, T. S. Eliot, Wallace Stevens, and Ezra Pound," Diss., Harvard U., 1972.

1386 Geisheker, Mary Rose. "Des Imagistes: Toward a Poetic Revolution," DAI, 33 (Milwaukee, Wisconsin: 1973), 3644A-45A.

2387 Geltman, Max. "The Poetry and Politics of Hate," Midstream, 22, #6 (1976), 57-68.

2388 _____. "Pound and/or Mussolini," Quadrant, 16 (November-December, 1972), 55-64.

2389 _____. "The Real Ezra Pound," Quadrant, 18 (January-February, 1974), 39-46.

2390 Gibbons, Reginald. "Pound and the Gods," Agenda, 17, #3-4, and 18, #1 (Autumn-Winter-Spring, 1979-80), 239-255.

2391 Gibson, Mary Ellis. "Browning and Pound: 'Pourquoi nier son pere?'" BSNotes, 10, ii (1980), 1-10.

2392 Gifford, Henry. "Pound, Mayakovsky and the Defence of Human Nature," PNR, 6 (1977), 15-18.

2393 Gil de Biedma, Jaime. "Postrera imagen de Ezra Pound," Plural, 18 (1973), 10-11.

2394 Gilkes, Martin. "Discovery of Ezra Pound," English, II, #8 (1938), 74-83.

2395 Ginsberg, Allen. "Encounters with Ezra Pound," Composed on the Tongue. Donald Allen, ed. Bolina, Calif.: Grey Fox Pr., 1980, pp. 1-17.

2396 Giuliani, Alfredo. "Ezra Pound e I colori della ta velezza," La Parrucca, III, #3 (Milan), (May 18, 1955), 32-33.

2397 _____. "The Metrical Recherche of Ezra Pound," [the Problem of the Lyre], Italian Images of Ezra Pound. Angela Jung and Guido Palandri, eds. Cf., #518, pp. 87-92.

2398 _____. "Le ragioni metriche di Ezra Pound (Il problema della cetra)," NC, Nos. 5-6 (genn.-giugno, 1956), 105-111.

2399 Goacher, Denis. "BBC Third Program: Ezra Pound--Translations from the Chinese," Cf., #125, pp. 210-219.

2400 _____. "Dr. Leavis or Mr. Pound," The European, #1 (March, 1953), 41-51.

2401 Godden, Richard. "Icons, Etymologies, Origins and Monkey Puzzles in the Languages of Upward and Fenollosa," Ezra Pound: Tactics for Reading. Ian F. A. Bell, ed., Cf., #449, pp. 221-244.

2402 Goekjian, Gregory F. "The Function and Effect of Rhyme," DAI, 31, #9 (Pittsburgh: 1970), 4714A.

2403 Going, William T. "A Peacock Dinner: The Homage of Pound and Yeats to Wilfrid Scawen Blunt," JML, 1, #3 (1971), 303-310.

2404 Goldman, Arnold. "Ezra Pound (1885-1972)," American Literature in Context, IV: 1900-1930. New York: London: Methuen, 1982, pp. 75-87.

2405 Goldring, Douglas. The Last Pre-Raphaelite: A Record of the Life and Writings of Ford Madox Ford. London: Macdonald & Co., Ltd., 1948, passim.

2406 _____. People and Places. Boston: Houghton Mifflin & Co., 1929, p. 264.

2407 _____. South Lodge. London: Constable & Co., Ltd., 1943, pp. 48-49, passim.

2408 _____. Trained for Genius: The Life and Writings of Ford Madox Ford. New York: E. P. Dutton & Co., Inc., 1949, passim.

2409 Goldsmith, Arnold L. "The Influence of Hulme, Richards, and Pound," American Literary Criticism: 1905-1965. Vol. III. Boston: G. K. Hall, 1979, pp. 103-104.

2410 Golffing, Francis, and Barbara Gibbs. "The Public Voice: Remarks on Poetry Today," Commentary, 28, #1 (July, 1959), 63-69.

2411 Goodwin, K. L. "Ezra Pound's Influence on Literary Criticism," MLQ, 29, #4 (December, 1968), 423-438.

2412 _____. "Some Corrections to Standard Biographies of Yeats," N&Q, 12, #5 (May, 1965), 260-262.

2413 Gordon, Ambrose, Jr. The Invisible Tent: The War Novels of Ford Madox Ford. Austin: U. of Texas Pr., 1964, pp. 29-30, passim.

2414 Gordon, David. "Academia Bulletin," Paideuma, 3 (Winter, 1974), 381-384.

2415 _____. "Ezra Pound Translating a Li Po Poem," Paideuma, 3, #1 (Spring, 1974), 55-59.

2416 _____. "From the Blue Serpent to Kati," Paideuma, 3, #2 (Fall, 1974), 239-244.

2417 _____. "Notes and Observations: The Pith of Del Mar," Paideuma, 6 (Spring, 1977), 41-42.

2418 _____. "'Root/Br./By Produce' in Pound's Confucian Ode, 166," Paideuma, 3, #1 (Spring, 1974), 13-32.

2419 Gordon, Robert. "'Old Yeats,' Young Willie, and 'this queer creature Ezra Pound,'" MJSS, 2, #1 (Summer, 1973), 68-73.

2420 Gorlier, Claudio. "Poesia e Civilta," NC, Nos. 5-6 (genn.-giugno, 1956), 112-122; "Poetry and Civilization," Italian Images of Ezra Pound, Angela Jung and Guido Palandri, eds., and trs., Cf., #518, pp. 93-101.

2421 _____. "Riflessioni su Ezra Pound," Approdo, 59-60 (1972), 51-56.

2422 Gorman, H. S. "Bolingbroke of Bards," NAR, 219 (June, 1924), 855-865.

2423 Grant, Joy. Harold Monro and the Poetry Bookshop. Berkeley and Los Angeles: U. of Calif. Pr., 1967, passim.

2424 Graves, Robert. The Common Asphodel: Collected Essays on Poetry: 1922-1949. London: H. Hamilton, 1949, passim.

2425 _____. "Dr. Syntax and Mr. Pound," The Crowning Privilege: The Clark Lectures, 1954-1955. London: Cassell & Co., c1955, pp. 212-214.

2426 _____. "Dr. Syntax and Mr. Pound," On Poetry: Collected Talks and Essays. New York: Doubleday, 1969.

2427 _____. "Letter to Editors of the Yale Literary Magazine," YLM, 127, #6 (January, 1959), 10.

2428 _____. "These Be Your Gods, O Israel!" EIC, 5 (April, 1955), 129-150; NR, 134 (February 27, 1956), 16-18; (March 5, 1956), 17-18.

2429 _____. "Working Models for Young Poets," TLS (October 29, 1954), 689.

2430 Greenbaum, Leonard. "The Hound & Horn Archive," YULG, 39, #3 (January, 1965), 137-146.

2431 Greene, Elizabeth. "Ezra Pound and Francois Villon: A Solution in Lyric Sequence," DAI, 32 (Toronto: 1969), 430A.

2432 Gregory, Horace. "The London Adventures," Amy Lowell: Portrait of the Poet in Her Time. Edinburgh; New York: Thomas Nelson & Sons, 1958, pp. 93-131.

2433 _____. "Pound's Sterling Age," NYT (July 9, 1950), 7.

2434 Griffin, Ernest. "'E. P. Ode Pour L'Election de Son Sepulchre' and Max Plowman's Pamphlet, 'The Right to Live,'" Paideuma, 5, #2 (Fall, 1976), 269-274.

2435 _____. "Pound in Perspective," TSEN, 1, #2 (1974), 13-15.

2436 Grigson, Geoffrey. "From Imagists to the Black Mountain," The Contrary View: Glimpses of Fudge and Gold. Rowman & Littlefield, 1974, pp. 221-229.

2437 Grillandi, Massimo and Lina Amgioletti. "Una poesia ardua e chiara," FLe, 48:46 (1972), 6-8.

2438 Gross, Dalton. "Ezra Pound's Early Literary Reputation: George Sterling's Dissent," Paideuma, 2, #2 (Fall, 1973), 203-204.

2439 Gross, Harvey S. "The 'Celebrated Metric' of Ezra Pound," Sound and Form in Modern Poetry: A Study of Prosody from Thomas Hardy to Robert Lowell. Ann Arbor, Mich: U. of Michigan Pr., 1964, pp. 130-168.

2440 _____. "The Contrived Corridor: A Study in Modern Poetry and the Meaning of History," DA, 15 (Michigan: 1955), 583.

2441 Grubb, Frederick. A Vision of Reality: A Study of Liberalism in Twentieth-Century Verse. London: Chatto & Windus, 1965; New York: Barnes & Noble, 1965, passim.

2442 Gugelberger, Georg M. Ezra Pound's Medievalism. (EurH, XVIII, 17). Frankfort: Lang, 1979.

2443 _____. "Medium Aevum Novum: Medieval European Literature and Ezra Pound," DAI, 33 (Iowa U.: 1972), 1724A.

2444 _____. "The Secularization of 'Love' to a Poetic Metaphor: Cavalcanti, Center of Pound's Medievalism," Paideuma, 2, #2 (Fall, 1973), 159-173.

2445 _____. "Zum Mittelaltereinfluss in der modernen Dichtung: Ezra Pounds Chaucerbild," OL, 35 (1980), 220-234.

2446 Guglielmi, Joseph E. "Pound ou la saturation livresque," CdS, 53 (July-September, 1966), 122-125.

2447 Guidacci, Margherita. "Ezra Pound," Stagione, 2, #7 (Rome: 1955), 7.

2448 _____. "Saggi, letteria di Ezra Pound," Humanitas, 4 (1975), 277-284.

2449 Guimond, James. The Art of William Carlos Williams: A Discovery and Possession of America. Urbana and Chicago: U. of Illinois Pr., 1968, passim.

2450 Gutchess, Elizabeth Denver. "Four Translators 'after' Pound: Studies of Richard Wilbur, Robert Lowell, Robert Bly and Galway Kinnell," DAI, 44, #3 (Notre Dame: 1983), 752A.

2451 Haas, Rudolf. "Ein erstes Modell: Masefields 'Cargoes' und Pounds 'melopoeia,' 'phaenopoeia,' 'logopoeia,'" Theorie und Paris der Interpretation: Modellanalysen englischer und amerikanischer Texte. (Grundlagen der Anglistik und Amerikanistik 5.) Berlin: Schmidt, pp. 68-83.

2452 Haase, Camilla Bunker. "Serious Artists: The Relationship between Ford Madox Ford and Ezra Pound," DAI, 45, #12, Part 1 (Harvard: 1984), 3635A.

2453 Haeusermann, H. W. "W. B. Yeats's Criticism of Ezra Pound," SR, 57 #3 (July-September, 1949), 437-455.

2454 Hagemann, E. R. "'Dear Folks ... Dear Ezra,' Hemingway's Early Years and Correspondence, 1917-1924," CollL, 7 (1980), 202-212.

2455 Hagenbüchle, Roland, ed. "Pound's Imagist Alba: Myth as Cognitive Method," Poetic Knowledge: Circumference and Center. Joseph Swann, ed. Bonn: 1980, n.p.

2456 Hall, Donald. "Poets Aloud," Poetry, 139, #5 (February, 1982), 297-305.

2457 _____. "The Poet's Place," Goatfoot, Milktongue Twinbird: Interviews, Essays, and Notes on Poetry, 1970-1976. Ann Arbor: U. of Michigan Pr., 1978, pp. 205, 208.

2458 _____. "Ezra Pound," Writers at Work: The Paris Review Interviews. 2nd ser. [Prepared for book publication by George Plimpton], Introduction by Van Wyck Brooks. Viking Pr., 1963, pp. 35-59.

2459 Halper, Nathan. "How Simple: A Tale of Joyce and Pound," PR, 44, #3 (1977), 438-446.

2460 Halperen, Max. "Ezra Pound: Poet-Priest, Poet-Propagandist," Warren French, ed. The Thirties: Fiction, Poetry, Drama. Cf., #2356, pp. 123-131.

2461 Hamburger, Michael. A Mug's Game: Intermittent Memoirs, 1924-1954. Cheadle: Carconet Pr., 1973, pp. 245, 247, 265.

2462 _____. The Truth of Poetry: Tensions in Modern Poetry from Baudelaire to the 1960's. New York: Harcourt, Brace & World, 1969, passim.

2463 Hamilton, Alastair. The Appeal of Fascism: A Study of Intellectuals and Fascism, 1919-1945. New York: Macmillan, 1971, passim.

2464 Hamilton, Ian. "A Conversation with Robert Lowell," MoOc, 2, #1 (Winter, 1972), 28-48.

2465 Hand, Alonzo. "Talk of the Town," New Yorker, 19 (August 14, 1943), 16-17.

2466 Hand, Claudius A. "Grow old along with me," Hamilton Alumni Review (July, 1955), 181-183.

2467 Hannah, J. M. "Ezra Pound," Manuscripts, No. 7 (Melbourne), (November, 1933), 33-40.

2468 Hansen, Miriam. Ezra Pounds frühe Poetik und Kulturkritik zwischen Aufklärung und Avantgarde. (SAVL, 16), Stuttgart: Metzler, 1979.

2469 Hargreaves, Frederic Kline, Jr. "The Concept of Private Meaning in Modern Criticism," DAI, 38, #12, Pt. I (Boston U.: 1978), 7324A.

2470 Harmer, J. B. Victory in Limbo: Imagism, 1908-1917. London: Secker & Warburg, 1975; New York: St. Martin's Pr., 1975, p. 76.

2471 Harmon, William R. "Ideas of Time in Ezra Pound's Work," DAI, 31 (Cincinnati: 1970), 3548A.

2472 Harper, Michael Frederick. "Beyond Romanticism: The Poetry of Ezra Pound," DAI, 34 (Pennsylvania: 1973), 5173A.

2473 Harris, Frank. "H. L. Mencken, Critic," Contemporary Portraits. 4th Series. New York: Brentano's Publishers, 1923, p. 149.

2474 Harris, Natalie Beth. "Aesthetics and/or Politics: Ezra Pound's Late Critical Prose," CentR, 23 (Winter, 1979), 1-19.

2475 _____. "A Map of Ezra Pound's Literary Criticism," SoR, 19 (1983), 548-572.

2476 _____. "New Pound Holdings at the Lilly Library," Paideuma, 8 (1979), 141-146.

2477 _____. "The Patterned Energy of Ezra Pound's Criticism," DAI, 38 (Indiana: 1977), 5478A.

2478 Harrison, Keith. "No Things But in Ideas: Doctor Williams and Mr. Pound," DR, 47, #4 (Winter, 1967-68), 577-580.

2479 Hart, Lawrence. "The New Face of Conformity," Works, I, #3 (Spring, 1968), 106-113.

2480 Hartman, Charles O. "Condensation: The Critical Vocabulary of Pound and Eliot," CE, 39 (October, 1977), 179-190.

2481 _____. "Some Notes on Poetic Value," ConP, 2, #3 (1977), 24-50.

2482 Hartman, Geoffrey. "The Maze of Modernism," Beyond Formalism: Literary Essays, 1958-1970. New Haven: Yale U. Pr., 1970, pp. 258ff, passim.

2483 Haruyama, Yukio. "Ezura Paundo," [Ezra Pound], Joisu Chushin no Bungaku Undo [The Joyce-Centered Literary Movement], December 15, 1933, pp. 21-50.

2484 _____. 20 Seiki Ei Bungaku Shin Undo, [New Developments in Twentieth Century English Literature], Tokyo: Daiichi Shobo, 1935.

2485 Hasbany, Richard. "The Shock of Vision: An Imagist Reading of In Our Time," Ernest Hemingway: Five Decades of Criticism. Linda Welshimer Wagner, ed. Michigan State U. Pr., 1974, pp. 224-240.

2486 Hassall, Christopher. A Biography of Edward March. New York: Harcourt, Brace & Co., 1959, p. 82.

2487 Hatlen, Burton. "Report on Work in Progress," Paideuma, 3, #2 (Fall, 1974), 275-277.

2488 _____. "Report on Work in Progress," Paideuma, 5, #3 (Winter, 1976), 469-470.

2489 Hattersley, Michael Elkins. "Poets of Light: Ezra Pound, William Carlos Williams, and Wallace Stevens," DAI, 37, #7 (Yale: 1976), 4353A.

2490 Hattum, Marinus van. "Der Pound-Text im Requiem," ABnG, 5 (1976), 103-109.

2491 Häusermann, H. W. "W. B. Yeats' Criticism of Ezra Pound," English Studies, 29, #4 (August, 1948), 97-109; SR, 57, #3 (1949), 437-455.

2492 Hayman, David. "Pound at the Wake or the Uses of a Contemporary," JJQ, 2 (Spring, 1965), 204-216.

2493 _____. "Tristan and Isolde in Finnegans Wake: A Study of the Sources and Evolution of a Theme," CL, 1, #2 (1964), 94-112.

2494 Healey, Eleanor Claire. "Ezra Pound: Poet in Rebellion," MJSS, 2, #1 (1973), 56-67.

2495 _____. "Imagist Dialogue," DAI, 29, #10 (Columbia: 1968), 3612A.

2496 Healy, J. V. "Addendum," Poetry, 68 (September, 1946), 347-349.

2497 Heap, J. "Ezra Pound's Critics," and "Pounding Ezra," The Little Review Anthology. Margaret Anderson, ed. New York: Hermitage House, Inc., 1953, pp. 211-212, 272-273.

2498 Heath-Stubbs, John. "The Last Humanist," Ezra Pound: A Collection of Essays. Peter Russell, ed. Cf., #114, pp. 249-256.

2499 _____. "Michael Alexander's The Poetic Achievement of Ezra Pound," Agenda, 17, #3-4; 18, #1 (Aut-Wntr-Spr., 1979-80), 278-280.

2500 Heinzelman, Kurt. "'Getting It' in Paterson: The Increment Defended," The Economics of the Imagination. Amherst: U. of Mass. Pr., 1980, pp. 234-275.

2501 Helmling, Steve. "A Homemade World by Hugh Kenner," Paideuma, 4, #1 (Spring, 1975), 171-173.

2502 Helwig, Werner. "Wesen, Werk und Wege des Ezra Pound," FH, 28 (1973), 49-56.

2503 Hemingway, Ernest. "Homage to Ezra," An Examination of Ezra Pound. Rev. & Enl. Peter Russell, ed. Cf., #114, pp. 73-76; This Quarter (Paris), I, 1 (Spring, 1925), 221-225.

2504 _____. "Hüldigung an Ezra," Ezra Pound: 22 Versuche über einen Dichter. Eva Hesse, ed., #1979, pp. 398-400.

2505 _____. "I sessantacinque anni di un significativo poeta, Ezra Pound," FLe, 46, #3 (November 19, 1950), 3.

2506 _____. "A Note on Ezra Pound," Ezra Pound: Perspectives. Noel Stock, ed., Cf., #125, pp. 151-153.

2507 _____. "The Soul of Spain, Part I," Der Querschmitt, (October, 1924); repr., in Sou'wester (October 30, 1970), p. 71.

2508 Henderson, Alice Corbin. Review: "Des Imagistes: An Anthology," Poetry, 5, #1 (October, 1914), 38-40.

2509 Henderson, Archibald, III. "Pound and Music: The Paris and Early Rapallo Years," DAI, 44, #1 (Los Angeles: 1983), 169A.

2510 Hendrickson, John R. "An Exchange on Pound," Poetry, 91, #3 (December, 1957), 209-211.

2511 Henn, T. R. The Lonely Tower: Studies in the Poetry of W. B. Yeats. London: Methuen & Co., Ltd., 1950, p. 97; New York: Barnes & Noble, 1965.

2512 Hesse, Eva. Ezra Pound: von Sinn und Wahnsinn. Münich: Kindler Verlag, 1978, pp. 414-415.

2513 _____. "Ezra Pounds ABC des Lesens," Dichten und Trachten, 9 (1957), 70-75.

2514 _____. "Mythopoiós," Paideuma, 8 (1979), 293-295.

2515 _____. "Pound oder der Verlangerte Konflikt," Diagonale, 5 (1967), 26-29.

2516 _____. "Schiavoni: 'That Chap on the Wood Barge,'" Paideuma, 4, #1 (Spring, 1975), 101-104; "Schiavoni: Or: When St. Hieronymus Turned His Back," Paideuma, 4, #1 (Spring, 1975), 105-110.

2517 _____. "Von der Nationalität des Dichters," Akzente, 15 (August, 1968), 354-382.

2518 _____. "The Vortex: On the Source of Pound's 'Vortex,'" Paideuma, 9 (1980), 329-331.

2519 _____ [a]; Dorothy Pound [b]; William Howell [c], "Notes and Queries/Letters to the Editor," Paideuma, 1, #2 (Winter, 1972), 271-277, 281-282.

2520 Heyen, William. "Toward the Still Point: The Imagistic Aesthetic," BSUF, 9, #1 (Winter, 1968), 44-48.

2521 Heymann, C. David. "Ezra Pound: A Portrait of the Artist as an Old Man," UDQ, 6 (Autumn, 1971), 1-12.

2522 _____. "The Pound Files," NYTB, VII (April 21, 1974), 47.

2523 Highet, Gilbert. "Homage to Ezra Pound," Nation, 154 (February 21, 1942), 228-230.

2524 Hillyer, Robert. "The Crisis in American Poetry," AmMercury, 70 (January, 1950), 65-71.

2525 _____. In Pursuit of Poetry. New York; London: McGraw-Hill Bk. Co., Ltd., 1960, pp. 187-190, 193-195, passim.

2526 Hindus, Milton. "Philip Rahv: The Critic and the Man," Images and Ideas in American Culture: The Functions of Criticism. Essays in Memory of Philip Rahv. Arthur Edelstein, ed. Hanover, New Hampshire: Pub. by Brandeis U. Pr., distributed by U. Pr. of Brandeis, New England, 1979, pp. 182-183.

2527 Hobhouse, Janet. Everybody Who Was Anybody: A Biography of Gertrude Stein. New York: G. P. Putnam's Sons, 1975, pp. 116, 125.

2528 Hobsbaum, Philip. "The Growth of English Modernism," WSCL, 6, #1 (Winter-Spring, 1965), 97-105.

2529 Hoffman, Daniel. "Old Ez and Uncle William," The Reporter, 37 (November 2, 1967), 59-63.

2530 Hoffman, Frederick John. The Imagination's New Beginning: Theology and Modern Literature. Notre Dame, Indiana; London: U. of Notre Dame Pr., 1967, passim.

2531 Hogg, Robert. "The Open Universe of Modern Poetry," Brave New Universe: Testing the Values of Science and Society. Tom Henighan, ed. Ottawa: Tecumseh: 1980, pp. 125-139.

2532 Holaday, Woon-Ping Chin. "From Ezra Pound to Maxine Hong Kingston: Expressions of Chinese Thought in American Literature," MELUS, 5, ii (1978), 15-24.

2533 _____. "Pound and Binyon: China via the British Museum," Paideuma, 6 (Spring, 1977), 27-36.

2534 Hölderlin, Friedrich. "Three Poems Translated by Richard Sieburth," Agenda, 17, #3-4; 18, #1 (Aut-Wntr-Spr., 1979-80), 118-121.

2535 Hollander, John, ed. "Ezra Pound: A Retrospect," Modern

Poetry: Essays in Criticism. London; New York: Oxford U. Pr., 1968, pp. 3-14.

2536 Holmes, John. "Pound Wise, Pound Foolish," Audience, 8, #3 (January, 1962), 109-112.

2537 Homberger, Eric. The Art of the Real: Poetry in England and America since 1939. London: Rowman & Littlefield, 1977, passim.

2538 _____. "Pound, Ford and 'Prose': The Making of a Modern Poet," JAmS, 5, #3 (December, 1971), 281-292.

2539 _____. "The Uncollected Plath," New Statesman, 84, #2166 (September 22, 1972), 404-405.

2540 Honig, Edwin. "That Mutation of Pound's," KR, 17, #3 (Summer, 1955), 349-356.

2541 Hough, Graham. "Imagism and Its Consequences," Image and Experience: Studies in a Literary Revolution. London: Duckworth, 1960; Lincoln: U. of Nebraska Pr., 1960, passim.

2542 Houserman, H. W. "W. B. Yeats' Criticism of Ezra Pound," ES, 29 (August, 1948), 97-109.

2543 Howarth, Herbert. Notes on Some Figures Behind T. S. Eliot. Boston: Houghton, Mifflin, 1964, pp. 216-222, passim.

2544 Howarth, R. G. "Ezra Pound," Southerly, 4 (Sidney: 1955), 237-238.

2545 _____. "Ezra Pound," Some Modern Writers. Australia: Extension Board of the University of Sydney, 1940, pp. [7]-31.

2546 _____. Two Modern Writers: Ezra Pound and Edith Sitwell. Cape Town: U. of Cape Town Editorial Board, 1963.

2547 Howe, Susan and Charles Ruas. "New Directions: An Interview with James Laughlin," The Art of Literary Publishing: Editors on Their Craft. Bill Henderson, ed. Yonkers, New York: Pushcart Pr., 1980, pp. 13-48.

2548 Hubbell, Jay B. "Ezra Pound," Who Are the Major American Writers? A Study of the Changing Canon. Durham, N.C.: Duke U. Pr., 1972, pp. 192-195, passim.

2549 Hubbell, L. W. "The Age of Pound," EigoS, 117 (1972), 670-673.

2550 Hubbell, Lindley. "Yeats, Pound, and Nō Drama," EWR, 1 (Spring, 1964), 70-78.

2551 Hume, Robert. "The Contribution of Ezra Pound," English, 8 (Summer, 1950), 60-65.

2552 Hummel, John. "The Provençal Translations," TQ, 10, #4 (Winter, 1967), 47-51.

2553 Hunting, Robert. "A Woodnote Wild," Paideuma, 6 (Fall, 1977), 177-179.

2554 Huntley, Carter. "The Imagistes," Poetry and Drama, I (June, 1913), 127-128.

2555 Hurtado, Gerardo César, ed. Ezra Pound. (Pensamiento de Amér. 12.) San José, Costa Rica: Ministerio de Cultura, Juventud y Deportes, 1978.

2556 Hurwitz, Harold M. "Ezra Pound and Rabindranath Tagore," AL, 36, #1 (March, 1964), 53-63.

2557 _____. "Hemingway's Tutor, Ezra Pound," MFS, 17, #4 (Winter, 1972), 469-482; Ernest Hemingway: Five Decades of Criticism. Linda Welshimer Wagner, ed. East Lansing: Michigan State U. Pr., 1974, pp. 8-21.

2558 Hutchins, Patricia. "Ezra Pound in Kensington," New World Writing. (11th Mentor Selection.) New York: New American Library of World Lit. (1957), pp. 203-213.

2559 _____. "Fifty Years of Ezra Pound," Time & Tide, 40 (May 23, 1959), 599-600.

2560 _____. James Joyce's World. London: Methuen & Co., Ltd., 1957, pp. 110-113, passim.

2561 Hynes, Samuel, ed. Introduction. Further Speculation by T. E. Hulme. Minn.: U. of Minnesota Pr., 1955; repr., Lincoln, Nebr., 1962, pp. xviiff.

2562 _____. "Some Views of the Village Explainer," SR, 69, #3 (Summer, 1961), 468-476.

2563 Ivănescu, Mircea. "'Il miglior Fabbro,'" SXX, 15, ix (1972), 38-46.

2564 Izubuchi, Hiroshi. "Kankei e no Shokushu--Pound no Giho," EigoS, 119 (1973), 5-6. [Feeling for relations--Pound's skill.]

2565 Izzo, Carlo. "Ezra Pound: 'Il miglior fabbro,'" Paragone, 280 (1973), 88-96.

2566 _____. "Ezra Pound," Storia della letteratura nord-americana. 2nd ed. Milan: Nuova accademia, 1958, pp. 584-590.

2567 Jackaman, Rob. "The Early and the Late Ezra Pound," SoRA, 12 (1979), 76-87.

2568 Jackson, Brendan. "'The Fulsomeness of her Prolixity': Reflections on H. D., 'Imagiste,'" SAQ, 83, #1 (Winter, 1984), 91-102.

2569 _____. "A Reluctant American: Pound's Response to Whitman, Whistler, and Henry James," Paideuma, 11 (1982), 326-334.

2570 Jackson, Thomas Herbert. The Early Poetry of Ezra Pound. Diss. Yale U., 1960; Harvard U. Pr., 1969.

2571 _____. "Herder, Pound, and the Concept of Expression," MLQ, 44, #4 (December, 1983), 374-393.

2572 _____. "The Poetic Politics of Ezra Pound," JML, 3 (April, 1974), 987-1011.

2573 Janssens, G. A. M. The American Literary Review: A Critical History, 1920-1950. Paris: The Hague-Mouton, 1968, passim.

2574 _____. "Perspectives on Pound," DQR, 3 (1973), 11-17.

2575 Jarrell, Randall. "Fifty Years of American Poetry." PrairieSch, 37, #1 (Spring, 1963), 1-27.

2576 Jeffares, Alexander Norman. W. B. Yeats: Man and Poet. London: Routledge & Kegan Paul, Ltd., 1949, pp. 176-177, passim.

2577 Jenkins, Alan. "Strange Correspondences: On Ezra Pound," Encounter, 58, #1 (January, 1982), 40-49.

2578 Jennings, Elizabeth. "Idea and Expression in Emily Dickinson, Marianne Moore and Ezra Pound," AmP, 31 (1965), 97-113; American Poetry. Ervin Ehrenpreis, ed. New York: St. Martin's Pr., 1965.

2579 Johnson, Carol. "The Translator as Poet," ArtInt, 16, #8 (October, 1972), 129-121.

2580 Johnson, Geoffrey. "English Poetry Today," LHY, 6, #1 (January, 1965), 30-35.

2581 Johnson, Scott. "The 'Tools' of the Ideogramic Method," Paideuma, 10, #3 (Winter, 1981), 525-532.

2582 Jones, A. R. "Notes Toward a History of History of Imagism: An Examination of Literary Sources," SAQ, 60 (Summer, 1961), 262-285.

2583 Jones, Dan Lewis. "The Poetics of Ezra Pound and T. S. Eliot," DAI, 34 (Utah: 1973), 777A.

2584 Jones, David. "Extract from a Letter to Father Desmond Chute," Agenda, 17, #3-4; 18, #1 (Aut-Wntr-Spr., 1979-80), 273-277.

2585 Joost, Nicholas. Ernest Hemingway and 'The Little Magazines': The Paris Years. Barre, Mass.: Barre Pubs., 1968, passim.

2586 _____. "Ezra Pound and The Dial--And a Few Translations," Sou'wester, Special Ezra Pound No., (October 30, 1970), 59-71.

2587 _____, and Alvin Sullivan. D. H. Lawrence and 'The Dial', Carbondale and Edwardsville: So. Ill. U. Pr., 1970, passim.

2588 Jordan, Barbara Scott. "Viola Jordan and Ezra Pound: Some Notes on Their Friendship," YULG, 51, #2 (1976), 98-103.

2589 Joseph, Terri Brint. "'Near Perigord': A Perplexity of Voices," Paideuma, 11 (1982), 93-98.

2590 Joyce, James. "Letter on Pound," Critical Writings of James Joyce. Ellsworth Mason and Richard Ellmann, eds. New York: Viking Pr., 1959, pp. 253-254.

2591 _____. "Letter to Ernest Walsh," This Quarter. Paris, I, i (Spring, 1925), 219.

2592 _____. The Letters of James Joyce. Stuart Gilbert, ed. New York: The Viking Pr., Ltd., 1957, pp. 23-24, passim.

2593 Juhasz, Suzanne H. "Patterns of Metaphor: Their Function in Some Modern Long Poems--Studies in Williams, Pound, Stevens, and Eliot," DAI, 32 (Calif., Berkeley: 1971), 920-21A.

2594 _____. "Williams, Pound, Stevens, and the Imagist Movement," Cf., #724, pp. 13-39.

2595 Jung, Angela Chih-ying. "Ezra Pound and China," DA, 15 (Seattle, U. of Washington: 1955), 2208-09. Ann Arbor, Univ. of Microfilms, 1955.

2596 _____, and Guido Palandri. "Uncle Ez," IQ, 64 (1973), 23-29.

2597 Junkins, Donald. "Mountain Interval: A Visit with Robert Frost in Ripton, Vermont," IndianLit (New Delhi), III (September, 1960), 30-37. [Frost's reminiscences of Pound.]

2598 Just, Klaus G. "Zur amerikanischen Literaturkritik: Ezra Pound und R. P. Blackmur," Merkur, 10 (December, 1956), 1230-1233.

2599 Kanaseki, Hisao. "Pound to Modernism--Passionate Simplicity," EigoS, 119 (1973), 7-8.

2600 Kappel, Andrew J. "Ezra Pound in Heaven," HudR, 35, #1 (Spring, 1982), 73-86.

2601 _____. "Ezra Pound, Thomas Carter, and the Making of an American Literary Magazine," Shenandoah, 31, #3 (1980), 3-22.

2602 _____. "Perception's Champion: The Affirmation and Refinement of Value in the Poetry of Ezra Pound," DAI, 39, #3 (Rice U.: 1978), 1550A.

2603 _____. "The Reading and Writing of a Modern Paradiso: Ezra Pound and the Books of Paradise," TCL, 27, #3 (Fall, 1981), 223-246.

2604 Karpinski, Joanne B. "Poetics and Polemics: Strategies of Ezra Pound and Vladimir Mayakovsky," DAI, 41, #8 (U. of Colorado at Boulder: 1980), 3566A.

2605 Kayman, Martin A. "A Contest for Hart's 'Complex': A Contribution to a Study of Pound and Science," Paideuma, 12, #2-3 (Fall-Winter, 1983), 223-235.

2606 _____. "Ezra Pound and the Phantasy of Science: An Investigation into the Relation Between Pound's Poetic Techniques and His Political Ideology, through the Image and Its Scientific Background," DAI, 39, #3119C.

2607 _____. "Report on the Ezra Pound Conference Held at the

University of Keele, September 20-23, 1976," Paideuma, 5, #3 (1976), 461-467.

2608 Kazin, Alfred. "Language as History: Ezra Pound's Search for the Authority of History," The Problem of Authority in America, Mark E. Kann, ed. Philadelphia: Temple U. Pr., 1981, pp. 113-125.

2609 _____. "The Writer as Political Crazy," Playboy, 20 (1973), pp. 207-8, 136, 206-9.

2610 Keller, David Michael. "Ezra Pound and Guido Cavalcanti: The Poetics of Translation," DAI, 35, #5 (Wisconsin: 1974), 2993A-94A.

2611 Kelly, Robert G. "The Premises of Disorganization: A Study of Literary Form in Ezra Pound, T. S. Eliot, James Joyce, and Dorothy Richardson," Diss. (Stanford: 1952), pp. 226-228.

2612 Kempf, Roger. "James Job Joyce," CritP, 24, #251 (April, 1968), 368-379.

2613 Kennedy, George. "Fenollosa, Pound, and the Chinese Character," YLM, 126 (December, 1958), 24-36.

2614 Kenner, Hugh. The Art of Poetry. New York: Holt, Rinehart & Winston, 1959.

2615 _____. "'As of Wings and of Water,'" Poetry, 85 (December, 1954), 159-165.

2616 _____. "Baker Street to Eccles Street: The Odyssey of a Myth," HudR, 1, #4 (Winter, 1949), 483.

2617 _____. Bucky: A Guided Tour of Buckminster Fuller. New York: Morrow, 1973, pp. 83-84, 152-153, passim.

2618 _____. "Dante tra Pound ed Eliot," Verri, #18 (1964), 35-40.

2619 _____. Review: Dichtung und Prosa of Ezra Pound, Trans. by Eva Hesse, Die Tat, #304 (Zurich: November 7, 1953), 11; and in Poetry, 83, #6 (March, 1954), 357-366.

2620 _____. "Douglas," Sou'wester (So. Ill. U.), Special Ezra Pound Number (Fall, 1970), 6-20.

2621 _____. "An Exchange on Ezra Pound," Poetry, 91, #3 (December, 1957), 210-221.

2622 _____. "Ezra Pound, RIP," NatlRev, 24, #43 (November 24, 1972), 1289.

2623 _____. "Ezra Pound and Chinese," Agenda, Special Issue in Honor of Ezra Pound's Eightieth Birthday, 4, #2 (October-November, 1965), 38-41.

2624 _____. "Ezra Pound and the Light of France," YFS, 10 (1953), 54-64; repr., and "Faces to the Wall," Gnomon: Essays on Contemporary Literature. New York: McDowell, Obolensky, 1958, pp. 80-100; 263-279.

2625 _____. "Ezra Pound and Provision of Measures," Poetry, 83, #1 (October, 1953), 29-35.

2626 _____. "Ezra Pound und das Geld," NDH, 114 (1967), 22-40.

2627 _____. "Ezra Pound und das Licht der Aufklarung," Ezra Pound: 22 Versuche über einen Dichter. Eva Hesse, ed., Cf., #2504, pp. 149-162.

2628 _____. "Faces to the Wall," Shenandoah, 6, #1 (Winter, 1954), 39-51.

2629 _____. "The Five Laws and Che Funge," Paideuma, I, #1 (Spring-Summer, 1972), 83-85.

2630 _____. "From a Lost World," NatlR, 20 (February 27, 1968), 195-197.

2631 _____. "Ghosts and Benedictions," Poetry, 113, #2 (November, 1968), 109-121.

2632 _____. A Homemade World: The American Modernist Writers. New York: Alfred A. Knopf, 1975, pp. 3-6, 8-12, passim.

2633 _____. "Horizontal Chords," Sumac, 2 (Winter-Spring, 1970), 227.

2634 _____. "The Invention of China," Spectrum, 9, #1 (Spring, 1967), 21-54.

2635 _____. "Leucothea's Bikini: Mimetic Homage," Ezra Pound: Perspectives in Honor of His Eightieth Birthday. Noel Stock, ed. Cf., #125, pp. 25-40.

2636 _____. "The Magic of Place: Ezra Pound," IQ, 16, #64 (1973), 5-10.

2637 _____. "MAO[4] or Presumption," Shen, 21, #3 (Spring, 1970), 84-93.

2638 _____. "The Muse in Tatters," Agenda, 6, #2 (Summer, 1968), 212-233; also in Arion, 7 (1968), 212-233.

2639 _____. "A Note on CX/778," Paideuma, 8 (1979), 51-52.

2640 _____. "The Persistent Past," Spectrum, 10 (Spring, 1969), 5-13.

2641 _____. "The Poetics of Error," TkR, 6, #2-7, #1 (1975-76), 89-98.

2642 _____. "Poets at the Blackboard," YR, 71 (Winter, 1982), 173-184.

2643 _____. "The Possum in the Cave," Allegory and Representation. Stephen Jay Greenblatt, ed. Johns Hopkins U. Pr., (Selected Papers from the English Institute [1979-1980], New Series, #5.)

2644 _____. "Pound and Around," Review, 3 (1981), 25-44.

2645 _____. "Pound on Joyce," Shenandoah, 3, #3 (Autumn, 1952), 3-8.

2646 _____. "The Rope in the Knot," KyR, 2, #3 (1968), 10-29.

2647 _____. "To the Editor of Poetry," Poetry, 91, #3 (December, 1957), 210-211; [Reply to John R. Hendrickson, Poetry, 91, #3 (1957), 209-210.]

2648 _____, ed. Introduction by Hugh Kenner. The Translations of Ezra Pound. London: Faber; New York: 1953. Review: NR, 130 (January 4, 1954), 18-19.

2649 _____. Ulysses. London; Boston: Geo. Allen & Unwin, 1980, pp. 2, 169, 170.

2650 Kent, Jay. "Der Fall Ezra Pound," Wort und Wahrheit (Vienna), VII, (1952), 880-882.

2651 Kereaski, Rodica. "Incercare de caracterizare a criticii lui Ezra Pound," AUB-LG, 22 (1973), 93-104.

2652 Kermode, Frank. "The New Apocalyptists," PR, 33, #3 (Summer, 1966), 339-361.

2653 _____. The Romantic Image. New York; London: Macmillan, 1957, passim.

2654 Ketchiff, David. "William James and/or Ezra Pound: Perceptions of Reality," DAI, 39 (North Carolina, Chapel Hill: 1978), 6757A.

2655 Kidney, Jennifer. "An American Prelude: Nostalgia and the Sense of Death in American Poetry," DAI, 36 (Yale: 1974), 275A.

2656 Kimpel, Ben D., and T. C. Duncan Eaves. "Ezra Pound on Hitler's Economic Policies," AL, 55, #1 (March, 1983), 48-54.

2657 _____, and _____. "Ezra Pound's Anti-Semitism," SAQ, 81, #1 (Winter, 1982), 56-69.

2658 _____, and _____. "Ezra Pound's Use of Sources as Illustrated by His Use of Nineteenth-Century French History," MP, 80 (August, 1982), 35-52.

2659 _____, and _____. "Herbert Hoover and the London Judge," Paideuma, 9 (1980), 505-507.

2660 _____, and _____. "The Intentional-Fallacy Fallacy and Related Contemporary Orthodoxies," SAQ, 83, #1 (Winter, 1984), 103-113.

2661 _____, and _____. "Note on 'e li mestriers ecoutes,'" Paideuma, 9 (1980), 311-312.

2662 _____, and _____. "Pound and Pumpelly," ELN, 17 (June, 1980), 293-294.

2663 King, Michael John. "An ABC of Ezra Pound's Library," LCUT, 17 (1981), 30-45.

2664 _____. "'Go, Little Book': Ezra Pound, Hilda Doolittle and 'Hilda's Book,'" Paideuma, 10, #2 (Fall, 1981), 347-360.

2665 Kirk, Russell. Eliot and His Age: T. S. Eliot's Moral Imagination in the Twentieth Century. New York: Random House, 1971, passim.

2666 _____. "Personality and Medium in Eliot and Pound," SR, 82 (Fall, 1974), 698-705.

2667 Kirstein, Lincoln. "Ezra Pound and the Visual Arts," NYTBR, 28 (April 20, 1982), 18.

2668 Klarman, Adolf D. "The Age of Abstraction in Modern European Literature," Four Quarters, 14, #4 (May, 1965), 19-29.

2669 Klein, Marcus. Foreigners: The Making of American

Literature, 1900-1940. Chicago: U. of Chicago Pr., 1981, passim.

2670 Klinck, Dennis R. "Pound, Social Credit, and the Critics," Paideuma, 5, #2 (Fall, 1976), 227-240.

2671 _____. "Pound's 'Economist Consulted of Nations,'" Paideuma, 5, #1 (Spring, 1976), 67-68.

2672 _____. "Pound's 'Gods': The Many and the One," SoRA, 11 (1978), 296-315.

2673 Knapp, James F. Ezra Pound. Boston: Twayne, 1979.

2674 Knoerle, Sister Jeanne. "Ezra Pound and the Literature of China," TamkR, 4, #1 (1973), 53-62.

2675 Kobayashi, Manji. "Marie Stopes to Pound," EigoS, 123 (1977), 397-399.

2676 Kodama, Jitsuei. "Pound no Naso to Fenollosa MSS no Hakken," EigoS, 115 (1969), 234-237.

2677 Kodama, Sanehide. "The Chinese Subject in Ezra Pound's Poetry," SELit, [Eng. No.], No. 37-62 (1970).

2678 _____. "Cosmopolitanism in Ezra Pound," Doshisha Women's College of Liberal Arts. Annual Reports of Studies. Vol. 24. Kyoto: Doshisha Women's College, 1973, pp. 125-137.

2679 _____. "Dappi no Itami--Shoki Shihen o megutte," EigoS, 119 (1973), 11-12.

2680 _____. "Ezra Pound," America Bungaku no Jiko Keisei: 20 seiki America Bungaku I. Toshihiko, Agata, ed. Kyoto: Yamaguchi, 1981, pp. 337-382.

2681 _____. "Persona, Pound, His Poetry," Doshisha Literature, (Kyoto), 22 (January, 1962), 9-19.

2682 _____. "The Road to Cathay: Ezra Pound's Experiments in Translation," AnRS, 28 (1977), 201-229.

2683 Kodoma, Sanchiko. "Swords and Aether: A Study on the Management of Tone in the Poetry of Ezra Pound," Gakujutsu Kenkyu Nempo, No. 11 (December, 1960), 47-58.

2684 Koehler, Stanley. "The Art of Poetry, VI," ParisR, 8, #32 (Summer-Fall, 1964), 111-51.

2685 Köhring, Klaus H. "The American Epic," SHR, 5, #3 (Summer, 1971), 265-280.

2686 Kojecky, Roger. T. S. Eliot's Social Criticism. London: Faber & Faber, 1971; New York: Farrar, Straus & Giroux, 1971, passim.

2687 Korg, Jacob. "Hulme and Pound," Language in Modern Literature Innovation and Experiment. New York: Barnes & Noble; Sussex: The Harvester Pr., 1979, pp. 84-92.

2688 _____. "T. S. Eliot," CLit, 13, #4, (Autumn, 1972), 535-540.

2689 Korn, Marianne. Ezra Pound: Purpose/ Form/ Meaning. London: Pembridge Pr., publ. for Middlesex Polytechnic Pr., 1983.

2690 _____. "Truth Near Perigord," Paideuma, 10, #3 (Winter, 1981), 571-579.

2691 Kostelanetz, Richard. "Reactions and Alternatives: Post-World War II American Poetry," Chelsea, 26 (May, 1969), 7-34.

2692 Kramer, Jane. "Paterfamilias--I," NY, 44, #26 (August 17, 1968), 32-73.

2693 Kreymborg, Alfred. "E. P.," The Little World, 1914 and After. New York: Coward-McCann, Inc., 1932, p. 141.

2694 _____. A History of American Poetry: Our Singing Strength. New York: Tudor Pub. Co., 1934, pp. 294-296, 333-347, passim.

2695 _____. Troubadour: An Autobiography. New York: Liveright, Inc., 1925, pp. 369-370.

2696 Kriegel, Leonard. "Poetry and Politics," PR, 42 (1975), 287-290.

2697 Kroll, Ernest. "With Ezra Pound before Rapallo," CimR, 2 (1973), 7-17.

2698 Kuberski, Philip. "Ezra Pound and the Calculations of Interest," NOR, 10, #2-3 (Summer-Fall, 1983), 69-74.

2699 Kumashiro, Sobu. Ezra Pound to T. S. Eliot. Tokyo: Hokuseido, 1970.

2700 Kunitz, Stanley J., and Howard Haycraft. "Ezra Pound," Twentieth Century Authors. New York: H. W. Wilson Co., 1942, pp. 1121-1123.

2701 Kwan-Terry, John. "Ezra Pound and the Invention of China," TkR, 10 (1979), 127-144.

2702 _____. "The Prosodic Theories of Ezra Pound," PLL, 9, #1 (Winter, 1973), 48-64.

2703 Laing, Alexander. "The Nation and Its Poets," Nation, 201, #8 (September 20, 1965), 212-218.

2704 Lander, Jeannette. Ezra Pound. New York: Ungar Pub. Co., 1971.

2705 Langbaum, Robert. "Ezra Pound's Dramatic Monologues," The Poetry of Experience. New York: Random House, 1957; repr., in Critics on Ezra Pound. E. San Juan, Jr., ed. Coral Gables, Fla.: U. of Miami Pr., 1972, pp. 47-48.

2706 _____. The Modern Spirit: Essays on the Continuity of Nineteenth and Twentieth Century Literature. New York: Oxford U. Pr., 1970, passim.

2707 _____. The Mysteries of Identity: A Theme in Modern Literature. New York: Oxford U. Pr., 1977, passim.

2708 Languasco, Nardo. "L'attésa di Pound," FLe, 47 (November 20, 1955), 6.

2709 _____. "Ezra Pound non scrive più versi," FLe, 8 (October 4, 1953), 5.

2710 Langumier, Eric. "Scarabs and Gold," Paideuma, 8 (1979), 57.

2711 Lattès, Jean-Claude. "Les silences d'Ezra Pound," NL (November 11, 1965), 3.

2712 Laughlin, James. "Gists and Piths: From the Letters of Pound and Williams," Poetry, 139, #4 (January, 1982), 229-244.

2713 _____. "A Portrait of Ezra Pound," UR, 6, #2 (December, 1939), 111-119.

2714 _____. "Pound the Teacher: The Ezuversity," StAR, 1, #1 (Fall-Winter, 1970), 17-18.

2715 _____. "Pound's Prose," New Democracy, 5 (December 1, 1935), 120.

2716 Laurie, Peter Hamilton. "Peacocks in Kore's House: A Note on Pound's Alchemy," Paideuma, 9 (1980), 333-337.

2717 _____. "The Poet and the Mysteries: Pound's Eleusis," DAI, 37 (Brown Univ.: 1975), 309A.

2718 Lawrence, D. H. The Letters of D. H. Lawrence. James T. Boulton, ed. New York; London: Cambridge U. Pr., 1979, passim.

2719 _____. D. H. Lawrence: A Composite Biography. Edward Nehls, ed. Madison: Wisconsin U. Pr., 1957-59, passim.

2720 Layton, Irving. "Shaw, Pound and Poetry," CIV/n, 7 (Montreal), 19-20.

2721 Leavis, Frank Raymond. "The Americanness in American Literature," Commentary, 14 (November, 1952), 466-474.

2722 _____. "Eliot and Pound," TLS, #3574 (August 28, 1970), 950; #3576 (September 11, 1970), 998.

2723 _____. "Ezra Pound: The Promise and the Disaster," PR, 18, #6 (November-December, 1951), 727-733; also in The Partisan Review Anthology. William Phillips and Philip Rahv, eds. New York: Holt, Rinehart & Winston, 1962, pp. 440-443.

2724 Le Breton, Eileen. "Ezra Pound," TLS, #3891 (October 8, 1976), 1280.

2725 Lechlitner, Ruth. "The Poetry of William Carlos Williams," Poetry, 54, #6 (September, 1939), 326-335.

2726 Ledbetter, Jack Tracy. "Modern Poetry and the American Idiom," Cresset, 32, #3 (January, 1969), 8-10.

2727 Lee, Pen-Ti, and Donald Murray. "The Quality of Cathay: Ezra Pound's Early Translations of Chinese Poems," LE&W, 10 (September, 1966), 264-277.

2728 Lehmann, John, ed. The Craft of Letters in England: A Symposium. London: Cresset, 1956; Boston: Houghton Mifflin Co., 1957.

2729 Lemaire, Marcel. "Some Recent American Novels and Essays," RLV, 28 (1962), 70-78.

2730 Lensing, George S. "Review: Ezra Pound: An Introduction to the Poetry by Sister Bernetta Quinn," Paideuma, 2 (1973), 327-329. Cf., #876.

2731 Leonello, Claudio. "Pound e la Cina," Galleria, 26 (1976), 17-21.

2732 Lesemann, Maurice. "Mr. Pound and the Younger Generation," Poetry, 30, #4 (July, 1927), 216-222.

2733 Levenson, Harry Michael. "A Genealogy of Modernism: Constituents of a Literary Doctrine, 1908-1922," DAI, 41, #8 (Stanford, 1980), 3573A.

2734 Levertov, Denise. "Grass Seed and Cherry Stones," AntigR, 8 (Winter, 1972), 29-33; repr., in The Poet in the World. New Directions, 1973, pp. 249-253.

2735 Levi, Albert W. "Three," [Poetics of Stevens, Pound, and T. S. Eliot], The Hidden Harmony: Essays in Honor of Philip Wheelwright. Oliver Johnson, David Harrah, Peter Fuss, and Theodore Guleserian, eds. New York: Odyssey, 1966, pp. 73-91.

2736 Levin, Gail. "Wassily Kandinsky and the American Literary Avant-Garde," Criticism, 21 (1979), 347-361. [Influence on Stein, Pound, and Williams].

2737 Levin, Harry. "Ezra Pound, T. S. Eliot, and the European Horizon," first presented as the Taylorian Special Lecture, 1974, at Oxford University; republished as pamphlet by Clarendon Pr., 1975; and in Memories of the Moderns. New York: New Directions, 1980, pp. 13-34.

2738 _____. "Ezra Pound, T. S. Eliot, and the Idea of Comparative Literature," Actes du VIIe congres de l'Association Internationale de Litterature Comparee/Proceedings of the 7th Congress of the International Comparative Literature Association. Milan V. Dimic, and Juan Ferrate, eds. (Lib. of CRCL 2.) Stuttgart: Bieber, 1979, pp. 545-552.

2739 _____. Grounds for Comparison. Cambridge, Mass.: Harvard U. Pr., 1972, pp. 280-282, 297, passim.

2740 _____. "Literature and Exile," Listener, 62 (1959), 613-617.

2741 _____. "Unfrocked Professor," YR, 43, #4 (Summer, 1954), 602-604.

2742 Levy, Alan. "Ezra Pound's Voice of Silence," NYTMS (January 9, 1972), 14-15, 59, 61-65, 68; Pub.: Ezra Pound: The Voice of Silence. Sag Harbor, NY: Permanent Pr., 1983.

2743 Lewis, John S. "Ezra Pound," TLS, (July 14, 1961), 433.

2744 Lewis, Roger. "Most Friendship Is Feigning," EIC, 34, #2 (April, 1984), 169-175.

2745 Lewis, Wyndham. "Early London Environment," T. S. Eliot: A Symposium from Conrad Aiken and Others. Richard March and M. J. Tambimuttu, eds. Chicago: Regnery, 1949, pp. 24-32.

2746 _____. "First Meeting with Ezra Pound," Blasting and Bombardiering. London: Eyre & Spottiswoode, 1937; Berkeley and Los Angeles: U. of Calif. Pr., 1967, pp. 271-281.

2747 _____. "To Ezra Pound," The Letters of Wyndham Lewis. W. K. Rose, ed. Norfolk, Conn.: New Directions, 1963, passim.

2748 Linati, Carlo. "Eliot e Pound," Letteratura (Florence), #7 (genn.-febb, 1954), 60-61.

2749 _____. "Ezra Pound," Scrittori anglo-americani d'oggi, Milan: Corticelli, 1944, pp. 87-98.

2750 Lindberg, Kathryne Victoria. "Reading, Writing, and Rhetoric: Nietzschean Traces in the Later Criticism of Ezra Pound," DAI, 45, #5 (Victoria: 1984), 1395A.

2751 Lindberg-Seyersted, Brita, ed., with Introduction, Commentary, and Notes. Pound/Ford: The Story of a Literary Friendship. Norfolk, Conn.: New Directions, 1982.

2752 Lindstrom, Naomi. "Ezra Pound: Creation and Play in Critical Discourse," BRMMLA, 35, #4 (1981), 291-303.

2753 Link, Franz H. "Mythos und Image in der frühen Dichtung Ezra Pounds," LJGG, 20 (1979), 209-260.

2754 _____. "Pound's 'A Girl' and Ovid's Metamorphoses, I, 547-555," Paideuma, 8 (1979), 409-410.

2755 Lipke, William C., and Bernard W. Rogran. "Ezra Pound and Vorticism: A Polite Blast," WSCL, 7 (Summer, 1966), 201-210.

2756 _____, and Walton Litz, eds. Modern Literary Criticism: 1900-1970. New York: Atheneum, 1972, passim.

2757 Lipman, Samuel. "Forms and Decorations," TLS, #3967 (April 14, 1978), 415-416.

2758 Lippincott, Henry F., Jr. "Pound, Richard Lattimore and Odyssey IX," Sou'wester (So. Ill. U.), Ezra Pound Birthday Issue (October 30, 1970), 36-45.

2759 Little, Matthew. "Corrections to Gallup's Pound and Some History of Pound's Essays on the Jefferson-Adams Letters," BSAP, 74, #3 (1980), 270-272.

2760 _____. "Pound and ylh: Bishop Carame's Translation of Avicenna as Background," Paideuma, 12, #1 (Spring, 1983), 33-40.

2761 _____. "Pound's Use of the Word Totalitarian," Paideuma, 11, #1 (Spring-Summer, 1982), 147-156.

2762 Litz, A. Walton. "Literary Criticism," Harvard Guide to Contemporary American Writing. Daniel Hoffman, ed. Cambridge, Mass., and London: Harvard U. Pr., 1979, pp. 79-80.

2763 _____. "Pound and Eliot on Ulysses: The Critical Tradition," JJQ, 10 (1972), 5-18; repr., Germanistische Streifzuge. Gert Mellbourn, et al., eds. Stockholm: Almqvist & Wiksell, 1974, pp. 5-18; Ulysses: Fifty Years. Thomas F. Staley, ed. Bloomington: Indiana U. Pr., 1974, pp. 5-18.

2764 Llona, Victor. "With Ezra Pound before Rapallo," CimR, 22 (1973), 7-17.

2765 Lloyd, Margaret Glynne. William Carlos Williams' Paterson: A Critical Appraisal. Rutherford and Madison, N.J.: Fairleigh Dickinson U. Pr., 1980, pp. 35-36, 39-41, passim.

2766 Logu, Pietro de. "Ezra Pound," Il Messaggero (Rome: July 19, 1954).

2767 Lombardo, Agostino. "Ezra Pound: The Last Decadent," Lo Spettatore Italiano, 8 (1955), 471-475; Realismo e simbolismo: saggi di letteratura americana contemporanea. Rome: Edizioni di storia e letteratura, 1957, pp. 75-84; Italian Images of Ezra Pound: Twelve Critical Essays. Angela Jung and Guido Palandri, eds. #518, pp. 16-25.

2768 _____. "Introduction," SR, 68, #3 (July-September, 1960), 353-374.

2769 _____. La poesia inglese dali estetismo al simbolismo. Roma: 1950, passim.

2770 Lopez, Enrique Hank. Conversations with Katherine Anne Porter: Refugee from Indian Creek. Boston: Little, Brown & Co., 1981, pp. 132-133, 268-269, passim.

2771 Lowell, Amy. A Fable for Critics. Boston; New York: Houghton Mifflin Co., 1922; repr., A Critical Fable. New York: AMS Pr., 1981, passim.

2772 _____. "The Imagists: 'H. D.' and John Gould Fletcher," Tendencies in Modern American Poetry. Boston; New York: 1917, 236, 251-254.

2773 Lowell, Robert. "Ezra Pound," [Poem], History. New York: Farrar, Straus & Giroux, 1973, p. 140; also in Notebook: 1967-1968, passim, p. 71.

2774 Luckett, Richard. "'Meaning Motion': Old Music and Some Modern Writers," E&S, 30 (1977), 88-97.

2775 Ludwig, Richard M. "Ezra Pound's London Years," Aspects of American Poetry: Essays Presented to Howard Mumford Jones. Richard Milton, ed. Columbus: Ohio U. Pr., 1962, pp. 99-119; Modern American Poetry: Essays in Criticism. Guy Owen, ed. Deland, Florida: Everett/Edwards, 1972, pp. 81-97.

2776 Lund, Mary Graham. "The Eliotian Cult of Impersonality," TexQt, 9 (Spring, 1966), 164-167.

2777 Lunkvist, Arthur. "Ezra Pound," Morgen-Tidningen (Stockholm), (October 17, 1953).

2778 MacAfee, Norman. "'I am a free man': Pasolini's Poetry in America," IQ, 21-22 (Fall-Winter, 1982-83), 99-105.

2779 McAfee, Thomas. "On Reading an Anthology of 'Most of the Boys Who Have ...,'" Sou'wester (October 30, 1970), p. 131.

2780 McAlister, Floyd L. "Milton and the Anti-Academics," JEGP, 61, #4 (October, 1962), 779-787.

2781 McCarthy, Dermot. Social Theory and Criticism of Ezra Pound. Diss., Queen's University, Kingston, Ontario, 1974-1975.

2782 Maccoby, Hyam. "The Jew as Anti-Artist: The Anti-Semitism of Ezra Pound," Midstream, 22, #3 (1976), 59-71.

2783 McCormick, John. "Poets," The Middle Distance: A Comparative History of American Imaginative Literature: 1919-1932. New York: Free Pr., 1971, 111-161.

2784 McCuaig, Ronald. "Ezra Pound," Bulletin (N.Y.P.L.), 72, #2 (April, 1951), 2.

2785 McDougal, Stuart Y. Ezra Pound and the Troubadour Tradition. London; Princeton, N.J.: Princeton U. Pr., 1972.

2786 _____. "A Parnassian in Provence: Ezra Pound and the Troubadour Tradition," DAI, 31, #10 (Pennsylvania: 1970), 5415A.

2787 MacDougall, Allan Ross. "Orpheus in Paris: Ida Rubenstein,

Ezra Pound and Much Gaiety," Arts and Decoration, 25 (October, 1926), 69, 98, 114.

2788 McFarland, Ronald E. "A Note on Monsieur Verog," Paideuma, 11 (1982), 446-448.

2789 McInnes, Marion Kaighn. "'The Discontinuous Gods' in the Poetry of Ezra Pound," DAI, 45, #4 (Yale: 1984), 1115A-1116A.

2790 MacKendrick, Louis K. "T. S. Eliot and the Egoist: The Critical Preparation," DR, 55 (1975), 140-154.

2791 McKeown, Thomas Wilson. "Ezra Pound's Early Experiments with Major Forms, 1904-1925," DAI, 44, #5 (U. of British Columbia: Canada, 1983), 1454A.

2792 Macksey, R. A. "The Old Poets," Johns Hopkins Mag, 19 (1968), 42-48.

2793 McLachian, W. I. "Translation and Critical Judgment: A Comparative Study of Ezra Pound and Gavin Douglas," DilR, 14, #2 (April, 1966), 166-191.

2794 MacLeish, Archibald. "Archibald MacLeish: Selected Letters," ParisR, 24, #84 (Summer, 1982), 104-144.

2795 _____. "In Praise of Dissent," NYTBR, 61, #51 (December 16, 1956), 5.

2796 _____. "The Most Compelling Acts of Love to Touch My Life," Today's Health, 51 (February, 1973), 40.

2797 _____. Poetry and Experience. Cambridge: Riverside Pr., 1961, passim.

2798 _____. "Poetry and the Public World," AtlM, 163 (1939), 829-830.

2799 _____. "Public Speech and Private Speech in Poetry," A Time to Speak. Boston: Houghton Mifflin Co., 1941, pp. 59-69.

2800 _____. "There Was Something about the Twenties," SatRL, 49 (December 31, 1966), 10-13.

2801 _____. "The Venetian Grave," SatRWorld, I, ii (February 9, 1974), 26, 28-29; repr., in Riders on the Earth: Essays and Recollections. Boston: Houghton Mifflin, 1978, pp. 115-122.

2802 _____. "Why Can't They Say What They Mean?" A Continuing Journey. Boston: Houghton Mifflin, 1968, pp. 194-195, passim.

2803 McLuhan, Marshall. "Pound, Eliot, and the Rhetoric of The Waste Land," NLH, 10 (Spring, 1979), 557-580.

2804 _____. "Pound's Critical Prose," An Examination of Ezra Pound: A Collection of Essays. Peter Russell, ed., Cf., # 114, pp. 165-171; also in The Interior Landscape: The Literary Criticism of Marshall McLuhan, 1943-1962. (Selected, Compiled and edited by Eugene McNamara.) New York: McGraw-Hill, 1969, pp. 75-81.

2805 MacShane, Frank. "The English Review," SAQ, 60 (Summer, 1961), 311-320.

2806 _____. The Life and Work of Ford Madox Ford. New York: Horizon Pr., 1965, passim.

2807 MacSween, R. J. "Yeats and His Language," AntigR, 14 (Summer, 1973), 17-24.

2808 McVeagh, John. Tradeful Merchants: The Portrayal of the Capitalist in Literature. Boston: Routledge & Kegan Paul, 1981, passim.

2809 Makin, Peter. "The American Poet, Ezra Pound, and Mediaeval Provençal Poetry," Diss. (London U.: 1972).

2810 _____. "Ezra Pound and Scotus Erigena," CLS, 10, #1 (March, 1973), 60-83.

2811 _____. "Ezra Pound's Abilities as a Translator of Provençal," Poetica (Tokyo), 4 (Autumn, 1975), 111-132.

2812 _____. "Kennedy, Fenollosa, Pound and the Chinese Character," Agenda, 17, #3-4; 18, #1 (Autumn-Winter-Spring, 1980), 220-237.

2813 _____. "Pound's Provence and the Medieval Paideuma: An Essay in Aesthetics," Ezra Pound: The London Years: 1908-1920. Philip Grover, ed. Cf., #52, pp. 31-60.

2814 _____. Provence and Pound. Berkeley and Los Angeles, U. of Calif. Pr., 1978.

2815 Malanga, Gerard. "Interview of Charles Olson," ParisR, 49 (Summer, 1970), 177-204.

2816 Malof, Joseph Fetler. "Ez Pound, Inc.," Ezra Pound: Perspectives.... Noel Stock, ed., Cf., #125, pp. 204-206.

2817 Mancuso, Girolamo. Pound e la Cina. Milan: Feltrinelli, 1974.

2818 Manganaris-Decavalles, Andonis. "Ezra Pound and the Mediterranean World," DA, 21 (Northwestern: 1961), 3770.

2819 Manganiello, Dominic. "Dante Among the Moderns," Selecta, 1 (1980), 15-18.

2820 Margolis, John D. T. S. Eliot's Intellectual Development: 1922-1939. London; Chicago: U. of Chicago Pr., 1972, pp. 197-198, passim.

2821 Mariani, Paul. "Two Essays on Ezra Pound," MassR, 14 (Winter, 1973), 118-129.

2822 Marin Morales, José A. "Radiografía epistolar: Joyce-Pound," Arbor, 318 (1972), 93-98.

2823 Mariorana, M. T., and M. C. Rezzano de Martini. "Un poema de Ezra Pound," Sur, #242 (1956), 22-30.

2824 Marschall, Hiltrud, et al. "Biographische Zeittafel," Ezra Pound: 22 Versuche über einen Dichter. Cf., #503, pp. 427-434.

2825 Marsh, Edward. A Number of People. London: W. Heinemann, Ltd.-H. Hamilton, Ltd., 1939, p. 82.

2826 Martin, Loy Davis. "The Literary Style of Robert Browning and Ezra Pound," DAI, 35, #5 (Virginia: 1974), 2947A.

2827 _____. "Pound and Fenollosa: The Problem of Influence," CritQ, 20, #1 (Spring, 1978), 48-60.

2828 Martin, Wallace. "Freud and Imagism," N&Q, 8, #12 (December, 1961), 470-471, 474.

2829 _____. "The Literary Significance of The New Age under the Editorship of A. R. Orage, 1907-1922," Diss., University of London, 1961.

2830 _____. The New Age under Orage: Chapters in English Cultural History. New York: Manchester U. Pr.; Barnes & Noble, Inc., 1967, pp. 151-154, passim.

2831 _____. "The Sources of the Imagist Aesthetic," PMLA, 85 (March, 1970), 196-204.

2832 Martz, Louis L. The Poem of the Mind: Essays on Poetry, English and American. New York: Oxford U. Pr., 1966, pp. 143-146, 147-153, passim.

2833 Materer, Timothy. "Doppelganger: Ezra Pound in His Letters," Paideuma, 11, #2 (1983), 241-256.

2834 _____. "The English Vortex: Modern Literature and the 'Pattern on Hope,'" JML, 3 (July, 1974), 1123-1139.

2835 _____. "Pound's Vortex," Paideuma, 6, #2 (Fall, 1977), 175-176.

2836 _____. "The Value of a Pound," Cw, 96 (July 28, 1972), 409-410.

2837 _____. Vortex: Pound, Eliot, and Lewis. London; Ithaca: Cornell U. Pr., 1979, passim.

2838 Matthiessen, F. O. The Achievement of T. S. Eliot. Boston; New York: Oxford U. Pr., 1935, passim.

2839 _____. "American Poetry, 1920-40," SR, 55, #1 (1947), 24-55.

2840 _____. American Renaissance. Art and Expression in the Age of Emerson and Whitman. New York: Oxford U. Pr., 1941, passim.

2841 Matz, C. A. "Menotti and Pound," OperaN, 30 (November 20, 1965), 14-15.

2842 Maxwell-Mahon, W. D. "Ezra Pound: Critical and Creative Influences," UES, 15, #2 (1977), 8-14.

2843 May, Henry F. The End of American Innocence: A Study of the First Years of Our Own Time, 1912-1917. New York: Alfred A. Knopf, 1959, pp. 269-277, passim.

2844 Mazzaro, Jerome. "Fusions," FarP, #5 (Winter-Spring, 1971), 70-73.

2845 _____. "The Legacy of Modernism," Salmagundi, Nos. 31-32 (Fall, 1975-Winter, 1976), pp. 303-308.

2846 _____, ed. Modern American Poetry: Essays in Criticism. New York: McKay, 1970, passim.

2847 _____. Postmodern American Poetry. Urbana: U. of Ill. Pr., 1980, passim.

2848 Mei, Francesco. "Il mito di Ezra Pound," FLe, 17 (November 12, 1962), 5.

2849 Meixner, John A. Ford Madox Ford's Novels: A Critical Study. Minneapolis: U. of Minn. Pr., 1962, passim.

2850 Melchiori, Giorgio. The Tightrope Walkers: Studies of Mannerism in Modern English Literature. New York: Macmillan, 1936; London: Routledge & Kegan Paul, 1956, pp. 176-177, passim.

2851 Mellow, James R. Charmed Circle: Gertrude Stein and Company. New York: Praeger Pubs., Inc., 1974, passim.

2852 Melote Castro, E. M. "Ezra Pound: Da obra," Coloquio, 11 (1973), 51-53.

2853 Mendes, Murilo. "Cocteau, Jouve, Pound," Coloquio, 12 (1973), 18-24.

2854 Menides, Laura Jehn. "The Use of the Past in Modern American Poetry: Eliot, Pound, Williams, Crane, Berryman, Olson, Lowell," DAI, 39, #6 (New York U.: 1978), 3583A.

2855 Merchant, W. Moelwyn. "Agenda," YLM, 126, #5 (December, 1958), 3-9.

2856 _____. "Ezra Pound," CritQ, 1 (Winter, 1959), 277-287.

2857 Meyer, G. P. "The Sage of Rapallo," SatRL, 33 (December 2, 1950), 24-25.

2858 Meyer, Peter. Die Finanz und wirtschaftspolitische Auffassung Ezra Pounds und ihre Bedeutung für seine Dichtung. Diss. Freiburg, [1959?].

2859 Meyerson, Edward L. The Seed Is Man: A Collection of Poetry and an Essay on Ezra Pound. New York: William-Frederick Pr., 1967, pp. 33-54.

2860 Michaels, Walter B. "Pound and Erigena," Paideuma, I, #1 (Spring and Summer, 1972), 37-54.

2861 Michelena, Margarita. "Breve nota sobre Pound y la epopeya," El Libro y el Pueblo, III (April-September, 1960), 75-77.

2862 Michelson, Max. "The Independents," Poetry, 8 (May, 1916), 94-96.

2863 Middleton, Christopher. "Documents on Imagism from the Papers of F. S. Flint," Review: A Magazine of Poetry and Criticism, 15 (April, 1965), 35-51.

2864 Miller, James E., Karl Shapireo, and Bernice Slote. Start with the Sun: Studies in Cosmic Poetry. Lincoln: Nebraska U. Pr., 1960, pp. 207-225, passim.

2865 Miller, Liam. "W. B. Yeats and Stage Design at the Abbey Theatre," MalR, #16 (October, 1970), 50-84.

2866 Miller, Vincent. "Eliot's Submission to Time," SR, 84 (Summer, 1976), 448-464.

2867 Mills, Ralph J., Jr. Cry of the Human: Essays on Contemporary American Poetry. Urbana; Chicago: U. of Ill. Pr., 1975, passim.

2868 Milner, Philip. "Life at All Its Points: An Interview with Robert Creeley," AntigR, #26 (Summer, 1976), 37-47.

2869 Miner, Earl. "Pound, Haiku, and the Image," HudR, 9 (Winter, 1956-57), 570-584.

2870 _____. "Pound's Debt to Japan," PoundN, #6 (April, 1955), 13-15.

2871 _____. "Vom Image zum Ideogram," Ezra Pound: 22 Versuche über einen Dichter. Eva Hesse, ed. Cf., #1979, pp. 104-124.

2872 Miyake, Akiko. "Ezra Pound's Vorticism," SEL, 52 (December, 1975), 49-66.

2873 _____. "A Note on So-shu," Paideuma, 6 (Winter, 1977), 325-328.

2874 _____. "Pound and Confucianism," St. AndrewsRev (Special Pound Issue), I, i (Fall-Winter, 1970), 45-47.

2875 Molesworth, Charles. "Frightful Fashions and Compulsive Occasions," Salmagundi, 50-51 (1980-81), 322-339.

2876 _____. The Fierce Embrace: A Study of Contemporary American Poetry. Columbia: U. of Missouri Pr., 1979, passim.

2877 Monk, Donald. "Pound: A Divergent Influence," CritQ, 25, #3 (Autumn, 1983), 29-34.

2878 Monro, Harold. Some Contemporary Poets. London: Leonard Parsons, 1920, pp. 87-93.

2879 Monroe, Harriet. "Ezra Pound," The New Poetry. New York: Macmillan, 1932, pp. 744-746.

2880 _____. "Miss Monroe re Ezra Pound," EJ, 20, #1 (January, 1931), 86-87.

2881 _____. "Notes and Announcements," Poetry, 1, #1 (October, 1912), 31; 1, #2 (November, 1912), 64.

2882 _____. "Some Imagist Poets--An Anthology," Poetry, 6, #3 (June, 1915), 150-153.

2883 Montale, Eugenio. "Se i biglietti da mille fossero quelli di Ezra Pound," Corriere d'informazione (Milan), (November 18-19, 1955). 3.

2884 _____. "Selva," Corriere della sera (Milan), Genn. 9, (1952), 3.

2885 _____. "The Second Life of Art," and "Voluntary Exile in Italy," The Second Life of Art: Selected Essays. Ed. & Trans. by Jonathan Gallassi. New York: Ecco Pr., 1982, pp. 203-208, 283-285.

2886 Montgomery, Marion. "Beyond Pound's Quarrel with Eliot's Text," GaR, 2 (1972), 415-425.

2887 _____. "Eliot and 'Il Miglior Fabbro,'" SCR, 6, i (November, 1973), 7-13.

2888 _____. "Eliot and the Particle Physicist: The Merging of Two Cultures," SoR, 10, #3 (July, 1974), 583-589.

2889 _____. Ezra Pound. (CWCP). Grand Rapids: Mich.: 1970.

2890 _____. "Ezra Pound's Angry Love Affair with America," JPC, 2 (Winter, 1968), 361-369.

2891 _____. "Ezra Pound's Arrogance," Sou'wester (So. Ill. U.), (Special Ezra Pound No.), (October 30, 1970), 46-54.

2892 _____. "Ezra Pound's Problems with Penelope," SHR, 3, #2 (Spring, 1969), 114-123.

2893 Moody, A. D. "Broken Images/Voices Singing," CamQ, 6 (1973), 45-56.

2894 Moore, Marianne. "Ezra Pound," QRL, 5, #2 (1949), 146.

2895 _____. "Marianne Moore on Ezra Pound, 1905-1915," MMN, 3, #2 (1979), 5-8.

2896 _____. "Teach, Stir the Mind, Afford Enjoyment," Ezra Pound: A Collection of Criticism. Grace Shulman, ed. Cf., #1084, pp. 39-44.

2897 _____. "The Ways Our Poets Have Taken in Fifteen Years Since the War," NY Herald Tribune Bk. Rev., (June 26, 1960), pp. 1, 11.

2898 Moramarco, Fred S. Edward Dahlberg. New York: Twayne Pub., Inc., 1972, passim.

2899 Morgan, Edwin. "Provenance and Problematics of 'Sublime and Alarming Images' in Poetry," PBA, 63 (1977), 293-313.

2900 Morgan, Frederick. "A Note on Ezra Pound," HudR, 4 (Spring, 1951), 156-160.

2901 Morrison, Blake. The Movement: English Poetry and Fiction of the 1950's. New York: Oxford U. Pr., 1980, passim.

2902 Motsch, Monika. Ezra Pound und China. Heidelberg: Winter, 1976.

2903 Mottram, Eric. "Pound, Merleau-Ponty and the Phenomenology of Poetry," Ezra Pound: Tactics for Reading. Ian F. A. Bell, ed. Cf., #449, pp. 121-147.

2904 _____. "Sixties American Poetry, Poetics and Poetic Movements," American Literature Since 1900. Marcus Cunliffe, ed. London: Barrie & Jenkins, 1975, pp. 271-311.

2905 Movius, Geoffrey H. "Caviar and Bread: Ezra Pound and William Carlos Williams, 1902-1914," JML, 5 (September, 1976), 383-406.

2906 Mowrer, Deane. "The Cracked Mirror and the Brazen Bull," NMQ, 20 #2 (Summer, 1950), 233-247.

2907 Munsi, Pradeep. "Prastutiparve Ejra Paund," Uttarasuri, 24 (1976-1977), 237-250.

2908 Munson, Gorham B. Robert Frost: A Study in Sensibility and Good Taste. New York: George H. Doran & Co., 1927; Haskell House, Pubs., 1967, passim.

2909 Murray, David. "Pound-signs: Money and Representation in Ezra Pound," Ezra Pound: Tactics for Reading. Ian F. A. Bell, ed., Cf., #449, pp. 50-78.

2910 Myake, Akiko. "Contemplation East and West: A Defense of Fenollosa's Language and Its Influence on Ezra Pound," Paideuma, 10, #3 (Winter, 1981), 533-570.

2911 Namjoshi, Suniti. "Ezra Pound and the Hex Hoax," AntigR, 23 (1975), 65-83.

2912 Nänny, Max. "Ezra Pound and the Menippean Tradition," Paideuma, 11 (1982), 395-405.

2913 _____. "Ezra Pounds letzte Texte," NZZ (November, 1976), 41.

2914 _____. "Ezra Pound's Visual Poetry and the Method of Science," ES, 43 (Autumn, 1962), 426-430.

2915 _____. "The Oral Roots of Ezra Pound's Methods of Quotation and Abbreviation," Paideuma, 8 (Winter, 1979), 381-387.

2916 Nathan, Leonard. "The Private 'I' in Contemporary Poetry," Shen, 22, #4 (Summer, 1971), 80-99.

2917 Nelson, F. William. "The Waste Land Manuscript," Wichita State U. Bulletin. University Studies #86, Vol. XLVII (February, 1971), #1, passim.

2918 Niikura, Shunichi. "Pound to Eliot--Arechi-teki naru mono," EigoS, 119 (1973), 9-10.

2919 Niikura, Toshikazu. "The American Identity of Ezra Pound," American Literature in the 1950's. Annual Report, 1976 (Tokyo Chap.,) American Lit. Soc. of Japan, pp. 105-110.

2920 Nims, Bruce Gladden. "Life-Powered Poetry: The Narration of Perception Processes in the Early Poetry of Ezra Pound and Wallace Stevens," DAI, 38 (Florida: 1977), 6717A.

2921 Nist, John. "Ezra Pound: Young Poets, Beware!" Approach, 38 (Winter, 1961), 5-9.

2922 Nolde, John J. "The Literary Revolutions of Hu Shih and Ezra Pound," Paideuma, 9 (Fall, 1980), 235-248.

2923 Nolte, William H., ed. "Ezra Pound," H. L. Mencken's Smart Set. Sel., and ed. by Wm. H. Nolte. Ithaca, New York: Cornell U. Pr., 1968, pp. 76-78, passim.

2924 North, Michael. "The Architecture of Memory: Pound and the Tempio Malatestiano," AL, 55, #3 (October, 1983), 366-387.

2925 Oakes, Randy Wayne. "The Discovery of Myth: Joyce, Pound, and Eliot, 1918-1923," DAI, 43, #6 (Georgia: 1982), 1969A.

2926 Oberg, Arthur. Modern American Lyric: Lowell, Berryman, Creeley, and Plath. New Brunswick, New Jersey: Rutgers U. Pr., 1978, passim.

2927 O'Connor, William Van. An Age of Criticism (1900-1950). Chicago: H. Regnery Co., 1952, pp. 68-69.

2928 _____. Sense and Sensibility in Modern Poetry. Chicago: U. of Chicago Pr., 1948, passim.

2929 Oderman, Kevin M. "'Calvalcanti': That the Body Is Not Evil," Paideuma, 11 (1982), 257-279.

2930 _____. "The Servants of Amor in Pound's Early Poems," Paideuma, 8 (1979), 389-403.

2931 Odlin, Reno. "Kati and Antef," Paideuma, 6 (1977), 181-182.

2932 O'Grady, Desmond. "Versions from Greek," Agenda, 17, #3-4; 18, #1 (Aut-Wntr-Spr., 1979-80), 187-192.

2933 [Olson, Charles]. "The Art of Poetry XII: Charles Olson," ParisRev, 13, #49 (Summer, 1970), 177-204.

2934 Oppenheim, Lois. "An Inheritance of Poetic Referentiality," CLS, 20, #3 (Fall, 1983), 329-345.

2935 Orsini, G. N. G. "Ezra Pound, critico letterario," Letterature moderne, VII (1957), 34-51.

2936 _____. "Ezra Pound and Italian Literature (1957)," SR, 68, #3 (July-September, 1960), 465-472.

2937 Orsini, Napoleone. "Ezra Pound, critico letterario," Letterature moderne, 7 (January-February, 1957), 34-51.

2938 Otto, Lon Jules. "Medieval Prosody and Four Modern Poets: The Accentual Poetry of Hopkins, Hardy, Pound, and Auden," DAI, 35, #7 (Indiana: 1974), 4447A.

2939 Owen, Guy, ed. Modern American Poetry: Essays in Criticism. Deland, Fla.: Everett/Edwards, 1972, pp. 254-255.

2940 Pack, Robert. "The Georgians, Imagism and Ezra Pound: A Study in Revolution," ArQ, 12 (Autumn, 1956), 250-265.

2941 Paden, William D., Jr. "Pound's Use of Troubadour Manuscripts," CompLit, 32 (Fall, 1980), 402-412.

2942 Paechter, Heinz. "Verrat der Intellektuellen?" Wirtschafts-Seitung (Stuttgart), 4, #41 (1949), 15.

2943 Paige, D. D. "Introductory Note," QRL, 5, #2 (November 2, 1949), 103-104.

2944 Palandri, Angela Jung. "Ezra Pound and His Italian Critics," TkR, 3, #2 (1972), 41-57.

2945 _____. "Ezra Pound Revisited," West Coast Review, 2 (Winter, 1968), 5-8.

2946 _____. "'La pietra mi è viva nella mano.' Le traduzioni dal cinese di Pound," Il Verri, 27 (1968), 3-19.

2947 _____. "'The Stone Is Alive in My Hand'--Ezra Pound's Chinese Translations," LE&W, 10 (September, 1966), 278-291.

2948 _____. "Le traduzioni dal cinese di Pound," Verri, 27 (1968), 3-19.

2949 Palm, Göran. "Tva bilder av Ezra Pound," BLM, 32 (February, 1963), 121-139.

2950 Panichas, George A. "Politics and Literature," Modern Age, 12, #1 (Winter, 1967-68), 84-89.

2951 Paolucci, Anne. "Ezra Pound and D. G. Rossetti as Translators of Guido Cavalcanti," RR, 51, #4 (December, 1960), 256-267.

2952 _____. "Benn, Pound, and Eliot: The Monologue Art of German Expressionism and Anglo-American Modernism," RNL, 9 (1978), 10-24.

2953 Parisi, Joseph. "Miss Monroe, Mr. Pound and the Boorzoi," Poetry, 131 (October, 1977), 39-51.

2954 Parisoff, Myra Jane Heinz. "A Study of the Relative Mode of Mind in Pound, Eliot, Stevens, and Williams," DAI, 41, #8 (Tulsa, Okla. U.: 1981), 3574A-75A.

2955 Parker, Andrew. "Ezra Pound and the 'Economy' of Anti-Semitism," Boundary, 11, #1-2 (Fall-Winter, 1982-83), 103-128.

2956 Parkinson, Thomas. "Pound among the Artists and Pound in His Later Years," OhR, 19, #1 (1978), 115-126.

2957 _____. "Yeats and Pound: The Illusion of Influence," CompLit, 6 (Summer, 1954), 256-264.

2958 Pasquier, Marie-Claire. "L'Ancien et le nouveau dans l'oeuvre poétique d'Ezra Pound," CRB, 94 (1977), 90-99.

2959 Pasquini, Luigi. "Incontro con Ezra Pound," Martinella, 21 (1967), 222-224.

2960 Patnaik, Deba P. "Ezra Pound and Naresh Guha," Paideuma, 3 (Spring, 1974), 67-68.

2961 _____. "Ezra Pound and Rabindranath Tagore," IJAS, 2, #2 (December, 1972), 53-69.

2962 _____. "Only the Quality of the Affection Endures," Paideuma, 3, #3 (Winter, 1974), 313-318.

2963 Patterson, Gertrude. "'The Waste Land' in the Making," CritQ, 14, #3 (Autumn, 1972), 269-283.

2964 Pattinson, John Patrick. "A Study of British Poetic Criticism between 1930 and 1965 as Exemplified in the Critics of Yeats, Pound, and Eliot," DAI, 30 (New York U.: 1970), 4460A-61A.

2965 Pea, Enrico. "Grazie, Ezra Pound," Stagione, 2, #7 (Rome: 1955), 3-4.

2966 Pearce, Roy Harvey. "Ezra Pound's Appraisal of Walt Whitman: Addendum," MLN, 74, #1 (January, 1959), 23-28.

2967 _____. "Pound and the New Poetry," and "Pound, Whitman and the American Epic," The Continuity of American Poetry. Cf., #857, pp. 163-177, 293-296.

2968 Pearlman, Daniel. "The Anti-Semitism of Ezra Pound," ConL, 22, #1 (Winter, 1981), 104-115.

2969 Peck, John. "Arras and Painted Arras," Paideuma, 3, #1 (Spring, 1974), 61-66.

2970 _____. "Pound and Hardy," Agenda, 10, ii-iii (Spring-Summer, 1972), 3-10.

2971 _____. "Pound's Idylls with Chapters on Catullus, Landor, and Browning," DAI, 34 (Stanford, 1973), 1290A.

2972 Peper, Jürgen. "Das imagistische 'Ein-Bild-Gedicht': Zwei Bildauffassungen," GRM, 22 (1972), 400-418.

2973 Pérez, Louis C. "Observations by Ezra Pound on the Dramatic Quality of Lope de Vega," Bulletin of the Comediantes, 7 (1955), 19-21.

2974 Peri, Jeffrey Michael. "The Return: Ideologies of 'Nostos' and the Nature of Modernism," DAI, 41, #4 (Princeton: 1980), 1581.

2975 Perkins, David. "Ezra Pound: The Early Career," A History of Modern Poetry: From the 1890's to the High Modernist Mode. Cambridge, Mass., and London: Belknap Pr., of Harvard U. Pr., 1976, pp. 449-489.

2976 Perlès, Alfred. My Friend Henry Miller. London: Neville Spearman, Ltd., 1955, pp. 32, 83-84, passim.

2977 Perloff, Marjorie G. "Charles Olson and the 'Inferior Predecessors': 'Projective Verse' Revisited," ELH, 40 (Summer, 1973), 285-306.

2978 _____. "A First Textbook," NR, 171, #26 (December 28, 1974), 21-22.

2979 _____. "'No Edges, No Convexities': Ezra Pound and the Circle of Fragments," The Poetics of Indeterminacy: Rimbaud to Cage. Princeton, New Jersey: Princeton U. Pr., 1981, pp. 155-199.

2980 _____. "The Poet and His Politics," NR, 170, #11 (March 16, 1974), 21-23.

2981 _____. "Pound and Rimbaud: The Retreat from Symbolism," IowaR, 6, #1 (1975), 91-117.

2982 _____. "Pound/Stevens: Whose Era?" NLH, 13 (Spring, 1982), 485-514.

2983 Permoli, Piergiovanni. "Appunti sull'imagismo in America e in Russia," NC, Nos. 5-6 (January-June, 1956), 155-164.

2984 Perrine, Laurence, and James M. Reid. 100 American Poems of the Twentieth Century. New York: Harcourt, Brace & World, Inc., 1966, pp. 82-83.

2985 Pettersson, Gunnar. "Ezra Pound, Il Miglior fabbro--Ezra Pound, Il fascista?" MSpr, 72 (1978), 15-18.

2986 Pinto, Vivian de Sola. "Imagists and D. H. Lawrence," Crisis in English Poetry, 1880-1940. London: Hutchinson U. Library, Rev. ed., 1961, pp. 153-155, passim.

2987 Pisanti, Tommaso. "Ezra Pound e Dante," Dante e l'Italia meridionale. Atti del Congresso nazionale di studi danteschi di Caserta. Florence: Olschki, 1966, pp. 329-336.

2988 _____. "Ezra Pound lettore di Dante," NA, 517:2066 (1973), 243-240.

2989 Pleynet, Marcelin. "La compromission poétique," Tel Quel, 70 (1977), 11-26.

2990 Poirier, Richard. "The Art of Poetry II," ParisR, 6, #24 (Summer-Fall, 1960), 89-120.

2991 Poli, Bernard J. Ford Madox Ford and the Transatlantic Review, Syracuse, New York: Syracuse U. Pr., 1967, passim.

2992 Pondrom, Cyrena N. "The Book of the Poets' Club and Pound's 'School of Images,'" JML, 3 (1973), 100-102.

2993 _____. "Modern French Poetry: Pound's First Important View," The Road from Paris: French Influence on English Poetry, 1900-1920. Cambridge: Cambridge U. Pr., 1974, pp. 172-174.

2994 Popescu, Adrian. "Duminica fără Ezra Pound," ["Sunday without Ezra Pound,"], Sreaua (n.s.), 23, #22 (November, 1972).

2995 Popescu, Petru. "Řeflectie unui poet după stingere," ["Thoughts for a poet after his death"], Cronica, 8, #1 (January 12, 1973).

2996 Porter, Katherine Anne. "From the Notebooks of Katherine Anne Porter--Yeats, Joyce, Eliot, Pound," SoR, 1, #3 (Summer, 1965), 570-573.

2997 _____. "It is hard to stand in the middle," The Days Before. New York: Harcourt, 1952, pp. 74-81; The Collected Essays and Occasional Writings of Katherine Anne Porter. New York: Delacorte Pr., 1970, pp. 40-46.

2998 Porteus, Hugh Gordon. "Ezra Pound and His Chinese Character," An Examination of Ezra Pound. Peter Russell, ed., Cf., #114, pp. 203-217.

2999 _____. "The Pound Errata," Encounter, 40 (June, 1973), 66-68.

3000 Pottorf, Michael. "The Great Gatsby: Myrtle's Dog and Its Relation to the Dog-God of Pound and Eliot," AN&Q, 14, #5 (1976), 88-90.

3001 Potts, P. "Poem about Ezra Pound," Commentary, 26 (November, 1958), 410.

3002 Pound, Dorothy Shakespear, ed. Etruscan Gate. Exeter: Rougemont Pr., 1971.

3003 _____, et al. "Notes and Queries--Letters to the Editor," Paideuma, 1, #2 (Winter, 1972); b, 271-277, 281-282.

3004 Pound, Omar, and A. Walton Litz, eds. Ezra Pound and Dorothy Shakespear: Their Letters: 1909-1914. New York: New Directions, 1984.

3005 Pratt, William C. "Imagism and Irony: The Shaping of the International Style," SAQ, 83, #1 (Winter, 1984), 1-17.

3006 _____. "Revolution without Betrayal: James, Pound, Eliot and the European Tradition," DA, 17 (Vanderbilt: 1957), 2600.

3007 Praz, Mario. "Gli scrittori e la tecnica," Tempo (Rome), 6 dic. 1954, p. 3.

3008 _____. "La critica americana d'oggi," Prospetti, #4 (1955).

3009 _____. Mnemosyne: The Parallel between Literature and the Visual Arts. Princeton: Princeton U. Pr., 1970, passim.

3010 _____. "T. S. and Dante," SoR, 2, #3 (Winter, 1937), 525-548; (Pound passim).

3011 _____. "Two Notes on Ezra Pound," Cronache letterarie anglosassoni. Rome: Edizioni di storia e letterature, 1950-1951, Vol. I, pp. 175-183.

3012 Precosky, Donald A. "'Make Ezra Pound and the Whole Caboodle of Them Sit Up': Florence Ayscough and the Lowell-Pound Feud," Four Decades of Poetry, 1890-1930, II (July, 1979), 204-209.

3013 Press, John. The Chequer'd Shade: Reflections on Obscurity in Poetry. London: Oxford U. Pr., 1958, passim.

3014 _____. "Ezra Pound, 1909-1919," A Map of Modern English Verse. London; New York: Oxford U. Pr., 1969, pp. 53-69.

3015 _____. The Fire and the Fountain: An Essay on Poetry. London: Oxford U. Pr., 1955, passim.

3016 _____. The Lengthening Shadows. London: Oxford U. Pr., 1971, passim.

3017 _____. Rule and Energy: Trends in British Poetry since the Second World War. London; New York: Oxford U. Pr., 1963, passim.

3018 Prestin, J. H. "Three American Poets," VQR, 3, #3 (July, 1927), 450-462.

3019 Prezzolini, Giuseppe. "Ezra Pound e il fascismo," Nazione, 2, #3 (1973).

3020 _____. "In attesta del risvogliamonte Ezra Pound sta in manicomie," Il Tempo (November 13, 1950), 3.

3021 _____. "Note Americane," Il Borghese, VI (Milan: February 10, 1956), 208.

3022 _____. "La polemica su Ezra Pound," America: con gli stivali. Firenze: Valecchi Editore, 1954, pp. 621-631.

3023 Pricop, Constantin. "Sisteme lirice [Lyrical Systems], ConvLit, 6 (1975), 14.

3024 Pritchard, William H. "Ezra Pound: Persistent Explorer," Lives of the Modern Poets. Cf., #1160, pp. 141-170.

3025 _____. "On Wyndham Lewis," PR, 35, #2 (Spring, 1968), 253-267.

3026 _____. "Paradise Lost," HudR, 25, #2 (Summer, 1972), 316-322.

3027 _____. Wyndham Lewis. New York: Humanities Pr., 1972, passim.

3028 _____. Seeing Through Everything: English Writers, 1918-1940. New York: Oxford U. Pr., 1977, passim.

3029 Pritchett, V. S. "Public Eye," NSt, 74 (July 28, 1967), 119-120.

3030 Puckett, Harry Thomas. "Encounter with the Gods: Form and Style in the Poetry of Ezra Pound," DAI, 32 (Indiana: 1971), 4630A.

3031 Puckett, Walter Edward. "The Nineteenth-Century Foundations of the Robert Browning-Ezra Pound Bridge to Modernity in Poetry," DA, 22, #9 (St. Louis: 1961), 3205.

3032 Puknat, E. M., and S. B. Puknat. "Goethe and Modern American Poets," GQ, 42 (1969), 21-36.

3033 Pulik, Ruth. "Pound and The Waste Land," UES, 15, #2 (1977), 15-24.

3034 Putnam, Samuel. "Ezra Pound: Cracker-barrel 'Revolutionist,'" Mosaic, 1, #5 (November-December, 1934), 3-8.

3035 _____. Paris Was Our Mistress. New York: Viking Pr., (1947), passim.

3036 Putz, Manfred. "A Conversation with William C. Chace," Occident, 8 (Spring, 1974), 51-65.

3037 Quartermaine, Peter. "'To Make Glad the Heart of Man': Bunting, Pound, and Whitman," Basil Bunting: Man and Poet. Carroll F. Terrell, ed. Orono, ME: National Poetry Foundation: 1981, pp. 145-158.

3038 Quinn, Mary Bernetta. "Ezra Pound and the Metamorphic Tradition," WR, 15 (Spring, 1951), 169-181.

3039 _____. Metamorphic Tradition in Modern Poetry: Essays on the Work of Ezra Pound, Wallace Stevens, William Carlos Williams, T. S. Eliot, Hart Crane, Randall Jarrell and William Butler Yeats. New Brunswick, N.J., Rutgers U. Pr., 1955; New York: Gordian Pr., 1966.

3040 Racey, Edgar F., Jr. "Pound and Williams: The Poet as Renewer," BuR, 11, #2 (March, 1963), 21-30.

3041 Raffel, Burton. Ezra Pound: Prime Minister of Poetry. Hamden, Conn.: Shoe String Pr., 1984.

3042 _____. Possum and Ole Ez: Contemporaries and Peers on T. S. Eliot and Ezra Pound. Hamden, Conn.: The Shoe String Pr., 1985.

3043 Rago, Henry. "Faith and the Literary Imagination: The Vocation of Poetry," Adversity and Grace: Studies in Recent American Literature. Nathan A. Scott, Jr., ed. Chicago; London: U. of Chicago Pr., 1968, pp. 249-252ff.

3044 Raine, Kathleen. "Besök i tjugonde seklet," BLM, 21 (October, 1952), 599-600.

3045 _____. "Il Miglior Fabbro," NS&N, 40 (November 25, 1950), 510-512.

3046 Ramsey, Warren. Jules Laforgue and the Ironic Inheritance. New York: Oxford U. Pr., 1953, passim.

3047 _____. "Pound, Laforgue, and Dramatic Structure," CL, 3 (Winter, 1951), 47-56.

3048 Rattray, David. "Der rapelköpfige Anhang," Ezra Pound: 22 Versuche über einen Dichter. Eva Hesse, ed. Cf., #1979, pp. 401-412.

3049 Ray, David. "Dealing with Mambrino's Helmet," The Art of Literary Publishing: Editors on Their Craft. Bill Henderson, ed. Yonkers, New York: Pushcart Pr., 1980, p. 267.

3050 Raymond, Marcel. From Baudelaire to Surrealism. New York: Wittenborn, Schultz, Inc., 1950, passim.

3051 Read, Forrest. "Pound, Joyce, and Flaubert: The Odysseans," New Approachs to Ezra Pound: A Coordinated Investigation of Pound's Poetry and Ideas. Eva Hesse, ed. Cf., #41, pp. 125-144.

3052 _____, ed. Pound/Joyce: Letters and Essays. With Introduction and Commentary. New York: New Directions, 1967.

3053 _____. "Storicamente Joyce, 1930: Ezra Pound's First Italian Essay, " TriQ, 15 (Spring, 1969), 100-107.

3054 _____. "'When will they ever learn': Sho-shu Again," Paideuma, 9 (1980), 327-328.

3055 Read, Herbert. "Révolte et réaction dans la poésie anglaise moderne," Présence, Geneva (April, 1946), 56.

3056 Reed, John. "A Word to Mr. Pound," Poetry, 2, #3 (June, 1913), 112-113.

3057 Reedy, William Marion. "What I Have Been Reading," Reedy's Mirror, 25 (July 14, 1916), 462-463; repr., in Ezra Pound: The Critical Heritage. Eric Homberger, ed., Cf., #1545, pp. 117-118.

3058 Rees, Thomas. "Ezra Pound and the Modernization of Yeats," JML, 4 (Fall, 1975), 574-592.

3059 Reeves, Gareth. "Obstetrics of The Waste Land," CritQ, 17 (Spring, 1975), 33-53.

3060 Regier, Willis G. "The Allusive Fabric of 'Apparuit,'" Paideuma, 9 (1980), 319-322.

3061 _____. "Ezra Pound and E. E. Cummings: Confrontations between Tradition and the Avant-Garde," DAI, 39 (Lincoln, Nebraska: 1978), 6766A.

3062 Reid, Benjamin L. "Four Winds," SR, 87 (Spring, 1979), 273-288.

3063 Reid, David, and Mark Turner. "A Conversation with Hugh Kenner," Occident, 7, #1 (1973), 18-48.

3064 Reid, Richard. "Pound's Radio Speeches," Agenda, 17, #3-4; 18, #1 (Aut-Wntr-Spr., 1979-80), 171-186.

3065 Rexroth, Kenneth. American Poetry in the Twentieth Century. New York: Herder & Herder, 1971, pp. 39-44.

3066 Rhys, Ernest. Everyman Remembers. London: J. M. Dent & Sons, Ltd., and Cosmopolitan Bk. Co., 1931, passim.

3067 _____, ed. The Prelude to Poetry: The English Poets in Defence and Praise of Their Own Art. New York: Dutton, Everyman Series, No. 789, 1970, passim.

3068 Ricciardi, Caterina. "La cosmologia della luce nel sincretismo poundiano," L'esotismo nella letteratura angloamericana. Elémire Zola. (Studi di Lett. Angloamer. 2.), Rome: Lucarini, 1979, pp. 83-119.

3069 Rich, W. "Ezra Pound and Poetry," Dial, 54 (May 1, 1913), 370-371.

3070 Richardson, Jack. "Looking Back at 'The Waste Land,'" Commentary, 60, #2 (August, 1975), 65-69.

3071 Ricks, Christopher. "Davie's Pound," New Statesman, 69 (April 16, 1965), 610.

3072 Riddel, Joseph N. "Decentering the Image: The 'Project' of 'American' Poetics?" Textual Strategies: Perspectives in Post-Structuralist Criticism. Josue V. Harai, ed. Ithaca, NY: Cornell U. Pr., 1979, pp. 322-358.

3073 _____. "'Neo Nietzschean Clatter'--Speculation and/on Pound's Poetic Image," Boundary, 2, IX, #3 (Spring, 1981); Ezra Pound: Tactics for Reading. Ian F. A. Bell, ed. London Vision Pr.; Noble Pr., 1982; Totowa, N.J.: Barnes & Noble, 1982, pp. 187-220.

3074 Ridge, Lola. "Ezra's Mind," Little Review Anthology. Margaret Anderson, ed. New York: Horizon Pr., 1953, pp. 273-274.

3075 Ringer, Gordon. "Notes on the Present State of Pound Studies," Shenandoah, 6, #3 (Summer, 1955), 64-66.

3076 Rizzardi, Alfredo. La condizione americana. Studi su poeli nord-americani. Bologna: Capelli, 1959, passim.

3077 _____, ed. "Inchiesta su Ezra Pound e la poesia americana," Studi e Opinioni su Ezra Pound, NC, Nos. 5-6 (1956), 205-236.

3078 _____. "Molte pagine per Pound," FLe, 3 luglio, 1955, p. 2.

3079 _____. "Una mostra bibliografica e iconografica di Ezra Pound," Conv, 27 (1959), 249-251.

3080 _____. "'Saeve indignatio' di Ezra Pound," NC, Nos. 5-6 (genn.-giugno, 1956), 1-8.

3081 Roberts, Michael. Critique of Poetry. London: Jonathan Cape, 1934, pp. 162-166.

3082 Robinson, James K. "Terror Lumped and Split: Contemporary British and American Poets," SoR, 6, #1 (January, 1970), 216-228.

3083 Robinson, Janice S. H. D.: The Life and Work of an American Poet. Boston: Houghton Mifflin, 1982, passim.

3084 Rodgers, Frederick George. "The Literary Background of Brazilian Concrete Poetry: The Impact of Pound, Mallarmé and Other Major Writers of the 'Noigandres' Group," DAI, 35, #12 (Indiana: 1974), 7922A.

3085 Roditi, Eduard. "Der Fall Ezra Pound oder Die Grenzen der esthetischen Wertschätzung," Der Monat (München), I, #10 (Munich: July, 1949), 107-113.

3086 Rorem, Ned. "Ezra Pound as a Musician," LonM, 7, #10 (January, 1968), 10, 27-41.

3087 Rose, W. K. "Ezra Pound and Wyndham Lewis: The Crucial Years," SoR, 4, #1 (January, 1968), 72-89; Agenda, 7, #3-4 (Autumn-Wntr, 1969-70), 117-132.

3088 Rosen, David Matthew. "Art and Economics in Pound," Paideuma, 9 (1980), 481-497.

3089 Rosenberg, Harold. "Sanity, Individuality and Poetry," The New Act, Vol. 2 (June, 1933), 59-75.

3090 Rosenthal, M. L. "Ezra Pound: The Poet as Hero," ForumH, 3 (1960), 29-32.

3091 _____. "New Works on Ezra Pound," Poetry, 106, #5 (August, 1965), 361-365.

3092 _____. "Volatile Matter: Humor in Our Poetry," MassR, 22 (Winter, 1981), 807-817.

3093 Rosmarin, Adena Margaret. "The Historical Imagination: Browning to Pound," VN, 61 (1982), 11-17.

3094 _____. "Lyric and Ironic Speakers in Modern Poetry: An Inquiry into the Modes and Methods of Our Literary Understanding," DAI, 39 (Berkeley: 1978), #5531.

3095 Ross, Robert H. The Georgian Revolt, 1910-1922: Rise and Fall of a Poetic Ideal. Carbondale: So. Ill. U. Pr., 1965, passim.

3096 Rossi, Aldo. "Ezra Pound," Paragone, #116 (Agosto, 1959), pp. 91-94.

3097 Rowe, Hershel Dale. "Basic Elements in the Criticism of Ezra Pound," DA, 20 (Florida: 1960), 2807-2808.

3098 Rubin, Louis D., Jr. The Curious Death of the Novel: Essays in American Literature. Baton Rouge: La. St. U., 1967, passim.

3099 Runte, Hans R. "Symbolist and Imagist Poetic Processes: Comparing Stéphane Mallarmé and Ezra Pound," Dimic, Milan V., and Juan Ferraté, eds. Actes du VII congres de l'Association Internationale de Litterature comparée/Proceedings of the 7th Congress of the International Comparative Literature Association, I: Litteratures americaines: .... (Lib. of CRCL 2.) Stuttgart: Bieber, 1979, pp. 173-177.

3100 Russell, Peter. "The Decay of Poetry," NatlRev, 17, #20 (May 18, 1965), 428-430.

3101 _____. "P, Q, and R," MalaR, 19 (July, 1971), 5-23.

3102 Ruthven, Greystiel. "Charles Tomlinson--An Introduction," Gemini/Dialogue, 3 (January, 1960), 30-33.

3103 Ruthven, K. K. "The Composite Mistress," AUMLA, #26 (November, 1966), 198-214.

3104 _____. "Ezra Pound, Alice Kenny, and the Triad," Landfall, 23 (1969), 73-84.

3105 _____. "The Poet as Etymologist," CritQ, 2 (Spring, 1969), 9-37.

3106 _____. "Some New Approaches to Ezra Pound," SoRA, 4, #4 (1971), 308-315.

3107 Ryan, Judith. "Ezra Pound und Gottfried Benn: Avantgarde, Faschismus und asthetische Autonomie," Faschismus und Avantgarde. Grimm, Reinhold, and Jost Hermand, eds. Königstein: Athenäum, 1980, pp. 29-34.

3108 Sahal, K. L. "The Objective Correlative and the Theory of Rasa," CalcR, 2, #2 (October-December, 1970), 237-240.

3109 Sala, Annamaria. "Some Notes on Vorticism and Futurism," Agenda, 7, #3-4/ 8, #1 (Autumn-Winter, 1969-70), 156-162.

3110 Saloman, Louis B. "The Pound-Ruskin Axis," CE, 16 (February, 1955), 270-276.

3111 Saltin, Myles. "More by Ezra Pound," YLG, 30 (October, 1955), 74-80.

3112 Salvalaggio, Nantas. "Ezra Pound sano di mente è tuttora in un manicomie," Il Giornale d'Italia (Rome: July 28, 1955), 1-2.

3113 Sanavio, Piero. Ezra Pound. Venezia, 1977.

3114 _____. "Politik-Gegebenheit oder Traum," Ezra Pound: 22 Versuche über einen Dichter. Eva Hesse, ed., Cf., #1979, pp. 378-386.

3115 Sandburg, Carl. "Poets Major and Minor," Home Front Memo. New York: Harcourt, 1943, pp. 258-260.

3116 _____. "The Work of Ezra Pound," Poetry, 7, #5 (February, 1916), 249-257.

3117 Sanders, Frederick K. "The View Beyond the Dinghey," SR, 79, #3 (Summer, 1971), 433-460.

3118 Satin, Joseph. "Ballatetta," Reading Poetry [Part Four of Reading Literature]. Boston: Houghton Mifflin Co., 1964, pp. 497-498.

3119 Schafer, R. Murray. "Der absolute Rhythmus," Ezra Pound: 22 Versuche über einen Dichter. Eva Hesse, ed. Cf., #1979, pp. 72-86.

3120 _____. "The Developing Theories of Absolute Rhythm and Great Bass," Paideuma, 2, #1 (Spring, 1973), 23-35.

3121 Schiffer, Reinhold. "Der zweimal verwandelte Dionysos: Zur Mythenrezeption bei Ovid und Pound," Arcadia, 8, #3 (1973), 235-247.

3122 Schiralli, Martin Guy. "Education and the Experience of Poetic Meaning," DAI, 39, #5 (Urbana-Champaign, Ill.: 1978), 2813A.

3123 _____. "The Educational Significance of Ezra Pound," JAE, 9, #3 (1975), 41-59.

3124 Schlauch, Margaret. Modern English and American Poetry: Techniques and Ideologies. London: Watts, 1956, passim.

3125 Schleppenbach, Barbara Aschemann. "Irony and Beyond:

The Mythic Method in Conrad, Eliot, and Pound," DAI, 38 (Stanford: 1977), 5467A.

3126 Schmidt, Gerd. "Conversations in Courtship: Ezra Pound als Ubersetzer altagyptischer Liebeslieder," Arcadia, 5 (1970), 296-302.

3127 _____. "'Et Vera Incessu Patuit Dea': A Note on Eliot, Pound, and the Aeneid," TSEN, 1, ii (Fall, 1974), 4-6, (#2-74).

3128 _____. "'I am thy soul, Nikoptis': Pound's The Tomb at Akr Caar," Archiv, 212 (1975), 127-129.

3129 Schmied, Wieland. "T. S. Eliot und Ezra Pound als Kritiker," WZ, V, xi (1959), 44-46.

3130 Schneditz, Wolfgang. Begegung mit Zeitgenossen. Bilder und Berichte. München: Prestel, 1959.

3131 Schneeman, Peter Henry. "Ezra Pound and the Act of Translation," DAI, 33 (Minnesota: 1972), 6373A-74A.

3132 _____. "Pound's 'Englischer Brief': A Look Toward Germany," Paideuma, 7 (Spring-Fall, 1978), 309-316.

3133 Schneidau, Herbert Newton. "Ezra Pound's Criticism and the Influence of His Literary Relationships in London, 1908-1920," DA, 24 (Princeton: 1963), #1177.

3134 _____. "Pound and Wordsworth on Poetry and Prose," Romantic and Modern: Revaluations of Literary Tradition. George Bornstein, ed. Pittsburgh: U. of Pittsburgh Pr., 1977, pp. 133-145.

3135 _____. "Pound and Yeats: The Question of Symbolism," ELH, 32 (June, 1965), 220-237.

3136 _____. "Pound, Olson, and Objective Verse," Paideuma, 5 (Spring, 1976), 15-30.

3137 _____. "Pound's Book of Cross-Cuts," Genre, 11, #4 (Winter, 1978), 505-521.

3138 _____. "Pound's Poetics of Loss," Ezra Pound: Tactics for Reading. Ian F. A. Bell, ed. Cf., #449, pp. 103-120.

3139 _____. "Vorticism and the Career of Ezra Pound," MP, 65, #3 (February, 1968), 214-227.

3140 _____. "Wisdom Past Metaphor: Another View of Pound,

Fenollosa, and Projective Verse," Paideuma, 5, #1 (Spring, 1976), 15-29.

3141 Schobert, Timothy. Review: "Pound, Ezra: 'Ezra Pound Speaking': Radio Speeches of WW.II," LibJ, 103, #16 (September 15, 1978), p. 1750.

3142 Schroth, Randall. "A Primer for Some of Pound's Chinese Characters," Paideuma, 9 (Fall, 1980), 271-288.

3143 Schulte, Edvige. "Omaggio a Ezra Pound," AION, SG, 1 (1958), 203-238.

3144 _____. "Ritmi Vecchi e nuovi nella poesia inglese moderna," AION, SG, 2 (1959), 191-238.

3145 Schultz, Robert Dale. "Ezra Pound's Developing Poetics: 1908-1915," DAI, 41, #12 (Cornell: 1981), 5103A.

3146 Schutz, Alexander H. "Pound as Provencalist," RomN, 3, #2 (Spring, 1962), 58-63.

3147 Schwartz, Delmore. "Graves in Dock--The Case for Modern Poetry," NR, 134 (March 19, 1956), 20-21.

3148 Schwartz, Sanford Ray. "The Relative Sublime: Pound, Eliot, Richards, and the Making of Modern English Poetics," DAI, 38 (Princeton: 1977), 4186A-87A.

3149 Schwartz, William Leonard. "L'Appel de l'extreme-orient dans la poesie des Etats-Unis," RLC (January, 1928), 113-126.

3150 Scott, Nathan A., Jr., ed. Adversity and Grace: Studies in Recent American Literature. Chicago: U. of Chicago Pr., 1968, passim.

3151 _____. The Broken Center: Studies in the Theological Horizon of Modern Literature. London; New Haven: Yale U. Pr., 1966, passim.

3152 Scott, Tom. "An Appreciation," Ezra Pound Perspectives: Essays in Honor of His Eightieth Birthday. Noel Stock, ed. Cf., #125, pp. 182-197.

3153 Scully, James. "A Prefatory Note," Modern Poetics. James Scully, ed. New York: McGraw-Hill Bk. Co., 1965, pp. 9ff.

3154 _____, ed. Modern Poets on Modern Poetry. London: Collins, 1966, passim.

3155 Sechi, Giovanni. "'Decadenza' e 'avanguardia' in Ezra

Pound," NC, Nos. 5-6 (genn.-giugno, 1956), 184-196; Cf., #518, pp. 26-36.

3156 Seed, David. "The Ezra Pound Conference at Sheffield University," Paideuma, 5, #2 (Fall, 1976), 339-342.

3157 Seidel, Frederick. "The Art of Poetry III," ParisR, 7 (Winter-Spring, 1961), 57-95.

3158 Sell, Frederick C. "The Fusion of Languages," MinnR, 4, #1 (Fall, 1963), 51-59.

3159 Senior, John. "E. P. Pour L'Erection," [poem], QRL, 5, #2 (1949), 145-146.

3160 Sergeant, Elizabeth Shepley. Robert Frost: The Trial by Existence. New York: Holt, Rinehart & Winston, 1960, pp. 101-112, passim.

3161 Seyersted, Brita L., ed. Pound-Ford: The Story of a Literary Friendship. New York: New Directions, 1982.

3162 Shaheen, Mohammed Y. "Pound and Blunt: Homage for Apathy," Paideuma, 12, #2-3 (Fall-Winter, 1983), 281-287.

3163 _____. "Pound in Arabic," Paideuma, 6 (1977), 399-410.

3164 Shapiro, Karl. "Ezra Pound: The Scapegoat of Modern Poetry," In Defense of Ignorance. New York: Random House, 1960, pp. 61-85; The Poetry Wreck: Selected Essays; 1950-1970. New York: Random House, 1975, pp. 29-54.

3165 _____. "Modern Poetry as a Religion," ASch, 28, #3 (Summer, 1959), 259-305.

3166 _____. Prose Keys to Modern Poetry. New York: Harper & Row, 1962, pp. 104, 136-137.

3167 _____. Trial of a Poet, and Other Poems. New York: Reynal & Hitchcock Pr., 1947.

3168 Sharp, Frederick Thomas. "'Objectivists' 1927-1934: A Critical History of the Work and Association of Louis Zukofsky, William Carlos Williams, Charles Reznikoff, Carl Rakosi, Ezra Pound, George Oppen," DAI, 43, #8 (Stanford: 1982), 2663A.

3169 Shaw, Peter. "Pound's Quantities and Absolute Rhythm," ELWIU, 4 (1977), 95-109.

3170 Shaw, Robert B., ed. American Poetry Since 1960: Some Critical Perspectives. Chester Springs, Pa.: Dufour, 1974; Cheadle: Carcanet Pr., 1973, passim.

3171 Sieburth, Richard Raymond. "Dada Pound," SAQ, 93, #1 (Winter, 1984), 44-68.

3172 _____. "Ezra Pound," American Writers in Paris: 1920-1939. Karen Lane Rood, ed. Detroit, Michigan: Gale Research Co., 1980, pp. 315-333.

3173 Simpson, David. "Pound's Wordsworth; or Growth of a Poet's Mind," ELH, 45 (Winter, 1978), 660-686.

3174 Simpson, Louis. "The California Poets," LonM, 11 (February-March, 1972), 56-63.

3175 Sinclair, Upton. "Ezra Pound," My Lifetime in Letters. Columbia: Missouri U. Pr., 1960, pp. 368-376.

3176 Singh, G. "Pound's Critical Credo," AJES, 6, #1 (1981), 48-75.

3177 Sisson, Charles Hubert. The Avoidance of Literature: Collected Essays. Michael Schmidt, ed. Manchester: Carcanet Pr., 1979.

3178 _____. "Ezra Pound," English Poetry, 1900-1950: An Assessment. London; New York: Methuen, 1971, pp. 96-124.

3179 _____. "Ezra Pound," Ishmael, 1, #2 (Summer, 1971), 49-74.

3180 _____. "Pound's Literary Programmes," Agenda, 17, #3-4; 18, #1 (Aut-Wntr-Spr., 1979-80), 200-207.

3181 Sitwell, Edith. "Yeats e la soluzione di Pound," FLe, No. 46 (November 16, 1950), 3.

3182 Skorina, Violet Cameron. "Leaving 'Wardour Street': An Examination of the Relationship between Ford Madox Ford and Ezra Pound during Their Years Together in London c. 1908-1915 and the Influence of Ford's Theory of the 'Prose Tradition' upon Pound's Verse Style," DAI, 40, #8 (Connecticut: 1979), 4592A-93A.

3183 Slatin, Myles. "'Mesmerism': A Study of Ezra Pound's Use of the Poetry of Robert Browning," DA, 29 (Yale: 1957), 1234A-35A.

3184 _____. "More by Ezra Pound," Yale U. Library Gazette, 30, #2 (October, 1955), 74-80, passim.

3185 Smith, Bernard. Forces in American Criticism: A Study in the History of American Literary Thought. New York: Harcourt, Brace & Co., 1939, pp. 351-352, passim.

3186 Smith, Chard P. "Semi-Classical Poetry and the Great Tradition," MassR, 3 (Autumn, 1961), 41-61.

3187 Smith, Lewis Worthington. "The New Naiveté," AtlM, 117 (April, 1916), 487-492.

3188 Smith, Paul. "Pound/Zukofsky," DR, 61, #2 (Summer, 1981), 356-362.

3189 Smith, Ray. Permanent Fires: Reviews of Poetry, 1958-1973. Metuchen, NJ: Scarecrow Pr., 1975, passim.

3190 Smith, Richard Eugene. Richard Aldington. Boston: Twayne Pub. Co., 1977, pp. 19-24, passim.

3191 Sokol, B. J. "What Went Wrong between Robert Frost and Ezra Pound," NEQ, 49, #4 (1976), 521-541.

3192 Sonne, Jørgen. "Ezra Pounds ideer," Horisonter. Introduktioner og essays. Copenhagen: Munksgaard, 1973, pp. 96-108.

3193 Soper, Brian. "Ezra Pound: Some Notes on His Philosophy," An Examination of Ezra Pound. Peter Russell, ed., Cf., #114, pp. 229-248.

3194 Sorda, Enrique. "Otra muerte en Venecia," Estafeta Literaria, #507 (January 1, 1973), 9-10.

3195 Sorrentino, Gilbert. The Sullen Art: Interviews by David Ossman with Modern American Poets. New York: Corinth Books, 1963, pp. 54-55.

3196 Southworth, James Granville. "Ezra Pound," More Modern American Poets. Freeport, New York: Bks. for Libraries Pr., 1954; repr., 1964; pp. 18-34.

3197 Spears, Monroe K. "The Beginnings of Modernism in English Verse," Dionysus and the City: Modernism in Twentieth-Century Poetry. New York: Oxford U. Pr., 1970, pp. 105-152, passim.

3198 Spector, Robert Donald. "Eliot, Pound, and the Conservative Tradition," HINL, 3, ii (April, 1957), 2-5.

3199 _____. "Pound as Pound," HINL, 4 (January, 1958), 9-10.

3200 Spencer, Benjamin T. "Eight Ways to Nationality," Patterns of Nationality: Twentieth-Century Literary Versions of America. New York: (American Cultural Heritage Series 7), Burt Franklin, 1981, passim.

3201 _____. "Pound: The American Strain," PMLA, 81, #7 (December, 1966), 457-466.

3202 Spender, Stephen. "Ebb Tide in England: The American Visitors," Love-Hate Relations: English and American Sensibilities. New York: Random House, 1974, pp. 149-163.

3203 _____. "On Literary Movements," Encounter, I, #2 (November, 1953), 66-68.

3204 _____. World Within World: The Autobiography of Stephen Spender. London: Hamish Hamilton, 1951, pp. 95, 164-165.

3205 _____. "Writers and Politics," PR, 34, #3 (Summer, 1967), 359-381, passim.

3206 Spiller, Robert E. The Cycle of American Literature: An Essay in Historical Criticism. New York: Macmillan, 1955, passim.

3207 _____, et al. Literary History of the United States. Vol. 2. New York: Macmillan Pub. Co., 1946, passim.

3208 _____. The Third Dimension: Studies in Literary History. London: Collier-Macmillan; New York: Macmillan, 1965, p. 146, passim.

3209 Stafford, Jack R. "Ezra Pound and Segregation," LonM, 9, #6 (September, 1969), 60-72.

3210 Stancioff, Marion Mitchell. "How I Remember Ezra Pound," America, 128, #10 (March 17, 1973), 240-241.

3211 Stanford, Ann. "Ezra Pound--Poetry 1910-1930," American Literary Scholarship: An Annual, 1964. Durham, N.C.: Duke U. Pr., 1966, pp. 184-186.

3212 Stanford, Donald E. "Elizabeth Daryush (1887-1977) and Ezra Pound (1885-1972)," SoR, 13, #4 (Autumn, 1977), 641-645.

3213 _____. Revolution and Convention in Modern Poetry: Studies in Ezra Pound, T. S. Eliot, Wallace Stevens, Edwin Arlington Robinson, and Yvor Winters. East Brunswick, N.J.: U. of Delaware Pr., 1983.

3214 _____. "Thoughts on the Pound Era," SoR, 9, #1 (Winter, 1973), viii-xv.

3215 Starkie, Enid. From Gautier to Eliot: The Influence of France on English Literature, 1851-1939. Hutchinson of London: Repub., 1971 by Scholarly Pr., 1971, pp. 155-161, passim.

3216 Stearns, Harold E., ed., with Introd. America Now: An Inquiry into Civilization in the United States. London; New York: Chas. Scribner's Sons, 1938, pp. 50-53, 56-58, passim.

3217 Stegman, Michael O. "William Carlos Williams and Paterson: An Exorcism of Pound and Eliot; Wallace Stevens at the Harmonium; Wallace Stevens and Music," DAI, 39, #6 (New York at Stony Brook: 1978), 3587A.

3218 Steiner, Francis George. "An Essay on the Situation of Modern Verse," Rivista di Letterature Moderne (Italy), I (July, 1950), 57-64.

3219 _____. "Cruellest Months," NY, 48 (April 22, 1972), 134ff.

3220 Stern, Richard. "Extracts from a Journal," Triquarterly, #50 (Winter, 1981), 261-273.

3221 Stewart, Mairi. "Ezra Pound," Poetry Review, 33, #5 (September-October, 1942), 285-289.

3222 Stewart, Peter. "Browning and Pound," BSNotes, 10, #3 (1980), 11-16.

3223 Stock, Noel. "Balancing the Books," PoetA, 30 (October, 1969), 42-52.

3224 _____. "Ezra Pound and an American Tradition," Agenda, 2, #4 (June, 1961), 4-10.

3225 _____. "Ezra Pound's Central Judgments on Contemporary Literature," Quadrant (Sydney), 6 (Winter, 1962), 5-17.

3226 _____. "Innovation Through Translation," TQ, 10, #4 (Winter, 1967), 40-46.

3227 _____. "Modern Poetry and the Norm of Language," TQ, 4, #4 (Winter, 1961), 134-144.

3228 _____. "Pound der Historiker," Ezra Pound: 22 Versuche über einen Dichter. Eva Hesse, ed., Cf., #1979, pp. 336-348.

3229 _____. "Thrones 1959," Reading the Cantos: A Study of Meaning in Ezra Pound. Cf., #954, pp. 104-117.

3230 _____. "The Young Poet," PoetA, 12 (October, 1966), 36-40.

3231 Stoenescu, Stefan. "Secretul celebrarii perpetue," SXX, 15, #9 (1972), 30-37.

3232 Stonier, G. W. "The Mystery of Ezra Pound," Purpose, 10, #1 (January-March, 1938), 21-26.

3233 Stough, Christina Carolina. "The Literary Relationship of T. S. Eliot and Ezra Pound after The Waste Land," DAI, 41, #4 (U. of So. Calif.: 1980), 1601A.

3234 Stovall, Floyd. American Idealism. Norman, Okla.: U. of Oklahoma Pr., 1943, passim.

3235 _____, ed. The Development of American Literary Criticism. Chapel Hill, NC: North Carolina U. Pr., 1955, passim.

3236 Strickland, G. R. "Flaubert, Pound and Eliot," CamQ, 2 (Summer, 1967), 242-263.

3237 Strough, Christina C. "The Skirmish of Pound and Eliot in The New English Weekly: A Glimpse at Their Later Literary Relationship," JML, 10, #2 (June, 1983), 231-246.

3238 Stuart, Duane R. "Modernistic Critics and Translators," PULC, 11 (Summer, 1950), 177-198.

3239 Sühnel, Rudolf. "Die Literarischen Voraussetzungen von Joyce's Ulysses," Germanisch-Romanische Monatsschrift, N.S., XII, #2 (April, 1962), 202-211.

3240 _____. "Ezra Pound und die homerische Tradition," Ezra Pound: 22 Versuche über einen Dichter. Eva Hesse, ed. Cf., #1979, pp. 206-210.

3241 Sullivan, J. P., ed. Preface and Introduction. Ezra Pound: A Critical Anthology. Harmondsworth: Penguin, 1970, pp. 11-13, 200-207.

3242 _____. "Ezra Pound as a Latin Translator," Arion, III, #3 (Autumn, 1964), 100-111.

3243 _____. "Ezra Pound on Classics and Classicists," Arion, 3, #1 (Spring, 1964), 9-22.

3244 Surette, Philip Leon. "Also Sprach Ezra: Pound Exposed," Mosaic, 15, #2 (June, 1982), 57-62.

3245 _____. "A Case for Occam's Razor: Pound and Spengler," Paideuma, 6 (Spring, 1977), 109-113.

3246 Sutherland, Donald. "What of Ezra Pound?" DenverQ, 8, #1 (Spring, 1973), 1-9.

3247 Swabey, Henry. "A Page without Which ...," Paideuma, 5, #2 (Fall, 1976), 329-337.

3248 _____. "Towards an A.B.C. of History," Ezra Pound: A Collection of Essays. Peter Russell, ed., Cf., #114, pp. 186-202.

3249 Sweeney, Richard Monnett. "'Editur Ez' and 'Old Hugger-Scrunch': The Influence of Ezra Pound on the Poems of William Carlos Williams," DAI, 31, #1 (Brown: 1970), 404A-405A.

3250 Symons, W. T. "A Public Scandal," New English Weekly, 7 (May 16, 1935), 100.

3251 Szasz, Thomas. "Ezra Pound," TLS, #3892 (October 15, 1976), 1306.

3252 Taggart, John Paul. "Intending a Solid Object: A Study of Objectivist Poetics," DAI, 36 (Syracuse: 1974), 332A.

3253 Tagliaferri, Aldo. "Ezra Pound's Jefferson and/or Mussolini," IQ, 16, #64 (1973), 109-115.

3254 Tagore, Rabindranath. "A Bundle of Letters," Ezra Pound: Perspectives. Noel Stock, ed., Cf., #125, pp. 109-110.

3255 Takada, Tomiichi. "'Kotoba' no Buto: Fenollosa-Pound no Baai," Phoenix o Motomete: Eibei Shosetsu no Yukue. Tokyo: Nan'undo, 1982, pp. 429-443.

3256 Takayanagi, Shunichi. "T. S. Eliot to Ezra Pound--The Waste Land no Seiritsu wo megutte," ELLS, 9 (1972), 100-144.

3257 Takuwa, Shinji. "The Difficulties of Ezra Pound," KAL, 5 (April, 1962), 42-47.

3258 Tanner, Tony. "Pound Revalued," Spectator, 223 (1969), 406-407.

3259 Tate, Allen. "Ezra Pound," The Man of Letters in the Modern World. Selected Essays. London: Meridian Bks., 1957, pp. 257-263.

3260 _____. "Ezra Pound: 1931," On the Limits of Poetry: Selected Essays, 1928-1949. New York: The Swallow Pr., and Wm. Morrow Co., 1948, pp. 350-357.

3261 _____, ed. Introduction by Allen Tate. Six American Poets from Emily Dickinson to the Present. Minneapolis: Minn. U. Pr., 1969, pp. 3-8.

3262 _____. "Ezra Pound," Sixty American Poets, 1896-1944. Selected with Preface and Critical Notes by Allen Tate. Library of Congress, General Reference and Bibliography Division, Washington, D.C., 1945, pp. 115-122; Rev. ed., 1954, pp. 93-101.

3263 Tatlow, Anthony. "Stalking the Dragon: Pound, Waley and Brecht," CL, 25 (Summer, 1973), 193-211.

3264 Taupin, René. "The Example of Remy de Gourmont," Criterion, 10 (July, 1931), 617-620.

3265 _____. "La poésie d'Ezra Pound," RAA, 8 (February, 1931), 221-236.

3266 Tay, William. "Fragmentary Negation: A Reappraisal of Ezra Pound's Ideogrammic Method," Chinese-Western Comparative Literature Theory and Strategy. John J. Deeney, ed. Chinese U. Pr., Distributed by University of Washington Pr., 1981, pp. 129-153.

3267 Taylor, Daniel William. "The Great London Vortex: Art as Patterned Energy," DAI, 35 (Emory: 1974), 4564A.

3268 Taylor, James. "The Difficult Individual," [poem], Sou' wester (October 30, 1970), p. 132.

3269 _____. "The Typical Critic of Pound," Sou'wester, Special Ezra Pound Number, (October 30, 1970), 118-123.

3270 Taylor, Mark. "The Value of Pound," Cw, 97, #10 (December 8, 1972), 226-227.

3271 Taylor, Thomas. "The Eleusinian and Bacchic Mysteries," Paideuma, 7 (Spring-Fall, 1978), 155-179.

3272 Taylor, Walter Fuller. The Story of American Letters. Chicago: Henry Regnery Co., Rev. ed., 1956, pp. 407-408, passim.

3273 Teele, Roy E. "Ezra Pound," TexQt, 10, #4 (Winter, 1967), 34-35.

3274 _____. Through a Glass Darkly: A Study of English Translations of Chinese Poetry. Ann Arbor: 1949. (Thesis: Columbia U.)

3275 Teodorescu, Virgil. "Ezra Pound," Secolul, 20, #7 (1969), 34-35.

3276 Terramagnino, Geronimo. "Kafka e Pound," Novite (Milan), (January, 1954).

3277 Terrell, Carroll F. "Conversations with Celia," Paideuma, 7 (1978), 585-600.

3278 _____. "A Couple of Documents," Paideuma, 6 (Winter, 1977), 359-361.

3279 _____. "John Adams Speaking: Some Reflections on Technique," Paideuma, 4, #2 (Fall-Winter, 1975), 533-538.

3280 _____. "K.R.H. [Katherine Ruth Heyman] and the Young E. P.," Paideuma, 2 (Spring, 1973), 49-51.

3281 _____. "Mang-Tsze, Thomas Taylor, and Madam YAH," Paideuma, 7 (Spring-Fall, 1978), 141-175.

3282 _____. "Meeting E. P. and Then....," Paideuma, 3, #3 (Winter, 1975), 343-360.

3283 Thatcher, David S., ed. "Richard Aldington's Letters to Herbert Read," MalR, 15 (July, 1970), 5-44.

3284 Theall, Donald F. "Communication Theories in Modern Poetry: Yeats, Pound, Eliot, Joyce," Diss., U. of Toronto, 1955.

3285 Thomas, C. T. "Link's 'Honey-Comb': A Rejoinder," Paideuma, 8 (1979), 541-542.

3286 Thomas, Ronald Edward. "Armstrong, Pound and Browning, or the Mystery of the Missing Bookcase," SBHC, 8, #1 (1980), 61-64.

3287 _____. "The Catullan Landscape in Pound's Poetry," ConP, 4, #1 (1981), 66-78.

3288 _____. "'Ere He His Goddis Brocht in Latio': On Pound's Appreciation of Gavin Douglas," Paideuma, 9 (1980), 509-517.

3289 _____. "The Latin Masks of Ezra Pound," DAI, 38 (Michigan: 1977), 6731A; Pub., UMI Research Pr., Ann Arbor, Michigan, 1983.

3290 Thompson, Douglas. "Pound and Brazilian Concretism," Paideuma, 6 (Winter, 1977), 279-294.

3291 Thompson, Harold. "Ezra Pound," Hamilton Alumni Review, I, #3 (March, 1936), 82-90.

3292 Thompson, Lawrance, ed. Selected Letters of Robert Frost. New York; Chicago: Holt, Rinehart & Winston, 1964, passim.

3293 _____, and R. H. Winnick. Robert Frost: The Later Years, 1938-1963. New York: Holt, Rinehart & Winston, 1976, passim.

3294 Thorp, Willard. "Make It New, 1920-1950," American Writing in the Twentieth Century. Cambridge, Mass.: Harvard U. Pr., 1960, pp. 198-203, passim.

3295 Thorwall, John C. "The Quality of Mercy Not Strained," Pound Newsletter, No. 8 (October, 1955), 22-23.

3296 Thurley, Geoffrey. The American Moment: American Poetry in the Mid-Century. New York: St. Martin's Pr., 1978, pp. 128-132, passim.

3297 _____. "The New Phenomenalist Poetry in the U.S.A.," SoRA, 4, #1 (1970), 15-28.

3298 Tierney, Bill. "Ezra Pound: State of the Poet," AntigR, 12 (Winter, 1973), 85-96.

3299 Tietjens, Eunice. "The End of Ezra Pound," Poetry, 60, #1 (April, 1942), 38-40.

3300 Todd, Olivier. "Pound in Paris," NSt, 70 (November 19, 1965), 801.

3301 Tolley, A. T. "Rhetoric and the Moderns," SoR, 6, #2 (April, 1970), 380-397.

3302 Tomlinson, Charles. "Dove sta memoria: In Italy," HudR, 33, #1 (Spring, 1980), 13-34.

3303 _____. "The Tone of Pound's Critics," Agenda (London), 4, #2 (October-November, 1965), 46-49.

3304 Torres, Aldo. "El reto de Ezra Pound," Atenea (Concepcion, Chile), 135 (December, 1959), 90-94.

3305 Trotter, David. The Making of the Reader: Language and Subjectivity in Modern American, English and Irish Poetry. New York: St. Martin's Pr., 1984.

3306 Tryford, John. "Wallace Stevens: John Tryford's Random Notes," Trace, 66 (Fall, 1967), 339-344.

3307 Tsukui, Nobuko. Ezra Pound and Japanese Noh Plays. Washington, D.C.: U. Pr. of America, 1983.

3308 Tucker, John Joseph. "Pound, Vorticism, and the New Esthetic," Mosaic, 16, #4 (Fall, 1983), 83-96.

3309 _____. "A Reading of Ezra Pound's Criticism, 1910-1920; The Fulcrums of Revolution," DAI, 39, #4 (Toronto: 1976), 2266A.

3310 Tucker, William P. "Ezra Pound, Fascism, and Populism," RPol, 18 (February, 1956), 105-107.

3311 Turco, Lewis. "The Age of Pound," ConP, 4, #3 (1982), 33-46.

3312 Turner, Mark. "Pound and Provence," Occident, 7, #1 (Berkeley, Calif.: 1973), 54-63.

3313 Uchino, Takako. "The Confucian Odes as a Case Study of Problems in Translating Oriental Classics into English," KAL, 11 (1968), 77-86.

3314 Uedo, Makoto. "Zeami, Basho, Yeats, Pound: A Study in Japanese and English Poetics," DA, 22 (U. of Washington: 1961), 4007-4008.

3315 _____. Zeami, Bashō, Yeats, Pound: A Study in Japanese and English Poetics. The Hague: Mouton, 1965.

3316 Uejio, Clifford Kiyoshi. "Romanticism to Modernism: The Force of the Personae-Self Relationship in the Poetry of Wordsworth, Pound, and Williams," DAI, 37 (State U., Buffalo, New York: 1976), 5100A-01A.

3317 Unger, Leonard, ed. "Ezra Pound," Seven Modern American Poets: An Introduction. Minneapolis: U. of Minnesota Pr., 1969, pp. 119-154.

3318 Untermeyer, Jean Starr. "Ezra Pound: The Mosaic of a Mandarin," Private Collection. New York: Alfred A. Knopf, 1965, pp. 208-217.

3319 Untermeyer, Louis. Bygones: The Recollections of Louis Untermeyer. New York: Harcourt, Brace & World, 1965, pp. 46, 61, 93-97.

3320 _____. "Ezra Pound," American Poetry Since 1900. New York: Henry Holt & Co., 1923, pp. 157-169.

3321 _____. "Ezra Pound," Makers of the Modern World. New York: Simon & Schuster, 1955, pp. 643-649.

3322 _____. "Ezra Pound," Modern American Poetry. New

York: Harcourt, Brace & Co., c1919; repub., Scholarly Pr., 1970, pp. 201-214.

3323 _____. "Ezra Pound," The New Era in American Poetry. New York: Henry Holt, 1919; repub., Scholarly Pr., 1970, pp. 201-214.

3324 _____. "Ezra Pound--Proseur," NR, 16 (August 17, 1918), 83-84.

3325 _____. "Ezra Pound," A Treasury of Great Poems. New York: Simon & Schuster, 1955, p. 1123, passim.

3326 Urdanivia-Bertarelli, Eduardo. "La poesía de Ernesto Cardenal: Fe cristiana y compromiso político," DAI, 44, #2 (August, 1983), 497A (Section A).

3327 Uribe Arce, Armando. Pound. Santiago de Edit (Chile): Editione Universitaria, 1963.

3328 Vallette, Jacques. "Ezra Pound," MdF, #1025 (January, 1949), 160-163.

3329 _____. "Faut-il lire Ezra Pound Essayiste?" MdF, 322 (October, 1954), 320-322.

3330 Valsecchi, Marco. "Si vuole liberare Ezra Pound," Tempo (Milan: November 17, 1955), 17-18.

3331 Van Doren, Mark. "The Garden," Introduction to Poetry. New York: Holt, Rinehart & Winston, 1951, pp. 46-49.

3332 Vázquez Amaral, José. "La poesía de los trovadores y Ezra Pound," RBA, 26 (1976), 10-18.

3333 Vietta, Susanne. "Zum Verhältnis von Subjektivität und Zeitlichkeit im Werk von Ezra Pound und Charles Olson," Amst, 22, #1 (1977), 147-166.

3334 von Hallberg, Robert. "Olson, Whitehead, and the Objectivists," Boundary, 2 (1973-74), 85-111.

3335 _____. "Olson's Relation to Pound and Williams," CLit, 15 (Winter, 1974), 15-48.

3336 _____. "The Poets' Politics: A View from the Archives," ChR, 28, #1 (1976), 147-157.

3337 von Koppenfels, Werner. "Ezra Pound: Der Modernist als Elegiker," Archiv, 212 (1975), 280-302.

3338 Vortriede, Werner. "Die Seefahrt zu den Herkünflen," Merkur, 19 (1966), 487-491.

3339 Waggoner, Hyatt Howe. American Visionary Poetry. Baton Rouge, La.: Louisiana St. U. Pr., 1982, passim.

3340 _____. The Heel of Elohim: Science and Values in Modern American Poetry. Norman, Oklahoma: U. of Oklahoma Pr., 1950, pp. 90-99, passim.

3341 _____. "The Legend of Ezra Pound," UKCR, 10, #4 (Summer, 1944), 275-285.

3342 Wagner, Geoffrey Atheling. Wyndham Lewis: A Portrait of the Artist as Enemy. New Haven: Yale U. Pr., 1957, passim.

3343 Wagner, Linda Welshimer, ed. "On Ezra Pound," Interviews with William Carlos Williams. New York: New Directions Pub. Corp., 1976, pp. 80-81, passim.

3344 _____. "The Poetry of Ezra Pound," JML, 1 (1970), 293-298.

3345 Wain, John. "Poetry," The Twentieth Century Mind: History, Ideas, and Literature in Britain. C. B. Cox and A. E. Dyson, eds. London: Oxford U. Pr., 1972, II, pp. 307-372.

3346 _____. "The Prophet Ezra v. 'The Egotistical Sublime,'" Encounter, 33 (August, 1969), 63-70.

3347 _____. "The Reputation of Ezra Pound," LonM, 2 (October, 1955), 55-64.

3348 _____. "The Reputation of Ezra Pound," Preliminary Essays. London: Macmillan; New York: St. Martin's Pr., 1957, pp. 157-169.

3349 Walkiewicz, E. P., and Hugh Witemeyer. "Ezra Pound's Contributions to New Mexican Periodicals and His Relationship with Senator Bronson Cutting," Paideuma, 9 (1980), 441-459.

3350 Wallace, Emily Mitchell. "Youthful Days and Costly Hours," Ezra Pound and William Carlos Williams. Daniel Hoffman, ed. The University of Pennsylvania Conference Papers. Philadelphia: U. of Pennsylvania Pr., 1983, pp. 14-58.

3351 Walsh, Chad. "The Postwar Revolt in England Against Modern Poetry," BuR, 13, #3 (December, 1965), 97-105.

3352 Walsh, Ernest. "Ezra Pound," This Quarter, I, 1 (Spring, 1925), 229-231.

3353 Walther, Ying Tai Shirley. "A Re-Examination of the Ideogrammic Method of Ezra Pound," DAI, 44, #5 (Kansas St. U.: 1983), 1456A.

3354 Wand, David Happell Hsin-Fu. "Cathay Revisited: The Chinese Tradition in the Poetry of Ezra Pound and Gary Snyder," DAI, 33 (So. Calif.: 1972), 5205A-6A.

3355 Wang, John C. "Ezra Pound as a Translator of Classical Chinese Poetry," SR, 73, #3 (Summer, 1965), 345-357.

3356 Wasserstrom, William, ed. "Introduction," A Dial Miscellany. Syracuse, N.Y.: Syracuse U. Pr., 1963, pp. xi-xxx.

3357 Waugh, Arthur. "The New Poetry," QRL, 226 (October, 1916), 365-368.

3358 _____. "Tradition and Change--the New Poetry," Tradition and Change. Studies in Contemporary Literature. Freeport, New York: Books for Libraries Pr., 1919; repr., 1969, pp. 38-39, passim.

3359 Weatherhead, A. Kingsley. The Edge of the Image: Marianne Moore, William Carlos Williams, and Some Other Poets. Seattle and London: U. of Washington Pr., 1967, pp. 12-19, passim.

3360 Webb, Mark S. "Ezra Pound's Literary Criticism: The Formation of a Modern Poet," DAI, 34 (Yale: 1973), 7252A.

3361 Weeks, Leroy Titus. "The New Beauty," Poetry, 6, #1 (April, 1915), 48-50.

3362 Wees, William C. "England's Avant-Garde: The Futurist-Vorticist Phase," WHR, 21 (1967), 117-128.

3363 _____. "Our Little Gang," Vorticism and the English Avant-Garde. Toronto: Toronto U. Pr., 1972, pp. 119-155.

3364 _____. "Pound's Vorticism: Some New Evidence and Further Comments," WSCL, 7 (Summer, 1966), 211-216.

3365 Weintraub, Stanley. The London Yankees: Portraits of American Writers and Artists in England, 1894-1914. New York: Harcourt Brace Jovanovich, 1979, passim.

3366 Weinzinger, Anita. "Graves's Criticism of Contemporary Poets," On Poets and Poetry: Second Series. Salzburg Studies in English/Poetic Drama and Poetic Theory, No. 27 (1980), pp. 49-101.

3367 Weiss, Theodore R. "The Blight of Modernism and Philip

Larkin's Antidote," The American Poetry Review, 6, #1 (January-February, 1977), 39-41.

3368 _____. "E. P.: The Man Who Cared Too Much," Parnassus, 5 (1977), 79-119; The Man from Porlock: Engagements, 1944-1981. Princeton U. Pr., 1982, pp. 17-57.

3369 _____. "The Many-Sidedness of Modernism," TLS, 1 (February, 1980), 124-125.

3370 Weisstein, Ulrich. "Vorticism: Expressionism English Style," Yearbook of Comparative and General Literature, 13 (1964), 28-40.

3371 Welke, Robert J. "Frobenius: Pound--Some Quick Notes," Paideuma, 2, #3 (Winter, 1973), 415-417.

3372 Wellek, Rene. "Cleanth Brooks, Critic of Critics," SoR, 10, #1 (January, 1974), 125-152.

3373 _____. "Ezra Pound's Literary Criticism," UDQ, 11, #1 (1976), 1-20.

3374 Wells, Henry Willis. New Poets from Old: A Study in Literary Genetics. New York: Russell & Russell, 1964, passim.

3375 Welsh, Andrew. "'Melos' and 'Opsis,'" DA, 31 (Pittsburgh: 1970), 2407A.

3376 West, Ray B. "Ezra Pound and Contemporary Criticism," QRL, 5, #2 (1949), 192-200.

3377 _____. "Ezra Pound and Contemporary Criticism," Critics on Ezra Pound: Readings in Literary Criticism. E. San Juan, Jr., ed. Coral Gables, Fla.: Miami U. Pr., 1972, pp. 36-37.

3378 West, Rebecca. "Imagisme," New Freewoman, I (August 15, 1913), 86-88.

3379 West, T. Wilson. "D. G. Rossetti and Ezra Pound," RES, 4, #13 (January, 1953), 52-56.

3380 Westlake, Neda. "Ezra Pound: A Retrospective of an American Poet: An Exhibition at the University of Pennsylvania, April-June, 1975," William Carlos Williams Newsletter, 1, #1 (1975), 6-7.

3381 Whicher, G. F. "Impressionists and Experimenters," Literature of the American Poeple: An Historical and Critical Survey. Arthur Hobson Quinn, ed. New York: Appleton-Century-Crofts, 1951, pp. 857-864.

3382 Whigham, Peter. "William Carlos Williams," Agenda, 3, #2 (October-November, 1963), 25-32.

3383 Whitehead, Cintra. "Essay I: Ezra Pound and James Legge. Essay II: Modern Personality Theory and Literary Criticism," DAI, 38 (Toledo: 1977), 6698A-99A.

3384 Whittemore, Reed. "Literature as Persuasion," SR, 68, #4 (October, 1960), 565-575.

3385 _____. "Little Magazines," UMPAW, #32, Minneapolis: U. of Minn. Pr., 1963.

3386 Wickes, George. "Hemingway's Arcadia," American Dialog, 3, #2 (Summer, 1966), 32-33.

3387 Widershien, Marc Alan. "The Presence of Modern French Literature in the Writings of Ezra Pound," DAI, 41, #5 (Boston: 1979), 2099A-2100A.

3388 Wiggs, Sharon J. "Pound's 'Greek Epigram': Indictment and Sentence for Inconstancy," StHum, 7, #1 (December, 1978), 48-51.

3389 Wildi, Max. "Pound and Eliot," NZZ, 12 (November, 1972), 51.

3390 Wilhelm, James J. "Arnaut Daniel's Legacy to Dante and to Pound," Italian Literature: Roots and Branches: Essays in Honor of Thomas Goodard Begin. Giose Rimanelli and Kenneth John Archity, eds. New Haven: Yale U. Pr., 1976, pp. 67-83.

3391 _____. Dante and Pound: The Epic of Judgement. Orono: U. of Maine Pr., 1974.

3392 _____. "Ezra Pound's Dante," Punto de Contacto Point of Contact, (New York), 1, #2 (1976), 55-60.

3393 _____. "Pound and the Troubadours," Paideuma, 2, #2 (1973), 133-137.

3394 _____. Seven Troubadours: The Creators of Modern Verse. London: University Park, 1977, pp. 145-172.

3395 _____. "The Troubadours as Guides to Poetry and Paradise," UES, 15, #2 (1977), 35-40.

3396 Willard, Charles B. "Ezra Pound and the Whitman 'Message,'" RLC, 31 (January, 1957), 94-98.

3397 _____. "Ezra Pound's Appraisal of Walt Whitman," MLN, 72 (January, 1957), 19-26.

3398 _____. "Ezra Pound's Debt to Walt Whitman," SP, 54 (October, 1957), 573-581.

3399 Williams, Ellen. Harriet Monroe and the Poetry Renaissance: The First Ten Years of Poetry, 1912-1922. London; Chicago: U. of Illinois Pr., 1977, pp. 33-37, passim.

3400 Williams, Raymond. "A Changing Social History of English Writing," Audience, 8 (Winter, 1961), 76-82.

3401 Williams, William Carlos. "A 1 Pound/Stein (1935)," Selected Essays of William Carlos Williams. New York: New Directions, 1954, pp. 162-166.

3402 _____. "The American Language--again," Pound Newsletter, (October, 1955), 2-7.

3403 _____. "Ezra Pound," The Autobiography of William Carlos Williams. New York: Random House, 1951, pp. 56-66, passim.

3404 _____. "Ezra Pound," The Critical Heritage. Charles Doyle, ed. London; Boston: Routledge & Kegan Paul, 1980, passim.

3405 _____. "Ezra Pound: Lord Ga-Ga!" Decision, 2 (September, 1941), 16-24.

3406 _____. "A Letter to Babette Deutsch," Pound Newsletter, 8 (October, 1955), 22-23.

3407 _____. "Letter to Edgar I. Williams," (April 12, 1905), The Selected Letters of William Carlos Williams. New York: McDowell, Obolensky, 1957, pp. 8-10.

3408 _____. "On Ezra Pound," Interviews with William Carlos Williams. Ed., with Introd., by Linda Welshimer Wagner. New York: New Directions, 1976, pp. 80-81.

3409 _____. "Public Speech and Private Speech in Poetry," A Time to Speak. Cambridge, Mass.: The Riverside Pr., 1941, pp. 61ff.

3410 _____. "Reply to Pound," New Democracy, Vol. 2 (March 30-April 15, 1934). 5.

3411 _____. "T. S. Eliot, or Religion," Three on a Tower: The Lives and Works of Ezra Pound, T. S. Eliot and William

Carlos Williams. New York: William Morrow & Co., Inc., 1975, pp. 93-191.

3412 Wilmer, Clive. "Definition and Flow: Thom Gunn in the 1970's," British Poetry Since 1970: A Critical Survey. Peter Jones and Michael Schmidt, eds. New York: Persea Books, c1980, pp. 64-74.

3413 Wilson, Edmund. Axel's Castle: A Study in the Imaginative Literature of 1870-1930. New York: Scribner's, 1931, pp. 100, 109, 111, 113.

3414 _____. The Devils and Canon Barham: Ten Essays on Poets, Novelists and Monsters. Foreword by Leon Edel. New York: Farrar, Straus and Giroux, 1973, pp. 27, 109, 112-117.

3415 _____. "Ezra Pound's Patchwork," The Shores of Light: A Literary Chronicle of the Twenties and Thirties. New York: Farrar, Straus and Young, Inc., 1952, pp. 44-48.

3416 _____. "The First Waste Land," NYRB, 17 (November 18, 1971), 16-17.

3417 _____. "Marxism at the End of the Thirties," The Shores of Light: A Literary Chronicle of the Twenties and Thirties. New York: Vintage Books, 1961, pp. 732-743.

3418 _____. "Mr. Pound's Patchwork," NR, 30, #385 (April 19, 1922), 232-233.

3419 _____. "The Permanence of Yeats," Selected Criticism. New York: Macmillan, 1950, pp. 22-23.

3420 _____. "T. S. Eliot," NR, 60, #780 (November 13, 1929), 345-346.

3421 Wilson, Suzanne M. "Emily Dickinson and Twentieth-Century Poetry of Sensibility," AL, 36, #3 (November, 1964), 349-358.

3422 Wimsatt, W. K., and Cleanth Brooks. "Eliot and Pound: An Impersonal Art," Literary Criticism: A Short History. New York: Random House, 1967, pp. 657-680.

3423 Winterich, John T. "Ezra Pound," SatRL, 28 (December, 1945), 10.

3424 Winters, Lee Eugene, Jr. "The Relationship of Chinese Poetry to British and American Poetry of the Twentieth Century," Diss. U. of California, Berkeley, 1956.

3425 Winters, Yvor. Forms of Discovery: Critical and Historical Essays on the Forms of the Short Poem in English. Denver: Alan Swallow Co., 1967, passim.

3426 Witemeyer, Hugh. "Ezra Pound," ConL, 14 (Spring, 1973), 240-246.

3427 _____. "Ezra Pound's Poetry, 1908-1916," DAI, 28 (Princeton: 1966), 2271A.

3428 _____. "Ezra Pound's Presence in Guy Davenport's Tatlin," Vort, 9 (1976), 57-61.

3429 _____. "Walter Savage Landor and Ezra Pound," Romantic and Modern: Revaluations of Literary Tradition. George Bornstein, ed. Pittsburgh: U. of Pittsburgh Pr., 1977, pp. 147-163.

3430 Wood, Michael. "Ezra Pound," NYRB, 20 (February 8, 1973), 7-11.

3431 Wood, Tom. "The Value of a Pound," LGJ, 1, #i (1973), 30-33.

3432 Woodard, Charles R. "Browning and Three Modern Poets: Ezra Pound, Yeats, and Eliot," Diss. Tennessee, 1953.

3433 Woodward, A. G. "Ezra Pound," UES, 15, #2 (1977), 1-7.

3434 _____. "Ezra Pound: From Enlightenment to Myth," Standpunte, 146 (1980), 32-43.

3435 _____. "Pound and Santayana," SAQ, 83, #1 (Winter, 1984), 80-90.

3436 Woodward, Anthony. "Ezra Pound, Mussolini and Fascism," Standpunte, 36, #3 (June, 1983), 20-30.

3437 Woodward, Daniel H. "John Quinn and T. S. Eliot's First Book of Criticism," PBSA, 56 (2nd Qt., 1962), 259-265.

3438 Woodward, Kathleen. "The Poetry of Old Age: The Late Poems of Eliot, Pound, Stevens, and Williams," DAI, 37 (Calif., San Diego: 1977), 5821A.

3439 Wright, Arthur F., (ed.) "Some Reflections on the Difficulty of Translation," Studies in Chinese Thought. Chicago: U. of Chicago Pr., 1953, passim.

3440 Wykes-Joyce, Max. "Some Considerations Arising from Ezra Pound's Conception of the Bank, [1949]," An Examination of

Ezra Pound: A Collection of Essays. Peter Russell, ed., Cf., #114, pp. 218-228.

3441 Yeats, William Butler. "Ezra Pound," Ezra Pound: A Collection of Critical Essays. Walter Sutton, ed. Cf., #2240, pp. 9-10.

3442 _____. "Ezra Pound," Critics on Ezra Pound: Readings in Literary Criticism. E. San Juan, Jr., ed., Cf., #535, p. 16.

3443 _____. "Ezra Pound," Introduction, The Oxford Book of Modern Verse. William Butler Yeats, ed. New York: Oxford U. Pr., 1936, pp. xxiv-xxvi.

3444 _____. Interviews and Recollections. E. H. Mikhail, ed. New York: Barnes & Noble, 1977, passim.

3445 _____. The King of the Great Clock Tower. New York: Macmillan Co., 1935, pp. v-vii.

3446 _____. "Letter to Lady Gregory," (December 10, 1909), The Letters of W. B. Yeats. Allan Wade, ed. London: Hart-Davis, 1954, p. 543.

3447 _____. Letters on Poetry from W. B. Yeats to Dorothy Wellesley. Dorothy Wellesley, ed. New York: Oxford U. Pr., 1964, p. 23.

3448 _____. Memoirs of W. B. Yeats: Autobiography-First Draft Journal. Trans. and Edited by Denis Donoghue. New York: Macmillan, 1972.

3449 _____. A Packet for Ezra Pound. Dublin: The Cuala Pr., 1929; repr., in A Vision (by Ezra Pound). London: Macmillan, 1937; New York: Macmillan, 1936, 1956.

3450 _____. "Speaking to the Psaltery," Essays and Introductions. New York: Macmillan, 1961, pp. 13-27.

3451 Yip, Wai-Lim. "Classical Chinese and Modern Anglo-American Poetry: Convergence of Languages and Poetry," CLS, 11, #1 (March, 1974), 21-47.

3452 Yoshino, Masaaki. "Luminous Eros: Ezra Pound and Provencal Alba," SELL, 29 (1978), 21-43. (In Jap.; Eng. sum., pp. 205-206.)

3453 _____. "Pound and His Method of Cognition--as Seen in Terms of His Language," SELL, 24 (1974), 63-77.

3454 Young, Kenneth. "Poets without Readers--and Why," Daily Telegraph (London), (August 7, 1954).

3455 Zabel, Morton Dauwen, ed. "Introduction: Criticism in America," Literary Opinion in America. New York: Rev. Ed., Harper, (1937), 1951, pp. 22-24.

3456 _____. "Recent Magazines," Poetry, 44, #3 (June, 1934), 173-174.

3457 _____. "Recent Magazines," Poetry, 46 (June, 1935), 172.

3458 Zach, Natan. "Imagism and Vorticism," Modernism, 1890-1930. (Pelican Guides to European Literature.) Malcolm Bradbury and James [Walter] McFarlane, eds. Hassocks, Eng.: Harvester; Atlantic Highlands, NJ: Humanities, 1978, pp. 228-242.

3459 Zapatka, Francis Edward. "Ezra Pound and Francois Villon," DAI, 34 (Catholic U. of America: 1973), 1262A.

3460 Zapponi, Niccolò. "Odi e amori futuristi di Ezra Pound," ["Ezra Pound and Futurism,"], SA, 18 (1972), 299-312; revised in "Odi e amori futuristi di Ezra Pound," L'Italia di Ezra Pound (1976); ed., and trans. by Angela Jung and Guido Palandri, Images of Ezra Pound: Twelve Critical Essays. Mei Ya Pubs., Inc., Taipei, Taiwan, 1979, pp. 128-139.

3461 Zardoya, Concha. "Espana en la poesia de Ezra Pound," Insula, (Madrid) 8 (April, 1953), 1-3, 8.

3462 Zilczer, Judith. "The Noble Buyer": John Quinn, Patron of the Avant Garde. Washington: Pub. for the Hirshhorn Museum and Sculpture Garden. Smithsonian Institution, by the Smithsonian Institution Pr., 1978.

3463 Zimmermann, Hans-Joachim. "Die Aphrodite mit dem goldenen Zweig des Argostöters: Betrachtungen zu Ezra Pound Canto I," Geschichte und Gesellschaft in der amerikanischen literature. Karl Schubert and Ursula Müller-Richter, eds., Heidelberg: Quelle & Meyer, 1975, pp. 166-174.

3464 _____. "'An Armour against Utter Consternation' Neuere Literatur zu Ezra Pound," Archiv, 217 (1980), 111-121.

3465 _____. "Ezra Pound," Englische Dichter der Moderne: Ihr Leben und Werk. Rudolf Sühnel and Dieter Riesner, eds. Berlin: Schmidt, 1971, pp. 230-251.

3466 _____. "Ezra Pound, 'A Song of the Degrees': Chinese Clarity versus Alchemical Confusion," Paideuma, 10 (1981), 225-241.

3467 Zinnes, Harriet, ed. Introduction. Ezra Pound and the Visual Arts. New York: New Directions Pub. Corp., 1980.

3468 Zukovsky, Louis. "Ezra Pound," Prepositions: The Collected Critical Essays of Louis Zukovsky. Expanded Ed., Cf., #1054, pp. 67-83.

3469 _____. An Objectivists Anthology. Le Beausset, France; New York: 1932, pp. 17-21.

3470 _____. "Objectivists, 1931," Poetry, 37, #5 (February, 1931), 268-272.

3471 _____. Louis Zukofsky: Man and Poet. Carroll F. Terrell, ed., with Introduction. National Poetry Foundation: U. of Maine, Orono, Maine, 1979, passim.

3472 Zverev, A. "Ezra Pound--literaturnaja teorija, poèzija, sud'ba," [Ezra Pound--literary theory, poetry, fate], VLit, 14, #6 (1970), 123-127.

3473 _____. "Der 'linke' Elitarismus und die Folgen: Ezra Pound," KuL, 4 (April 29, 1981), 427-444. [Tr. from Modernizm v literature, SShA, 1979.]

V. INTERVIEWS

3474 Bridson, D. G. "An Interview with Ezra Pound," New Directions, 17, (1961), 159-184.

3475 Dembo, L. S., and Cyrena N. Pondrom, eds. The Contemporary Writer: Interviews with Sixteen Novelists and Poets. Madison, Wis.: University of Wisconsin Pr., 1972, passim.

3476 Hall, Donald. "Ezra Pound: An Interview," ParisR, 7, #28 (Summer-Fall, 1962), 22-51; repr., in Ezra Pound: A Collection of Criticism. Grace Schulman, ed., Cf., #1084.

3477 _____. "The Paris Review Interviews with T. S. Eliot and Ezra Pound," Remembering Poets: Reminiscences and Opinions: Dylan Thomas, Robert Frost, T. S. Eliot, Ezra Pound. New York: Harper & Row, 1978, pp. 201-244.

3478 Henderson, Archie. "Pound's Stretlets Interview (1915)," Paideuma, 11, #3 (Winter, 1982), 473-486.

3479 Johnson, Edd. Interview with Ezra Pound. Philadelphia Record. (May 9, 1945).

3480 Kerblat-Blanchenay, Jeanne. "End to Torment: Etude de l'interrogation dans la memoire de H. D." in All Men Are Created Equal: Ideologies, Reves et realites. Martin, Jean-Pierre, ed. Aix-en-Provence: Pubs. Univ. de Provence, 1983, pp. 147-167.

3481 Pound, Homer L. [Father of Ezra Pound]. Interview. Evening Bulletin of Philadelphia (February 20, 1928), quoted in Imagism and the Imagists: A Study in Modern Poets by Glenn Hughes. New York: Humanities Pr., c1931, 1960, pp. 227-28.

3482 Reid, B. L. "Four Winds," SR, 87 (Spring, 1979), 273-288.

3483 Reid, David, and Mark Turner. "A Conversation with Hugh Kenner," Cf., #3063, pp. 18-48.

3484 Remnick, David. "An Interview with Charles Wright," PR, 50, #4 (1983), 567-575.

3485 Yoshikawa, Kojiro. "An Interview with Ezra Pound," EWR, 1 (1964), 212-217.

VI. LETTERS

3486 Anceschi. Luciano. "Due lettere su Dante," NC, Nos. 5-6 (1956), 58-69.

3487 _____. "Lettere di Pound," Aut-Aut, No. 2 (marzo 1951), 157-159.

3488 _____. "Tre lettere di Ezra Pound al Dr. Rouse sul tradurre poesia, e una lettera di Joyce," LetM, I (September, 1950), 220-226.

3489 Atkinson, F. G. "Ezra Pound's Reply to an 'Old-World' Letter," AL, 46, #3 (November, 1974), 357-359.

3490 Barnard, Mary. "Ezra Pound, Sappho, and My Assault on Mount Helicon," MHRev, 66 (October, 1983), 140-144.

3491 Bartlett, Lee, and Hugh Witemeyer. "Ezra Pound and James Dickey: A Correspondence and a Kinship," Paideuma, 11, #2 (Fall, 1982), 290-312.

3492 Bergman, Petter. "Ezra Pounds brev," Dagstidningen Arbetaren. Stockholm: (November 9, 1954). (Review: Letters).

3493 Bodini, Vittorio. "Alcune lettere di Ezra Pound," SA, 4 (1958), 421-423.

3494 Brown, Ray C. B. "The Ounce of Prevention," Voices, No. 144 (1951), pp. 45-48.

3495 Bryer, Jackson R. "Pound to Joyce on Ulysses: A Correction," AN&Q, 4 (April, 1966), 115-116.

3496 Carpenter, Humphrey. Ezra Pound and Dorothy Shakespear: Their Letters: 1909-1914. Omar Pound and A. Walton Litz, eds. New York: New Directions (1984).

3497 Casillo, Robert. "Letters of Ezra Pound to Clark Emery in the University of Miami Library," Carrell, 21 (1983), 24-35.

3498 Connolly, Cyril. "Nor Could the Muse Defend Her Son," The Observer, (April 22, 1951). 7.

3499 Cowley, Malcolm. "Mad about Poetry; and Other Things, Too," New York Herald Tribune, Book Review (November 12, 1950), 4. (Review: The Letters.)

3500 Creeley, Robert. "A Note Followed by a Selection of Letters from Ezra Pound," Agenda, 4, #2 (October-November, 1965), 11-21.

3501 Cummings, E. E. "Letters to Ezra Pound," PaR, 39 (Fall, 1966), 55-87.

3502 _____. "To Ezra Pound," Selected Letters of E. E. Cummings. F. W. Dupee and George Stade, eds. New York: Harcourt, Brace & World, Inc., 1969, passim.

3503 Curci, Lino. "Alcune letters," SA, 4 (1958), 421-430.

3504 Dudek, Louis. "Correspondence," Canadian Forum, 29 (November, 1949), 185-186.

3505 _____, ed. Some Letters of Ezra Pound. Montreal: Dudek-Collins, 1974.

3506 Dupee, F. W., and George Stade. "Letters of E. E. Cummings to Ezra Pound," PaR, 10 (Fall, 1966), 55-87.

3507 _____, and _____, eds. Selected Letters of E. E. Cummings. New York: Harcourt, Brace & World, 1969, passim.

3508 Eliot, T. S. "Letter to Ezra Pound from T. S. Eliot," Ezra Pound: Perspectives. Cf., #125, pp. 110-111.

3509 _____. "Mr. Pound and His Poetry," Athenaeum, (November 7, 1919), 1163. (Reply to Pound's Letter, Athenaeum [October 31, 1919], 1132.)

3510 Ellman, Richard, ed. "Joyce Letters," TriQ, 8 (Winter, 1967), 166-176.

3511 Farmer, David. "The Bibliographical Potential of a 20th Century Literary Agent's Archive: The Pinker Papers," LCUT, 2 (November, 1970), 26-35.

3512 _____. "An Unpublished Letter by Ezra Pound," TexQt, 10 (Winter, 1967), 95-104.

3513 Fitts, Dudley. "O Dulce Convivium," Cf., #2316.

3514 Fitz Gerald, Mary. "Ezra Pound and Irish Politics: An Unpublished Correspondence," Paideuma, 12, #2-3 (Fall-Winter, 1983), 377-417.

3515 Ford, Ford Madox. "Letter," Ezra Pound: Perspectives. Cf., #125, p. 126.

3516 Fuller, Roy. [Review: The Letters], The London Magazine, I, #4 (May, 1954), 94-100.

3517 Gallup, Donald, ed. "Ezra Pound: Letters to Viola Baxter Jordan," Paideuma, 1 (Spring-Summer, 1972), 107-111.

3518 Gershman, Herbert S. "Ezra Pound to 'Littérature,'" MLN, 74 (November, 1959), 608-609. Reprint of Pound's Letter to Littérature, #16 (1920), 48.

3519 Gillespie, Don C. "John Becker's Correspondence with Ezra Pound: The Origins of a Musical Crusader," BRH, 83 (1980), 163-171.

3520 Hagemann, E. R. "Incoming Correspondence to Dorothy and Ezra Pound at the Lilly Library," Paideuma, 12, #1 (Spring, 1983), 131-156.

3521 Helsztynski, Stanislaw, ed. "Ezra Pound's Letters to an Editor of His Anthology," KN, 20 (1973), 59-65.

3522 _____. "Ezra Pound's Letters to a Polish Scholar," KN, 17 (1970), 299-323.

3523 Herdeck, Donald E. "A New Letter by Ezra Pound about T. S. Eliot," MassR, 12 (1971), 287-292.

3524 Hungiville, Maurice. "Ezra Pound, Educator: Two Uncollected Pound Letters," AL, 44, #3 (November, 1972), 462-469.

3525 _____. "Ezra Pound's Letters to Olivet," TexQt, 16, #2 (Summer, 1973), 77-87.

3526 Hutchins, Patricia. "Letters from Ezra Pound," TC, 164 (October, 1958), 355-363.

3527 _____. "Ezra Pound and Thomas Hardy," SoR, 4 (n.s.) #1 (January, 1968), 90-104.

3528 Izzo, Carlo. Civiltà americana. Vol. II: impressioni e note. Rome: Edizioni di Storia e Letteratura, 1967.

3529 _____. "Three Unpublished Letters by Ezra Pound," IQ, 64 (1973), 117-118.

3530 _____. "23 lettere e 9 cartoline inedite," NC, Nos. 5-6 (genn.-giugno, 1956), pp. 123-154.

3531 _____. "Twenty-three Unpublished Letters and Nine Post Cards of Ezra Pound," Italian Images of Ezra Pound: Twelve Critical Essays. Angela Jung and Guido Palandri, eds. Taipei, Taiwan: Mei Ya, 1979, pp. 139-159.

3532 Joyce, James. Ezra Pound: Perspectives: Essays in Honor of His Eightieth Birthday. Noel Stock, ed. Cf., #125, pp. 112-113, 115-116.

3533 Kenner, Hugh. "Praestantibusque Ingeniis," KR, 13, #2 (Spring, 1951), 342-345.

3534 Laughlin, James. "Gists and Piths: From the Letters of Pound and Williams," Cf., #2712, pp. 229-243.

3535 Lawton, Harry. "The Ezra Pound Correspondence: Letters of the Lost Legion," Sadakichi Hartmann N, 1 (Winter, 1970), 1-3.

3536 Leary, Lewis. "Book Reviews," SAQ, 50 (October, 1951), 595-596.

3537 _____. "Ezra Pound: A Letter to Jay Hubbell," Paideuma, 5, #3 (Winter, 1976), 417-418.

3538 _____. "Pound-Wise, Penny Foolish: Correspondence on Getting Together a Volume of Criticism," St. Andrews Rev, 1, #1 (Fall-Winter, 1970), 5-9. See also #772.

3539 Leavis, F. R. "Pound in His Letters," Scrutiny, 18, #1 (June, 1951), 74-77.

3540 Lewis, Wyndham. "The Rock Drill," NS&N, 41 (April, 1951), 398.

3541 Lilly Library, Indiana University, Bloomington, Indiana. Reception of more than 12,000 letters from Ezra Pound Estate, donated by Pound's widow, Dorothy Shakespear Pound.

3542 Lindberg-Seyersted, Brita, ed. "Letters from Ezra Pound to Joseph Brewer," Paideuma, 10, #2 (Fall, 1981), 369-382.

3543 _____. "A Note on Ezra Pound as Letter-Writer," Edda, 1 (1981), 59-60.

3544 _____, ed. Pound/Ford: The Story of a Literary Friendship: The Correspondence between Ezra Pound and Ford Madox Ford and Their Writings about Each Other. Cf., #2751.

3545 Lowe, Robert Liddell. "High Thought," Furioso, 6, #2 (Spring, 1951), 71-74.

3546 McShane, Frank, et al. "Letters: The Case for Pound," Cf., #357.

3547 Materer, Timothy. "Doppelganger: Ezra Pound in His Letters," Cf., #2833.

3548 _____. "A Letter by Ezra Pound," MissouriRev, 6, #1 (Fall, 1982), 117-135.

3549 Meacham, Harry M. "Illustrations and Facsimile Letters," The Caged Panther: Ezra Pound at St. Elizabeth's. Cf., #361, pp. 97-102.

3550 Mencken, H. L. Letters of H. L. Mencken. Selected and Edited by Guy J. Forgue. New York: Alfred A. Knopf, 1961, passim.

3551 Meyer, George Previn. "The Sage of Rapallo," SatRL, 33 (December 2, 1950), 24-25.

3552 Meyerson, Edward L. "Letters, Essays, Poetry," The Seed Is Man: A Collection of Poetry and an Essay on Ezra Pound. New York: Wm. Frederick Pr., 1967, pp. 34ff.

3553 Mondolfo, Vittoria I., and Margaret Hurley. Introduction by Walter Pilkington. Ezra Pound: Letters to Ibbotson, 1935-1952. Orono, Maine: National Poetry Foundation, University of Maine, 1979.

3554 Monroe, Harriet. "Poetry's Old Letters," Poetry, 47 (October, 1935), 38-39.

3555 Moore, Arthur V. Letter to Ronald Duncan, December 19, 1945; Letter to Ronald Duncan, February 20, 1946. Humanities Research Center, University of Texas.

3556 Moore, Marianne. Letters. Ezra Pound: Perspectives: Essays in Honor of His Eightieth Birthday. Cf., #125, pp. 116-120.

3557 Morgan, Frederick. "A Note on Ezra Pound," HudR, 4, #1 (Spring, 1951), 156-160.

3558 Namjoshi, S., ed. "Ezra Pound: Letters to John Buchan, 1934-1935," Paideuma, 8 (1979), 462-483.

3559 Nassivera, J. C. "Leaf is a Leaf: A Look at DK/Some Letters of Ezra Pound," Paideuma, 4, #1 (Spring, 1975), 175-178.

3560 Neame, Alan. "Ezra Pound Reconsidered," Blackfriars (May, 1951), Review: Money Pamphlets and The Letters.

3561 Newbolt, Henry. "A Bundle of Letters," Ezra Pound: Perspectives. Noel Stock, ed. Cf., #125, pp. 109-128.

3562 Oldani, Louis. "Two Unpublished Pound Letters: Pound's Aid to Dreiser," LC, 42 (1977), 67-70.

3563 Österling, Anders. "Ezra Pounds brev," Stockholms-Tidningen (January 24, 1951). Review: The Letters.

3564 Paige, D. D. "Letters of Ezra Pound," HudR, 3, #1 (Spring, 1950), 53-56.

3565 _____, ed. The Letters of Ezra Pound, 1907-1941. New York; London: Harcourt Brace, 1950; repr., Norfolk, Conn.: New Directions, 1950.

3566 _____, ed. The Selected Letters of Ezra Pound, 1907-1914. London: Faber, 1971; New York: New Directions Pub. Co., 1971.

3567 Pearlman, Daniel D. "Fighting the World: The Letters of Ezra Pound to Senator William E. Borah of Idaho," Paideuma, 12, #2-3 (Fall-Winter, 1983), 419-426.

3568 Perrine, Laurence. "Ezra Pound's Ideas," SWR, 36 (Winter, 1951), xvi-xix. (Review of Pound's Letters.)

3569 Peschman, Herman. Review: ABC of Reading and The Letters, PoetryRev, 42, #5 (September-October, 1951), 273-275.

3570 Porter, Katherine Anne. "Yours, Ezra Pound," NYT (October 29, 1950), 4.

3571 Pound, Dorothy Shakespear. Letter to Julian Cornell. The Trial of Ezra Pound, Cf., #291, pp. 59-60.

3572 _____. Letter to E. E. Cummings, November 4, 1945, Houghton Library, Harvard University.

3573 _____. Gift of letters from Ezra Pound Estate to Lilly Library. Cf., #3541.

3574 Pound, Ezra. E. P. to L. U.: Nine Letters Written to Louis Untermeyer. Bloomington: Univ. of Indiana Pr., 1963, pp. 46. Review by Marvin Magalaner, BA, 38, #3 (Summer, 1964), 317.

3575 _____. "A Letter by Ezra Pound," MissouriRev, 6, #1 (Fall, 1982), 117-135. Notes by Timothy Materer.

3576 _____. "A Letter to Jay Hubbell," (Lewis Leary, ed.) Paideuma, 5 (Winter, 1976), 417-418.

3577 _____. "Letters from Ezra Pound to Benito Mussolini," ed. by C. D. Heymann; tr. by R. Connolly. Encounter, 46, #5 (May, 1976), 35-41.

3578 _____. "Letters to Elizabeth Winslow," Paideuma, 9 (Fall, 1980), 340-356.

3579 _____. Letters to Ibbotson, 1935-1952. Vittoria I. Mondolfo and Margaret Hurley, eds. Introduction by Walter Pilkington. Orono: National Poetry Foundation, University of Maine, 1979.

3580 _____. "Letters to John Buchan, 1934-1935," Paideuma, 8 (Winter, 1979), 461-483.

3581 _____. "Letters to Natalie Barney," Edited with Commentary by Richard Sieburth. Paideuma, 5 (Fall, 1976), 279-299.

3582 _____. "Letters to Viola Baxter Jordan," Paideuma, 1 (Spring-Summer, 1972), 107-112.

3583 _____. "Letters to a Young Poet from Ezra Pound," Poetry, 76 (September, 1950), 342-351.

3584 _____. "Letters to the Editor," SatRL, 32 (June, July, 1949), 21-24.

3585 _____. "A Prison Letter," PaR, 28 (Summer-Fall, 1962), 17.

3586 _____. "Tidings from Pound to Joyce: Letter," Esquire, 64 (December, 1965), 152ff.

3587 _____, and T. S. Eliot. "[An Exchange of Letters on The Waste Land,]" Nine, 4 (Summer, 1950), 176-179.

3588 Pound, Omar, and A. Walton Litz, eds. Ezra Pound and Dorothy Shakespear: Their Letters, 1909-1914. New York: New Directions, 1984.

3589 Read, Forrest, ed. Pound/Joyce: The Letters of Ezra Pound to James Joyce, with Pound's Essays on Joyce. New York: New Directions, 1970.

3590 Robbins, J. Albert, ed. EP to LU: Nine Letters Written to Louis Untermeyer by Ezra Pound. Bloomington: Indiana University Pr., 1963.

3591 Sieburth, Richard. "Ezra Pound: 'Letters to Natalie Barney,'" Paideuma, 5 (Fall, 1976), 279-299.

3592 Sinclair, Upton. "Ezra Pound," My Lifetime in Letters. Cf., #3175, pp. 368-376.

3593 Singh, G. "Ezra Pound as a Letter Writer," AJES, 2 (1977), 167-193.

3594 Steele, John L. "Ezra at the DTC: A Correspondence between Carroll F. Terrell and John L. Steele," Paideuma, 12, #2-3, (Fall-Winter, 1983), 293-303. [DTC: Disciplinary Training Center]

3595 Stein, Sol. Reviews: The Letters and An Examination of Ezra Pound, ArizQt, 7, #2 (Summer, 1951), 180-186.

3596 Stock, Noel, ed. "A Bundle of Letters," Ezra Pound: Perspectives, Cf., #125, pp. 109-128.

3597 _____. "Ezra Pound and the Sense of Responsibility," ModAge (Chicago), 5 (Spring, 1961), 173-178.

3598 _____. "Verse Is a Sword: Unpublished Letters of Ezra Pound," XQtRev, I, #4 (October, 1960), 258-265.

3599 Symington, R. T. K. "'I Like to Get Letters': Ezra Pound and a Canadian Correspondent," MHRev, 66 (October, 1983), 129-139.

3600 Tanselle, G. Thomas. "Two Early Letters of Ezra Pound," Cf., #1781, pp. 114-119.

3601 Terrell, Carroll F. "An Interlude: Creating and Sweeping Up: [Letters to Marcella Booth and Her Replies]," Paideuma, 4, #1 (Spring, 1975), 189-195.

3602 _____. "Ezra Pound's Letters to William Butler Yeats," Antaeus, 21 (1976), 34-49.

3603 Thirlwall, John C. "The Quality of Mercy was not strained: a Footnote Followed by a Letter," Pound Newsletter, 8 (October, 1955), 22-23.

3604 Thompson, James H., ed. "Letters to Elizabeth Winslow," Paideuma, 9 (1980), 341-356.

3605 Traverso, Leone. "Letture de Ezra Pound," Studi urbinati di storia, filosofia e letteratura, 45 (1971), 300-303.

3606 Tseng, Pao Swen. "Letter to Mr. and Mrs. Pound," YLM, 127, #6 (January, 1959), 11.

3607 Van Doren, Mark. Preface. The Letters of Ezra Pound, 1907-1941. D. D. Paige, ed. Cf., #3565, pp. v-ix.

3608 Wade, Allan, ed. The Letters of W. B. Yeats. London: Rupert Hart-Davis; New York: Macmillan, 1954, passim.

3609 Weissman, David L., et al. "Correspondence," Cf., #252.

3610 West, Ray B., Jr. "Letters of an American," SR, 59 (Spring, 1951), 342-347.

3611 Wigginton, Waller B. "A Homer Pound Letter," Cf., #149, pp. 27-29.

3612 Williams, William Carlos. "Letter," Ezra Pound: Perspectives. Noel Stock, ed. Cf., #125, pp. 124-125.

3613 Yeats, W. B. "A Packet for Ezra Pound," A Vision. New York: Macmillan, [c1938], 1956, pp. 26-30.

3614 Z[abell], M[orton]. "Recent Magazines," [Letters]. Cf., #3456, pp. 173-174.

VII. BIBLIOGRAPHY

3615 Agenda, Ezra Pound Number, #2, IV (October-November, 1965); Nos. 3-4, VIII (1970), William Cookson, ed.

3616 Altieri, Charles, Comp. "Ezra Pound," Modern Poetry. AHM Pub. Co., Arlington Hts., Ill., 1979, pp. 76-79.

3617 The Analyst, ed. Robert Mayo. Evanston: Northwestern University, 1953- .

3618 Angus, Ian D. A List with Description of the Books of Ezra Pound. London: [Microfilm copy of typescript.], 1952.

3619 Arms, George, and Joseph Kuntz. Poetry Explication. New York: Swallow Press and William Morrow & Co., Inc., 1950.

3620 Bornstein, George. "Pound and Eliot," American Literary Scholarship: An Annual/1977. Durham, N.C.: Duke U. Pr., 1979, pp. 119-133.

3621 _____, and Stuart Y. McDougal. "Pound and Eliot," American Literary Scholarship: An Annual/1978. J. Albert Robbins, ed. Durham, N.C.: Duke U. Pr., 1980, pp. 111-125.

3622 _____, and Stuart Y. McDougal. "Pound and Eliot," American Literary Scholarship: An Annual/1979. James Woodress, ed. Durham, N.C.: Duke U. Pr., 1981, pp. 115-132.

3623 _____, and Stuart Y. McDougal. "Pound and Eliot," American Literary Scholarship: An Annual/1980. J. Albert Robbins, ed. Durham, N.C.: Duke U. Pr., 1982, pp. 121-141.

3624 _____, and Stuart Y. McDougal. "Pound and Eliot," American Literary Scholarship: An Annual/1981. James Woodress, ed. Durham, N.C.: Duke U. Pr., 1983, pp. 127-136.

3625 "A Checklist of Explications." Pound Newsletter, #5 (January, 1955), 20-21; #6 (April, 1955), 16-19, 24-30; #7 (July, 1955), 6-10; #8 (October, 1955), 33-35.

3626 Corrigan, Robert A. "An Annotated Checklist of Ezra Pound Criticism: Part I," Paideuma, 1 (Winter, 1972), 229-263; (supersedes author's "The First Quarter Century of Ezra Pound Criticism," RALS, 2, 157-207.

3627 Crosland, Andrew. "An Annotated Checklist of Criticism on Ezra Pound, 1961-1965," Paideuma, 8 (Winter, 1979), 523-538.

3628 Crowder, Richard. "Ezra Pound: Poetry, 1900 to the 1930's," American Literary Scholarship: An Annual, 1969. J. Albert Robbins, ed. Durham, N.C.: Duke U. Pr., 1971, pp. 253-261.

3629 _____. "Ezra Pound: Poetry, 1900 to 1930's," American Literary Scholarship: An Annual, 1970. J. Albert Robbins, ed. Durham, N.C.: Duke U. Pr., 1972, pp. 280-288.

3630 _____. "Ezra Pound: Poetry: 1900 to the 1930's," American Literary Scholarship: An Annual, 1971. J. Albert Robbins, ed. Durham, N.C.: Duke U. Pr., 1973, pp. 278-283.

3631 _____. "Ezra Pound: Poetry: 1900 to 1930's," American Literary Scholarship: An Annual, 1973. James Woodress, ed. Durham, N.C.: Duke U. Pr., 1975, pp. 305-311.

3632 Davis, Charles T. "Pound--Poetry: 1910-1930," American Literary Scholarship: An Annual, 1963. James Woodress, ed. Durham, N.C.: Duke U. Pr., 1965, pp. 173-177.

3633 Dilligan, Robert J., James W. Parins, and Todd K. Bender. A Concordance to Ezra Pound's Cantos. New York; London: Garland Pub., Inc., 1981.

3634 Edwards, John. A Preliminary Checklist of the Writings of Ezra Pound. New Haven: Kirgo-Books, 1953.

3635 _____, and W. W. Vasse. Annotated Index to the Cantos of Ezra Pound. Berkeley: U. of Calif. Pr., 1958.

3636 Espey, John. "Ezra Pound: Bibliography," Fifteen Modern American Authors. Jackson R. Bryer, ed. Durham, N.C.: Duke U. Pr., 1969, pp. 323-344.

3637 _____. "Ezra Pound: Bibliography," Sixteen Modern American Authors. Jackson R. Bryer, ed. Durham, N.C.: Duke U. Pr., 1974, pp. 445-471.

3638 Froula, Christine. A Guide to Ezra Pound's Selected Poems. New York: New Directions, 1983.

3639 Gallup, Donald Clifford. A Bibliography of Ezra Pound. London: Rupert Hart-Davis, 1963.

3640 _____. "Corrections and Additions to the Pound Bibliography (Part 3)," Paideuma, 1, #1 (Spring-Summer, 1972), 113-125; 2, #2 (Fall, 1973), 315-324; 3, #3 (Winter, 1974), 403-404.

3641 _____. On Contemporary Bibliography, with Particular Reference to Ezra Pound. Austin, Texas: Humanities Research Center, U. of Texas, 1970.

3642 Hatlen, Burton. "Work in Progress," Paideuma, 3, #2 (Fall, 1974), 275-277.

3643 Havlice, Patricia Pate. "Ezra Pound," Index to American Author Bibliographies. Metuchen, N.J.: Scarecrow Pr., Inc., 1971, pp. 132-133.

3644 Henault, Marie P. Guide to Ezra Pound. Merrill Guides. Columbus, Ohio: Charles E. Merrill, 1970.

3645 Jones, Howard Mumford, and Richard M. Ludwig. "The Thirties," and "The Poetic Renaissance," Guide to American Literature and Its Backgrounds Since 1890. 4th ed., Rev. & Enlarged. Cambridge, Mass.: Harvard U. Pr., 1972, pp. 174, 198-199.

3646 Jung, Angela, and Guido Palandri, eds., and trs. Italian Images of Ezra Pound: Twelve Critical Essays. Taipei, Taiwan: Mei Ya, 1979, pp. 163-167.

3647 Koster, Donald N. "Ezra Pound (1885-1972)," American Literature and Language: A Guide to Information Sources. Detroit, Mich.: Gale Research Co., 1982, pp. 224-232.

3648 Kunitz, Stanley J., ed. Twentieth Century Authors: A Bibliographical Dictionary of Modern Literature. New York: H. W. Wilson Co., 1955, pp. 1121-1123.

3649 Kuntz, Joseph M., and Nancy C. Martinez. "Ezra Pound," Poetry Explication: A Checklist of Interpretation Since 1925 of British and American Poems, Past and Present. Boston: G. K. Hall & Co., 1950; 1980, pp. 351-354.

3650 Lane, Gary. A Concordance to Personae: The Shorter Poems of Ezra Pound. New York: Haskell House Pubs., 1972.

3651 Leary, Lewis. "Ezra Pound," Articles on American Literature, 1900-1950. Durham: Duke U. Pr., 1954, pp. 252-254.

3652 _____. "Ezra Pound," Articles on American Literature, 1950-1967. Durham, N.C.: Duke U. Pr., 1970, pp. 450-561.

3653 _____, with John Auchard. "Ezra Pound," Articles on American Literature, 1968-1975. Durham, N.C.: Duke U. Pr., 1979, pp. 426-437.

3654 Libman, Valentina A., com. "Ezra Pound," Russian Studies in American Literature. Clarence Gohdes, ed. Chapel Hill: U. of North Carolina Pr., 1969, p. 155f.

3655 Little, Matthew. "Corrections to Gallup's Pound and Some History of Pound's Essays on the Jefferson-Adams Letters," BSAP, 74 (1980), 200-272.

3656 Ludwig, Richard M. "Pound and Eliot," American Literary Scholarship: An Annual, 1974. James Woodress, ed. Durham, N.C.: Duke U. Pr., 1976, pp. 101-121.

3657 McDougal, S. Y. "Pound and Eliot," American Literary Scholarship: An Annual, 1975. James Woodress, ed. Durham, N.C.: Duke U. Pr., 1977, pp. 131-142.

3658 _____. "Pound and Eliot," American Literary Scholarship: An Annual, 1976. J. Albert Robbins, ed. Durham, N.C.: Duke U. Pr., 1978, pp. 109-118.

3659 Millett, Fred Benjamin. "Ezra Pound," Contemporary American Authors. New York: AMS Pr., 1970, pp. 529-533.

3660 Mondolfo, Vittoria. "Annotated Bibliography of Criticism of Ezra Pound, 1918-1924," Paideuma, 5, #2 (Fall, 1976), 303-328.

3661 _____, and Helen Shuster. "Annotated Checklist of Criticism on Ezra Pound, 1930-1935," Paideuma, 5, #1 (Spring, 1976), 155-184.

3662 Morrow, Bradford, and Bernard Lafourcade. With Introduction by Hugh Kenner. A Bibliography of the Writings of Wyndham Lewis. Santa Barbara, Calif.: Black Sparrow Pr., 1978, Pound passim.

3663 Munson, Gorham. "Ezra Pound," American Literary Scholarship: An Annual, 1966. James Woodress, ed. Durham, N.C.: Duke U. Pr., 1968, pp. 193-196.

3664 _____, and Ann Stanford. "Ezra Pound--Poetry: 1900 to 1930's," American Literary Scholarship: An Annual, 1968. Durham, N.C.: Duke U. Pr., 1970, pp. 228-232.

3665 Nilon, Charles H. "Ezra Pound," Bibliography of Bibliographies in American Literature. New York; London: R. R. Bowker Co., 1970, p. 232.

3666 O'Connor, William Van, and Edward Stone, eds. A Casebook on Ezra Pound. New York: Thomas Y. Crowell Co., 1959.

3667 Paideuma: A Journal Devoted to Ezra Pound Scholarship. Hugh Kenner and Eva Hesse, eds. U. of Maine, Orono, 1972.

3668 Pound Newsletter. John H. Edwards, ed. Berkeley, U. of Calif. 1954-1966.

3669 Quarterly Review of Literature. Ezra Pound Issue, 5, #2 (1949). Bard College, Annandale, N.Y.

3670 Richardson, Kenneth ed. "Ezra Pound," Twentieth Century Writing: A Reader's Guide to Contemporary Literature. Levittown, New York: Transatlantic Arts, Inc., 1971, pp. 499-501.

3671 Rizzardi, Alfredo, ed. "Studi e Opinioni su Ezra Pound," Nuova Corrente, Nos. 5-6 (January-June, 1956).

3672 Rooks, George. "An Annotated Checklist of Criticism on Ezra Pound, 1976," Paideuma, 8, (Fall, 1979), 303-316.

3673 Rosenfeld, Alvin H. "Ezra Pound--Poetry: 1900 to the 1930s," American Literary Scholarship: An Annual/1972. Durham, N.C.: Duke U. Pr., 1974, pp. 312-319, passim.

3674 Russell, Peter, ed. Ezra Pound: A Collection of Essays edited by Peter Russell to be Presented to Ezra Pound on His Sixty-fifth Birthday. Norfolk, Conn.: New Directions, 1950.

3675 San Juan, Jr., E[pifanio]. Critics on Ezra Pound: Readings in Literary Criticism. Coral Gables, Florida: U. of Miami Pr., 1972.

3676 Schneeman, Peter. "Pound in Romania," Paideuma, 10, #2 (Fall, 1981), 421-434.

3677 Schulman, Grace, ed. Ezra Pound: A Collection of Criticism. New York: McGraw-Hill, 1974.

3678 Schwartz, Joseph. "Books on Pound," Spirit, 37, #2 (1970), 42-46.

3679 Seymour-Smith, Martin. "Ezra Pound," Guide to Modern World Literature. New York: Funk & Wagnalls, 1973, pp. 67-73.

3680 Sickles, Hollis. "An Annotated Checklist of Pound Criticism," Paideuma, 8 (Spring, 1979), 97-140.

3681 Slatin, Myles. "More by Ezra Pound," YULG, 30 (October, 1955), 74-80.

3682 Somer, John, and Barbara E. Cooper. American and British Literature, 1945-1975: An Annotated Bibliography of Contemporary Scholarship. Lawrence, Kansas: Regents Pr. of Kansas, 1980, passim.

3683 Spiller, Robert E., et al, eds. Literary History of the United States. Bibliography Supplement II. New York: Macmillan, 1972, Vol. 3, pp. 240-244.

3684 Stanford, Ann. "Ezra Pound--Poetry 1910-1930," American Literary Scholarship: An Annual, 1964. James Woodress, ed. Durham, N.C.: Duke U. Pr., 1966, pp. 184-186.

3685 _____. "Ezra Pound--Poetry: 1900 to the 1930's," American Literary Scholarship: An Annual, 1965. James Woodress, ed. Durham, N.C.: Duke U. Pr., 1967, pp. 204-208.

3686 Stock, Noel, ed. Ezra Pound: Essays in Honour of His Eightieth Birthday. Chicago: Henry Regnery Co., 1965.

3687 _____, Guest-ed. Helix. Special Issue Nos. 13 and 14 (1983). (119 Maltravers Road, Ivanhoe, Australia 3079).

3688 Sutton, Walter, ed. Ezra Pound: A Collection of Critical Essays. Englewood Cliffs, New Jersey: Prentice-Hall, 1963, Cf., #2240.

3689 Tate, Allen. "Ezra Pound," Essays of Four Decades. Chicago: The Swallow Pr., 1968, pp. 364-371, 509-513; Cf., #240, #970.

3690 _____. Sixty American Poets, 1896-1944. Washington: Library of Congress and Biblio Division, 1954, Rev. ed., pp. 93-101. Cf., #3262.

3691 Vasse, William. "Bibliography," The Pound Newsletter, [Ten issues], (January, 1954-April, 1956).

3692 _____. "A Checklist of Explications: I: The Pre-Canto Poetry," Pound Newsletter, 5 (January, 1955), 20-21.

3693 _____. "A Checklist of Explications: II: The Cantos," Pound Newsletter, 6 (April, 1955), 16-19.

3694 Weber, Brom, and James Woodress. "Ezra Pound--Poetry:

1900 to the 1930's," American Literary Scholarship: An Annual, 1967. James Woodress, ed. Durham, N.C.: Duke U. Pr., 1969, pp. 212-216.

3695 Wenzel, Gernot. "Addenda to Robert A. Corrigan's Bibliographical Contributions on Pound," Paideuma, 5, #1 (Spring, 1976), 214-215.

3696 Williams, William Carlos. The William Carlos Williams Reader. Edited with Introduction by M. L. Rosenthal. New York: New Directions Pub. Corp., 1966, pp. 308-318. Cf., #423.

INDEX OF CRITICS

A. M. 1453
Aaron, Daniel 1784
Abad, Gemino H. 1774
Abbs, Peter 1785
Abiru, Shin 427
Abse, Dannie 1786, 1787
Accrocca, E[lio] F[illippo] 1762, 1788
Ackroyd, Peter 1, 1789
Adams, Leonie 157
Adams, Robert M. 1790, 1791
Adams, Stephen Jon 428, 429, 430, 1630, 1792, 1793, 1794, 1795, 1796, 1797, 1798
Agnoletti, Enriques E. 158
Agresti, Olivia Rosetti 1799, 1800, 1801
Aiken, Conrad 260, 1543, 1548, 1549, 1550, 1802, 1803, 1804, 1805, 1806
Alden, Raymond Macdonald 1620
Aldington, Richard 1807, 1808, 1809, 1810, 1811, 1812, 1813, 1814, 1815, 1816, 1817, 1818, 1819
Aleksic, Branko 1820
Alexander, Michael 431, 432, 1631, 1821, 1822
Allen, Robert L. 261
Alpert, Barry S. 1823, 1824, 1825
Alsterlund, B. 1826, 1827
Altieri, Charles 1828, 3616
Alvarez, A[lfred] 262, 263, 1199, 1683, 1829, 1830, 1831
Amaral, Jose Vazquez 1065, 1066, 1832, 1833, 1834
Amdur, Alice Steiner 433, 1835
Ames, Alfred C. 159
Amgioletti, Lina 2437
Anant, Victor 1836
Anceschi, Luciano 1837, 1838, 1839, 1840, 3486, 3487, 3488
Anderson, David 1279, 1280, 1841, 1842
Anderson, Margaret 1843
Angoff, Allan 1546, 1844
Angoff, Charles 1845
Angus, Ian D. 3618
Antheil, George 1676, 1677, 1846, 1847
Antonini, A. 1848
Apter, Ronnie Susan 1849
Arce, Armando Uribe 1850
Arendt, Hannah 1851
Armanini, Ante 1852
Arms, George 3619
Arnold, Thurman 264
Arns, K. 1603, 1604
Arvin, Newton 1742
Ashleigh, Charles 1853
Astaldi, Maria Louisa 1067
Atkinson, F. G. 3489
Auchard, John 3653
Auden, W. H. 2, 160
Avedon, Richard 17, 1854
Awiszus, Sabine 1855, 1856, 1857
Axelrod, Steven Gould 434, 1858
Ayscough, Florence 1859

Baar, Ron 435, 1860
Bab, Julius 1861
Bachinger, Katrina 436
Bacigalupo, Massimo 437, 438, 439, 440, 441, 1068, 1200, 1339, 1862, 1863
Baconsky, A. E. 1864
Bailey, Bruce 1865
Baisch, Dorothy 1866

Baker, Carlos 3, 1867
Balagot, Thelma C. 442
Baldner, Ralph W. 1868
Banerjee, Ron D. K. 443, 1869
Banta, R. E. 4
Barbour, Douglas 1870
Barbour, Linda Lee 1871
Barfoot, Gabriele 1872, 1873
Barilli, Renato 1874
Barker, George 444
Barnard, Harry 1875
Barnard, Mary 1876, 3490
Barrett, William 161
Barricelli, Gian Piero 1877
Barry, Elaine 1599, 1878
Barry, Iris 266, 1879
Bartlett, Lee 3491
Barton, David 1069
Batavia, Ludovico von 1880
Bates, Eveline 1881
Bates, Margaret 1882
Baumann, Walter 445, 446, 447, 448, 1201, 1883, 1884, 1885, 1886, 1887
Bayes, Ronald H. 267
Beach, Joseph Warren 1888, 1889
Beach, Sylvia 1890, 1891
Beatty, Richard Croom 1967
Beaujour, Michel 1892
Beck, Warren 1429
Bednář, Kamil 1893
Beer, J. B. 1894
Bell, Ian F. A. 449, 1340, 1341, 1342, 1343, 1430, 1621, 1895, 1896, 1897, 1898, 1899, 1977, 2401, 2606, 2903, 2909, 3138
Bender, Todd K. 569, 3633
Benet, William Rose 162, 268, 269, 1070, 1551, 1900, 1901
Bennett, John 1252
Bennett, Mitchell Bruce 1902
Benton, Richard P. 1903
Berezin, Charles 450, 1904
Berger, T. L. 1905
Bergman, Herbert 1906
Bergman, Petter 3492
Bergonizi, Bernard 451, 1907
Bernard, Mary 1908
Bernstein, Michael Andre 452, 453, 454, 455, 456
Berri, Pietro 1909
Berryman, Jo Brantley 1344, 1345, 1346, 1347, 1348, 1349, 2332
Berryman, John 5, 6, 163, 1071, 1910, 1911
Bertacchini, Renato 1072, 1912, 1913
Berti, Luigi 1914, 1915
Bertolucci, Attilio 1916
Betocchi, Carlo 1917
Bessinger, J. B. 1632
Bevilaqua, Ralph 1431
Bewley, Marius 1918, 1919
Beyer, W. H. 1920
Bhatnagar, I. 1921
Bianchi, Ruggero 1922, 1923
Bibesco, H. 7
Bigongiari, Piero 1924, 1925
Bilenchi, Romano 1926, 1927
Bishop, Elizabeth 270
Bishop, John Peale 457, 1580, 1928, 1929
Bishop, Philip E. 458
Blackburn, Paul 1930
Blackburn, Thomas 1931
Blackmur, R. P. 459, 1286, 1349, 1552, 1932, 1933, 1934
Blamires, David 460
Blish, James 164, 271, 461
Blissett, William 1240
Bloom, E. A. 1458
Blum, W. C. 1447
Bly, Robert 1935
Bock, Layeh Aronson 1936
Bode, Carl 1937
Bodenheim, Maxwell 462, 1478, 1581
Bodini, Vittorio 3493
Boensch, Maria R. 1938
Boer, Charles 1939
Bogan, Louise 463, 464, 465, 1073, 1268, 1269, 1940, 1941, 1942, 1943, 1944
Bonfante, Jordan 272
Bonner, Paul Hyde 1945
Booth, Frederick Joseph 1946
Booth, Marcella Spann 273, 1947
Bornstein, Daniel 466

Bornstein, George 467, 468, 1350, 1948, 1949, 1950, 1951, 1952, 1953, 3134, 3620, 3621, 3622, 3623, 3624
Boselli, Mario 1954, 1955
Bosha, Francis J. 274, 469, 470
Bosschère, Jean de 1956
Bottome, Phyllis 8, 9
Bottrall, Ronald 471, 472, 473, 1957
Boussard, Léon 1958
Boveri, Margaret 1959
Bowen, Stella 1960
Bowers, Faubion 10
Bowers, Fredson 1571
Bowers, Frederick 1961
Bowra, Cecil Maurice 473, 1074, 1646, 1715, 1962
Boyd, Ernest L. 11
Boyers, Robert 1963
Bradbrook, Muriel C. 1964
Bradbury, Malcolm 12, 275, 1965, 1966
Bradford, Curtis B. 474
Bradley, Edward Sculley 1967
Braidwood, John 13
Braithwaite, William Stanley 1968
Brandabur, Edward 1969
Braybrooke, Neville 1553
Bregy, Katherine 1743
Breit, Harvey 276, 1706
Brenner, Milton 1253
Breslin, James E. 1970
Breunig, Le Roy 1971
Bridgman, Richard 1972
Bridson, D. G. 277, 475, 476, 1744, 1973, 1974, 1975, 3474
Brinnin, John Malcolm 626, 1374, 1614, 1976
Bronner, Milton 1554
Brooke, Rupert 1555, 1556
Brooker, Peter 477, 1977, 1978
Brooke-Rose, Christine 478, 479, 480, 481, 1979
Brooks, Cleanth 165, 278, 1432, 3422
Brooks, David Gordon 482
Brooks, Van Wyck 1448, 1980, 1981, 1982, 1983
Brown, Ashley 1459
Brown, C. 1984
Brown, E. K. 1588
Brown, Ivor 1745
Brown, John 1985
Brown, John L. 14, 1986, 1987
Brown, Merle 1988
Brown, Peter 280
Brown, Ray C. B. 3494
Browne, Robert M. 1989
Broyard, A. 1990
Bruce, Elizabeth Esther 1991
Brulé, A. 1329, 1330
Brumm, Anne-Marie 1351
Bruns, Gerald L. 1992
Bryer, Jackson R. 1433, 1434, 1521, 1993, 1994, 1995, 2271, 2272, 3495
Bryher, Annie Winfred Ellerman 1996
Brynos, Robert S. 1529
Bueltmann, Faith 1352
Bullaro, John Joseph 1997
Bullough, Geoffrey 1998
Bunting, Basil 483, 484
Burchardi, Johannis 485
Burford, William 1647
Burgess, Anthony 1999
Burke, Kenneth 1746
Burne, Glenn S. 2000
Burns, Gerald 486
Burt, Struthers 166
Bush, Douglas 2001, 2002
Bush, Ronald L. 487, 1287, 2003
Buss, Kate 1479
Butor, Michel 2004
Butterick, George 488, 2068
Butturff, Douglas R. 2005
Buxbaum, Katherine 1775
Bynner, Witter 2006
Byrd, Don 2007
Byrnos, Robert S. 1529

C. R. A. 1494
Cady, Frank C. 2008
Caesar, Terry Paul 2009

Calinescu, Matei 2010, 2011
Callaghan, Morley 2012
Caloro, Bonaventura 2013
Cambon, Glauco 1202, 2014, 2015, 2016, 2017, 2018, 2019, 2020, 2021, 2022, 2023
Campbell, K. T. S. 489
Campbell, Sue Ellen 2024
Campos, Augusto de 1353, 2025, 2026
Campos, Haroldo de 2026, 2027
Canby, Henry Seidel 167, 281
Cann, Louise Beghard 15
Cantrell, Carol Helmstetter 490, 491, 1075
Caparelli, Giuseppe 1076
Capellan Gonzalo, Angel 16, 2028, 2029
Capote, Truman 17, 1854
Caproni, Giorgio 2030, 2031, 2032
Cargill, Oscar 2033
Carleton, Samuel 2034
Carmichael, Frank Charles, Jr. 2035
Carne-Ross, D. S. 492, 493, 494, 2036, 2203
Carnevali, Emanuel 1544
Carpenter, Humphrey 3496
Carruth, Hayden 18, 168, 169, 170, 282, 2037, 2038, 2039
Carruthers, Ian 2040
Carter, Thomas H. 1460
Cary, Joseph 2041
Casamayor, Enrique 2042
The Case Against the Saturday Review 283
Casillo, Robert 495, 2043, 2044, 3497
Casper, Leonard 2045
Cassell, Richard A. 2046, 2047
Castellani, Leonardo 2048
Cayley, John 496
Cenci, Lino 2049
Cerf, Bennett 284, 285, 2050
Chace, William M. 497, 1077, 2051, 2052, 2053, 2054, 2055
Chakravarty, Amiya 2056
Chan, Wing-tsit 1707
Chaplin, Sherry 1633
Chapman, Robert T. 2057
Charlesworth, Barbara 2058, 2059
Charters, Jimmie 2060
Chase, Richard 2061
Chauvet, Paul 1288, 1495
Cheadle, Brian 498
Cherchi, Luciano 2062
Chesterton, G. K. 1496
Chiara, Piero 2063
Chiareno, Aldo 2064
Chiari, Joseph 2065
Chilanti, Felice 286, 2066
Child, Harold 1622
Childs, Harwood Lawrence 171
Childs, John Steven 499, 500
Chisolm, Lawrence W. 2067
Christensen, Paul 2068, 2069
Chung, Ling 2070
Chute, Desmond 2071, 2072
Cianci, Giovanni 2073
Ciardi, John 1203, 2074
Cimatti, Piettro 2075
Claes, Paul 2076
Clare, John 2077
Clark, David R. 2078
Clark, Thomas 501
Clark, William Bedford 19
Clarkson, William Ellis 2079, 2080
Clearfield, Andrew 2081
Clemons, Walter 2082
Coblentz, Stanton A. 2083
Coffman, Stanley K., Jr. 1667, 2084, 2085
Cohane, J. J., Jr. 287
Cohen, J. M. 2086
Colaneri, John 2087
Cole, Thomas 1461, 1648, 2088, 2089
Coles, R. 2090
Colinas, Antonio 2091
Collinge, N. E. 1530
Colum, Mary M. 2092, 2093
Colum, Padriac 1449
Conarroe, Joel 2094
Connolly, Cyril 20, 288, 502, 2095, 2096, 2097, 3498
Connolly, Thomas E. 1354, 1511

Conquest, Robert 2098
Contini, Gianfranco 2099
Contino, Vittorugo 1078
Cook, Albert S. 503, 504
Cook, Howard Willard 2100
Cook, Reginald L. 2101
Cookson, William 2102
Cooney, Douglas L. 511
Cooper, Barbara Eck 3682
Cork, Richard 2103
Cornell, Julien 289, 290, 291
Cornevali, Emanuel 2104
Coronel-Urtecho, José 2105
Corrigan, Matthew 2106
Corrigan, Robert A. 172, 173, 174, 292, 293, 1079, 2107, 2108, 2109, 2110, 3626
Corsare, Antonio 1080
Corsini, Renato 2111
Cory, Daniel 21, 512, 2112
Coulter, John W. 1738
Cournos, John 22
Courtney, W. L. 1557
Cousins, Norman 175, 176, 177, 234, 1081
Covell, Roger 1529
Cowan, James C. 513
Cowley, Edmund 23
Cowley, Malcolm 178, 294, 295, 514, 1082, 2113, 2114, 2115, 2116, 2117, 3499
Cox, Kenneth 515, 2118
Coxe, Louis O. 1649
Craig, Cairns 2119, 2120
Craig, David 2121
Crane, Hart 2122
Creeley, Robert 2123, 2124, 2125, 2126, 3500
Crick, Bernard 2127
Crinò, Anna Maria 1083
Cronin, Anthony 2128
Cronin, G. W. 1480
Crosland, Andrew 3627
Crosman, Robert 2129
Crowder, Richard 2130, 3628, 3629, 3630, 3631
Cruvant, Bernard A. 296
Culver, Michael 516
Cummings, Annette 179
Cummings, E. E. 297, 2131, 3501, 3502
Cunard, Nancy 517, 2132
Cunha, Carlos 2133
Cunliffe, Marcus 2134, 2904
Curci, Lino 3503
Curtui, Aurel 2135

D'Agostino, Nemi 518, 519, 520, 1355, 2136, 2137, 2138, 2139
Dahlberg, Edward 24, 2140, 2141
Daiches, David 2142, 2143
Dale, Peter 1450, 2144
Damon, S. Foster 2145
Daniels, Earl 1531, 2146
Danojlić, Milovan 2147
Darrach, Brad 25
Dasenbrock, Reed Way 2148, 2149
D'Avanzo, Mario L. 1527
Davenport, Guy 26, 298, 521, 522, 523, 524, 525, 526, 527
Davey, Frank 2157
Davidsen, Carol 528
Davidson, Gustav 180, 181
Davidson, Peter 2158, 2159
Davie, Donald 529, 530, 531, 532, 533, 534, 535, 536, 537, 538, 1084, 1085, 1206, 1207, 1348, 1356, 1357, 1462, 1684, 2160, 2161, 2162, 2163, 2164, 2165, 2166, 2167, 2168, 2169, 2170, 2171, 2172, 2173, 2174, 2175, 2176, 2177, 2178, 2179
Davis, Charles T. 3632
Davis, Clyde Brion 299
Davis, Earl 182, 539, 2180
Davis, Gary W. 2181
Davis, Helen Kathryn 540
Davis, Kay 541, 542, 543, 1058, 2182, 2183
Davis, Robert Gorham 183, 184, 185, 2184
Dawson, Christopher M. 1532
Day, Douglas 2185
Deane, Hugh 544
De Bedts, Ruth 545
De Bosschère, Jean 2186
De Campos, Augusto 1358, 2187

Decavalles, Anthony M. 546, 1087
de Chasca, Edmund S. 2188
Dekker, George 547, 548, 549
Delehanty, Elizabeth 300
Dell, Floyd 1606, 1607, 2189
Delmer, F. Sefton 2190
de Mailla, Père Joseph 2191
Dembo, L. S. 2192, 2193, 3475
Demetz, Peter 550, 2194
Demirovic, Hamdija 1359
Demott, Robert 551
de Nagy, N. Christoph 552, 553, 554, 2195
Dennis, Helen M. 1087, 2196
D'Epiro, Peter Francis 555, 556, 557
de Rachewiltz, Boris 558, 2198, 2199
de Rachewiltz, Mary 27, 28, 559, 560, 2200, 2201, 2202, 2203
DeSchloezer, Boris 1685
Deutsch, Albert 301, 302
Deutsch, Babette 29, 186, 561, 562, 563, 564, 565, 567, 1088, 1089, 1090, 1271, 1360, 1463, 1482, 1497, 1537, 1559, 1612, 1747
Devlin, Vianney M. 30, 2197
Di Canzio, William 2204
Dick, Bernard F. 1716
Dickey, R. P. 303, 568
Diesendorf, Margaret 31, 1763
Diggins, John P. 187
Diggory, Terrence 1091
Dilligan, Robert 569, 3633
Dillon, George 570
Dilworth, Thomas 2205
Dobree, Bonamy 1498
Dodworth, Edmund 2206
Dodsworth, Martin 571
Donath, Andreas 2207
Donati, Franco 2208
Donoghue, Denis 572, 1361, 1717, 2209, 2210
Doob, Eveline Bates 32
Doob, Leonard W. 33
Doody, M. A. 34
Doolittle, Hilda 35, 2211
Doria, Charles 573
Dos Passos, John 2212
Dougherty, James P. 188
Drew, Elizabeth 2213, 2214
Drew-Bear, Thomas 1289
Driscoll, John 574, 575
Drummond, Donald F. 2215
Drummond, John 304, 305, 306, 307, 308, 309, 576
Drummond, Roberta 2216
Duberman, Martin 2217
DuBois, A. E. 1499
Duclos, Jacques 577, 1464
Dudek, Louis 310, 311, 578, 1686, 2218, 2219, 3504, 3505
Duffey, Bernard I. 579, 1362, 2220, 2221
Duncan, Robert 1650, 2222
Duncan, Ronald 36, 1363, 2223, 2224, 2225
Dupee, F. W. 3506, 3507
DuPlessis, Rachel Blau 1092
Duran, Manuel 2226
Durand, Regis 882
Durant, Alan 580
Durant, Ariel 946
Dyson, William 2227

Earp, F. R. 1718
Eastham, Scott Thomas 2228, 2229
Eastman, Barbara C. 37, 581, 582, 583
Eaves, T. C. Duncan 341, 584, 745, 746, 747, 748, 749, 750, 751, 752, 753, 754, 755, 756, 1127, 1128, 1217, 2656, 2657, 2658, 2659, 2660, 2661, 2662
Eberhart, Richard 1093, 1094, 1095
Eckman, Frederick 2230
Ede, Harold Stanley 1257
Eder, Doris L. 585, 2231
Editors, Hudson Review 312
Edwards, John Hamilton 38, 586, 587, 588, 1687, 3634, 3635
Edwards, Thomas R. 2232
Edwards, William W. 1005

Egudu, Romanus N. 1364, 2233
Ehrenpreis, Irwin 2234
Eisenhauer, Robert G. 589
Eliot, T. S. 590, 591, 592, 1465, 1515, 1560, 1561, 1651, 1718, 1719, 2235, 2236, 2237, 2238, 2239, 2240, 2241, 2242, 2243, 2244, 2245, 2246, 2247, 2248, 2249, 3508, 3509
Elliott, Angela 594, 595, 2250
Elliott, George P. 2251
Elliott, Robert C. 189
Ellis, Stephen Paul 2252
Ellman, Richard 598, 2253, 2254, 2255, 2256, 2257, 2258, 2259, 3510
Ellmann, Maud 597
Emerson, Dorothy 599
Emery, Clark M. 600, 1096, 1365, 2260
Emslie, Macdonald 1366
Engel, Bernard F. 1850, 2261
Engel, Carl 1767, 2262
Engel, Ilse 2263
Engelking, Leszek 2264
Enright, D. J. 39, 2265
Enriques Agnoletti, E. 313
Eoyang, Eugene 2266
Epstein, Jacob 2267
Epstein, Joseph 2268
Eriksson, Pamela 2269
Espey, John J. 601, 602, 603, 1290, 1291, 1367, 1435, 1652, 1653, 1668, 1720, 1721, 2270, 2271, 2272, 2273, 2274, 2275, 2276, 3636, 3637
Espmark, Kjell 2277
Essary, Loris 2278
Evans, B. I. 1589
Evans, David W. 314
Evans, Luther H. 40
Evans, Oliver W. 2279
Everett, B. 2280

Faas, Egbert 1368, 2281
Fabiani, Enzo 2282
Fabri, Renata 2283
Fairchild, Hoxie N. 2284
Falbo, Ernest S. 1454
Falck, Colin 1764
Fallacara, Luigi 2285
Falqui, Enrico 2286
Fang, Achilles 604, 605, 1097, 1533, 1534, 1708, 2287, 2288, 2289
Farmer, David R. 2290, 3511, 3512
Fauchereau, Serge 2291, 2292, 2293
Faulkner, Peter 2294
Feder, Lillian 1369, 2295, 2296, 2297
Feldman, A. Bronson 606
Feldman, David 315
Fender, Stephen 607, 2298
Fenton, Charles 2299
Ferkiss, Victor L. 2300
Ferlinghetti, Lawrence 1688, 1709, 2301
Ferran, Jaime 2302
Ferril, Thomas Harnsby 1098, 1654
Feuchtwanger, Lion 316
Fiedler, Leslie 41, 1689, 2303, 2304, 2305, 2306
Fields, Kenneth Wayne 2307
Fields, Rick 2308
Figgis, Darrell 2309
Filler, Louis 2310
Findley, Timothy 1370
Fink, Jon-Stephen 608
Finkelstein, Norman Mark 2311
Finkelstein, Sidney 2312
Firchow, P. E. 2313
Fischer, Walther L. 2314
Fisher, Esther Safer 2315
Fitts, Dudley 609, 610, 1208, 1243, 1272, 1423, 1424, 1690, 2316, 2317, 3513
Fitzgerald, Edward J. 611
Fitz Gerald, Mary 3514
Fitzgerald, Robert 193, 612, 613, 614, 615, 616, 1099, 1100, 2318
Fleming, Rudd 398
Fleming, William 317, 318, 319, 617, 1101, 2319, 2320, 2321
Fletcher, John Gould 618, 1292, 1655, 2322, 2323, 2324
Flint, F. S. 1255, 1256, 1562, 1623, 2325, 2326, 2327, 2328

Flint, R. W. 619, 2329, 2330
Flory, Wendy Jane Stallard 620, 621, 622, 1102, 2331, 2332, 2333
Foote, Edward 42
Forbes, Clarence A. 1293
Ford, Boris 1357
Ford, Ford Madox 43, 125, 1232, 1244, 1331, 1563, 2334, 2335, 2336, 2337, 2338, 3515
Forde, S. Victoria M. 2339
Forgue, Guy J. 2340
Forrest-Thompson, Veronica 2141
Forsell, Lars 2342, 2343, 2344
Foster, John L. 623
Fraire, Isabel 2345
Franciosa, Massimo 2346
Franck, J. 2347
Frank, Mortimer H. 1768
Frankel, Haskell 2348
Frankenberg, Lloyd 624, 1103, 2349
Franzen, Erich 194
Fraser, George Sutherland 1371, 2350, 2351, 2352, 2353, 2354
Freedman, Ralph 1466
French, A. L. 1372, 1373
French, Warren G. 671, 1421, 2355, 2356, 2460
French, William 2357, 2358, 2359
Freudenheim, Richard Jesse 625
Frair, Kimon 320, 626, 1294, 1374, 1614
Friedman, Melvin J. 2360
Friedrich, Otto 1273
Friend, Joseph H. 1436
Frohock, W. M. 627, 628
Frost, Robert 321, 2361, 2362, 2363, 2364
Froula, Christine 1656, 2365, 3638
Frye, Northup 2366
Fuchs, Daniel 2367
Fukuda, Rikutaro 2368, 2369
Fuller, Buckminster 2370
Fuller, Dorothy V. 629
Fuller, Roy 1467, 2371, 2372, 2373, 3516
Furia, Philip 630, 631
Fussell, Edwin 632, 633, 2374, 2375
Fussell, Paul 1245, 2376

Gage, John T. 2377, 2378
Galigani, Giuseppe 634
Gall, Sally M. 635, 2379
Gallup, Donald Clifford 44, 2380, 2381, 2382, 2383, 3517, 3639, 3640, 3641
Gannett, Lewis 285, 322
Garcia-Terres, Jaime 1246
Gardner, Helen 2384
Garelick, Judith Spritzer 2385
Garrison, Omar 323
Gatter, Carl 45
Geddes, Virgil 46, 1582
Gefin, Laszlo 636
Geisheker, Mary Rose 2386
Geltman, Max 2387, 2388, 2389
Gerhardt, Rainer M. 1104
Gershman, Herbert S. 3518
Giannone, Richard J. 1600
Gibbons, Reginald 2390
Gibbs, Alonzo 637
Gibbs, Barbara 2410
Gibson, Mary Ellis 2391
Gifford, Henry 2392
Gil de Biedma, Jaime 2393
Gilkes, Martin 2394
Gillespie, Don C. 3519
Gilson, Etienne 1281
Ginsberg, Allen 47, 48, 2395
Giovacchini, Graziella 1105
Giovannini, Giovanni 324, 638, 1375
Giuliani, Alfredo 2396, 2397, 2398
Glenn, Edgar M. 639, 640, 641, 642, 643
Glicksberg, Charles I. 325, 326
Goacher, Denis 49, 644, 645, 1722, 1723, 2399, 2400
Godden, Richard 2401
Goekjian, Gregory F. 2402
Going, William T. 2403
Gold, Michael 327, 328

Goldman, Arnold 2404
Goldring, Douglas 2405, 2406, 2407, 2408
Goldsmith, Arnold L. 2409
Golffing, Francis 1106, 2410
Goodspeed, George 646
Goodwin, K. L. 50, 647, 648, 2411, 2412
Gordon, Ambrose, Jr. 2413
Gordon, Arthur 329
Gordon, David M. 51, 196, 649, 650, 651, 652, 653, 654, 655, 992, 1059, 1107, 1209, 2414, 2415, 2416, 2417, 2418
Gordon, Robert 2419
Gorlier, Claudio 2420, 2421
Gorman, H. S. 1564, 2422
Graham, D. B. 1665
Graham, John F. 330
Graham, Stephen 1691
Grant, Joy 2423
Graves, Robert 1779, 2424, 2425, 2426, 2427, 2428, 2429
Greenbaum, Leonard 2430
Greene, Elizabeth 2431
Greenspan, Cory Robert 1108
Gregory, Horace 657, 1109, 1110, 1111, 1376, 1500, 1739, 1748, 1749, 2432, 2433
Grieder, Josephine 1601
Grieve, Thomas 1210
Griffin, Ernest 2434, 2435
Grigsby, Gordon Kay 658, 659
Grigson, Geoffrey 660, 661, 2436
Grillandi, Massimo 2437
Gross, Dalton 2438
Gross, Harvey S. 662, 663, 2439, 2440
Grover, Philip 52, 1342, 1377, 1483
Grubb, Frederick 2441
Guenther, Charles 1692
Gugelberger, Georg N. 664, 2442, 2443, 2444, 2445
Guglielmi, Joseph E. 2446
Guidacci, Margherita 1112, 2447, 2448
Guidi, Augusto 1113, 1114
Guidotti, Mario Colombi 1115
Guiliani, Alfredo 665
Guimond, James 2449
Gutchess, Elizabeth Denver 2450
Guthrie, Ramon 53

H. S. 197
Haas, Rudolf 2451
Haase, Camilla Bunker 2452
Haberstroh, Patricia Boyle 666
Haefner, Gerhard 1437
Haeusermann, H. W. 2453
Hagelstango, Rudolf 1602
Hagemann, E. R. 2454, 3520
Hagenbüchle, Roland 2455
Haggin, Bernard H. 1769
Halawatsch, Wolfhard 667
Hale, William G. 1295, 1545
Haley, Martin 331, 1693, 1750
Hall, Donald 54, 55, 668, 669, 2456, 2457, 2458, 3476, 3477
Hall, Ian Roger 670
Halper, Nathan 2459
Halperen, Max 671, 672, 673, 2460
Halsband, Robert 1669, 1751
Hamburger, Michael 1116, 2461, 2462
Hamilton, Alastair 2463
Hamilton, Ian 2464
Hand, Alanzo 2465
Hand, Claudius A. 2466
Hankins, John E. 674, 675
Hannah, J. M. 2467
Hansen, Miriam 2468
Hanzo, Thomas A. 1438
Hargreaves, Frederic Kline, Jr. 2469
Harmer, J. B. 2470
Harmon, William 676, 677, 2471
Harnwell, Anna Jane 198
Harper, Michael Frederick 678, 2472
Harris, Frank 1565, 2473
Harris, Natalie Beth 2474, 2475, 2476, 2477
Harrison, John 679
Harrison, Keith 2478
Hart, Lawrence 2479

Hartley, Anthony 680
Hartman, Charles O. 2480, 2481
Hartman, Geoffrey 2482
Haruyama, Yukio 2483, 2484
Hasbany, Richard 2485
Hasegawa, Mitsuaki 1484
Hassall, Christopher 1566, 2486
Hatlen, Burton 2487, 2488, 3642
Hattersley, Michael Elkins 2489
Hattum, Marinus van 2490
Häusermann, H. W. 2491
Havlice, Patricia Pate 3643
Hawkins, A. Desmond 1455
Haycraft, Howard 2700
Hayman, David 2492, 2493
Hazlitt, Henry 1740
Healey, Eleanor Claire 2494, 2495
Healy, J. V. 1117, 1274, 1590, 1741, 2496
Heap, J. 2497
Heath-Stubbs, John 2498, 2499
Heinzelman, Kurt 2500
Helmling, Steven 681, 682, 2501
Helsztynski, Stanislaw 3521, 3522
Helwig, Werner 2502
Hemingway, Ernest 2503, 2504, 2505, 2506, 2507
Hénault, Marie P. 683, 3644
Henderson, Alice Corbin 2508
Henderson, Archibald, III 1282, 2509, 3478
Hendrickson, John R. 2510
Henn, T. R. 2511
Heppenstall, Rayner 684, 1296
Herdeck, Donald Elmer 685, 3523
Herzbrun, Philip 1634
Herzinger, Kim 56
Hesse, Eva 41, 503, 686, 687, 688, 689, 690, 691, 692, 693, 694, 695, 696, 697, 698, 1118, 1119, 1297, 1635, 1979, 2058, 2260, 2270, 2273, 2314, 2504, 2512, 2513, 2514, 2515, 2516, 2517, 2518, 2519, 2871, 3048, 3051, 3240
Heyen, William 699, 2520
Heymann, C. David 57, 332, 1425, 2521, 2522
Hölderlin, Friedrich 2534
Hollander, John 1567, 2535
Holmes, John 2536
Homberger, Eric 58, 334, 1381, 1545, 1606, 1608, 1675, 2537, 2538, 2539, 3057
Highet, Gilbert 700, 1298, 1535, 2523
Hildesheimer, Wolfgang 701
Hillyer, Robert 199, 200, 201, 2524, 2525
Hindus, Milton 2526
Hlawatsch, Wolfhard 702
Hobhouse, Janet 2527
Hobsbaum, Philip 2528
Hoffa, William W. 703
Hoffman, Daniel 704, 2529
Hoffman, Frederick J. 1378, 2530
Hogg, Robert 2531
Holaday, Woon-Ping Chin 705, 2532, 2533
Holbrook, David 1379
Holder, Alan 333, 706, 707, 708, 1299, 1380
Hombitzer, Eleonore 1382, 1579
Honig, Edwin 2540
Hopes, David Brendan 709
Hopkins, Harry L. 202
Horrocks, R. J. 710
Hough, Graham 2541
Hoult, Thomas Ford 203
Houserman, H. W. 2542
Houston, John Porter 711, 1383
Howard, Brian 1583
Howarth, Herbert 2543
Howarth, R. G. 2544, 2545, 2546
Howe, Irving 204, 335, 336
Howe, Susan 2547
Hubbell, Jay B. 2548
Hubbell, L. W. 2549
Hubbell, Lindley 2550
Hueffer, Ford Madox [See Ford, Ford Madox]
Huett, Richard 205

Hugen, Dorothy Jean 712, 713
Hughes, Glenn 1776
Hughes, Robert 714, 1678
Hume, Robert 2551
Hummel, John 2552
Humphries, Rolphe 337, 1120
Hungiville, Maurice 3524, 3525
Hunting, Robert 2553
Huntley, Carter 2554
Hurley, Margaret 3553
Hurtado, Gerardo César 2555
Hurwitz, Harold M. 2556, 2557
Hutchens, John K. 338
Hutchens, Patricia 59, 60, 61, 62, 1121, 1773, 2558, 2559, 2560, 3526, 3527
Hynes, Samuel 206, 715, 2561, 2562

Ingber, Richard Geoffrey 1624, 1724
Ismail Jamila 716
Israel, Calvin 1615
Ivănescu, Mircea 2563
Iwamoto, Yoshiyuki 1440
Iwasaki, Ryozo 63, 717, 1300
Izubuchi, Hiroshi 2564
Izzo, Carlo 2565, 2566, 3528, 3529, 3530, 3531

Jack, Peter Monro 1275
Jackamon, Bob 2567
Jackson, Brendan 2568, 2569
Jackson, Thomas Herbert 718, 2571, 2572
James, Roberta 207
Janssens, G. A. M. 2573, 2574
Jarrell, Randall 719, 720, 2575
Jeffares, Alexander Norman 2576
Jenkins, Alan 2577
Jenner, E. A. B. 721, 1384
Jennings, Elizabeth 2578
John, K. 1501, 1752
John, Roland 722
Johnson, Carol 2579
Johnson, Edd 3479
Johnson, Geoffrey 2580
Johnson, Scott 2581
Jones, A. R. 2582
Jones, Dan Lewis 2583
Jones, David 2584
Jones, Howard Mumford 3645
Joost, Nichols 2585, 2586, 2587
Jordan, Barbara Scott 2588
Joseph, Terry Brint 1301, 1385, 1386, 1512, 2589
Joyce, James 723, 2590, 2591, 2592, 3532
Juhasz, Suzanna 724, 2593, 2594
Jung, Angela [Chik-y] 518, 1247, 1248, 1955, 2397, 2595, 2596, 3531, 3646
Junkins, Donald 2597
Just, Klaus G. 2598

Kahn, Sholom J. 1528
Kanaseki, Hisao 2599
Kann, Hans-Joachim 1439
Kapp, Jack 208
Kappel, Andrew John 64, 725, 2600, 2601, 2602, 2603
Karpinski, Joanne B. 2604
Kavka, Jerome 339
Kay, Bernard 1451
Kayman, Martin A. 2605, 2606, 2607
Kazin, Alfred 65, 66, 2608, 2609
Kearns, George W. 726, 727
Keith, Nobuko Tsuki 728, 1516, 1517, 1694
Keller, David Michael 2610
Kelly, Robert G. 2611
Kempf, Roger 2612
Kennedy, George 2613
Kennedy, Leo 1122
Kenner, Hugh 67, 68, 69, 70, 340, 581, 729, 730, 731, 732, 733, 734, 735, 736, 737, 738, 739, 740, 741, 742, 743, 771, 1123, 1124, 1125, 1126, 1211, 1212, 1213, 1214, 1215, 1216, 1230, 1276, 1302, 1303, 1387, 1388, 1389, 1390, 1426, 1456, 1513, 1538, 1616, 1625, 1636,

1637, 1638, 1670, 1695, 1725, 1726, 2614, 2615, 2616, 2617, 2618, 2619, 2620, 2621, 2622, 2623, 2624, 2625, 2626, 2627, 2628, 2629, 2630, 2631, 2632, 2633, 2634, 2635, 2636, 2637, 2638, 2639, 2640, 2641, 2642, 2643, 2644, 2645, 2646, 2647, 2648, 2649, 3533, 3667
Kenny, Herbert A. 744
Kent, Jay 2650
Kerblat-Blanchenay, Jeanne 3480
Kereaski, Rodica 2651
Kermode, Frank 534, 1357, 2652, 2653
Ketchiff, David 2654
Keynes, Geoffrey 1556
Kidney, Jennifer 2655
Killigrew, Michael 2333
Kimpel, Ben D. 341, 584, 745, 746, 747, 748, 749, 750, 751, 752, 753, 754, 755, 756, 1127, 1128, 1217, 2656, 2657, 2658, 2659, 2660, 2661, 2662
King, George T. 757
King, Michael 35, 1129, 2663, 2664
King, William 1502
Kirk, Russell 2665, 2666
Kirsch, Hans-Christian 2207
Kirstein, Lincoln 2667
Klarman, Adolf D. 2668
Klein, Marcus 2669
Klinck, Dennis R. 2180, 2670, 2671, 2672
Knapp, James F. 2673
Knight, Robert M. 758
Knoerle, Sister Jeanne 2674
Knoll, Robert E. 342
Knox, Bryant 71
Knox, George 1391, 1392
Koch, Adrienne 209
Kobayashi, Manji 2675
Kodama, Jitsuei 2676
Kodama, Sanehide 759, 1235, 2677, 2678, 2679, 2680, 2681, 2682
Kodoma, Sanchiko 2683
Koehler, Stanley 2684
Kohli, Raj K. 760
Kohring, Klaus H. 2685
Kojecky, Roger 2686
Koppenfels, Wermer von 761
Korg, Jacob 762, 1218, 1219, 2687, 2688
Korn, Marianne 2689, 2690
Kostelanetz, Richard 763, 764, 2691
Koster, Donald N. 3647
Kramer, Jane 2692
Kreyborg, Alfred 2693, 2694, 2695
Kriegel, Leonard 2696
Kroll, Ernest 2697
Kuberski, Philip 2698
Kumashiro, Sobu 2699
Kunitz, Stanley J. 2700, 3648
Kuntz, Joseph M. 3619, 3649
Kurumisawa, Atsuo 1130
Kutler, Stanley I. 343
Kwan-Terry, John 765, 2701, 2702

Lafourcade, Bernard 3662
Laing, Alexander 2703
Lander, Jeannette 2704
Landini, Richard George 766, 767, 768
Lane, Gary 3650
Langbaum, Robert 2705, 2706, 2707
Languasco, Nardo 2708, 2709
Langumier, Eric 2710
Larkin, Greg 1131
Lasser, Michael L. 1440
Lattès, Jean-Claude 2711
Lattimore, Richmond 1718, 1727
Lauber, John 769
Laughlin, James 344, 1304, 2712, 2713, 2714, 2715, 3534
Laurie, Peter Hamilton 2716, 2717
Law, Richard 770
Lawrence, D. H. 72, 73, 2718, 2719
Lawson, John Howard 345
Lawton, Harry 3535
Layton, Irving 2720
LaZebnik, Jack 346
Leary, Lewis 771, 772, 3536, 3537, 3538, 3651, 3652, 3653

Leavis, Frank R[aymond] 773, 774, 1332, 1333, 1334, 1393, 2721, 2722, 2723, 3539
Le Breton, Eileen 2724
Lechlitner, Ruth 2725
Ledbetter, Jack Tracy 2726
Lee, Pen-Ti 1233, 2727
Le Gallienne, Richard 1584
Lehmann, John 2728
Leibowitz, Herbert 775
Lemaire, Marcel 2729
Lenberg, Lore Marianne 1132, 1133
Lennig, Arthur George 776
Lensing, George S. 2730
Leonello, Claudio 2731
Lesemann, Maurice 2732
Levenson, Harry Michael 2733
Levertov, Denise 2734
Levi, Albert W. 2735
Levi, Peter 777, 1305, 1728, 1729, 1765
Levin, Gail 2736
Levin, Harry 2737, 2738, 2739, 2740, 2741
Levy, Alan 2742
Lewin, Bruno 1518
Lewis, Anthony 349
Lewis, John S. 2743
Lewis, Roger 2744
Lewis, Wyndham 74, 778, 1220, 1306, 2745, 2746, 2747, 3540
Libby, Gary R. 1394
Libera, Sharon Mayer 779, 780
Libman, Valentina A. 3654
Library of Congress 210
Lilly Library, Indiana U. 3541, 3573
Linati, Carlo 2748, 2749
Lindberg, Kathryne Victoria 2750
Lindberg-Seyersted, Brita 2751, 3542, 3543, 3544
Lindstrom, Naomi 2752
Link, Franz H. 1395, 1441, 1777, 2753, 2754
Lipke, William C. 2755, 2756
Lipman, Samuel 2757
Lippincott, Henry F., Jr. 2758
Little, Matthew 2759, 2760, 2761, 3655
Littlefield, Walter 1671
Litz, A. Walton 2756, 2762, 2763, 3004, 3588
Liu, Wu-Chi 1249
Livi, Grazia 75
Llona, Victor 2764
Lloyd, Margaret Glynne 2765
Loftus, Beverly J. G. 211
Logu, Pietro de 2766
Logue, Christopher 781
Lombardo, Agostino 2767, 2768, 2769
Long, Hudson 1967
Long, Richard A. 1396
Lopez, Enrique Hank 2770
Lottman, Herbert R. 76, 351
Louchheim, Aline B. 212, 352
Lowe, Robert Liddell 3545
Lowell, Amy 1859, 2771, 2772
Lowell, Robert 77, 2773
Lowry, W. M. 209
Lucas, F. L. 1639, 1640, 1657
Lucas, John 1221, 1679
Luckett, Richard 2774
Ludwig, Richard M. 2775, 3645, 3656
Lund, Mary Graham 2776
Lunkvist, Arthur 2777
Lyall, Larry 1680

M. M. 1617
M. T. 1486
MacAfee, Norman 2778
McAfee, Thomas 2779
McAlister, Floyd L. 2780
McAlmon, Robert 78, 79
McCabe, Victoria 353
McCarthy, Dermot 2781
McClure, John 1585
Maccoby, Hyam 2782
McCole, Camille 1503
McCormick, John 80, 2783
McCracken, Van 81
McCuaig, Ronald 1397, 2784
MacDiarmid, Hugh 782, 1307, 1308, 1309, 1310
MacDonald, Dwight 213, 354
McDonald, Gerald 1658
McDonald, James R. 1060, 1061

McDougal, Stuart Y. 1782, 1951, 1952, 2785, 2786, 3621, 3622, 3623, 3624, 3657, 3658
MacDougall, Allan Ross 2787
McDowell, Colin 783
MacFall, Russell 1539
McFarland, Ronald E. 1568, 2788
McGreevy, Thomas 1335
McGrory, Mary 355
McInnes, Marion Kaighn 2789
McGuire, William 214
MacKendrick, Louis K. 2790
McKenzie, Donald 356
McKeown, Thomas Wilson 2791
Macksey, R. A. 2792
McLachian, W. I. 2793
MacLeish, Archibald 1134, 1135, 2794, 2795, 2796, 2797, 2798, 2799, 2800, 2801, 2802
McLuhan, Marshall 1472, 2803, 2804
McNaughton, William 82, 784, 785, 786, 1696
MacNeice, Louis 787
MacShane, Frank 357, 2805, 2806, 3546
MacSween, R. J. 2807
McVeagh, John 2808
Madge, Charles 788, 1136, 1398
Maia, Joao 83
Mairet, Philip 1753
Makin, Peter 2809, 2810, 2811, 2812, 2813, 2814
Malanga, Gerard 2815
Malkoff, Karl 789, 1399, 1400
Malof, Joseph Fetler 2816
Mancuso, Girolamo 2817
Mandanis, Alice Subley 790
Mangan, Sherry 1283
Manganaris-Decavalles, Anthony 791, 2818
Manganiello, Dominic 2819
Mangum, Geoff 792
Margolis, John D. 2820
Mariani, Paul 2821
Marin Morales, José A. 2822
Mariorana, M. T. 2823
Marschall, Hiltrud 2824
Marsh, Edward 2825
Marshall, Margaret 358
Martin, B. K. 793
Martin, Loy Davis 2826, 2827
Martin, Wallace 2828, 2829, 2830, 2831
Martinez, Nancy C. 3649
Martini, M. C. Rezzano de 2823
Martz, Louis L. 1137, 2832
Mason, H. A. 1730
Materer, Timothy 794, 795, 796, 1264, 1265, 1760, 2359, 2833, 2834, 2835, 2836, 2837, 3547, 3548
Mathews, Elkin 1569
Matthias, John E. 1266
Matthiessen, F. O. 359, 2838, 2839, 2840
Matz, C. A. 2841
Maxwell-Mahon, W. D. 2842
May, Henry F. 2843
Mayfield, John S. 360
Mayo, Robert 797, 798, 799
Mayor, A. Hyatt 1284
Mazzaro, Jerome 2844, 2845, 2846, 2847
Mazzeno, Laurence W. 1401
Meacham, Harry M. 84, 361, 362, 3549
Mei, Francesco 2848
Meixner, John A. 2849
Melchiori, Giorgio 2850
Mellow, James R. 2851
Melote Castro, E. M. 2852
Mencken, H. L. 1608, 1778, 3550
Mendes, Murilo 2853
Menides, Laura Jehn 2854
Merchant, Moelwyn 800, 2855, 2856
Meredith, William 215
Messing, Gordon M. 1311
Meyer, G[eorge] P[revin] 1659, 2857, 3551
Meyer, Peter 2858
Meyer, William J. 1666
Meyers, Jeffrey 363
Meyerson, Edward L. 2859, 3552
Michaels, Walter B. 801, 2860
Michelena, Margarita 2861

Michelson, Max 1487, 2862
Middleton, Christopher 2863
Miller, Felicia 1519
Miller, James Edwin 802, 2864
Miller, Liam 2865
Miller, Nolan 216
Miller, Vincent 803, 1312, 2866
Millett, Fred B. 804, 3659
Mills, Lloyd L. 1402
Mills, Ralph J., Jr. 2867
Milner, Philip 2868
Miner, Earl Roy 805, 2869, 2870, 2871
Miyake, Akiko 806, 807, 2872, 2873, 2874
Mizener, Arthur 364
Molesworth, Charles 2875, 2876
Mondolfo, Vittoria I. 3553, 3660, 3661
Monk, Donald 1138, 2877
Monroe, Harold 2878
Monroe, Harriet 85, 86, 808, 1586, 1626, 2627, 2879, 2880, 2881, 2882, 3554
Montale, Eugenio 87, 1139, 1140, 1141, 2883, 2884, 2885
Montgomery, Marion 88, 89, 2886, 2887, 2888, 2889, 2890, 2891, 2892
Moody, A. D. 71, 809, 810, 1142, 2893
Moore, Arthur V. 3555
Moore, Marianne 90, 811, 812, 813, 814, 815, 816, 2894, 2895, 2896, 2897, 3556
Moramarco, Fred 817, 818, 819, 820, 1143, 2898
Morgan, Edwin 2899
Morgan, Frederick 2900, 3557
Morrison, Blake 2901
Morrow, Bradford 821, 822, 3662
Morse, Jonathan 823
Mortimer, Raymond 1591
Motsch, Monika 2902
Mottram, Eric 2903, 2904
Movius, Geoffrey H. 2905
Mowrer, Deane 1144, 1592, 2906
Muir, Edwin 824, 825, 826, 1250, 1403, 1697
Mullins, Eustace Clarence 91, 92, 365, 827
Munsi, Pradeep 2907
Munson, Gorham B. 2908, 3663, 3664
Murphy, Richard 828, 1698
Murray, David 769, 2909
Murray, Donald 1233, 2727
Murray, Robert Duff, Jr. 1536
Musselman, M. M. 217
Myake, Akiko 2910
Myers, Peter 829

N. C. 197
Namjoshi, Suniti Manohar 830, 2911, 3558
Nanny, Max 831, 832, 833, 1570, 2912, 2913, 2914, 2915
Nassar, Eugene Paul 834, 835, 1144
Nassivera, J. C. 3559
Nathan, Leonard 2916
Neame, Alan 366, 367, 781, 1146, 1147, 1148, 1149, 1150, 3560
Neault, D. James 1222, 1223, 1224
Neidhardt, Frances E. 836
Nelson, Francis William 2917
Newbolt, Henry 3561
Nicholls, P. 837
Nichols, Robert 1313
Nicolaisen, Peter 1442
Nicolescu, Vasile 838
Niikura, Shunichi 1151, 2918
Niiura, Toshikazu 839, 1152, 2919
Nilon, Charles H. 3665
Nims, Bruce Gladden 2920
Nist, John 2921
Nolde, John J. 840, 841, 842, 2922
Nolte, William H. 1609, 1778, 2923
Norman, Charles 93, 94, 218, 368, 369, 843, 1153
North, Michael 2924
Nyren, Dorothy 1154

Oakes, Lois Ann 844
Oakes, Randy Wayne 2925
Oberg, Arthur 2926
O'Connor, William Van 219, 370, 845, 1155, 2927, 2928, 3666
Oderman, Kevin M. 1285, 2929, 2930
Odlin, Reno 371, 846, 2931
O'Grady, Desmond 220, 2932
Oldani, Louis 3562
Olmstead, Edwin G. 372
Olson, Charles 95, 373, 374, 847, 1457, 2933
Olson, Paul A. 221, 848, 1156
Olsson, Theodore C. A. 849
Oppen, George 96
Oppenheim, Lois 2934
Orage, A[lfred] R[ichard] 1234, 1314, 1315, 2488
Orsini, G. N. G. 2935, 2936
Orsini, Napoleone 2937
Orwell, George 222
Österlung, Anders 3563
Otto, Lon Jules 2938
Øverland, Orm 850
Owen, Earl Ben 851
Own, Guy 2939

Pack, Robert 2940
Packard, William 1520
Paden, William D., Jr. 2941
Paechter, Heinz 2942
Paige, D. D. 852, 2943, 3564, 3565, 3566
Palandri, Angela & Guido 97, 518, 1231, 1955, 2397, 2596, 2944, 2945, 2946, 2947, 2948, 3531, 3646
Palm, Göran 2949
Palmer, Leslie H. 1754
Panichas, George A. 2950
Paolucci, Anne 2951, 2952
Parins, James W. 569, 3633
Parisi, Joseph 2953
Parisoff, Myra Jane Heinz 2954
Parker, Andrew 2955
Parkes, H[enry] B[amford] 1605
Parkinson, Thomas 2956, 2957
Pasquier, Marie-Claire 1732, 2958
Pasquini, Luigi 2959
Patchen, Kenneth 375
Patmore, Brigit 98, 99, 1157
Patmore, Derek 99
Patnaik, Deba P. 2960, 2961, 2962
Patterson, Gertrude 2963
Pattinson, John Patrick 2964
Paz, Octavio 853, 854
Pea, Enrico 2965
Peachy, Frederic 855, 1733
Peacock, Alan J. 856
Pearce, Donald 100
Pearce, Roy Harvey 857, 858, 2966, 2967
Pearlman, Daniel D. 101, 859, 860, 861, 862, 863, 864, 865, 866, 2968, 3567
Pearson, Norman Holmes 35
Pearson, R. M. 376
Peck, John 867, 868, 869, 2969, 2970, 2971
Pecorino, Jessica Prinz 1158
Peel, Robert 102, 1755
Pegler, Westbrook 377, 378, 379
Pellizzi, Camillo 103
Peper, Jürgen 2972
Pepper, Bill 380
Pérez, Louis C. 2973
Peri, Jeffrey Michael 2974
Perkins, David 2975
Perlès, Alfred 870, 2976
Perloff, Marjorie G. 1267, 2977, 2978, 2979, 2980, 2981, 2982
Permoli, Piergiovanni 2983
Perrine, Laurence 2984, 3568
Peschman, Herman 1756, 3569
Peterson, Leland D. 871
Petrocchi, Giorgio 1159
Petter, C. G. 1571
Pettersson, Gunnar 2985
Pevear, Richard 872
Phillips, William 1689
Pinck, Dan 104
Pinto, Vivian de Sola 2986
Pisanti, Tommaso 2987, 2988
Pleynet, Marcelin 2989
Poirier, Richard 2990

Poli, Bernard J. 2991
Pondrom, Cyrena N. 2992, 2993, 3475
Popescu, Adrian 2994
Popescu, Petru 2995
Porter, Katherine Anne 2996, 2997, 3570
Porteus, Hugh Gordon 1316, 2998, 2999
Pottorf, Michael 3000
Potts, P. 3001
Pound, Dorothy Shakespear 3002, 3003, 3571, 3572, 3573
Pound, Ezra 3574, 3575, 3576, 3577, 3578, 3579, 3580, 3581, 3582, 3583, 3584, 3585, 3586, 3587
Pound, Homer L. 3481
Pound, Omar 3004, 3588
Powell, Dilys 1504
Powell, James A. 873
Pratt, William C. 1404, 3005, 3006
Praz, Mario 3007, 3008, 3009, 3010, 3011
Precosky, Donald A. 3012
Press, John 3013, 3014, 3015, 3016, 3017
Prestin, J. H. 3018
Prezzolini, Giuseppe 3019, 3020, 3021, 3022
Pricop, Constantin 3023
Pritchard, William H. 874, 1160, 3024, 3025, 3026, 3027, 3028
Pritchett, V. S. 3029
Puckett, Harry Thomas 3030
Puckett, Walter Edward 3031
Puknat, E. M. 3032
Puknat, S. B. 3032
Pulik, Ruth 3033
Putnam, Samuel 3034, 3035
Putz, Manfred 3036

Quartermain, Peter 1405, 3037
Queneau, Raymond 1277
Quinn, Mary Bernetta, O.S.F. 875, 876, 877, 878, 879, 1406, 3038, 3039

Raaberg, Gloria Gwen 880
Rabate, Jean-Michel 881, 882
Raboni, Giovanni 883
Racey, Edgar Francis, Jr. 884, 3040
Raddatz, Fritz J. 383
Rader, James E. 105, 106
Raffel, Burton 3041, 3042
Rago, Henry 3043
Raine, Kathleen 1161, 1710, 3044, 3045
Rainer, Dachine 1757
Ramsey, Warren 3046, 3047
Ransom, John Crowe 1758
Ratte, Eva 1162
Rattray, David 107, 3048
Ray, David 3049
Raymond, Marcel 3050
Read, Forrest, Jr. 885, 886, 887, 888, 889, 1163, 1664, 3051, 3052, 3053, 3054, 3589
Read, Herbert E. 24, 890, 891, 892, 893, 3055
Reboni, Giovanni 894
Rebora, Piero 1164
Reche, Denis 895
Reck, Michael 108, 109, 384, 896, 1165
Redman, Tim 110
Reed, John 3056
Reed, Victor B. 897
Reedy, William Marion 3057
Rees, Thomas 3058
Reeves, Gareth 3059
Regier, Willis G[oth] 898, 3060, 3061
Regnery, Henry 111
Reid, Benjamin L. 1489, 3062, 3482
Reid, David 3063, 3483
Reid, James M. 2984
Reid, Richard 3064
Reinhold, Robert 385
Reiss, Christopher 1407
Reit, Seymour V. 223
Remnick, Davis 3484
Revell, Peter 899
Rexroth, Kenneth 3065
Rhys, Ernest 3066, 3067
Ricciardi, Caterina 3068
Rice, Philip Blair 900

Rice, Wallace 1628
Rich, W. 3069
Richardson, Jack 3070
Richardson, Kenneth 3670
Richie, Donald 1540
Richardson, Lawrence 1317
Ricks, Christopher 3071
Riddel, Joseph N. 901, 3072, 3073
Ridge, Lola 3074
Riding, Laura 1779
Ringer, Gordon 224, 3075
Rittenhouse, J. B. 1490
Rizzardi, Alfredo 1166, 1167, 3076, 3077, 3078, 3079, 3080, 3671
Robbins, J. Albert 3590
Roberts, Michael 902, 903, 1505, 1597, 1660, 3081
Robinson, E. 1770
Robinson, Fred C. 1641
Robinson, James K. 3082
Robinson, Janice S. 3083
Robson, W. W. 1474
Roche, Denis 112
Rodgers, Frederick George 3084
Roditi, Eduard 3085
Rodker, John 1681
Rogers, William D. 113
Rogran, Bernard W. 2755
Rooks, George 3672
Rorem, Ned 1771, 3086
Rose, W. K. 3087
Rosen, Aaron 1225
Rosen, David Matthew 3088
Rosenberg, Harold 3089
Rosenfeld, Alvin H. 3673
Rosenfeld, Paul 386
Rosenthal, M[achia] L[ouis] 904, 905, 906, 907, 908, 909, 910, 911, 912, 1168, 1226, 1318, 1408, 1409, 1443, 1618, 1761, 3090, 3091, 3092
Rosenthal, Marilyn 913
Roskolenko, Harry 914, 1169, 1661
Rosmarin, Adena Margaret 3093, 3094
Ross, Robert H. 3095
Rossi, Alberto 1170
Rossi, Aldo 3096
Rosten, Norman 225
Rovere, Richard 387, 388
Rowe, Hershel Dale 3097
Ruas, Charles 2547
Rubin, Louis D., Jr. 915, 3098
Ruggeri, Cosimo 226
Runnquist, Åke 1541
Runte, Hans R. 3099
Russell, Francis 389, 916
Russell, Peter 114, 115, 116, 1573, 1662, 2999, 3100, 3101, 3440, 3674
Ruthven, Greystiel 3102
Ruthven, K. K. 1319, 1572, 3103, 3104, 3105, 3106
Ryan, Judith 3107

S. C. C. 1506
Sahal, K. L. 3108
Saitoh, Kuniharu 1521
Sala, Annamaria 3109
Saloman, Louis B. 3110
Saltin, Myles 3111
Salvalaggio, Nantas 3112
Sanavio, Piero 1411, 3113, 3114
Sandburg, Carl 3115, 3116
Sanders, Frederich K[irkland] 917, 1062, 1063, 3117
Sanehide, Kodama 1235
Sanesi, Roberto 1171
Sanguineti, Edoardo 1172
San Juan, E., Jr. 535, 548, 1093, 1410, 3442, 3675
Sarang, Vilas 1642
Satin, Joseph 3118
Sato, Toshihiko 1522
Savery, Pancho 117
Savoia, Dianella 1643
Sawyer, Richard James 918
Scalero, Liliano 1173
Scarfoglio, Carlo 390
Schafer, R. Murray 919, 1772, 3119, 3120
Schaffner, Perdita 118
Schiffer, Reinhold 3121
Schimmel, Harold 920
Schiralli, Martin Guy 3122, 3123

Schlauch, Margaret 1174, 3124
Schleppenbach, Barbara Aschemann 3125
Schmidt, A. V. C. 1412
Schmidt, Gerd 921, 1514, 1766, 3126, 3127, 3128
Schmied, Wieland 3129
Schneditz, Wolfgang 3130
Schneeman, Peter Henry 3131, 3132, 3676
Schneidau, Herbert Newton 922, 1780, 3133, 3134, 3135, 3136, 3137, 3138, 3139, 3140
Schneideman, Robert 923
Schneider, Isidor 391, 392
Schobert, Timothy 3141
Schroth, Randall 3142
Schuldiner, Michael 1175
Schulman, Grace 1084, 2896, 3476, 3677
Schulte, Edvige 3143, 3144
Schultz, Alexander H. 3146
Schultz, Robert Dale 119, 3145
Schwartz, Delmore 924, 925, 926, 927, 3147
Schwartz, Joseph 3678
Schwartz, Sanford Ray 3148
Schwartz, William Leonard 3149
Scott, Nathan A., Jr. 3150, 3151
Scott, Tom 393, 928, 3152
Scully, James 3153, 3154
Sechi, Giovanni 3155
Seed, David 3156
Seelye, Catherine 373
Seferis, George 929
Seidel, Frederick 3157
Sell, Frederick C. 3158
Senior, John 3159
Sergeant, Elizabeth Shepley 3160
Sergeant, Howard 1413
Seyersted, Brita L. 3161
Seymour-Smith, Martin 3679
Shaheen, Mohammed Y. 930, 931, 3162, 3163
Shapiro, Karl 227, 228, 229, 395, 1176, 2864, 3164, 3165, 3166, 3167
Sharp, Frederick Thomas 3168
Shaw, Peter 932, 3169
Shaw, Robert B. 3170
Sheerin, J. B. 230
Sheldon, Michael 120
Shere, Charles 933
Sherman, William David 396
Shirer, William L. 397
Shlaes, Jared 781
Shuster, Helen 3661
Sickles, Hollis 3680
Sieber, H. A. 398, 399
Sieburth, Richard Raymond 934, 935, 1177, 1452, 3171, 3172, 3591
Sillen, Samuel 231, 1178
Simpson, David 3173
Simpson, Louis A. 121, 3174
Sinclair, May 1320
Sinclair, Upton 3175, 3592
Singh, G. 936, 937, 938, 939, 940, 941, 3176, 3593
Sisam, Kenneth 1644
Sisson, Charles Hubert 3177, 3178, 3179, 3180
Sitwell, Edith 942, 943, 944, 1414, 1573, 3181
Sjostrand, Osten 1759
Skorina, Violet Cameron 3182
Slatin, Myles 945, 3183, 3184, 3681
Slavitt, David 1735
Slocum, John J. 122
Slote, Bernice 2864
Smith, A. J. M. 1443
Smith, Bernard 3185
Smith, Chard P. 3186
Smith, G. I. Gilling 1251
Smith, Harrison 175, 176, 177, 232, 233, 234, 400, 1081, 1179
Smith, Lewis Worthington 3187
Smith, P. H. 946
Smith, Paul 3188
Smith, Ray 3189
Smith, Richard Eugene 1444, 3190
Snodgrass, W. D. 947
Sokol, B. J. 3191
Somer, John 3682
Sonne, Jorgen 3192
Sontag, Susan 1699

Soper, Brian 3193
Sorda, Enrique 3194
Sorrentino, Gilbert 3195
Southworth, James Granville 3196
Spagnoletti, Giacinto 1180
Spann, Marcella 948
Spanos, William V. 1415
Sparrow, John 1416
Spears, Monroe K. 3197
Spector, Robert Donald 3198, 3199
Speirs, John 1321
Spencer, Benjamin T. 3200, 3201
Spender, Stephen 949, 1322, 3202, 3203, 3204, 3205
Spiller, Robert E. 3206, 3207, 3208, 3683
Spingarn, Natalie Davis 401
Splitter, Randolph 950
Squires, Radcliffe 235, 1181
Stade, George 3506, 3507
Stafford, Clayton 1336
Stafford, Jack R. 3209
Stancioff, Marion Mitchell 3210
Stanford, Ann 3211, 3664, 3684, 3685
Stanford, Derek 1475
Stanford, Donald E. 3212, 3213, 3214
Starkie, Enid 3215
Stauffer, Donald A. 951
Stearns, Harold E. 3216
Steele, John L. 3594
Stegman, Michael O. 3217
Stein, Sol 3595
Steiner, Francis George 3218, 3219
Stern, Richard G. 123, 1674, 1700, 3220
Steven, James C. 952
Stevens, Peter 1182
Stevenson, Anne 1701
Stewart, Mairi 3221
Stewart, Peter 3222
Stock, Noel 45, 124, 125, 126, 127, 128, 402, 403, 953, 954, 1183, 1227, 1228, 1309, 1427, 1428, 1476, 1610, 2506, 3223, 3224, 3225, 3226, 3227, 3228, 3229, 3230, 3561, 3596, 3597, 3598, 3612, 3686, 3687
Stoenescu, Stefan 3231
Stoicheff, Richard Peter 955, 956
Stone, Douglas 957
Stone, Edward 370
Stonier, G. W. 3232
Stough, Christina Carolina 3233
Stovall, Floyd 3234, 3235
Straus, H. 1682
Strickland, G. R. 3236
Strough, Christina G. 3237
Struthers, Burt 236
Stuart, Duane R. 3238
Sühnel, Rudolf 3239, 3240
Sullivan, Alvin 2587
Sullivan, John Patrick 129, 1323, 1324, 1325, 1326, 1327, 3241, 3242, 3243
Surette, Philip Leon 958, 959, 960, 961, 962, 963, 964, 965, 1584, 1585, 3244, 3245
Sutherland, Donald 1736, 3246
Sutherland, James R. 1645
Sutton, Walter E. 773, 966, 967, 1186, 1187, 1417, 1418, 2240, 3441, 3688
Swabey, Henry 968, 3247, 3248
Sweeney, John L. 2214
Sweeney, Richard Monnett 3249
Symington, R. T. K. 3599
Symons, W. T. 3250
Szasz, Thomas S. 404, 405, 3251

Taggart, John Paul 3252
Tagliaferri, Aldo 3253
Tagore, Rabindranath 3254
Takada, Tomiichi 3255
Takayanagi, Shunichi 3256
Takuwa, Shinji 3257
Tanner, Tony 3258
Tanselle, G. Thomas 130, 131, 1611, 1781, 3600
Tate, Allen 237, 238, 239, 240, 241, 242, 243, 244, 245, 246, 969, 970, 971, 972, 973, 974, 975, 976, 977, 1337, 1338,

3259, 3260, 3261, 3262, 3689, 3690
Tatlow, Anthony 3263
Taupin, René 1619, 3264, 3265
Tay, William Shu-sam 978, 1188, 1229, 1711, 1712, 2276, 3266
Taylor, Daniel William 3267
Taylor, James 132, 3268, 3269
Taylor, Mark 3270
Taylor, Richard 1523
Taylor, Thomas 3271
Taylor, Walter Fuller 3272
Teele, Roy E. 1524, 1525, 3273, 3274
Teodorescu, Virgil 3275
Terramagnino, Geronimo 3276
Terrell, Carrol F. 10, 133, 134, 406, 979, 980, 981, 982, 983, 984, 985, 986, 987, 988, 989, 990, 991, 992, 1064, 1947, 3277, 3278, 3279, 3280, 3281, 3282, 3601, 3602
Thaniel, George 993
Thatcher, David S. 3283
Thayer, Mary Dixon 135
Theall, Donald F. 3284
Theroux, Paul 994
Thirlwall, John C. 3603
Thomas, C. T. 3285
Thomas, Edward 136, 1574, 1675
Thomas, Ronald Edward 1491, 1783, 3286, 3287, 3288, 3289
Thompson, Douglas 3290
Thompson, Francis J. 137
Thompson, Harold W. 138, 3291
Thompson, J. S. 995
Thompson, James H. 3604
Thompson, Lawrance 3292, 3293
Thorp, Willard 3294
Thorwall, John C. 3295
Thurley, Geoffrey 3296, 3297
Tichenor, George 247
Tierney, Bill 3298
Tietjens, Eunice 3299
Tillyard, E. M. W. 1419
Todd, Olivier 3300
Toki, Tsuneji 1236
Tolley, A. T. 3301
Tomlinson, Charles 1477, 3302, 3303
Torres, Aldo 3304
Torrey, E. Fuller 139, 407, 408
Traverso, Leone 3605
Trevisan, Lucio 996
Trewin, J. C. 1737
Tritschler, D. M. 997
Trotter, David 3305
Tryford, John 3306
Tseng, Pao Swen 3606
Tseng, Yueh-nung 998
Tsukui, Nobuko 1526, 3307
Tucker, John Joseph 3308, 3309
Tucker, William P. 3310
Turco, Lewis 3311
Turner, Mark 1328, 3063, 3312, 3483

Uberti, Riccardo M. degli 140
Uchino, Takako 3313
Uedo, Makoto 3314, 3315
Uejio, Clifford 3316
Ullyatt, A. G. 999
Unger, Leonard 3317
Untermeyer, Jean Starr 3318
Untermeyer, Louis 410, 1000, 1001, 1492, 1547, 3319, 3320, 3321, 3322, 3323, 3324, 3325
Urdanivia-Bertarelli, Eduardo 3326
Uribe Arce, Armando 3327

Vallette, Jacques 3328, 3329
Valsecchi, Marco 3330
Van Doren, Mark 248, 1575, 3331, 3607
Varney, H. L. 411
Vasse, William W. 588, 1002, 1003, 1004, 1005, 3691, 3692, 3693
The Vatican 412
Vázquez Amaral, José 3332
Vettori, Vittorio 1006, 1007
Véza, Laurette 1008

Viator [sic] 413
Vidan, Ivo 1009
Viereck, Peter 249, 250, 251, 252, 1189, 1190, 1875
Vietta, Susanne 3333
von Hallberg, Robert 3334, 3335, 3336
Von Hendy, Andrew John 1010
von Koppenfels, Werner 3337
Vortriede, Werner 3338

Wade, Allan 3608
Waggoner, Hyatt H. 3339, 3340, 3341
Wagner, Geoffrey Atheling 3342
Wagner, Linda Welshimer 2367, 2485, 3343, 3344
Wagstaff, A. Christopher 1011
Wain, John 1012, 1013, 3345, 3346, 3347, 3348
Walkiewicz, E. P. 1014, 3349
Wallace, Emily Mitchell 141, 142, 143, 3350
Wallace-Crabbe, Chris 1420
Walsh, Chad 3351
Walsh, Ernest 3352
Walther, Ying Tai Shirley 3353
Walton, Edna Lou 414, 1015, 1016, 1507
Wand, David Happell Hsin-Fu 1017, 3353
Wang, David R. 107
Wang, John C. 3355
Wanning, Andres 1018
Ward, Charlotte 1703
Warren, Eugene 1019
Warren, Robert Penn 1432
Wasserstrom, William 3356
Watts, Harold 415, 1020, 1021, 1022, 1191
Waugh, Arthur 3357, 3358
Weatherhead, A. Kingsley 3359
Webb, Mark S. 3360
Weber, Brom 3694
Weeks, Leroy Titus 3361
Wees, William C. 1023, 3362, 3363, 3364
Weintraub, Stanley 3365
Weinzinger, Anita 3366
Weiss, Theodore R. 3367, 3368, 3369
Weissman, David L. 252, 1192, 3609
Weisstein, Ellrich 3370
Welke, Robert J. 3371
Wellek, René 3372, 3373
Wells, Henry W. 3374
Wells, Tanya 1237
Welsh, Andrew 3375
Wenning, Henry W. 253
Wenzel, Gernot 3694
Wertham, Frederic 416, 417, 418
West, Ray B., Jr. 254, 3376, 3377, 3610
West, Rebecca 3378
West, T. Wilson 3379
Westcott, Glenway 1024
Westlake, Neda 3380
Weston, K. Noel 1025
Weyl, Nathaniel 113, 255, 419, 420
Whicher, George E. 1704, 1705, 3381
Whigham, Peter 144, 145, 146, 1026, 3382
Whitehead, Cintra 3383
Whittemore, Reed 147, 1193, 3384, 3385
Whitton, John B. 171
Wickes, George 3386
Widershien, Marc Alan 3387
Widmer, Kingsley 1421
Wieners, John 148
Wigginton, Waller B. 149, 150, 3611
Wiggs, Sharon J. 3388
Wildi, Max 3389
Wilhelm, James J. 151, 152, 1027, 1028, 1029, 1030, 1031, 1032, 1033, 3390, 3391, 3392, 3393, 3394, 3395
Willard, Charles B. 3396, 3397, 3398
Williams, David Park 1194
Williams, Ellen 3399
Williams, John K., Jr. 1034
Williams, Raymond 3400
Williams, William Carlos 153,

154, 155, 423, 424, 1035, 1036, 1037, 1038, 1195, 1278, 1576, 3401, 3402, 3403, 3404, 3405, 3406, 3407, 3408, 3409, 3410, 3411, 3612, 3695
Wilmer, Clive 3412
Wilson, Donald D. 1445
Wilson, Edmund 1542, 1587, 3413, 3414, 3415, 3416, 3417, 3418, 3419, 3420
Wilson, Suzanne M. 3421
Wilson, T. C. 1039, 1508
Wimsat, W. K. 1446, 2258, 3422
Winnick, R. H. 3293
Winterich, John T. 3423
Winters, Lee Eugene, Jr. 3424
Winters, Yvor 256, 1040, 1041, 1042, 3425
Witemeyer, Hugh H. 1043, 1044, 1045, 1046, 1422, 1493, 1629, 1953, 3349, 3426, 3427, 3428, 3429, 3491
Wolfe, Humbert 1047
Wood, Lewis 425
Wood, Michael 3430
Wood, Tom 3431
Woodard, Charles R. 3432
Woodfin, Henry A., Jr. 257
Woodress, James 3694
Woods, John 1196
Woodward, A. G. 3433, 3434, 3435
Woodward, Anthony 1197, 3436
Woodward, Daniel H. 3437
Woodward, Kathleen M. 1198, 3438
Wright, Arthur F. 3439
Wright, Cuthbert 1598
Wright, George T. 1577, 1578
Wuletich, Sybil 799
Wykes-Joyce, Max 3440

Yeats, William Butler 3441, 3442, 3443, 3444, 3445, 3446, 3447, 3448, 3449, 3450, 3613
Yip, Wai-Lim 1238, 1239, 3451
Yoder, Jonathan 156
Yoshikawa, [Kōjirō] 3485
Yoshino, Masaaki 3452, 3453
Young, G. M. 1509, 1510
Young, Gordon 258
Young, Kenneth 3454
Young, Thomas Daniel 259
Yueh-nung, Tseng 1048

Zabell Morton, Dauwen 973, 3455, 3456, 3457, 3614
Zach, Natan 3458
Zapatka, Francis Edward 1049, 3459
Zapponi, Niccolò 3460
Zardoya, Concha 3461
Zaturenska, Marya 1111
Zilczer, Judith 3462
Zimmermann, Hans-Joachim 3463, 3464, 3465, 3466
Zinnes, Harriet 3467
Zolla, Elémire 1050
Zukovsky, Louis 1051, 1052, 1053, 1054, 1055, 1056, 1057, 3468, 3469, 3470, 3471
Zverev, A. 3472, 3473

INDEX OF TOPICS

Abstraction 2668
Adams, John 1064
Aesthetic 2119, 2149, 2474, 2813, 2831
African Poetry 2233
The Age [Era] of Pound 2549
Aiken, Conrad 1806
Alba, Provencal 3452
Alchemy, Pound's 2716
Alchemy of the Word 1760
Aldington, Richard 3283
Alexander, Michael 2499
Alison, Archibald 2119
Allegory 2643
"Allen Upward" 2118
Allston, Oliver 1982
Allusions 607
America, Pound's Angry Love-affair 2890
The American Strain: Pound's 3201
Anglo Saxon Studies, Pound's 1641
Antheil, George 703, 2205
Anti-Democratic Intelligentsia 679
Anti-Humanism of Pound 1174
Anti-Semitism 685, 2995, 2968
Arabic, Pound in Arabic 3163
Arensberg, Walter Conrad 2307
Armstrong, Edward 3286
Arnold, Matthew 1754
Arrogance, Pound's 2891
Art 175, 668, 3088, 3267; of Poetry 1807; of the Real 2537; Visual Arts 2667, 3009, 3467
Atmosphere 2200
Auden, W. H. 2253
Audience 2129
Avant-Garde 2736, 3155; English Avant-Garde 2073
Ayscough, Florence 3012
Baker Street 2616
Barney, Natalie, Letters to 3581, 3591
Bartlett, John T. 2362
Beauty 948
Becker, John, Correspondence 3519
Belief 2142
Berryman, John 699, 839, 2854
Binyon, Laurence 2533
"Bishop Carame's Translation of Avicenna," 2760
Blackmur, R. P. 2598
Blake, William 622, 630
Blunt, Wilfrid Scawen 2403, 3162
"Boobliography" 2380
Books and People 2114
Booth, Marcella 3601
Borah, William E. [Senator from Idaho] 3567
The Boticellian Vision 875
Bowlker, Charles 551
Bradstreet, Anne 1299
Brancusi, Constantin 2135
Brazilian Concrete Poetry 3084
Brecht, Bertolt 3263
Brewer, Jospeh [Olivet College President] 3525, 3542
Browning, Robert 503, 554, 1219, 1950, 2391, 2826, 2971, 3031, 3183, 3222, 3286, 3432
Buchan, John 3558, 3580
Buckminster Fuller, A Guided Tour of 2617
Buddhism 652
Bunting, Basil 2339

Campo, Luchino Dal 712
Cantos--The Malatesta Cantos 755
Cardenal, Ernesto 3326
Carter, Thomas 2601
Case--Ezra Pound's Case 2105
Castration 2043
Cathay 1232
Catullus 144, 1491, 2971
Cavalcanti, Guido 2444, 2610, 2951
Censorship 2382
Cerf, Bennett 174
Chace, William C. 3036
China and Chinese--History and Literature 561, 575, 604, 705, 842, 882, 980, 1131, 1210, 1229, 1244, 1479, 1492, 1665, 2399, 2532, 2533, 2595, 2613, 2623, 2634, 2674, 2677, 2701, 2727, 2731, 2812, 2817, 2902, 2947, 2948, 2998, 3142, 3274, 3424, 3354, 3355, 3439, 3451, 3466
Chute, Father Desmond 2584
Cicero 2034
Civilization in the United States 1942, 2420
Clarification 646
The Classics--Pound and the Classics 777, 1624, 3243
Clough, Arthur Hugh 1961
Cocteau, Jean 2853
Cognition, Pound and His Method 3453
Coherence 1132
Coke, Edward 651, 1107
Communism 1784
Comparatist, Ezra Pound 1986
Concretism--Brazilian Concretism 3290
Condensation 2480
Conformity 2479
Confucius 649, 766, 978, 1198, 2102, 2266, 2288, 3313; Confucianism 2874; Confucian Odes 2649, 2762, 2763, 2800, 4203
Conservatism 1588
Contact 1570
Context 1570
Contiguity 1570
Contribution of Pound 2551
Convictions 2097
Cornell, Julian 291, 3571
Cosmopolitanism 2678
Coxe, Louis 1647, 1650
Craft [Craft and Morals] 1829, 2738
Crane, Hart 2122, 2221, 2854
Credit, Social Credit 2670
Creeley, Robert 2125, 2868
Critic(s) 1507, 1508, 1546, 1895, 2944, 3133, 3238, 3303
Criticism 1472, 1881, 1988, 2107, 2108, 2134, 2185, 2469, 3360, 3373, 3376, 3377, 3383, 3455
Culture, Breakdown of 1785
Cummings, E. E. 94, 3061, 3502, 3506, 3507, 3572
Cutting, Bronson 3349
Dada 2081
Dahlberg, Edward 2140, 2141
Dame Fortune 861
Daniel, Arnaut 3390
Dante Alighieri 638, 664, 937, 1033, 1399, 1869, 1872, 1873, 1997, 2014, 2099, 2148, 2252, 2618, 2819, 2987, 2988, 3010, 3390, 3391, 3392
Daryush, Elizabeth 3212
Davey, Frank 2218
Decadence 1041, 2033, 2767, 3155
Dell, Floyd 130
Democracy 810
Design 1341
Device 1577
The Dial 2586, 2587
Dialect 39
Dickey, James 3491
Dickinson, Emily 3421
Dictatorship, Freedom through 2083
Dissertations [and Abstracts] 38, 429, 458, 482, 487, 500, 526, 540, 556, 594, 625, 658, 666, 670, 673, 685, 705, 707, 709, 710, 712, 767, 776, 780, 790, 806, 830, 866, 880, 884, 897, 918, 952, 955, 958, 978,

1004, 1010, 1011, 1061, 1063, 1092, 1097, 1108, 1132, 1224, 1237, 1238, 1301, 1346, 1452, 1526, 1577, 1624, 1792, 1825, 1849, 1863, 1866, 1871, 1902, 1936, 1946, 1989, 1997, 2008, 2009, 2035, 2044, 2054, 2059, 2079, 2084, 2110, 2149, 2197, 2228, 2307, 2311, 2332, 2385, 2386, 2402, 2431, 2440, 2443, 2450, 2452, 2469, 2471, 2472, 2477, 2489, 2495, 2509, 2570, 2583, 2593, 2595, 2602, 2604, 2606, 2610, 2611, 2654, 2655, 2717, 2733, 2750, 2781, 2786, 2789, 2791, 2809, 2818, 2826, 2854, 2858, 2920, 2925, 2938, 2954, 2964, 2971, 2974, 3006, 3030, 3031, 3061, 3084, 3094, 3097, 3122, 3125, 3131, 3133, 3145, 3148, 3168, 3182, 3183, 3217, 3233, 3249, 3252, 3267, 3274, 3284, 3289, 3309, 3314, 3316, 3326, 3353, 3354, 3360, 3375, 3383, 3387, 3424, 3427, 3432, 3438, 3459

Don Quixote [Modern] 331

Doolittle, Hilda 2664

Douglas, Gavin 2793, 3288

Dreiser, Theodore 3562

Dryden, John 822

Dublin 137

"The Duce" 2099

Duncan, Ronald 3555

The East--the Far East 2067

Economics 539, 837, 2111, 2180, 3088

Educational Significance 3123

The Edwardians 2165

Edwards--King Edward's Court 2109

Elements, Magic Elements 558

The Eleusinian and Bacchic Mysteries 3271

Eleusis 964, 965, 1711, 2717

Eliot, T. S. 24, 44, 54, 111, 121, 194, 253, 579, 670, 677, 679, 701, 707, 708, 906, 1077, 1465, 1560, 1561, 1577, 1578, 1600, 1798, 1812, 1865, 1869, 1871, 1872, 1902, 1919, 1948, 1949, 1951, 1952, 1990, 2011, 2018, 2054, 2065, 2106, 2119, 2120, 2138, 2170, 2171, 2221, 2236, 2231, 2244, 2245, 2253, 2280, 2281, 2292, 2307, 2341, 2383, 2384, 2385, 2480, 2543, 2583, 2593, 2611, 2618, 2665, 2666, 2686, 2688, 2699, 2722, 2735, 2737, 2738, 2745, 2763, 2776, 2790, 2803, 2820, 2837, 2838, 2854, 2866, 2886, 2887, 2888, 2918, 2925, 2952, 2954, 2964, 2996, 3006, 3042, 3127, 3129, 3148, 3198, 3213, 3215, 3217, 3233, 3236, 3237, 3256, 3284, 3389, 3411, 3420, 3422, 3432, 3437, 3438, 3508, 3525, 3587, 3620, 3621, 3622, 3623, 3624, 3656, 3657, 3658

Emerson, Ralph Waldo 1897, 2840

Emery, Clark 3497

Encounters with E.P. 2395

The English--and Pound 2166

Enlightenment 3434

Environment--Early London Environment 2745

Epic 456, 492, 744, 802, 884, 1013, 2042, 2967

Epic, Modern Verse Epic 773, 1256, 1337

Era, The Pound Era 1637, 3214

Erigena, Scotus 1711, 2810, 2860

Error, The Poetics of Error 2641

Ethical [or Ethics] 2042

Etymologies 2401

Evangelism 2042

Evans, Donald 2307

Evil--Moral Evil 189

Exhibition 2290

Exile and Literature 2740

Expression 2578

Failure 1583

Fallacy--Intentional Fallacy 2660

Fascism 187, 325, 326, 451,

685, 769, 1907, 2173, 2300, 2463, 3106, 3310, 3436
Faulkner, William 274
Fenollosa 728, 1235, 1517, 1923, 2067, 2287, 2308, 2401, 2613, 2676, 2812, 2827, 2910, 3140, 3166, 3255
Festus 867
Fiction, the Art of 2113
Flaminius 1491
Flaubert, Gustave 3051, 3236
Fletcher, John Gould 2188, 2323, 2772
Flint, F. S. 1971, 2863
Ford, Ford Madox 1866, 2046, 2334, 2405, 2408, 2413, 2538, 2751, 2806, 2849, 2991, 3161, 3182, 3544
Form--Modernist Form 500, 2689, 2791, 3030
Formal Structure 501
The Forties 173, 2355
France and Pound 1892, 2624
Free Verse 967, 2077
French--Symbolism and Language 1619, 2319, 3387
Freud, Sigmund 2828
Frobenius, Leo 692, 2151, 2153, 2201, 3371
Frost, Robert 321, 1599, 1601, 1878, 1902, 2101, 2327, 2361, 2597, 2908, 3160, 3191, 3292, 3293
Fugue 428, 541, 2182
Futurism 2073, 3109, 3460
Gastronomy of Letters 1746
Gaudier, Henry 795
Gautier, Theophile 1868, 3215
The Genius of Ezra Pound 1975, 2082
The Georgians 2940
German Studies, Pound's, and Germany 3132
Gloom and Gold 612
Goethe, Johann Wolfgang von 3032
Gomme, Lawrence 131
Gourmont, Remy de 1450, 1452, 2153, 3264
Greek and Egyptian Mysteries 807, 3388
Guba, Naresh 2960
Gunn, Thom 3412
H. D. 2568, 2772
Hades 2297
Haiku 1444, 2869
Hardy, Thomas 2970, 3527
Harmony 1795
Hate 2234, 2387
"A Hawk and a Handsaw" 1790
Heaven, Pound in 2600
Heidegger, Martin 2008
Helen of Tyre 962
Hell, Dante's 2148
Hemingway, Ernest 1928, 1972, 2299, 2367, 2454, 2485, 2557, 2585, 3386
Heracles 2159
Hero, the Poet as Hero 3090
Hiss, Alger 251, 1875
Historian 435, 466, 479
Historical and Semi-Historical Sources and Allusions 478, 607
History and Historical: 662, 663, 924, 932, 945, 968; American History 745, 760, 1002, 1004; 19th century French History 746; General 1919, 2440, 2608, 2609, 2658, 3228, 3248, 3400, 3425; Use and Abuse 871; Sources 917
Hitler's Economic Policies 2656
Hoover, Herbert 2659
Horizon, The European Horizon 2737
Hubbell, Jay 3537, 3576
Hulme, T. E. 1623, 1923, 2084, 2409, 2561, 2687
Human Nature 2392
Humanist--The Last Humanist 2498
Humor 3092
Ibbotson, Joseph Darling 3553, 3579
Icons 2401
Idealism 3234
Ideas 534, 2578; Ideogram 499; Ideas in Action 892
Identity, American 2919; Mysteries of 2707

Ideogram 2871; Ideogrammic Method of Ezra Pound 3353; Tools of Ideogramic Method 2581
Ideology, Literary Ideology and Politics 1977
Ignorance, In Defense of 3164
Image(s) 1394, 1404, 1515, 1828, 2393, 2397, 2653, 2753, 2869, 2871, 2893, 2899, 2992, 3072, 3073; The Art of 2341; Image Complex 2341; Racial Image 1998
Imagination 2531, 3043, 3093
Imagism and Imagists 451, 1034, 1437, 1666, 1776, 1803, 1810, 1811, 1816, 1853, 1889, 1907, 1923, 1936, 1968, 1971, 2073, 2084, 2085, 2143, 2188, 2220, 2221, 2230, 2269, 2313, 2321, 2325, 2326, 2351, 2375, 2377, 2378, 2386, 2436, 2455, 2470, 2485, 2495, 2508, 2520, 2541, 2554, 2569, 2582, 2594, 2772, 2828, 2831, 2863, 2882, 2940, 2972, 2983, 2986, 3005, 3099, 3378, 3458
Imitation 1615
Impressionists 3381
Individuality 3089
The Inferno 2231
Influence(s): Creative and Critical 2842; Divergent 2877; Formative 1624; Influence in London 3133
Inheritance, Ironic 3046
Innocence 915, 2304, 2843
Innovations 1929
Instaurations 494
Intelligence of Poets 1929, 1580
Interlude 1947
Interpretation 2129
Interviews 54, 55, 2457, 3444, 3474, 3485
Intuition of Prose Fiction 2106
Ireland 2294
Irony 3005, 3125
Isolation 1581
Italian Images of Ezra Pound 2019, 2420, 3531; Italian Literature 2936, 3390; Italian Ministry for Popular Culture 292; Italian Translation 1083; Italy 1078, 2885, 2987
Jacobins 2372
Jakobson's Method 480
James, Henry 706, 707, 708, 1351, 1380, 2570, 3006
James, William 1899, 1936, 2654
"Janequin's 'Song of the Birds'" 757
Japan, Pound's Debt to 2870; Japanese Elements 2369; Japanese and English Poetics 3315; Japanese Noh Plays 728, 3307; Japanese Tradition 805
Jefferson-Adams Letters, Pound's Essays on 2759
Jefferson, Thomas 758, 1456
The Jew as Anti-Artist 2782
Jordan, Viola Baxter 2588, 3517, 3582
Joyce, James 723, 1994, 2216, 2231, 2253, 2256, 2459, 2560, 2590, 2592, 2611, 2612, 2645, 2822, 2925, 2996, 3051, 3052, 3053, 3239, 3284, 3495, 3510, 3586, 3589
K. R. H. [Katherine Ruth Heyman] 3280
Kandinsky, Wassily 1969, 2736
Kenny, Alice 3104
Kensington [W. London] 2558
Kingston, Maxine Hong 2532
Kung Futzu [Chinese name of Confucius] 1711, 1855
Laforgue, Jules 2116, 2144, 2195, 3046, 3047
Landor, Walter Savage 2971, 3429
Landscape 868, 2094, 3287
Language(s) 2609, 2807, 3158, 3402
Lattimore, Richard 2758
Laughlin, James 2547
Law 113
Lawrence, D. H. 679, 1866, 2587, 2718, 2719, 2986
Lawrence, T. E. 793
Layamon's Brut 446, 1886

Leavis, Frank Raymond 2400
Lectures--Oxford Lectures on Poetry 2371
Legacy, Pound's 1870
Legge, James 3383
Leopardi, Count Giacomo 1877
Letters: EP in His Letters 2833, 2988; Letters of Yeats 3446, 3447
Lewis, Wyndham 111, 2024, 2057, 2149, 2747, 2837, 3087, 3342
Liberals 1875, 2441
Literary, [Theory of Literary Collage] 880
Literary Criticism, Pound's Influence 2411
Literary Tradition 552
Literature: Comparative 2738, 2739; Imaginative 3412; Persuasive 3384
Logos 455
London Years, Pound's 2775
Loss, Poetics of 3138
Love 2234, 2796
Lowell, Amy 2145, 2432
Lowell, Robert 2464, 2854
The Lowell-Pound Feud 3012
Loy, Mina 2307
Lucifer 555, 595, 863, 2155, 2250
The Lyric 2329
Magic, Pound and Magic 1884, 2198
Magnanimity 2177
Magnum Opus, Pound's 624
The Malatesta Cantos 819
Mallarmé, Stéphane 3099
Man--Modern Man 1659
Mannerism 2850
Manuscripts--Sienese Manuscripts 751
Marginalien 550
Marx, Karl 898; Marxism 3417; Marxist Temptation 2051
Masks 1552, 1569, 3289
Mayakovsky, Vladimir 2392, 2604
Meaning 954, 1615, 2129, 2689; Poetic Meaning 3122
The Mediterranean Man 2210
The Mediterranean World 2818
Medievalism 2442, 2443, 2813
Medieval Provencal Poetry 2809
Medieval Prosody 2938
Melopoesia 1696, 1793
Memory 1513; Memoirs 2461, 2924
Mencken, H. L. 1608, 1609, 1778, 1937, 2340, 2473, 3550
Menippean Tradition 2912
Menotti, Gian Carlo 2841
Merton, Thomas 3326
The Metamorphic Tradition 3038, 3039
The Metamorphoses of Ezra Pound 878, 1946
Metaphor 724, 2444, 3140
Metaphysics 1534, 1708
Meters 784 (see also Rhythm)
Method, Ideogrammatic 545, 749
Methodism 661
Metonymy 946
Metric--Greek Metric 1876, 1908; Pound's Metric 2036
Michio, Ito 2040
Milton, John 2780
Ming, Cheng Ming 1712
Modernism 704, 711, 1941, 1965, 2128, 2131, 2482, 2528, 2599, 2733, 2845, 2974, 3144, 3147, 3197, 3337, 3369
Money 68; Money-Making 1534, 1708; Money and Power 1740
Monologues 2379, 2705
Monroe, Harriet 2880, 3399
Moore, Marianne 2385, 2895, 3359
Morals 1829
Mosher, John T. 2363
Motive, Poetic and Strategic 548
The Muse--the Tenth Muse 891; Muses 1677, 1847, 1932; Muse in Tatters 2638
Music 429, 609, 703, 896, 919, 1682, 1768, 1772, 1792, 1795, 2509, 2774
Musician, Ezra Pound as 3086
Musonius, Homage to 1211, 1726

Mussolini, Benito 187, 1456, 2388, 3436, 3577
Mutation of Pound's 2540
The Mystery of Ezra Pound 3232
Myth(s) 455, 506, 1371, 1946, 2002, 2514, 2616, 2753, 3125, 3434
Mythography, Lexical 869
Mythology, Chinese 1017
Napoleon Bonaparte 725
Nassar, Eugene, Lyric Mode of 585
Nationality 3200
Nature 1887
Neofism--Musical Neofism 1795
The Noh Plays 1515, 1516, 1517, 1518, 1519, 1520, 1521, 1522, 1523, 1524, 1525, 1526
"The 'Noigandres' Group" 3084
The Novel 2106
Objectivity 2378
The Objectivists 3334, 3469, 3470
Odysseus, Pound as 156
Okigbo, Christopher 2233
Olson, Charles 373, 573, 1939, 2068, 2815, 2854, 2933, 3136, 3333, 3334, 3335
Opera, Pound's 1678
Oppen, George 1904, 3168
The Orient and/or Orientalism 2308, 2324, 2368, 3149
Orwell, George 1905
Ovid 643, 1946, 3121
Ovid's Metaphorphoses 2754
Pagan Elements in Pound 558
Painting 2149
Paradise 2228
Paradox 400, 2378
Paris and Pound 2081, 3300
Parody 2009
Partisans--and Poets 2127
The Past--the Persistent Past 2640; Use of the Past 2854
Pater, Walter 1782
Patriots 337
Pattern, Historical 963
"Penny-Wise"--Pound 1445
Perfection, Visions of 677
Permissiveness, Limits of 893
Perspectives on Pound 2574
Phenomenalist Poetry 3297
Philistines 2372
Philosophers, Literary 1809
Philosophy, Pound's 3193
Philosophy 568
Pisa--Pound at Pisa 1129
Place, Magic of 2636
Plath, Sylvia 2539
Poet--The American Poet 2050
Poetics of Ezra Pound and T. S. Eliot 2583, 2604, 3145
Poetics of Loss 3138
Poetry, The Art of Reading Poetry 1531, 2146
Poetry--English and American since 1939 2537, 2580
Poetry--From 1900 to 1930's 2130
Poetry and Politics 1962, 2696, 3205, 3336
Poetry: Translation of 1683-1705
"A Pointless Pointillist" 1543, 1804
Poland 2264
Polemics 2604
Politics and Poetry 57, 245, 293, 320, 404, 405, 450, 564, 837, 977, 1602, 1962, 1977, 2049, 2054, 2079, 2120, 2330, 2353, 2387, 2474, 2572, 2950, 2980, 3205, 3336
"Polyglot"--A Creative Writer as Polyglot 2360
Populism 3310
Porter, Katherine Anne 2770, 2996
Pound-Abercrombie Feud 2315
Pound, Dorothy Shakespear 2357, 3004, 3496, 3588
The Pound Era 732, 2174
The Pound Conference at Sheffield University 3156
Pound, Homer 149, 3611
Pound, Thaddeus Coleman 141
Power--Money and Power 1740
The Pre-Imagist Stage 553
Price, John 1823
Primitivism 1041
Prisms 504

Process, Poetics of 2181
The Promise and the Disaster [of Pound] 2723
Propertius, Sextus 1319, 1321
Prose 2538, 3166
Prose Tradition 715, 1857, 2715, 3166
Prosody 511
Protest, Poetry of 2169
Provence--and Medieval Provencal Aspects and Translations 1492, 2045, 2197, 2552, 2813, 2814, 3146, 3312
Psychiatry 405, 407, 418
Pumpelly, Ralph 2662
Purpose, Pound's 2689
Quantities, Pound's 3169
Quinn, John 1489, 3437, 3462
Quotations and Abbreviations, Pound's Methods 2915
Racial Image [Cf., Image, Racial]
Radio Speeches, Pound's 3064, 3141
Rakosi, Carl 3168
Rapallo 2697, 2857, 3551
Reactionaries 679, 701
Read, Herbert 3283
Readers 2129
Reality 830, 2193
Rebellion--by a Poet 2494
Rebirth 2296
Recapitulation 1629
Religion, Modern Poetry as 3165
Religion, Pound's 2059, 3411
The Renaissance--Pateresque Renaissance 2204
Renaissance, Prophets of 741, 1538
The Reputation of Ezra Pound 3347
Responsibility, Sense of 3597
"Reviewer's Notebook" 1448
Revolt, Images of 627, 628
Revolution, Modern 967
Reznikoff, Charles 3168
Rhetoric 2354
Rhetoric and the Moderns 3301
Rhyme 543, 2183, 2402
Rhythm 498, 784, 1039, 3119, 3120, 3169
Richards, I. A. 2409
Richardson, Dorothy 2611
Rimbaud, Arthur 2979, 2981
"Risveglio Vivaldiano" 1796
Robinson, Edwin Arlington 3213
Romance, Spirit of 1667, 1668, 1671, 1672, 1673
Romanticism 2035
Rossetti, D. G. 1869, 2951, 3379
Rubenstein, Ida 2787
Rudge, Olga 1796
Ruskin, John 1046, 2044, 3110
Russia 2983
Russian Studies in American Literature 3654
Sacchetti, Franco 691
Sacrament 1780
The Sacred Edict 653, 654
Salons de Paris 1676
The San Francisco Chinese World 1714
Sandburg, Carl 1889
Sanity 3089
Santayana, George 80, 2112, 3435
Sappho 1536, 1876, 1908, 3490
Satire--Post-War Satire 2143
Saviotti, Gino 2206
Science, Method of 2914
Science, Phantasy of 2606
Science, A Study of Pound and Science 2605
Science and Values in Modern American Poetry 3340
Sculpture 536
Segregation and Ezra Pound 3209
Semiotic Aspects 499
Semitism and Anti-Semitism 2043, 2657, 2955
Sensibility 656, 3421
"Sestina," Eliot's 1798
Sexual Mockery 1484
Shaw, George Bernard 2720
Sicily 537
The Silences of Ezra Pound 2711

Sitwell, Edith 2546
The Sixties 2904
The Smart Set Mystique 1845
Smith, Adam 898
Snyder, Gary 3354
Social Change 2121
Social Responsibility 1987
Social Theory 2781
The Sophisticated, Studies in 1449
Sophocles 1728, 1974, 2034
Space 1339
The Spanish-Speaking World and Pound 2226
Speech, Public and Private 2799, 3409
Spender, Stephen 3204
Spengler, Oswald 2003
Stalin, Joseph V. 470
Steele, John L. 3594
Steffens, Lincoln 801
Stein, Gertrude 1976, 2851
Sterling, George 2438
Stevens, Wallace 724, 2307, 2489, 2594, 2735, 2920, 2954, 2982, 3213, 3217, 3306, 3438
Stopes, Marie 2675
Strater, Henry 516
Stravinsky, Igor Fedorovich 1685
Structure, Formal Structure 501
Structural Reading 647, 673, 918
Style 1377, 1778, 2037, 2826, 3005
Subject 1649
Superiority 1561
Symbolism 711, 886, 1383, 1535, 1619, 1888, 2011, 2085, 2198, 2981, 3099, 3135
Symphony, Color Symphony 1984
Syntax, English Poetry Syntax 2161
Synergy 2370
Tagore, Rabindranath 1921, 2556, 2961
Talleyrand-Perigord, Charles Maurice de 725
Taufers, Margarethe von 695
Taylor, Thomas 3281
Teacher, Pound as Teacher 2714
Techniques 1040, 3279
Temperament 1649
Tennyson, Alfred Lord 1934
Terrell, Carroll F. 3594
Texas 2203
Theme, International 2374
Theme, Lack of 1379
Theology and/or Theological Aspects 2530, 3151
Theories, Prosodic Theories of Pound 2702
Thinking, Symbolic 951
The Thirties 1587, 2356, 2373, 2460, 3415, 3417, 3645
Time 2202, 2221
Time in Ezra Pound's Work 670, 676, 803, 865, 866, 1487, 2471
Tomlinson, Charles 2125
Tone in Ezra Pound's Poetry 2683
"Totalitarian," Pound's Use of the Word 2761
Tradition:
American Tradition 1967, 3224
Avant-Garde 3061
Classical 573
Conservative 3198
European 3006
Genteel Tradition 2115
Medieval Tradition 2005
Real Tradition 1340
Tradition and Change 3358
Traduzione Integral 559
Troubadour Tradition 2785, 2786
Traitors 337
Translations 1323, 1324, 1325, 1326, 1439, 1666, 1674, 1698, 1699, 1705, 1830, 1849, 2144, 2289, 2551, 2552, 2579, 2586, 2610, 2682, 2811, 2877, 3131, 3226, 3238, 3239, 3242, 3331
Translucencies, Chinese 544
Treason 360, 408, 419, 420, 425
Troubadour(s) 2785, 2786,

2941, 3393, 3394, 3395
Truth 678, 2690
The Twenties 671, 1378, 1421, 1587, 2800, 3415
Ulysses 2763
The Universe 2178, 2531
Unpopularity [of Ezra Pound] 1660
Untermeyer, Louis 3574, 3590
Upward, Allen 2401
Usury 836, 1873, 2043, 2152
The Utopian 2311
"Verog, Monsieur" 1568
Verse: Modern 2095; Objective 3136; Projective 3140
Villain to Visionary 1953
Villon, Francois 1953, 2431, 3459
Vision, Messianic 2295
Vision and Rhetoric 2354
Visual Arts 3467
Vocabulary, Critical 2480
Voice, The Public Voice 2410
Voltaire, Francois Marie Arouet de 935
Vortex 2834, 2835, 2837, 3267
Vorticism 768, 1023, 1482, 1991, 2073, 2103, 2149, 2154, 2359, 2518, 2755, 2872, 3109, 3139, 3308, 3362, 3363, 3364, 3370, 3458
Wadsworths, The 152
Waley, Arthur 3263
War 439, 2143
The Westons 152
Whistler, James McNeill 2570
Whitman, Walt 1528, 1906, 2221, 2570, 2840, 2966, 2967, 3037, 3396, 3397, 3398
Wilde, Oscar 2253
Williams, William Carlos 121, 143, 153, 579, 724, 1092, 2023, 2088, 2089, 2094, 2152, 2331, 2449, 2478, 2489, 2500, 2594, 2712, 2725, 2765, 2854, 2905, 2954, 3040, 3168, 3217, 3249, 3316, 3335, 3343, 3350, 3359, 3382, 3411, 3438, 3534
Winslow, Elizabeth 3578, 3604
Winters, Yvor 2307, 3213
Woolf, Virginia 1866
Wordsworth, William 1319, 3134, 3173, 3316
Writing 847
Writing--American Writing 1844
Yankees--The "London Yankees" 3365
Yeats, William Butler 374, 468, 679, 906, 1001, 1091, 1319, 1457, 1577, 1578, 1948, 2078, 2120, 2179, 2243, 2253, 2255, 2259, 2294, 2403, 2412, 2419, 2453, 2491, 2511, 2542, 2550, 2576, 2807, 2865, 2957, 2964, 2996, 3058, 3135, 3181, 3284, 3314, 3315, 3419, 3432, 3446, 3447, 3448, 3602, 3608
The Younger Generation 2732
Zukofsky, Louis 3168, 3188